AF683970

# Injia on Contempt of Court in Papua New Guinea and the Pacific

Salamo Injia

University of Papua New Guinea Press and Bookshop, 2013

**Injia on Contempt of Court in Papua New Guinea and the Pacific**

© Copyright 2013, The Independent State of Papua New Guinea

ISBN: 978-9980-87-919-6

This publication is copyright. Other than for the purposes of and subject to the conditions prescribed under the Copyright and Neighbouring Rights Act 2000, no part of it may in any form or by any means (electronic, mechanical, microcopying, recording or otherwise) be reproduced, stored in a retrieval system or transmitted without prior written permission.

Inquiries should be addressed to the publisher.

**PUBLISHED BY:**

The University of Papua New Guinea Press and Bookshop
PO Box 413
University PO, NCD
Papua New Guinea
Email: upngpress@gmail.com

# FOREWORD

This textbook is one of eight (8) textbooks written under my hand and supervision:

***'Injia on Criminal Offences in Papua New Guinea and the Pacific'***

***'Injia on Criminal Practice and Procedure in Papua New Guinea and the Pacific'***

***'Injia on Sentencing in Papua New Guinea and the Pacific'***

***'Injia on Statutory Interpretation in Papua New Guinea and the Pacific'***

***'Injia on Coronial Proceedings in Papua New Guinea and the Pacific'***

***'Injia on Investigatory Practice in Papua New Guinea and the Pacific'***

***'Injia on Contempt of Court in Papua New Guinea and the Pacific'***

***'Injia on Evidence in Papua New Guinea and the Pacific'***

Each of those textbooks is an effort to offer to Judicial officers, legal practitioners and students of law a comprehensive set of principles and practical guidelines on criminal law and practice in Papua New Guinea and the Pacific. The work undertaken under the auspices of AusAID through the PNG-Australia Law and Justice Partnership Project is an extension of a similar project undertaken previously in writing the textbook *Criminal Law and Practice in Papua New Guinea* co-authored by myself, Professor Don Chalmers, Dr Weisbrot and Justice Andrew.

The textbooks will be of great benefit to the criminal justice system in Papua New Guinea and the Pacific and specifically will assist judges, magistrates, lawyers, law students and police officers in the performance of their duties.

The assistance of AusAID and its development practitioner Mr Errol Gibson who provided research and spent countless hours in the production of these textbooks is acknowledged.

Sir Salamo Injia, Kt

Chief Justice of Papua New Guinea

22nd September 2013

# TABLE OF CONTENTS

| TABLE OF CONTENTS |
|---|

# TABLE OF CONTENTS

# TABLE OF CONTENTS

## TABLE OF CONTENTS

# TABLE OF CONTENTS

# INTRODUCTION

## [1.0] SUPREME AND NATIONAL COURTS OF JUSTICE[1]

The *Constitution of the Independent State of Papua New Guinea* vests contempt powers on the two superior courts (the Supreme and National Courts of Justice) to punish offences against themselves under sections 160(2) and 163(2) respectively.[2]

This is, of course, an inherent power[3] translated into statutory form under the Constitution. The courts, therefore, have undoubted powers to compel observance of their processes and obedience of and compliance with their orders and directions. These powers are inherent in the sense that they 'are necessary attributes to render the judicial function effective in the administration of justice'. Expressed in another way, the power to punish for contempt is inherent in the judiciary. The contempt power enables the courts to perform their functions without interference, to control courtroom behaviour and to enforce orders and compel obedience.[4]

---

[1] The Bougianville High Court when established will also be a superior court of record and will have the power to punish the offence against itself commonly known as 'Contempt of Court', see section 116 of the *Constitution of the Autonomous Region of Bougainville.*

[2] See *Peter Luga v Richard Sikani Commissioner, Correctional Services and The State* (2002) N2285; *Agnes Okona Meten v William Seneka and Magisterial Services* (2011) N4462, [2011] PGNC 169 and *Review Pursuant to Constitution, Section 155(2)(B); Application by Herman Joseph Leahy* (2006) SC855.

[3] See also:

- *Luchya Mussa Tikuye v Patrick Haines* (2009) N4434, [2009] PGNC 259; *R v Dunbavin; ex parte Williams* (1935) 53 CLR 434 at 442, [1935] HCA 34; *R v Metal Trades Employers' Federation; ex parte Amalgamated Engineering Union* (1951) 82 CLR 208 at 241 and 254, [1951] HCA 3; *R v Forbes; ex parte Bevan* (1972) 128 CLR 1 at 7, [1972] HCA 21; *Balogh v Crown Court at Saint Albans* [1974] 3 All ER 283, [1975] QB 73, per Lawton LJ at 92; *McDermott v Beaumont* [1868] LR 2 PC 341; *Taylor v Attorney-General* [1975] 2 NZLR 675 and *Skouvakis v Skouvakis* [1976] 2 NSWLR 29 at 34; and
- Oswald, 1910, 'Contempt of Court' 3rd ed., Butterworths, England, p. 12 and G Borrie and N Lowe, 1983, 'The Law of Contempt' 2nd ed., Butterworths, London, p. 314.

[4] See *Review Pursuant to Constitution, Section 155(2)(B); Application by Herman Joseph Leahy* (2006) SC855; *Peter Luga v Richard Sikani Commissioner, Correctional Services and The State* (2002) N2285 and *Stephen John Rose and another v Neville Devete, Acting Solicitor-General and The State* (2007) N3327.

## INTRODUCTION

The law of contempt is concerned with judicial process[5] and the exercise of judicial power[6], and is the mechanism by which a Court ensures the integrity of the system of justice that it administers, and therefore the effective administration of justice[7].

Obstructions to the exercise of executive power, administrative power, legislative power or other governmental power are not within the conception of the offence of 'Contempt of Court'.[8]

The purpose of contempt powers is to preserve and protect the general community interest, not the Court's own dignity, in suppressing unjustifiable interference in the authority of the Courts of the land[9].[10]

---

[5] See *Attorney-General v Times Newspapers Ltd* [1973] 3 All ER 54, [1974] AC 273 at 294.

See also: *R v Taylor; ex parte Roach* (1951) 82 CLR 587 at 598, [1951] HCA 22 and *Victoria v Australian Building Construction Employees' and Builders Labourers' Federation* (1981-82) 152 CLR 25, per Brennan J at 161, [1982] HCA 31.

[6] See *R v Taylor; ex parte Roach* (1951) 82 CLR 587at 598, [1951] HCA 22 and *Victoria v Australian Building Construction Employees' and Builders Labourers' Federation* (1981-82) 152 CLR 25, per Brennan J at 161, [1982] HCA 31.

[7] See *Australasian Meat Industry Employees' Union v Mudginberri Station Pty Ltd* (1986) 161 CLR 98, 107, (1986) 66 ALR 577, [1986] HCA 46; *Miller v Eurovox Pty Ltd* [2004] VSCA 211 and *Registrar of the Court of Appeal v Maniam (No. 2)* (1992) 26 NSWLR 309 at 313.

[8] See *Ex parte Brown* [1864] EngR 447, (1864) 5 B and S 280, (1864) 122 ER 835.

[9] See *Attorney-General v Leveller Magazine Ltd and others* [1979] AC 440, per Diplock LJ at 449; *Australian Building Construction Employees' and Builders Labourers' Federation v David Syme and Company Ltd* (1982) 59 FLR 48 at 49, [1982] FCA 43; *Keegan v De Burca* [1973] I IR 223; *Poje v Attorney-General for British Columbia* [1953] 1 SCR 516, [1953] SCC 34 and *Witham v Holloway* (1995) 183 CLR 525 at 530, (1995) 131 ALR 401, (1995) 69 ALJR 847, [1995] HCA 3.

See also: D Eady and ATH Smith, 1999, 'Arlidge, Eady and Smith on Contempt' 2nd ed., Sweet and Maxwell, London, para. 3-1 and Chief Justice McRuer of the High Court of Justice of Ontario, 1952, 'Criminal Contempt of Court Procedure: A Protection to the Rights of the Individual', 130 Canadian Bar Review 225, p. 226.

[10] See *Andrew Kwimberi of Paulus M Dowa Lawyers v The State* (1998) SC545, [1998] PGSC 9 and *Paul Metta v The State* [1992] PNGLR 176 at 184.

See also: *Attorney-General v Times Newspapers Ltd* [1973] 3 All ER 54, [1974] AC 273 at 302.

## INTRODUCTION

As stated by Lord Denning MR in *R* v *Commissioner of Police of the Metropolis; ex parte Blackburn (No. 2)*[11]:

> Let me say at once that we will never use this jurisdiction as a means to uphold our own dignity. That must rest on surer foundations. Nor will we use it to suppress those who speak against us. We do not fear criticism, nor do we resent it. For there is something far more important at stake. It is no less than freedom of speech itself.

Contempt of court is a very serious matter.[12]

It amounts to:

- an interference in the administration of justice; and
- a subjugation of the Rule of Law[13].[14]

The contempt powers exist to protect the justice system and the Rule of Law.[15]

---

[11] [1968] 2 QB 150 at 155.

[12] See *Public Prosecutor v Nahau Rooney (No. 2)* [1979] PNGLR 448, [1979] PGSC 23; *Sr Dianne Liriope v Dr Jethro Usurup, Chief Executive Officer, Modilon General Hospital and others* (2009) N3572, [2009] PGNC 2; *Pioneers Health Services Ltd v Gabriel Yer, Secretary of Department of Finance and The State* (2008) N3326 and *Pius Mark for and on behalf of the Council of the Mount Hagen Technical College v Korali Iki* [1995] PNGLR 116, [1995] PGNC 134.

See also: *Varnavides v Victorian Civil and Administrative Tribunal and another* [2005] VSCA 231; *Registrar of the Court of Appeal v Maniam (No. 2)* (1992) 26 NSWLR 309 at 314; *Attorney-General (NSW) v Whiley* (1993) 31 NSWLR 314 and *Bydand Holdings Pty Limited v Pineland Property Holdings Pty Limited and others* [2009] NSWSC 584.

[13] As regards the legal principles in relation to the 'Rule of Law', refer also to the chapter titled 'Introduction To Criminal Law' in the text titled 'Injia on Criminal Practice and Procedure in Papua New Guinea and the Pacific'.

[14] See *Public Prosecutor v Nahau Rooney (No. 2)* [1979] PNGLR 448, [1979] PGSC 23; *Newsat Limited v Telikom PNG Ltd and others* (2008) N3673, [2008] PGNC 227 and *Sr Dianne Liriope v Dr Jethro Usurup, Chief Executive Officer, Modilon General Hospital and others* (2009) N3572, [2009] PGNC 2.

See also: *Attorney-General v Punch Ltd* [2003] 1 All ER 289, [2003] HRLR 14, [2003] 2 WLR 49, [2002] UKHL 50, [2003] AC 1046, [2003] EMLR 7, per Nicholls LJ.

[15] See *In re Section 57 of the Constitution of Papua New Guinea, Application by John Bosco* [2007] PGNC 195, (2007) N4999.

## INTRODUCTION

No one can question the extreme public importance of preserving an efficient and impartial system of justice in today's society which appears to be subject to growing dangers of direct action in its various forms. It is to that end, and that end alone, that the law of contempt exists.[16]

The Rule of Law is directly dependent on the ability of the courts to enforce their process and maintain their dignity and respect.[17]

The course of justice must not be deflected or interfered with. To maintain law and order, the judges have, and must have, power at once to deal with those who offend against it.[18]

The Rule of Law is central to a democratic way of life.[19]

It is unfortunate that the offence of 'Contempt of Court' should continue to be known by a name that suggests to the modern mind that its essence is a supposed affront to the dignity of the Court.[20]

---

[16] See *Solicitor-General v Radio Avon Ltd* [1978] 1 NZLR 225.

[17] See *United Nurses of Alberta v Alberta (Attorney-General)* [1992] 1 SCR 901, per McLachlin J at 931, [1992] SCC 99.

[18] See *Morris v The Crown Office* [1970] 1 All ER 1079 at 1081, [1970] 2 QB 114.

See also: *British Columbia Government Employees Union v British Columbia (Attorney-General)* [1988] 2 SCR 214, [1988] SCC 3.

[19] See *Public Prosecutor v Nahau Rooney (No. 2)* [1979] PNGLR 448, per Saladanha J at 482, [1979] PGSC 23; *Peter Luga v Richard Sikani Commissioner, Correctional Services and The State* (2002) N2285; *Bewa Tou on his own behalf and on behalf of Isou Clan of Krissa Village, Vanimo, Sandaun Province v Papua New Guinea Forest Authority and others* (2003) N2490; *Kapil Salo and others v Peter Terry Gerari and others* (2005) N2923 and *Luga v Sikani, Commissioner of Correctional Services (No. 2)* [2002] PGNC 60, (2002) N2286.

[20] See *Attorney-General v Times Newspapers Ltd* [1973] 3 All ER 54, [1974] AC 273, per Cross LJ at 322.

See also: Western Australia Law Reform Commission, 2003, 'Final Report on Report on the Law of Contempt'.

# INTRODUCTION

However, nothing could be further from the truth.[21]

The contempt powers of the Court do not exist to protect the personal feelings or dignity of the presiding Judge.[22]

It is justice itself[23] and the fundamental supremacy of the law[24] that is flouted by the 'Contempt of Court'.

The dignity of an individual judicial officer is of very subordinate importance compared with the dignity of the Court.[25]

---

[21] See *Pioneers Health Services Limited v Gabriel Yer, Secretary of Department of Finance and The State* (2008) N3326.

See also: *Jennison v Baker* [1972] QB 52 at 61; *Gisborne Herald Co Ltd v Solicitor-General* [1995] 3 NZLR 563 and *Solicitor-General v Radio Avon Ltd* [1978] 1 NZLR 225 at 229.

[22] See *In re Section 57 of the Constitution of Papua New Guinea, Application by John Bosco* [2007] PGNC 195, (2007) N4999.

See also: *R v Fowler* (1905) 1 Tas LR 53, per Dodds CJ at 56; *Helmore v Smith (No. 2)* (1886) 35 Ch D 449, per Bowen LJ; *R v Dunbabin; ex parte Williams* (1935) 53 CLR 434, per Rich J at 442; [1935] HCA 34; *Anthony Radcliffe Lewis v His Honour Judge Ogden* (1984) 153 CLR 682, [1984] HCA 26; *Ex parte Ferandez* [1861] EngR 556, (1861) 30 LJCP 321 at 332; *Skipworth's case* (1873) LR 9 QB 219 at 232 and *Balanto* [1963] SRNSW 200 at 202.

[23] See *The State v Foxy Kia Tala, Re Detective Constable Corney Winjan* [1995] PNGLR 303.

See also: *Attorney-General v Leveller Magazine Ltd and others* [1979] AC 440, per Diplock LJ at 449; *Jennison v Baker* [1972] 2 QB 52 at 61; *Anthony Radcliffe Lewis v His Honour Judge Ogden* (1984) 153 CLR 682 at 693, [1984] HCA 26 and *Attorney-General (NSW) v Willesee* [1980] 2 NSWLR 143 at 161.

[24] See *Johnson v Grant* [1923] SC 789, per Lord President Clyde at 790.

[25] See *Davenport v Vose* [2003] WASCA 44, per Pullin J.

# INTRODUCTION

The fundamental importance of the law on contempt of court is enduring, as it continues to play a significant role in the protection of the due administration of justice.[26]

The wisdom of history is that the Court must be free to deal directly and decisively with any contempt against its process.[27]

---

[26] See:

- *Re Colina; ex parte Torney* (1999) 200 CLR 386, (1999) 73 ALJR 1576, (1999) 166 ALR 545, per Hayne J at 579, [1999] HCA 57; *R v Kirby; ex parte Boilermakers' Society of Australia* (1956) 94 CLR 254 at 287, [1956] HCA 10; *Attorney-General v British Broadcasting Corporation* [1981] AC 303 and *Attorney-General (Cth) v R* (1957) 95 CLR 529 at 534, [1957] AC 288 at 308, [1957] HCA 12; and
- K Mason, 1983, 'The Inherent Jurisdiction of the Court', 57 Australian Law Journal 449.

The law in relation to Contempt of Court has been the subject of a number of reports including:

- Canadian Law Reform Commission, 1977, 'Contempt of Court: Offences Against the Administration of Justice', Working Paper No. 20;
- Canadian Law Reform Commission, 1982, 'Contempt of Court, Report No. 17;
- Ireland Law Reform Commission, 1991, 'Contempt of Court', Consultation Paper;
- Ireland Law Reform Commission, 1994, 'Contempt of Court', Report No. 47;
- United Kingdom, Committee on Contempt of Court, 1974, 'Report of the Committee on Contempt of Court', HMSO, London, Cmnd 5794, as referred to as the Phillimore report;
- Justice (British Section of the International Commission of Jurists), 1959, 'Contempt of Court', Report, Stevens and Sons, London;
- United Kingdom, Home Office and Scottish Home and Health Department, 'Report of the Interdepartmental Committee on the Law of Contempt As It Affects Tribunals of Inquiry', 1969, HMSO, London, Cmnd 4078;
- Australian Law Reform Commission, 1987, 'Contempt', Report No. 35;
- Australian Law Reform Commission, 1986, 'Contempt: Disruption, Disobedience and Deliberate Interference', Discussion Paper No. 27;
- New South Wales Law Reform Commission, 2000, 'Contempt by Publication', Report 100;
- New South Wales Law Reform Commission, 2000, 'Contempt by Publication', Discussion Paper No. 43;
- Law Reform Commission of Western Australia, 2001, 'Discussion Paper on Contempt in the Face of the Court', Project No. 93(I);
- Law Reform Commission of Western Australia, 2001, 'Discussion Paper on Contempt by Publication', Project No. 93(II);
- Law Reform Commission of Western Australia, 2002, 'Discussion Paper on Contempt by Disobedience to the Orders of the Court', Project No. 93(III); and
- Law Reform Commission of Western Australia, 2003, 'Final Report on Report on the Law of Contempt'.

[27] As stated by McEachern CJ in *MacMillan Bloedel Ltd v Simpson* (1997) 113 DLR (4th) 368 at 390.

## INTRODUCTION

Contempt powers are given to the Courts in order for Judges to:

- uphold and protect the effective administration of justice[28];
- prevent interference with the due administration of justice[29];
- maintain the supremacy of the law and the due and unobstructed administration of justice[30];
- protect the public interest in the integrity of the Court and its administration of justice[31];
- protect the dignity, quietness, and regularity of its proceedings, and to prevent defiance of its orders, to deal with acts of contempt[32];
- vindicate the integrity of the Court and of its proceedings[33];

---

[28] See *Attorney-General v Times Newspapers Ltd* [1973] 3 All ER 54, [1974] AC 273.

See also: *Australasian Meat Industry Employees Union v Mudginberri Station Pty Ltd* (1986) 161 CLR 98 at 107, (1986) 66 ALR 577 at 584, [1986] HCA 46; *R v West Australian Newspapers Ltd; ex parte Director of Public Prosecutions (WA)* (1996) 16 WAR 518; *Miller v Eurovox Pty Ltd* [2004] VSCA 211 and *Registrar of the Court of Appeal v Maniam (No. 2)* (1992) 26 NSWLR 309 at 313.

[29] See *Helmore v Smith (No. 2)* (1886) 35 Ch D 449, per Bowen LJ.

See also: *Attorney-General v Times Newspapers Ltd and another* [1991] 2 All ER 398, [1991] 2 WLR 994, [1992] 1 AC 191, per Ackner LJ at 209.

[30] See *Ruby Moy and others v Chan Luen Ying and another* [1964] HKLR 579 at 587.

[31] See *Bewa Tou on his own behalf and on behalf of Isou Clan of Krissa Village, Vanimo, Sandaun Province v Papua New Guinea Forest Authority and others* (2003) N2490.

[32] See *Petrie v Angus* (1889) 2 White 358, per Lord Justice Clerk Macdonald.

[33] See *Ex parte Ferandez* [1861] EngR 556, [1861] 30 LJCP 321 at 332 and *Skipworth's case* (1873) LR 9 QB 219 at 232.

See also: *Balanto* [1963] SRNSW 200 at 202 and *Anthony Radcliffe Lewis v His Honour Judge Ogden* (1984) 153 CLR 682 at 688, [1984] HCA 26.

- protect the integrity of its operations and to prevent interference with its administration of justice[34];
- keep the course of justice free for by the exercise of them law and order prevails[35];
- punish acts of contempt so as to maintain the dignity and authority of the Court and to ensure a fair trial[36];
- ensure that justice will be done and solely to this end, it prohibits acts and words tending to obstruct the administration of justice[37];
- ensure that justice shall be done by prohibiting acts and words tending to obstruct the administration of justice[38], either in a particular case or more generally as a continuing process in the case of criminal contempts[39];
- preserve and protect the general community interest, not the Court's own dignity[40], in suppressing unjustifiable interference in the authority of the Courts of the land[41];

---

[34] See *Commissioner of Taxation v De Vonk* (1995) 61 FCR 564, per Foster J at 569.

See also: Australian Law Reform Commission, 1987, 'Contempt', Report No. 35, p. 16.

[35] As stated by Dodds CJ in *R v Fowler* (1905) 1 Tas LR 53 at 56.

[36] See *Balogh v Crown Court at Saint Albans* [1974] 3 All ER 283, per Denning LJ at 288, [1975] QB 73.

See also: *British Columbia Government Employees Union v British Columbia (Attorney-General)* [1988] 2 SCR 214, per Dickson CJ at 238, [1988] SCC 3.

[37] See *The State v Foxy Kia Tala, Re Detective Constable Corney Winjan* [1995] PNGLR 303.

See also: *Jennison v Baker* [1972] 2 QB 52, per Salmon LJ at 61.

[38] As stated by Salmon LJ in *Jennison v Baker* [1972] 2 QB 52 at 61.

[39] As stated by Diplock LJ in *Attorney-General v Leveller Magazine Ltd and others* [1979] AC 440 at 449.

[40] See *Helmore v Smith (No. 2)* (1886) 35 Ch D 449, per Bowen LJ.

[41] See *Paul Metta v The State* [1992] PNGLR 176 at 184 and *Andrew Kwimberi of Paulus M Dowa Lawyers v The State* (1998) SC545, [1998] PGSC 9.

See also: *Attorney-General v Times Newspapers Ltd* [1973] 3 All ER 54, [1974] AC 273 at 302.

- ensure that justice shall be done and solely to this end, it prohibits acts and words tending to obstruct the administration of justice[42];

- secure a better and more secure administration of justice. Every writing, letter or publication which has for its object to divert the course of justice is a contempt of the Court[43];

- protect the authority of the Courts and preserve the impartial administration of justice[44];

- uphold the undisturbed and orderly administration of justice in the Courts according to law[45];

- enforce the process and orders of the Court, disobedience to which has been described as 'civil contempt'[46]; and

---

[42] See *Pioneers Health Services Limited v Gabriel Yer, Secretary of Department of Finance and The State* (2008) N3326.

See also: *Jennison v Baker* [1972] QB 52 at 61; *Gisborne Herald Co Ltd v Solicitor-General* [1995] 3 NZLR 563 and *Solicitor-General v Radio Avon Ltd* [1978] 1 NZLR 225 at 229.

[43] As stated by Cottenham LC in *Re Ludlow Charities; Mr Lechmere Charlton's Case* (1837) 2 My and Cr 316 at 339, [1837] EngR 524, (1837) 40 ER 661 at 670.

[44] See *R v David Syme and Co* [1982] VicRp 16, [1982] VR 173.

[45] See *C v Registrar, Court of Appeal No. Ca 40130/94 Contempt* [1996] NSWSC 103; *Director of Public Prosecutions v John Fairfax and Sons Ltd* (1987) 8 NSWLR 732 at 741; *Kennedy v Lovell* [2002] WASCA 226; *Phelan* (1993) 66 A Crim R 446 at 449; *GDR* (1994) 35 NSWLR 376 at 378, (1994) 75 A Crim R 319 at 321; *Wood v Staunton (No. 5)* (1995) 86 A Crim R 183; *Registrar of the Court of Appeal v Maniam (No. 2)* (1992) 26 NSWLR 309, per Kirby P at 314 and *Pelechowski v The Registrar of the Court of Appeal of New South Wales* (1999) 198 CLR 435, per McHugh J at 462 and Kirby J at 484, [1999] HCA 19.

[46] See *Australasian Meat Industry Employees' Union and others v Mudginberri Station Pty Ltd* (1986) 161 CLR 98 at 106, (1986) 66 ALR 577, [1986] HCA 46 and *Witham v Holloway* (1995) 183 CLR 525 at 533, (1995) 131 ALR 401, (1995) 69 ALJR 847, [1995] HCA 3.

See also: J Fox, 1927, 'History of Contempt of Court', p. 1.

- punish other acts which impede the administration of justice, such as obstructing proceedings in court while it is sitting or publishing comments on a pending case, which have both been described as 'criminal contempt'[47].

However, the law of contempt does not exist to protect the private interests of a person.[48]

Contempt of court involves two ideas:

- contempt of their power, referring to the deference and respect which is paid to Judges and their acts, from an opinion of their justice and integrity; and

- contempt of their authority which is used to express both the right of declaring the law, which is properly called jurisdiction, and enforcing obedience to it.[49]

The Supreme and National Courts, have undoubted powers to compel:

- observance of their processes; and

- obedience of and compliance with their orders and directions.[50]

However, judges ought to remember the purpose of their contempt powers.[51]

---

[47] See *Australasian Meat Industry Employees' Union and others v Mudginberri Station Pty Ltd* (1986) 161 CLR 98 at 106, (1986) 66 ALR 577, [1986] HCA 46.

See also: J Fox, 1927, 'History of Contempt of Court', p. 1.

[48] See *Attorney-General v Times Newspapers Ltd* [1973] 3 All ER 54, [1974] AC 273.

See also: *R v West Australian Newspapers Ltd; ex parte Director of Public Prosecutions (WA)* (1996) 16 WAR 518.

[49] As stated by Wilmot J in *R v Almon* (1765) 97 ER 94 at 100, (1765) Wilm 243 at 256, [1765] EngR 25.

[50] See *Review Pursuant to Constitution, Section 155(2)(B); Application by Herman Joseph Leahy* (2006) SC855 and *Peter Luga v Richard Sikani Commissioner, Correctional Services and The State* (2002) N2285.

[51] See *Paul Metta v The State* [1992] PNGLR 176.

## INTRODUCTION

Committal for contempt of Court is a weapon to be used sparingly[52] and exercised strictly for the purposes of the prevention of interference with the fair and due administration of justice.[53]

Contempt powers are inherent in the sense that they 'are necessary attributes to render the judicial function effective in the administration of justice'. Expressed in another way, the power to punish for contempt is inherent in the Courts. The contempt power enables the Courts to:

- perform their functions without interference;
- control courtroom behavior; and
- enforce orders and compel obedience.[54]

In the general interests of the community it is imperative that:

- the authority of the Courts should not be imperiled; and
- recourse to the Courts should not be subject to unjustifiable interference.[55]

The enforcement in proper cases of committal for 'Contempt of Court' for attacks on the Court may be absolutely necessary to preserve in the community the dignity of and respect for the Court.[56]

---

[52] See *SCR No 3 of 1984; Ex parte Callick and Koroma* [1985] PNGLR 67, [1985] PGSC 20 and *Public Prosecutor v Nahau Rooney (No. 2)* [1979] PNGLR 448, [1979] PGSC 23.

See also: *Drummoyne Municipal Council v Lewis* [1974] 1 NSWLR 655, per Holland J at 658 and *R v WA Newspapers Ltd; ex parte Director of Public Prosecutions (WA)* (1996) 16 WAR 518.

[53] See *McLeod v St. Aubyn* [1899] AC 549 at 561.

See also: the comments of Montgomery J in *Re Ouellet (Nos. 1 and 2)* (1977) 72 DLR (3d) 95 at 102 and *Attorney-General for New South Wales v Mundey* (1972) 2 NSWLR 887 at 907.

[54] See *Peter Luga v Richard Sikani Commissioner, Correctional Services and The State* (2002) N2285.

[55] See *Paul Metta v The State* [1992] PNGLR 176.

[56] See *Ambard v Attorney-General for Trinidad and Tobago* [1936] AC 322, per Morris LJ at 335.

## INTRODUCTION

Contempt proceedings are distinct from those proceedings that gave rise to the contempt.[57]

However, a contempt of court can occur although no proceedings are on foot or the conduct is not tied to:

- specific proceedings; or
- a particular court.[58]

Notwithstanding that the contempt provisions as provided for by section 277 of the *District Courts Act* (Ch. 40) ['Contempt of Court'] are limited to the matters therein[59], the National Court, has an inherent power to watch over the proceedings of inferior courts, such as the District Court, to, inter alia, prevent persons from interfering with the course of justice in inferior courts. The power of the National Court derives from the unlimited jurisdiction conferred upon it by the *Constitution of the Independent State of Papua New Guinea.*[60]

---

[57] See *O'Shea v O'Shea and Parnell* (1890) 15 PD 59, per Cotton LJ at 63.

See also: *R v B* [1972] WAR 129, per Hale J; *Viner (Minister of State for Industrial Relations) v Australian Building Construction Employees and Builders' Labourers' Federation* (1981) 38 ALR 550, per Northrop J at 555; *Gregory v Phillip Morris Ltd* (1987) 74 ALR 300 at 308; *Jeray v Blue Mountains City Council* [2011] NSWLEC 28 and *Witham v Holloway* (1995) 183 CLR 525 at 530, (1995) 131 ALR 401, (1995) 69 ALJR 847, [1995] HCA 3.

[58] As explained by McHugh JA in *Pelechowski v Registrar, Court of Appeal of New South Wales* (1999) 198 CLR 435, (1999) 162 ALR 336, (1999) 73 ALJR 687, [1999] HCA 19.

Order 14, rule 42(2) of the *National Court Rules 1983* ['Procedure Generally'] states:

> 'Where contempt is committed, but not in connexion with proceedings in the court, proceedings for punishment of the contempt must be commenced by originating summons, but an application for punishment of the contempt is made by motion on notice in any proceedings, the application may be heard and disposed of in the latter proceedings, unless the court otherwise orders'.

[59] See *Marko Iatinata v Denison Toiwat and Penington Valaun* (1994) N1204 and *Agnes Okona Meten v William Seneka and Magisterial Services* (2011) N4462, [2011] PGNC 169.

[60] See *Pius Mark for and on behalf of the Council of the Mount Hagen Technical College v Korali Iki* [1995] PNGLR 116, [1995] PGNC 134 and *Roy Koroka v Michael Kapal and The State* (2011) N4384, [2011] PGNC 112.

As to such power at common law, see *In re an application by Liu Lee Yuk-ching* [1982] HKLR 399; *R v Davies* [1906] 1 KB 32; *John Fairfax and Sons Pty Ltd v McRae* (1955) 93 CLR 351 at 606, [1955] HCA 12; *R v McKinnon* (1909) 12 NZ Gaz LR 423 at 424; *R v Daily Mail; ex parte Farnsworth* [1921] 2 KB 733; *Ex parte Bishop of Norwich* [1932] 2 KB 402; *Attorney-General v Soundy* (1938) 33 Tas LR 143; *R v Edwards* (1933) 49 Times LR 383; *Ex parte Collins; Re Hlentzos* (1935) 52 WN (NSW) 65; *Attorney-General (NSW) v Mundey* [1972] 2 NSWLR 887, per Hope JA at 905 and *R v Hoser and Kotabi Pty Ltd* [2001] VSC 443.

## INTRODUCTION

The National Court may act on its own motion to institute contempt proceedings[61] and there is no interposition of a prosecuting authority since the function that is exercised by the Court is not to be exercised or controlled by the Executive[62].

However, when deciding whether to lay a charge of 'disobedience contempt[63]' a Judge should consider:

- the extent of non-compliance with the Court's orders;
- whether non-compliance appears to be manifestation of a deliberate snubbing of or disrespect for the Court;
- whether the purpose of making the orders might be defeated by laying a charge; and
- whether the persons in whose favour the orders were made have applied or agitated for the laying of charges.[64]

---

[61] Order 14, Division 6, rule 47(1) of the *National Court Rules 1983* ['Motion or Proceedings by Registrar'] states:

> 'Where it is alleged, or appears to the Court on its own view, that a person is guilty of contempt of the court or of any other court, the Court may, by order, direct the Registrar to apply by motion for, or to commence proceedings for, punishment of the contempt'.

[62] See *Re Colina; ex parte Torney* (1999) 200 CLR 386 at 429, (1999) 73 ALJR 1576, (1999) 166 ALR 545, [1999] HCA 57.

[63] See *Stephen John Rose and another v Neville Devete, Acting Solicitor-General and The State* (2007) N3327 and *Public Officers Superannuation Fund Board v Paul Paraka Trading as Paul Paraka Lawyers and Paul Paraka Trading as Paul Paraka Lawyers v Public Officers Superannuation Fund Board* (2005) N2791.

See also: Australian Law Reform Commission, 1987, 'Contempt', Report No. 35, Ch. 5.

[64] See *In re Section 57 of the Constitution of Papua New Guinea, Application by John Bosco* (2007) N4999, [2007] PGNC 195.

## [2.0] INFERIOR COURTS

## [2.1] INTRODUCTION

At common law inferior courts of record have jurisdiction to deal summarily with contempt in the face of the court.[65]

However, the contempt provisions as provided for by section 277 of the *District Courts Act* (Ch. 40) ['Contempt of Court'] and section 28 of the *Coroners Act* (Ch. 32) are limited to the matters therein[66] and therefore, both those courts are not empowered to punish contemptuous behavior that is not specified in such statutory provisions.

The offences are non-indictable and therefore may be dealt with summarily.[67]

This textbook examines the law in relation to that offence as it applies in the Supreme and National Courts.

## [2.2] DISTRICT COURT

### STATUTORY PROVISION

Section 277 of the *District Courts Act* (Ch. 40) ['Contempt of Court'] states:

> '(1) A person who –
>
> (a) wilfully interrupts the proceedings of a Court; or
>
> (b) conducts himself disrespectfully to the Court during the sittings of the Court; or
>
> (c) obstructs or assaults a person in attendance, or an officer of the Court, in view of the Court; or

---

[65] See *R v Brompton County Court Judge* [1893] QB 195.

See also: *R v Metal trades Employers' Association; ex parte Amalgamated Engineering Union* (1951) 82 CLR 208, per Latham CJ at 241, [1951] HCA 3.

[66] See *Marko Iatinata v Denison Toiwat and Penington Valaun* (1994) N1204 and *Agnes Okona Meten v William Seneka and Magisterial Services* (2011) N4462, [2011] PGNC 169.

[67] Refer also to the chapter titled 'Classification Of Offences' in the text titled 'Injia on Criminal Practice and Procedure in Papua New Guinea and the Pacific'.

(d) wilfully disobeys an order made by the Court under Section 63[68],

may be excluded from the Court and is guilty of an offence.

Penalty: A fine not exceeding K200.00[69].

(2) A person who, in the opinion of the Court, wilfully prevaricates in giving evidence is guilty of an offence.

Penalty[70]: A fine not exceeding K100.00[71].

(3) The Court in the presence of which an offence under this section is committed may immediately convict the person guilty of the offence, on its own view or on the oath of some credible witness.

(4) If a person convicted of an offence against Subsection (1) makes to the Court, before its rising, such apology as it considers satisfactory, the Court may remit the fine wholly or in part'.

## GENERAL PRINCIPLES

Section 277 of the *District Courts Act* (Ch. 40) prescribes;

- the elements of the offence of 'Contempt of Court';
- the procedure for dealing with a person alleged to be guilty of that offence; and

---

[68] Section 63 of the *District Courts Act* (Ch. 40) ['Ordering Witnesses Out of Court'] states:

> At any time during the hearing, a Court may if it thinks fit, and shall if required by a party, order that all witnesses, other than the complainant and the defendant and the witnesses under examination, go and remain outside and beyond the hearing of the Court until required to give evidence, except in so far as in particular cases and in special circumstances it sees fit to do otherwise'.

[69] As regards the law in relation to 'Sentencing', refer to the text titled 'Injia on Sentencing in Papua New Guinea and the Pacific'.

[70] This is not an indictable offence [see section 21(b) of the *Interpretation Act* (Ch. 2)] and therefore can be dealt with summarily [see section 22 of the *Interpretation Act* (Ch. 2)].

Refer also to the chapter titled 'Classification Of Offences' in the text titled 'Injia on Criminal Practice and Procedure in Papua New Guinea and the Pacific'.

[71] As regards the law in relation to 'Sentencing', refer to the text titled 'Injia on Sentencing in Papua New Guinea and the Pacific'.

- the punishment that may be imposed upon conviction.[72]

An Information (a written charge) may be laid under section 28 of the *District Courts Act* (Ch. 40) ['Information and Complaints'], but that is not a mandatory procedure.[73]

Section 277(3) allows the District Court to deal with a person alleged to be guilty of the offence of 'Contempt of Court' summarily.[74]

That section states:

> 'The Court in the presence of which an offence under this section is committed may immediately convict the person guilty of the offence, on its own view or on the oath of some credible witness.'

However, whichever procedure is used, it must be fair: it must comply with the principles of 'natural justice'.[75]

The person alleged to be guilty of contempt must be:

- given adequate notice of the charge;
- told in reasonably precise terms what the charge is; and
- given a reasonable opportunity to be heard.[76]

[72] See *Agnes Okona Meten v William Seneka and Magisterial Services* (2011) N4462, [2011] PGNC 169.

[73] See *Agnes Okona Meten v William Seneka and Magisterial Services* (2011) N4462, [2011] PGNC 169.

[74] See *Agnes Okona Meten v William Seneka and Magisterial Services* (2011) N4462, [2011] PGNC 169.

Section 59 of the *Constitution of the Independent State of Papua New Guinea* ['Principles of Natural Justice'] states:

> '(1) Subject to this Constitution and to any statute, the principles of natural justice are the rules of the underlying law known by that name developed for control of judicial and administrative proceedings.
> (2) The minimum requirement of natural justice is the duty to act fairly and, in principle, to be seen to act fairly'.

[75] See *Andrew Kwimberi of Paulus M Dowa Lawyers v The State* (1998) SC545, [1998] PGSC 9 and *Agnes Okona Meten v William Seneka and Magisterial Services* (2011) N4462, [2011] PGNC 169.

[76] See *Agnes Okona Meten v William Seneka and Magisterial Services* (2011) N4462, [2011] PGNC 169.

## INTRODUCTION

### [2.3] CORONERS COURT

Section 28 of the *Coroners Act* (Ch. 32) ['Power to Punish for Contempt'] states:

'Where a person –

(a) insults the Coroner during the holding of an inquest; or

(b) wilfully interrupts the proceedings at an inquest; or

(c) obstructs or assaults a person in attendance at an inquest; or

(d) refuses or neglects to obey a lawful order of the Coroner,

the Coroner may impose on him a fine not exceeding K40.00[77],[78].

[77] This is not an indictable offence [see section 21(b) of the *Interpretation Act* (Ch. 2)] and therefore can be dealt with summarily [see section 22 of the *Interpretation Act* (Ch. 2)].

Refer also to the chapter titled 'Classification Of Offences' in the text titled 'Injia on Criminal Practice and Procedure in Papua New Guinea and the Pacific'.

As regards the law in relation to 'Sentencing', refer to the text titled 'Injia on Sentencing in Papua New Guinea and the Pacific'.

[78] Refer also to the text titled 'Injia on Coronial Proceedings in Papua New Guinea and the Pacific'.

## GENERAL CONSTITUTIONAL RIGHTS

### [1.0] GENERAL PRINCIPLE

It is the duty of courts to zealously guard the rights entrenched in the *Constitution of the Independent State of Papua New Guinea*, especially the National Court and the Supreme Court. Before any of these rights are denied to a person the Courts must ensure that the circumstances of the particular person come within the exceptions (if any) specifically outlined in the *Constitution*.[79]

### [2.0] CONSTITUTIONAL PROVISIONS

Section 160(2) of the *Constitution of the Independent State of Papua New Guinea* ['Establishment of the Supreme Court'] states:

> 'The Supreme Court is a superior court of record and accordingly, subject to any Act of the Parliament, has the power to punish the offence against itself commonly known as contempt of court'.

Section 163(2) ['Establishment of the National Court'] states:

> 'The National Court is a superior court of record and accordingly, subject to any Act of the Parliament, has the power to punish the offence against itself commonly known as contempt of court'.

Section 37 of the *Constitution of the Independent State of Papua New Guinea* ['Protection of the Law'][80] states (in part):

> '(1) Every person has the right to the full protection of the law, and the succeeding provisions of this section are intended to ensure that that right is fully available, especially to persons in custody or charged with offences.[81]

---

[79] As stated by Kidu CJ in *Thomas Kavali v Thomas Hoihoi* [1986] PNGLR 329 at 332.

See also: *Tom Longman Yaul v The State* (2005) SC803, [2005] PGSC 29.

[80] See also: section 178 of the *Constitution of the Autonomous Region of Bougainville* ['Basic Rights'].

[81] This constitutional provision applies to contempt charges, see *Stephen John Rose and another v Neville Devete, Acting Solicitor-General and The State* (2007) N3327.

(2) Except, subject to any Act of the Parliament to the contrary, in the case of the offence commonly known as contempt of court, nobody may be convicted of an offence that is not defined by, and the penalty for which is not prescribed by, a written law.

(3) A person charged with an offence shall, unless the charge is withdrawn, be afforded a fair hearing within a reasonable time, by an independent and impartial court.[82]

(4) A person charged with an offence –

(a) shall be presumed innocent until proved guilty according to law, but a law may place upon a person charged with an offence the burden of proving particular facts which are, or would be, peculiarly within his knowledge[83]; and

(b) shall be informed promptly in a language which he understands, and in detail, of the nature of the offence with which he is charged[84]; and

(c) shall be given adequate time and facilities for the preparation of his defence[85]; and

(d) shall be permitted to have without payment the assistance of an interpreter if he cannot understand or speak the language used at the trial of the charge; and

(e) shall be permitted to defend himself before the court in person or, at his own expense, by a legal representative of his own choice, or if he is a person entitled to legal aid, by the Public Solicitor or another legal representative assigned to him in accordance with law[86]; and

---

82 This constitutional provision applies to contempt charges, see *Stephen John Rose and another v Neville Devete, Acting Solicitor-General and The State* (2007) N3327.

83 This constitutional provision applies to contempt charges, see *Stephen John Rose and another v Neville Devete, Acting Solicitor-General and The State* (2007) N3327.

84 This constitutional provision applies to contempt charges, see *Stephen John Rose and another v Neville Devete, Acting Solicitor-General and The State* (2007) N3327.

85 This constitutional provision applies to contempt charges, see *Ross Bishop and others v Bishop Brothers Engineering and Pty Ltd* [1998-89] PNGLR 533, [1988] PGSC 8 and *Stephen John Rose and another v Neville Devete, Acting Solicitor-General and The State* (2007) N3327.

86 This constitutional provision applies to contempt charges, see *Ross Bishop and others v Bishop Brothers Engineering and Pty Ltd* [1998-89] PNGLR 533, [1988] PGSC 8.

(f) shall be afforded facilities to examine in person or by his legal representative the witnesses called before the court by the prosecution, and to obtain the attendance and carry out the examination of witnesses and to testify before the court on his own behalf, on the same conditions as those applying to witnesses called by the prosecution[87].

(5) Except with his own consent, the trial shall not take place in his absence unless he so conducts himself as to render the continuance of the proceedings in his presence impracticable and the court orders him to be removed and the trial to proceed in his absence, but provision may be made by law for a charge that a person has committed an offence the maximum penalty for which does not include imprisonment, (except in default of payment of a fine), to be heard summarily in his absence if it is established that he has been duly served with a summons in respect of the alleged offence.[88]

(10) No person shall be compelled in the trial of an offence to be a witness against himself'.

Section 42(1) ['Liberty Of The Person'][89] states (in part):

'No person shall be deprived of his personal liberty except –

(b) in the execution of the sentence or order of a court in respect of an offence of which he has been found guilty, or in the execution of the order of a court of record punishing him for contempt of itself or *another court* or tribunal'. (emphasis added)

[87] This constitutional provision applies to contempt charges, see *Ross Bishop and others v Bishop Brothers Engineering and Pty Ltd* [1998-89] PNGLR 533, [1988] PGSC 8 and *Stephen John Rose and another v Neville Devete, Acting Solicitor-General and The State* (2007) N3327.

[88] This constitutional provision applies to a charge of contempt of court, see *Ross Bishop and others v Bishop Brothers Engineering and Pty Ltd* [1998-89] PNGLR 533, [1988] PGSC 8 and *21 ILGS Gobe Project Area Inc Land Groups v Pawih* [2006] PGNC 10, (2006) N3066.

However, a charge on contempt may be heard in the absence of a contemnor, depending on the circumstances, see *Seth L Daniels as Senior Vice President of Papua New Guinea Football (Soccer) Association Inc v David Chung as the President of Papua New Guinea Football (Soccer) Association Inc and another* (2009) N3610, [2009] PGNC 24 and *Bank of South Pacific Ltd v Sekum* [2011] PGNC 176, (2011) N4588.

Refer also to the section titled 'Right To Be Present' in the chapter titled 'Rights Of An Accused Person' in the text titled 'Injia on Criminal Practice and Procedure in Papua New Guinea and the Pacific'.

[89] See also: section 178 of the *Constitution of the Autonomous Region of Bougainville* ['Basic Rights'].

## ORIGIN OF CONTEMPT OF COURT

'Contempt of Court' is said to have its origins in the medieval devolution of royal powers to the courts from a monarch who was believed to be divinely appointed and accountable only to God.[90]

The jurisidiction of 'Contempt of Court' dates back to at least the 12th century[91] and has been regarded as inherent in courts throughout the recorded history of the Common Law[92].

In 1900 Lord Russell CJ in *R v Gray*[93] described it as:

> not a new-fangled jurisdiction; it is a jurisdiction as old as the common law itself, of which it forms a part.

At common law all courts have the jurisdiction to defend their own authority.[94]

---

[90] See Australian Law Reform Commission, 1987, 'Contempt', Report No. 35, p. 16.

[91] 'Contemptus curiae' was referred to by Glanvill, an English legal historian writing about 1187, apparently referring to a failure by a litigant to appear before the court: see D Eady and ATH Smith, 1999, 'Arlidge, Eady and Smith on Contempt' 2nd ed., Sweet and Maxwell, London, Ch. 1.

See also: *United Nurses of Alberta v Alberta (Attorney-General)* [1992] 1 SCR 901, per McLachlin J at 931, [1992] SCC 99.

[92] As stated by O'Higgins CJ in *The State (Director of Public Prosecutions) v Walsh* [1981] IR 412 at 429.

[93] [1900] 2 QB 36 at 40.

This jurisdiction is not known to the civil law countries, see *Times Newspapers Limited v United Kingdom* [1979] 2 EHRR 245 and *Director of Public Prosecutions v Independent Newspapers Ireland Ltd and others* [2003] IEHC 624.

[94] See *British Columbia Government Employees Union v British Columbia (Attorney-General)* [1988] 2 SCR 214, [1988] SCC 3, per Dickson CJ and *Cordiner v Petr* [1973] JC 16, per Lord Justice General Emslie at 18.

See also: H Jacob, 1970, 'The Inherent Jurisdiction of the Court', 23 Current Legal Problems 23, p. 27.

## ORIGIN OF CONTEMPT OF COURT

In 1765 Wilmot J in *R v Almon*[95] stated:

> The power of the courts to punish for contempt 'stancis upon the same immemorial usage as supports the whole fabric of the Common Law'; the power of 'vindicating their own authority is coeval with their first foundation and institution'.

The contempt jurisdiction is inherent in the very idea of a Court[96] and provides great coercive powers of proceedings for contempt[97].

Historically, the settled rule was that a court of record[98] was the sole and exclusive judge of what amounted to a contempt of court.[99]

The contempt jurisdiction is a summary remedy for obstructions in the course of justice and causing the process of the law to be obeyed.[100]

---

[95] [1765] EngR 25, (1765) 97 ER 94, (1765) Wilm 243.

The principles enunciated in that case have been applied in numerous cases including: *Packer v Peacock* (1912) 13 CLR 577, [1912] HCA 8; *Porter v R; ex parte Yee* (1926) 37 CLR 432, [1926] HCA 9; *Consolidated Press Ltd v McRae* (1955) 93 CLR 325, [1955] HCA 11; *John Fairfax and Sons Pty Ltd v McRae* (1955) 93 CLR 351, [1955] HCA 12; *R v Clarke; ex parte Crippen* (1910) 103 LT 636; *R v Daily Mirror; ex parte Smith* (1927) 1 KB 845; *R v Davies; ex parte Delbert-Evans* (1945) 1 KB 435 and *R v Duffy; ex parte Nash* (1960) 2 QB 188.

[96] See *R v Almon* [1765] EngR 25, (1765) 97 ER 94, (1765) Wilm 243 at 254 and *Hamilton v Anderson* (1858) 3 Macq 363, per Chelmsford LC at 373.

See also:

- *British Columbia Government Employees Union v British Columbia (Attorney-General)* [1988] 2 SCR 214, [1988] SCC 3, per Dickson CJ; *Cordiner v Petr* [1973] JC 16, per Lord Justice General Emslie at 18; *R v Kirby; ex parte Boilermakers' Society of Australia* (1956) 94 CLR 254, [1956] HCA 10; *Ex Parte Robinson* (1873) 86 US 505 at 510; *Attorney-General v British Broadcasting Corporation* [1981] AC 303 and *R v Vermette* [1987] 1 SCR 577, [1987] SCC 51, per McIntyre J; and
- H Jacob, 1970, 'The Inherent Jurisdiction of the Court', 23 Current Legal Problems 23, p. 27; K Mason, 1983, 'The Inherent Jurisdiction of the Court', 57 Australian Law Journal 449 and J Fox, 1972, 'The History of Contempt of Court', p. 1.

[97] As described by Woodhouse J in *Taylor v Attorney-General* [1975] 2 NZLR 675 at 690.

[98] A 'court of record' is a court whereof the acts and judicial proceedings are enrolled for a perpetual memory and testimony, and which has authority to fine and imprisonment for contempt of its authority, see *Simon Mali and others v The State* (2002) SC690.

[99] See *Rainy v The Justices of Sierra Leone* [1853] EngR 788, (1853) 8 Moo PC 47 at 54, (1853) 14 ER 19 at 21.

[100] As stated by Parke B in *Miller v Knox* [1838] EngR 648, (1838) 4 Bing (NC) 574 at 614, (1838) 132 ER 910 at 925, (1838) Scott 1.

## ORIGIN OF CONTEMPT OF COURT

Contempt is the only criminal offence punishable summarily at common law.[101]

Historically, the litigant and private citizens[102] have the power to apply to the Court to exercise its contempt jurisdiction.

At common law 'Contempt of Court', other than a 'civil' contempt referred to as 'contempt in procedure', was a misdemeanour[103] and was able to be prosecuted either by indictment[104] or criminal information.[105]

---

[101] As observed by Lindley LJ in *O'Shea v O'Shea and Parnell* (1890) 15 PD 59 at 64.

[102] See *R v Henningham* (1869) Mac (NZ) 712; *R v Fletcher; ex parte Kisch* (1935) 52 CLR 248, per Evatt J at 258, [1935] HCA 1; *R v Dunbavin; ex parte Williams* (1935) 53 CLR 434, per Rich J at 445, [1935] HCA 34; *European Asian Bank AG v Wentworth* (1986) 5 NSWLR 445 at 459; *Director of Public Prosecutions v Australian Broadcasting Corporation* (1987) 7 NSWLR 588 at 595 and *United Telecasters Sydney Ltd v Hardy* (1991) 23 NSWLR 323 at 328.

See also:

- G Borrie and N Lowe, 1983, 'The Law of Contempt' 2nd ed., Butterworths, London, p. 327; and
- Order 14, Division 6, rule 47(2) of the *National Court Rules 1983* ['Motion or Proceedings by Registrar'].

[103] See *Skipworth's Case* (1873) LR 9 QB 230 at 233.

See also: Hawkins, 1824, 'Pleas of the Crown' 8th ed., Book 1, Ch. 6, s. 8, vol. I., p. 63; Book 2, Ch. 25, s. 4, vol. II., p. 289.

[104] See *R v Revel* (1719) I Str. 420, (1719) 93 E.R. 609; *R v Fisher* (1811) 2 Camp. 563, (1811) 170 ER 1253 and *Skipworth's case* (1873) LR 9 QB 230 at 233.

See also: Hawkins, 1824, 'Pleas of the Crown' 8th ed., Book 1, Ch. 6, s. 8, vol. I., p. 63; Book 2, Ch. 25, s. 4, vol. II., p. 289.

The last reported case in England was *R v Tibbits* [1902] 1 KB 97, see *Registrar of the Court of Appeal v Willesee* [1984] 2 NSWLR 378, per Samuels JA at 381.

In Australia the procedure is still available, see *Maslen v Official Receiver* (1947) 74 CLR 602 at 610, [1947] HCA 30, although not used.

[105] See *Re Davies* (1888) 21 QBD 236 at 238; *R v McKinnon* (1909) 12 GLR 423 at 424; *Scott v Scott* [1913] AC 417 at 460; *Morris v The Crown Office* [1970] 1 All ER 1079, [1970] 2 QB 114 at 123 and *Balogh v Crown Court at Saint Albans* [1974] 3 All ER 283, [1975] QB 73, per Lawton LJ at 91.

See also:

- *Re Dunn; Re Aspinall* [1906] VicLawRp 84, [1906] VLR 493 at 501; *John Fairfax and Sons Pty Ltd v McRae* (1955) 93 CLR 351 at 364 and 370, [1955] HCA 12; *Fraser v R (No. 2)* (1985) 1 NSWLR 680 at 692 and *R v Vermette* (1987) 32 CCC (3d) 519; and
- Oswald, 1910, 'Contempt of Court' 3rd ed, Butterworths, London, p. 6.

## DEFINITION OF CONTEMPT OF COURT

Neither the *Constitution of the Independent State of Papua New Guinea*[106] nor any statutory provision[107], including the *National Court Rules 1983,* define the term 'Contempt of Court'.

The offence of 'Contempt of Court' in relation to the Supreme and National Courts is not defined by written law[108], a scenario that is expressly authorised by section 37(2) of the *Constitution of the Independent State of Papua New Guinea* ['Protection of the Law'][109].

It is left to the Court to define in accordance with principles established by precedent.[110]

'Contempt of Court' is historically, and by its name and nature, concerned with:

- the position of courts;
- proceedings in court; and
- the protection of parties to proceedings in court.[111]

'Contempt of Court' is, however, an unfortunate and misleading phrase.[112]

'Contempt of Court' is a generic term, the definition of which conceals a certain degree of complexity.[113]

---

106 See *Andrew Kwimberi of Paulus M Dowa Lawyers v The State* (1998) SC545, [1998] PGSC 9.

107 See *Andrew Kwimberi of Paulus M Dowa Lawyers v The State* (1998) SC545, [1998] PGSC 9.

108 See *Nombri Waine Ambre v The State* [1995] PNGLR 453, [1995] PGNC 101 and *The State v Joseph Waine and others* (2002) N2276.

109 See *Agnes Okona Meten v William Seneka and Magisterial Services* (2011) N4462, [2011] PGNC 169.

110 See *Nombri Waine Ambre v The State* [1995] PNGLR 453, [1995] PGNC 101.

111 See *James v Robinson* (1963) 109 CLR 593, [1963] HCA 32, per Windeyer J.

112 See *The State v Foxy Kia Tala, Re Detective Constable Corney Winjan* [1995] PNGLR 303 and *Pioneers Health Services Limited v Gabriel Yer, Secretary of Department of Finance and The State* (2008) N3326.

See also: *Jennison v Baker* [1972] 2 QB 52, per Salmon LJ at 61.

113 See *Vidéotron Ltée v Industries Microlec Produits Électroniques Inc.* [1992] 2 SCR 1065, [1992] SCC 29, per L'Heureux-Dubé J.

## DEFINITION OF CONTEMPT OF COURT

At common law 'Contempt of Court' is also an unfortunate[114] and misleading expression that covers the various ways in which words or conduct unlawfully interfere[115] with the due administration of justice[116].[117]

Due administration of justice requires that:

- all citizens should have unhindered access to the constitutionally established Courts of criminal or civil jurisdiction for the determination of disputes as to their legal rights and liabilities;

- all citizens should be able to rely upon obtaining in the Courts the arbitration of a tribunal which is free from bias against any party and whose decision will be based upon those facts only that have been proved in evidence adduced before it in accordance with the procedure adopted in Courts of law; and

---

[114] See *Attorney-General v Punch Ltd* [2003] 1 All ER 289, [2003] HRLR 14, [2003] 2 WLR 49, [2002] UKHL 50, [2003] AC 1046, [2003] EMLR 7, per Nicholls LJ.

[115] See *Re: Johnson* (1887) 20 QBD 68, per Bowen LJ.

See also: J Fox, 1909, 25 Law Quarterly Review 238.

[116] See *Andrew Kwimberi of Paulus M Dowa Lawyers v The State* (1998) SC545, [1998] PGSC 9 and *Paul Metta v The State* [1992] PNGLR 176 at 184.

See also: *Attorney-General v Times Newspapers Ltd* [1973] 3 All ER 54, [1974] AC 273 at 302; *Attorney-General v Times Newspapers Ltd and another* [1991] 2 All ER 398, [1991] 2 WLR 994, [1992] 1 AC 191, per Ackner LJ at 209; *Helmore v Smith (No. 2)* (1886) 35 Ch D 449, per Bowen LJ; *Australasian Meat Industry Employees' Union v Mudginberri Station Pty Ltd* (1986) 161 CLR 98 at 107, (1986) 66 ALR 577, [1986] HCA 46 and *Witham v Holloway* (1995) 183 CLR 525 at 530, (1995) 131 ALR 401, (1995) 69 ALJR 847, [1995] HCA 3.

[117] See *Attorney-General (NSW) v John Fairfax and Sons Ltd and Bacon* (1985) 6 NSWLR 695, per McHugh JA at 707.

- once the dispute has been submitted to a Court of law, they should be able to rely upon there being no usurpation by any other person of the function of that Court to decide it according to law.[118]

Contempt law has been fashioned by the courts to protect the administration of justice. This is an activity, self-evidently of the greatest importance to society. It represents a vital part of the peaceful government of a community.[119]

It is axiomatic that a party to a proceeding, or a potential party to a proceeding in any court of law is entitled to expect that the proceeding will be determined according to law and that the law will be duly and justly administered without undue interference.[120]

'Contempt of Court' has been defined as:

- a generic term descriptive of conduct in relation to particular proceedings in a court of law which tends to undermine that system or to inhibit citizens from availing themselves of it for the settlement of their disputes[121];

---

[118] See *SCR No 3 of 1984; Ex parte Callick and Koroma* [1985] PNGLR 67, [1985] PGSC 20; *The Attorney-General, Mr Michael Gene; The State and Internal Revenue Commissioner, Mr David Sode v Dr Pirouz Hamidian-Rad* [1999] PNGLR 278; *Public Prosecutor v Nahau Rooney (No. 2)* [1979] PNGLR 448, [1979] PGSC 23 and *The State v Re Awaita; Contempt Proceedings* [1985] PNGLR 179, [1985] PGNC 29, (1985) N508.

See also: *Helmore v Smith* (1887) 35 Ch D 436, per Bowen LJ at 445; *Attorney-General v Times Newspapers Ltd* [1973] 3 All ER 54, [1974] AC 273, per Diplock LJ at 309 and *Victoria v Australian Building Construction Employees' and Builders' Labourers' Federation* (1981-1982) 152 CLR 25, [1982] HCA 31, per Brennan J.

[119] As stated by Kirby P in *Registrar of the Court of Appeal v Maniam (No. 2)* (1992) 26 NSWLR 309 at 313.

[120] See *BHP v Dagi* [1996] VicRp 62, [1996] 2 VR 117, per Tadgell JA at 157.

[121] See *The Attorney-General, Mr Michael Gene; The State and Internal Revenue Commissioner, Mr David Sode v Dr Pirouz Hamidian-Rad* [1999] PNGLR 278 and *Public Prosecutor v Nahau Rooney (No. 2)* [1979] PNGLR 448, [1979] PGSC 23.

See also: *Attorney-General v Times Newspapers* [1973] 3 All ER 54, [1974] AC 273, per Diplock LJ at 307.

## DEFINITION OF CONTEMPT OF COURT

- a contempt is in disobedience to the Court, or an opposing or despising the authority, justice or dignity thereof. It consists in a party's doing otherwise than he or she is enjoined to do, or not doing what he or she is commanded to do or required by the process, order or decree of the Court[122];

- any conduct that is 'an act or omission calculated to interfere with the due administration of justice'[123];

- words spoken or otherwise published, or acts done, outside court which are intended or likely to interfere with or obstruct the fair administration of justice are punishable as criminal contempts of court[124];

- any act or omission committed in the face of the court or outside court which is intended to or calculated to or likely to interfere or obstruct the fair or due administration of justice[125];

---

[122] See *Ome Ome Forests Ltd v Ray Cheong and others* (2002) N2289.

See also: *Miller v Knox* [1838] EngR 648, (1838) 4 Bing (NC) 574 at 614, (1838) 132 ER 910, (1838) Scott 1, per Patterson J.

[123] See *Richard Sikana v The State and Peter Luga* (2003) SC807; *Stephen John Rose and another v Neville Devete, Acting Solicitor-General and The State* (2007) N3327; *The State v Re Awaita; Contempt Proceedings* [1985] PNGLR 179, [1985] PGNC 29, (1985) N508; *The State v Raymond Tupundu* (1996) N1536, [1996] PGNC 10 and *In re Section 57 of the Constitution of Papua New Guinea, Application by John Bosco* [2007] PGNC 195, (2007) N4999.

See also: *Helmore v Smith* (1886) 35 Ch D 436, per Bowen LJ at 455.

[124] See *David Gwaya Poka v The State* [1988-89] PNGLR 218, [1988] PGSC 27; *Re: Contempt of Court; Re: Assistant Registrar, Philip Kaumba* (2004) N2763; *The State v Joseph Waine and others* (2002) N2276; *The State v Lucas Sasoruo* [1997] PNGLR 676 and *Nombri Waine Ambre v The State* [1995] PNGLR 453, [1995] PGNC 101.

See also: 'Halsbury's Laws of England' 4th ed., Vol. 9, para. 7.

[125] See *Andrew Kwimberi of Paulus M Dowa Lawyers v The State* (1998) SC545, [1998] PGSC 9; *Paul Metta v The State* [1992] PNGLR 176 at 184; *David Gwaya Poka v The State* [1988-89] PNGLR 218 at 219, [1988] PGSC 27; *SCR No 3 of 1984; Ex parte Callick and Koroma* [1985] PNGLR 67 at 75, [1985] PGSC 20; *Re Passingan Taru and Contempt Proceedings* [1982] PNGLR 292 at 295; *Public Prosecutor v Nahau Rooney (No. 2)* [1979] PNGLR 448 at 473, [1979] PGSC 23; *Ian Augerea, Registrar of the National Court v David Tigavu* (2010) N4185, [2010] PGNC 182; *Ian Augerea in his Capacity as Registrar of The National and Supreme Courts v Jack Pambel as the Acting Public Prosecutor and others* (2008) N3332 and *Elias Padura v Stephanie Valakvi* (2012) N4894, [2012] PGNC 254.

- action or inaction amounting to an interference with, or obstruction to, or having a tendency to interfere with or obstruct the due administration of justice, using that term in a broad sense[126];

- conduct that denotes wilful defiance of, or disrespect towards, the Court[127];

- conduct that wilfully challenges or affronts the authority of the Court or the supremacy of the law itself[128];

- conduct that undermines legal proceedings in a Court[129];

- conduct that inhibits citizens from availing themselves of a Court for the settlement of their disputes[130];

---

[126] See *Lane v Registrar of the Supreme Court of New South Wales* (1981) 148 CLR 245 at 257, (1981) 55 ALJR 529 at 534, (1981) 35 ALR 322, [1981] HCA 35 and *Re Dunn; Re Aspinall* [1906] VicLawRp 84, (1906) VLR 493, per Cussen J at 497.

[127] See *HM Advocate v Airs* [1975] JC 64, per Lord Justice General Emslie at 69 and *Manson v Petr* [1977] SCCR (Supp) 176 at 178.

[128] See *HM Advocate v Airs* [1975] JC 64, per Lord Justice General Emslie at 69 and *Manson v Petr* [1977] SCCR (Supp) 176 at 178.

[129] See *The Attorney-General, Mr Michael Gene; The State and Internal Revenue Commissioner, Mr David Sode v Dr Pirouz Hamidian-Rad* [1999] PNGLR 278 and *Public Prosecutor v Nahau Rooney (No. 2)* [1979] PNGLR 448, [1979] PGSC 23.

See also: *Attorney-General v Times Newspapers* [1973] 3 All ER 54, [1974] AC 273, per Diplock LJ at 307.

[130] See *The Attorney-General, Mr Michael Gene; The State and Internal Revenue Commissioner, Mr David Sode v Dr Pirouz Hamidian-Rad* [1999] PNGLR 278 and *Public Prosecutor v Nahau Rooney (No. 2)* [1979] PNGLR 448, [1979] PGSC 23.

See also: *Attorney-General v Times Newspapers* [1973] 3 All ER 54, [1974] AC 273, per Diplock LJ at 307.

- any act done or writing published calculated to bring a Court or a judge of the Court into contempt, or to lower his or her authority[131]; and

- any act done or writing published calculated to obstruct or interfere with the due course of justice or the lawful process of the Courts[132].

Irrespective, the elements of the offence of 'Contempt of Court' are:

- any act or omission[133];

- committed in the face of the court ('*in facie curiae*') or outside court ('*ex facie curiae*')[134]; and

[131] As stated by Russell LCJ in *R v Gray* [1900] 2 QB 36 at 40.

See also: *Ambard v Attorney-General for Trinidad and Tobago* [1936] AC 322; *Solicitor-General v Radio Avon Ltd and another* (1978) 1 NZLR 225; *Wong Yeung Ng v Secretary for Justice* [1999] 2 HKLRD 293 and *Izuora v R* [1953] 1 All ER 827, per Tucker LJ at 829.

[132] See *The Attorney-General, Mr Michael Gene; The State and Internal Revenue Commissioner, Mr David Sode v Dr Pirouz Hamidian-Rad* [1999] PNGLR 278.

See also: *R v Gray* [1900] 2 QB 36, per Russell LCJ at 40; *Ambard v Attorney-General for Trinidad and Tobago* [1936] AC 322; *Solicitor-General v Radio Avon Ltd and another* (1978) 1 NZLR 225; *Wong Yeung Ng v Secretary for Justice* [1999] 2 HKLRD 293 and *Izuora v R* [1953] 1 All ER 827, per Tucker LJ at 829.

[133] See *Andrew Kwimberi of Paulus M Dowa Lawyers v The State* (1998) SC545, [1998] PGSC 9 and *Agnes Okona Meten v William Seneka and Magisterial Services* (2011) N4462, [2011] PGNC 169.

[134] See *Andrew Kwimberi of Paulus M Dowa Lawyers v The State* (1998) SC545, [1998] PGSC 9 and *Agnes Okona Meten v William Seneka and Magisterial Services* (2011) N4462, [2011] PGNC 169.

- which is intended to, calculated[135] to or likely[136] to interfere or obstruct the fair or due administration of justice;[137] or

- which has the tendency to interfere with or obstruct the fair or due administration of justice in the case of 'publication contempt'[138].

  The requisite tendency has frequently been described as a real and definite tendency as a matter of practical reality to interfere with the administration of justice.[139]

---

[135] See *John Fairfax and Sons Pty Ltd v McRae* (1955) 93 CLR 351, [1955] HCA 12; *Hinch and Macquarie Broadcasting Holdings Ltd v The Attorney-General for the State of Victoria* (1987) 164 CLR 15, [1987] HCA 56; *Davis v Baillie* [1946] VicLawRp 76, [1946] VLR 486 at 492; *Watts v Hawke* [1976] VicRp 77, [1976] VR 707, per Kaye J at 711; *ANZ Banking Group v Richard Ellis* [1994] VicRp 20, [1994] 1 VR 328, per Coldrey J at 330; *R v MacDonald* [1994] VicRp 29, [1994] 1 VR 414, per Hampel J at 419 and *Hamersley Iron Pty Ltd v Lovell* (1998) 19 WAR 316 at 320 and 346.

[136] See *John Fairfax and Sons Pty Ltd v McRae* (1955) 93 CLR 351, [1955] HCA 12; *Hinch and Macquarie Broadcasting Holdings Ltd v The Attorney-General for the State of Victoria* (1987) 164 CLR 15, [1987] HCA 56 and *Davis v Baillie* [1946] VicLawRp 76, [1946] VLR 486 at 492.

[137] See *Paul Metta v State* [1992] PNGLR 176 at 184; *David Gwaya Poka v The State* [1988-89] PNGLR 218 at 219, [1988] PGSC 27; *SCR No. 3 of 1984; Ex parte Callick and Koroma* [1985] PNGLR 67 at 75, [1985] PGSC 20; *Re Passingan Taru and Contempt Proceedings* [1982] PNGLR 292 at 295; *Public Prosecutor v Nahau Rooney (No. 2)* [1979] PNGLR 448 at 473, [1979] PGSC 23; *Andrew Kwimberi of Paulus M Dowa Lawyers v The State* (1998) SC545, [1998] PGSC 9 and *Agnes Okona Meten v William Seneka and Magisterial Services* (2011) N4462, [2011] PGNC 169.

See also: *Helmore v Smith* (1986) 35 Ch D 436, per Bowen LJ at 455; *R v O'Neill* (1885) 6 NSWLR 43, per Marton CJ at 45; *R v Mathews* (1887) 8 NSWLR 45, per Darley CJ at 50; *In re Dunn; In re Aspinall* [1906] VicLawRp 84, [1906] VLR 493 at 497; *Lane v Registrar of Supreme Court of New South Wales* (1981) 148 CLR 245 at 257, (1981) 55 ALJR 529, (1981) 35 ALR 322, [1981] HCA 35; *Anthony Radcliffe Lewis v His Honour Judge Ogden* (1984) 153 CLR 682 at 688, [1984] HCA 26 and *R v Slaveski (contempt)* [2011] VSC 643. [2011] VSC 643.

The law in relation to this principle is examined in the section titled 'Risk And Tendency' in the chapter titled 'Sub-judice Rule'.

[138] See *Parshuram Detaram Shamdasani v King-Emperor* [1945] AC 264 at 268.

See also: *In re Dunn; In re Aspinall* [1906] VicLawRp 84, [1906] VLR 493, per Cussen J at 497; *Lane v Registrar of Supreme Court of New South Wales* (1981) 148 CLR 245 at 257, (1981) 55 ALJR 529, (1981) 35 ALR 322 at 331, [1981] HCA 35; *Anthony Radcliffe Lewis v His Honour Judge Ogden* (1984) 153 CLR 682 at 688, [1984] HCA 26; *R v Slaveski (contempt)* [2011] VSC 643 and *Witham v Holloway* (1995) 183 CLR 525, per McHugh J at 538, (1995) 131 ALR 401, (1995) 69 ALJR 847, [1995] HCA 3.

[139] The law in relation to this principle is examined in the section titled 'Risk And Tendency' in the chapter titled 'Sub-judice Rule'.

> Therefore, the contemptuous behavior must present as a real risk, as opposed to a mere possibility, of interference with the due administration of justice.[140]
>
> It is sufficient if the alleged contemnor had the intention to do the act which, objectively, had the tendency to interfere.[141]

The question whether there is an actual intention or purpose[142] to interfere with proceedings is always relevant, but never decisive.[143]

Notwithstanding that:

- an intention to interfere with or obstruct[144]; or

---

[140] See *Public Prosecutor v Nahau Rooney (No. 2)* [1979] PNGLR 448 at 467, [1979] PGSC 23; *SCR No. 3 of 1984; Ex parte Callick and Koroma* [1985] PNGLR 67 at 73 and 77, [1985] PGSC 20; *Charles Maino v Moi Avei and Electoral Commission* [1998] PNGLR 165; *Ian Augerea in his Capacity as Registrar of The National and Supreme Courts v Jack Pambel as the Acting Public Prosecutor and others* (2008) N3332; *The State v Joel Donne and others* (2007) N3133, [2007] PGNC 47 and *Andrew Kwimberi of Paulus M Dowa Lawyers v The State* (1998) SC545, [1998] PGSC 9.

See also: *Attorney-General v Times Newspapers Ltd* [1973] 3 All ER 54, [1974] AC 273, per Reid LJ at 298; *R v Duffy; ex parte Nash* [1960] 2 QB 188, per Parker LCJ at 200; *Hinch and Macquarie Broadcasting Holdings Ltd v The Attorney-General for the State of Victoria* (1987) 164 CLR 15, [1987] HCA 56; *Re Coroner's Court of Western Australia; ex parte Porteous*, [2002] WASCA 144; *Victoria v Australian Building Construction Employees' and Builders' Labourers Federation* (1981-82) 152 CLR 25, [1982] HCA 31; *Solicitor-General v Radio Avon Ltd* [1978] 1 NZLR 225 at 234; *R v Kopyto* (1988) 47 DLR (4th) 213 at 290; *Wong Yeung Ng v Secretary for Justice* [1999] 2 HKLRD 293; *Secretary for Justice v The Oriental Press Group Ltd and others* (1998) 2 HKLRD 123, [1998] 2 HKC 627; *John Fairfax and Sons Pty Ltd v McRae* (1955) 95 CLR 351 at 370, [1955] HCA 12; *Attorney-General (NSW) v John Fairfax and Sons Ltd and Bacon* (1985) 6 NSWLR 695, per Samuels JA at 697; *Attorney-General (NSW) v John Fairfax and Sons Ltd* [1980] NSWLR 362 at 368 and *Hammond v The Commonwealth* (1982) 152 CLR 188, per Gibbs CJ at 198, [1982] HCA 42.

See however: *Ian Augerea, Registrar of the National Court v David Tigavu* (2010) N4185, [2010] PGNC 182.

[141] See *Attorney-General (New South Wales) v Dean* (1990) 20 NSWLR 650 at 655 and *R v Slaveski* [2011] VSC 643.

[142] See *Ex parte Tuckerman; Re Nash* [1970] 3 NSWR 23 at 28.

[143] See *John Fairfax and Sons Pty Ltd v McRae* (1955) 93 CLR 351 at 371, [1955] HCA 12.

[144] See *Hinch and Macquarie Broadcasting Holdings Ltd v The Attorney-General for the State of Victoria* (1987) 164 CLR 15, [1987] HCA 56 and *R v Slaveski (contempt)* [2011] VSC 643.

- the successful interference of[145]

the due administration of justice are not essential elements of a charge of 'Contempt of Court'[146], proof of such an intention renders the offence more serious[147].

Where an alleged contemor deliberately, abusively and offensively addresses the presiding Judge it is sufficient if the Court is satisfied that such behavior was performed consciously and voluntarily.[148]

[145] See *Smith v Lakeman* (1857) 26 LJ Ch 305.

See also: *Harkianakis v Skalkos* (1997) 42 NSWLR 22 and *R v Slaveski (contempt)* [2011] VSC 643.

[146] See *Attorney-General v Butterworth* [1963] 1 QB 696, per Donovan LJ at 726 and *R v Gray* [1900] 2 QB 36, per Russell LCJ at 40.

See also: *Brambles Holdings Ltd v Trade Practices Commission and another* (1980) 32 ALR 328, [1980] FCA 120; *Supreme Court Registrar, Equity Division v McPherson* [1980] 1 NSWLR 688 at 700; *R v Hill* (1976) 73 DLR (3d) 621, per McIntyre JA at 629; *Attorney-General (New South Wales) v Dean* (1990) 20 NSWLR 650 at 655 and *R v WA Newspapers Ltd; ex parte Director of Public Prosecutions (WA)* (1996) 16 WAR 518.

See however: *Attorney-General v Punch Ltd* [2003] 1 AC 1046; *Attorney-General v Newspaper Publishing Plc* [1988] Ch 333 at 383 and *Davis v Baillie* [1946] VicLawRp 76, [1946] VLR 486 at 493.

However, the test propounded in *Attorney-General v Newspaper Publishing Plc* (supra) has to be considered in light of the English legislative regime, ie., the *Contempt of Court Act 1981*, as per the observation of Bingham LCJ in *Attorney-General v Newspaper Publishing Plc and others* [1997] WLR 926 at 936.

[147] See *Attorney-General (New South Wales) v Dean* (1990) 20 NSWLR 650; *Director of Public Prosecutions v Johnson* [2002] VSC 583 and *R v Slaveski (contempt)* [2011] VSC 643.

[148] See *Attorney-General (Victoria) v Rich* [1999] VSCA 14.

## DEFINITION OF CONTEMPT OF COURT

'Contempt of court' may arise in many different ways and take many different forms[149] and has as a consequence been characterised as 'the Proteus of the legal world[150]'.

Furthermore, it is not possible to particularise the acts which can or cannot constitute contempt in the face of the court.[151]

As observed by Hayne J in *Re Colina; ex parte Torney*[152]:

> there is no single 'offence' of the kind that the criminal law knows.

The offence of 'Contempt of Court' is matter of underlying law[153] and based on the common law. The elements of the offence are very broad; so it is often said that the categories of contempt are never closed[154].

It all depends on the circumstances of each case.

---

149 See *The Attorney-General, Mr Michael Gene; The State and Internal Revenue Commissioner, Mr David Sode v Dr Pirouz Hamidian-Rad* [1999] PNGLR 278 and *Public Prosecutor v Nahau Rooney (No. 2)* [1979] PNGLR 448, [1979] PGSC 23.

See also: *Attorney-General v Times Newspapers* [1973] 3 All ER 54, [1974] AC 273, per Diplock LJ at 307 and *United Nurses of Alberta v Alberta (Attorney-General)* [1992] 1 SCR 901, [1992] SCC 99, per Cory J.

150 See *Attorney-General v Newspaper Publishing Plc* [1988] Ch 333, per Sir John Donaldson MR at 361.

See also: *S v Mamabolo* 2001 (3) SA 409, per Kriegler J.

Proteus, according to Greek mythology, was a 'minor sea god who had the power of prophecy but who would assume different shapes to avoid answering questions', see *The Australian Oxford Dictionary* (1999).

See also: J Moskovitz, 1943, 'Contempt of Injunctions, Civil and Criminal', 43 Colorado LR 780 and G Borrie and N Lowe, 1996, 'The Law of Contempt' 3rd ed., Butterworths, London, p. 2.

151 See *Izuora v R* [1953] AC 327, per Tucker LJ at 336.

152 (1999) 200 CLR 386, (1999) 73 ALJR 1576, (1999) 166 ALR 545, [1999] HCA 57.

153 See *The Attorney-General, Mr Michael Gene; The State and Internal Revenue Commissioner, Mr David Sode v Dr Pirouz Hamidian-Rad* [1999] PNGLR 278 and *Public Prosecutor v Nahau Rooney (No. 2)* [1979] PNGLR 448, [1979] PGSC 23.

154 See *Andrew Kwimberi of Paulus M Dowa Lawyers v The State* (1998) SC545, [1998] PGSC 9 and *Agnes Okona Meten v William Seneka and Magisterial Services* (2011) N4462, [2011] PGNC 169.

Refer also to the section titled 'Underlying Law' in the chapter titled 'Sources Of Law' in the text titled 'Injia on Criminal Practice and Procedure in Papua New Guinea and the Pacific'.

## DEFINITION OF CONTEMPT OF COURT

Any conduct which presents an effective challenge to:

- the authority of the Court;
- the supremacy of the law; or
- the due administration of justice

may constitute a 'Contempt of Court'[155] and includes:

- contempt in the face of the Court ('*in facie curiae*') which includes outside Court ('*ex facie curiae*');
- disobedience contempt;
- scandalising the Court; and
- breaches of the sub-judice rule.

[155] See *Andrew Kwimberi of Paulus M Dowa Lawyers v The State* (1998) SC545, [1998] PGSC 9 and *The State v Re Awaita; Contempt Proceedings* [1985] PNGLR 179, [1985] PGNC 29, (1985) N508.

## DISTINCTION BETWEEN CRIMINAL AND CIVIL CONTEMPT OF COURT

The distinction between the civil and criminal contempt is well recognised.[156]

The distinction which has often been made seems to have originated in the 17th century.[157]

A criminal 'Contempt of Court' is a common law offence; whereas at common law a civil 'Contempt of Court' does not involve an offence.[158]

The distinction is based on the difference between:

- proceedings which are remedial or coercive in the interest of a private individual (civil contempt)[159]; and

[156] See *In re Armstrong* [1892] 1 QB 327 at 329.

See also: *R v Metal Trades Employers' Association; ex parte Amalgamated Engineering Union, Australian Section* (1951) 82 CLR 208, per Dixon J at 253-254, [1951] HCA 3; *Keegan v De Burca* [1973] I IR 223; *Savings Bank, Savings and Investment Bank Ltd v Gasco Investments (Netherlands) BV (No. 2)* [1988] Ch 422 at 438; *John Fairfax and Sons Pty Ltd v McRae* (1955) 93 CLR 351 at 363, [1955] HCA 12; *Australian Consolidated Press Ltd v Morgan* (1965) 112 CLR 483 at 489 and 497, [1965] HCA 21; *Markisic v Commonwealth of Australia* (2007) 69 NSWLR 737 at 744, [2007] NSWCA 92; *Matthews v ASIC* [2009] NSWCA 155 and *John Fairfax Publications Pty Ltd v Attorney-General (NSW)* (2000) 181 ALR 694, [2000] NSWCA 198.

[157] See *Australasian Meat Industry Employees' Union v Mudginberri Station Pty Ltd* (1986) 161 CLR 98 at 106, (1986) 66 ALR 577, [1986] HCA 46.

See also: United Kingdom, Committee on Contempt of Court, 1974, 'Report of the Committee on Contempt of Court', HMSO, London, Cmnd 5794, para. 22.

[158] See *Doyle v The Commonwealth* (1985) 156 CLR 510 at 516, [1985] HCA 46; *Australian Consolidated Press Ltd v Morgan* (1965) 112 CLR 483, per Windeyer J at 497, [1965] HCA 21 and *Ahnee v Director of Public Prosecutions* [1999] 2 WLR 1305 at 1314, [1999] 2 AC 294 at 306.

[159] See *Australasian Meat Industry Employees' Union v Mudginberri Station Pty Ltd* (1986) 161 CLR 98 at 106, (1986) 66 ALR 577, [1986] HCA 46; *Witham v Holloway* (1995) 183 CLR 525 at 530, (1995) ALR 410, (1995) 69 ALJR 847, [1995] HCA 3; *Allbeury v Corruption And Crime Commission* [2012] WASCA 84, per McLure P and *Hearne v Street* (2008) 235 CLR 125, per Kirby J, [2008] HCA 36.

See also: Lightman QC, 1987, 'A Trade Union in Chains: Scargill Unbound -- The Legal Constraints of Receivership and Sequestration', CLP 25, p. 27 and Lord Wedderburn, 1992, 'Contempt Of Court: Vicarious Liability of Companies and Unions' 21 IndLJ 51, p. 53.

- proceedings in the public interest to vindicate judicial authority or maintain the integrity of the judicial process (criminal contempt).[160]

  Criminal contempt serves a broader social interest; it finds its justification in the desire to protect the rights of society generally.[161]

The critical point is whether the contempt proceedings are in essence punitive (in which case they will be classified as 'criminal') or whether they are in essence remedial or coercive (in which case they will be classified as 'civil').[162]

The theoretical distinction between the two classes overlooks the underlying rationale of every exercise of the contempt power, namely that it is necessary to uphold and protect the effective administration of justice.[163]

Criminal contempts have been classified as all contempts, other than the disobedience of:

- a court order[164]; or

- an undertaking given to a Court.

[160] See *Australasian Meat Industry Employees' Union v Mudginberri Station Pty Ltd* (1986) 161 CLR 98 at 106, (1986) 66 ALR 577, [1986] HCA 46; *Witham v Holloway* (1995) 183 CLR 525 at 530, (1995) ALR 410, (1995) 69 ALJR 847, [1995] HCA 3; *Allbeury v Corruption And Crime Commission* [2012] WASCA 84, per McLure P and *Hearne v Street* (2008) 235 CLR 125, per Kirby J, [2008] HCA 36.

See also: Lightman QC, 1987, 'A Trade Union in Chains: Scargill Unbound -- The Legal Constraints of Receivership and Sequestration', CLP 25, p. 27 and Lord Wedderburn, 1992, 'Contempt Of Court: Vicarious Liability of Companies and Unions' 21 IndLJ 51, p. 53.

[161] See Law Reform Commission of Canada, 1977, 'Criminal Law: Contempt of Court -- Offences Against the Administration of Justice', Working Paper 22, p. 12.

[162] See *Hearne v Street* (2008) 235 CLR 125, [2008] HCA 36.

[163] See *Australasian Meat Industry Employees' Union v Mudginberri Station Pty Ltd* (1986) 161 CLR 98 at 107, (1986) 66 ALR 577, [1986] HCA 46.

[164] See *Attorney-General v Times Newspapers Ltd* [1973] 3 All ER 54, [1974] AC 273, per Diplock LJ at 307.

## DISTINCTION BETWEEN CRIMINAL AND CIVIL CONTEMPT OF COURT

Such contempts are said to consist of:

- words spoken or otherwise published, or acts done; outside court[165] which are intended or likely to interfere with or obstruct the fair administration of justice[166];

- words spoken or acts done obstructing, or tending to obstruct, the administration of justice[167]; and

- words spoken, acts done and writings published[168] which tend to:

    - wrongfully interfer with the due administration of justice[169]; or

    - bring the administration of justice into scorn[170].

---

[165] But not necessarily only outside of Court, refer to the chapter titled 'Contempt In The Face Of The Court'.

[166] See *Re Passingan Taru* [1982] PNGLR 292 at 295; *David Gwaya Poka v The State* [1988-89] PNGLR 218 at 219, [1988] PGSC 27 and *The State v Lucas Sasoruo* [1997] PNGLR 676.

See also: 'Halsbury's Laws of England' 4th ed., Vol. 9, para. 7.

[167] See *Bell v Stewart* (1920) 28 CLR 419, per Isaacs and Rich JJ at 428, [1920] HCA 68 and *R v Arrowsmith, Miller and Little* [1950] VicLawRp 17, [1950] VLR 78, per Dean J at 81.

See also: 'Halsbury's Laws of England' 2nd ed., Vol. 7, p. 2; 3rd ed., Vol. 8, p. 2 and 4th ed., Vol. 9, p. 3.

[168] See Law Reform Commission of Canada, 1977, 'Criminal Law: Contempt of Court -- Offences Against the Administration of Justice', Working Paper No. 22, p. 12.

[169] See *Attorney-General v Leveller Magazine Ltd and others* [1979] AC 440, per Diplock LJ at 449; *Australian Building Construction Employees' and Builders Labourers' Federation v David Syme and Company Ltd* (1982) 59 FLR 48 at 49, [1982] FCA 43; *Keegan v De Burca* [1973] I IR 223; *Poje v Attorney-General for British Columbia* [1953] 1 SCR 516, [1953] SCC 34 and *Witham v Holloway* (1995) 183 CLR 525 at 530, (1995) 131 ALR 401, (1995) 69 ALJR 847, [1995] HCA 3.

See also: D Eady and ATH Smith, 1999, 'Arlidge, Eady and Smith on Contempt' 2nd ed., Sweet and Maxwell, London, para. 3-1 and Chief Justice McRuer of the High Court of Justice of Ontario, 1952, 'Criminal Contempt of Court Procedure: A Protection to the Rights of the Individual', 130 Canadian Bar Review 225, p. 226.

[170] See *Poje v Attorney-General for British Columbia* [1953] 1 SCR 516, [1953] SCC 34.

See also: Chief Justice McRuer of the High Court of Justice of Ontario, 1952, 'Criminal Contempt of Court Procedure: A Protection to the Rights of the Individual', 30 Canadian Bar Review 225, p. 226.

## DISTINCTION BETWEEN CRIMINAL AND CIVIL CONTEMPT OF COURT

Criminal contempts of court are characterised as common law offences.[171]

Criminal contempt involves an interference with the due administration of justice either:

- in a particular case; or
- more generally as a continuing process.[172]

The essence of criminal contempt is that it is an obstruction to public justice.[173]

Defiance of the court or its procedures, publication of matters scandalising the court, actions calculated to prejudice the fair trial of a pending case, threats to parties or witnesses and misconduct within the court are examples of criminal contempts.[174]

The harm in criminal contempt, therefore, is primarily of a general character: if the course of justice is tampered with, society as a whole suffers the consequences.[175]

However, civil contempt has always been regarded both in substance and as a matter of procedure as being within the Court's civil jurisdiction[176] and has been referred to as 'contempt in procedure[177]'.

---

[171] See W Hawkins, 1824, 'The Pleas of the Crown' 8th ed., Ch. 6.

[172] See *Attorney-General v Leveller Magazine Ltd and others* [1979] AC 440, per Diplock LJ at 449; *Witham v Holloway* (1995) 183 CLR 525 per McHugh J at 538, (1995) 131 ALR 401, (1995) 69 ALJR 847, [1995] HCA 3; *John Fairfax and Sons Pty Ltd v McRae* (1955) 93 CLR 351, [1955] HCA 12; *Hinch and Macquarie Broadcasting Holdings Ltd v The Attorney-General for the State of Victoria* (1987) 164 CLR 15, [1987] HCA 56 and *Attorney-General for New South Wales v Dean* (1990) 20 NSWLR 650.

[173] As stated by Bowen LJ in *In the Matter of a Special Reference from the Bahama Islands* [1893] AC 138 at 148.

[174] See *Witham v Holloway* (1995) 183 CLR 525 per McHugh J at 538, (1995) 131 ALR 401, (1995) 69 ALJR 847, [1995] HCA 3; *John Fairfax and Sons Pty Ltd v McRae* (1955) 93 CLR 351, [1955] HCA 12; *Hinch and Macquarie Broadcasting Holdings Ltd v The Attorney-General for the State of Victoria* (1987) 164 CLR 15, [1987] HCA 56 and *Attorney-General for New South Wales v Dean* (1990) 20 NSWLR 650.

[175] See Law Reform Commission of Canada, 1977, 'Criminal Law: Contempt of Court -- Offences Against the Administration of Justice', Working Paper No. 22, p. 12.

[176] See *Allbeury v Corruption and Crime Commission* [2012] WASCA 84, per McLure P.

[177] See *Bell v Stewart* (1920) 28 CLR 419, per Isaacs and Rich JJ at 428, [1920] HCA 68 and *R v Arrowsmith, Miller and Little* [1950] VicLawRp 17, [1950] VLR 78, per Dean J at 81.

See also: 'Halsbury's Laws of England' 2nd ed., Vol. 7, p. 2; 3rd ed., Vol. 8, p. 2 and 4th ed., Vol. 9, p. 3.

## DISTINCTION BETWEEN CRIMINAL AND CIVIL CONTEMPT OF COURT

The purpose of civil contempt is to secure compliance with the process of a Court, including but not limited to, the process of a Court.[178]

It is a Civil Contempt:

- to refuse to or neglect to do an act required by a judgement or order or to disobey a judgement or the order requiring a person to abstain from doing a specified act stipulated in order of the Court[179]; or

- to fail to compy with an undertaking given to a Court[180],

and involves an interference with the due administration of justice.[181]

An undertaking in a civil action has the same force as an injunction made by the Court. Its breach is misconduct amounting to contempt.[182]

---

[178] See *British Columbia Government Employees Union v British Columbia (Attorney-General)* [1988] 2 SCR 214, [1988] SCC 3; *R v Hill* (1976) 73 DLR (3d) 621 at 629 and *Poje v Attorney-General for British Columbia* [1953] SCR 516.

[179] See *Concord Pacific Ltd and Paiso Company Ltd v Thomas Nen – Managing Director, Papua New Guinea Forest Authority and the State* [2000] PNGLR 47; *Philip Soon Kiat Yap v Tin Siew Tan, B and T Engineering Pty Ltd, Robert L Wong, William Baptiste and David F Tau* [1987] PNGLR 227, [1987] PGSC 21 and *21 ILGS Gobe Project Area Inc Land Groups v Pawih* [2006] PGNC 10, (2006) N3066.

[180] See *Spokes v Banbury Board of Health* (1865) LR 1 Eq 42 at 48.

See also:

- *Australian Consolidated Press Limited v Morgan* (1965) 112 CLR 483, per Windeyer J at 496, [1965] HCA 21; *Re L (a Ward) (Publication of Information)* [1988] 1 FLR 255 at 259; *Australian Building Construction Employees' and Builders Labourers' Federation v David Syme and Company Ltd* (1982) 59 FLR 48 at 49; [1982] FCA 43 and *Witham v Holloway* (1995) 183 CLR 525 at 530, (1995) 131 ALR 401, (1995) 69 ALJR 847, [1995] HCA 3; and
- D Eady and ATH Smith, 1999, 'Arlidge, Eady and Smith on Contempt' 2nd ed., Sweet and Maxwell, London, para. 3-1 and New South Wales Law Reform Commission, 2000, 'Contempt by Publication', Discussion Paper No. 43.

[181] See *Australasian Meat Industry Employees' Union v Mudginberri Station Pty Ltd* (1986) 161 CLR 98 at 107, (1986) 66 ALR 577, [1986] HCA 46 and *Witham v Holloway* (1995) 183 CLR 525 at 530, (1995) 131 ALR 401, (1995) 69 ALJR 847, [1995] HCA 3.

[182] See *Midland Marts Ltd v Hobday* [1989] 1 WLR 1143; *Williams v Fawcett* [1986] 1 QB 604 at 607 and *Capel v Caram Finance Aust Ltd* [1998] QSC 110.

See also: 'Halsbury's Laws of England' 4th ed., para. 75.

## DISTINCTION BETWEEN CRIMINAL AND CIVIL CONTEMPT OF COURT

The harm done by civil contempt is primarily of a private character.[183]

Disobedience to the process and orders of a Court in civil proceedings is said to be a civil wrong, a matter between party and party, enforcement being for the private benefit or interest of the party seeking enforcement, whereas impeding the administration of justice is a public wrong.[184]

In these cases, the purpose of the imposition of the contempt sanction has been seen as primarily 'coercive[185]' or 'remedial[186]', rather than punitive[187].

Civil contempt was not necessarily an offence.

---

[183] See *Bell v Stewart* (1920) 28 CLR 419, per Isaacs and Rich JJ at 428, [1920] HCA 68 and *R v Arrowsmith, Miller and Little* [1950] VicLawRp 17, [1950] VLR 78, per Dean J at 81.

See also: 'Halsbury's Laws of England' 2nd ed., Vol. 7, p. 2; 3rd ed., Vol. 8, p. 2 and 4th ed., Vol. 9, p. 3 and Law Reform Commission of Canada, 1977, 'Criminal Law: Contempt of Court -- Offences Against the Administration of Justice', Working Paper No. 22, p. 12.

[184] See *Ansah v Ansah* [1977] Fam 138 at 144.

[185] See *Gompers v Bucks Stove and Range Co.*(1911) 221 US 418 at 442; *Turner v Rogers* (2011) 564 US 8, per Breyer J at 10; *Ansah v Ansah* [1977] Fam 138 at 144; *Street and others v Hearne and another* (2007) 70 NSWLR 231, [2007] NSWCA 113 and *Witham v Holloway* (1995) 183 CLR 525 at 532, (1995) 131 ALR 401, (1995) 69 ALJR 847, [1995] HCA 3.

[186] See *Witham v Holloway* (1995) 183 CLR 525 at 532, (1995) 131 ALR 401, (1995) 69 ALJR 847, [1995] HCA 3.

See also: D Eady and ATH Smith, 1999, 'Arlidge, Eady and Smith on Contempt' 2nd., Sweet and Maxwell, London, para. 3-1.

[187] See *Ansah v Ansah* [1977] Fam 138 at 144 and *Street and others v Hearne and another* (2007) 70 NSWLR 231, [2007] NSWCA 113.

## DISTINCTION BETWEEN CRIMINAL AND CIVIL CONTEMPT OF COURT

The distinction has been blurred by cases that have recognised a species of civil contempt which 'savours of criminality' involving disobedience[188] though not necessarily referred to as an 'offence[189]'.

As a consequence the dividing line between the two forms of contempt is, in some cases, unclear[190] and difficult to draw[191].

The distinction has been criticized[192] and has been variously described as:

- unhelpful[193];
- largely meaningless[194];

---

[188] See *Wellesley v The Duke of Beaufort* [1831] EngR 809, (1831) 2 Russ and M 639 at 677; *Scott v Scott* [1913] AC 417, per Atkinson LJ at 455; *Attorney-General v Times Newspapers Ltd* [1973] 3 All ER 54, [1974] AC 273, per Diplock LJ at 307 and *Comet Products v Hawkox Plastics* [1971] 2 QB 67, per Lord Denning MR at 73 and Cross LJ at 77.

See also: *Witham v Holloway* (1995) 183 CLR 525, per McHugh J at 538, (1995) 131 ALR 401, (1995) 69 ALJR 847, [1995] HCA 3 and *R v Metal Trades Employers' Association; ex parte Amalgamated Engineering Union, Australian Section* (1951) 82 CLR 208, per Dixon J at 253-254; [1951] HCA 3.

[189] See *Pooley v Whetham* (1880) 15 Ch D 435 at 440, 443 and 445 and *Scott v Scott* [1913] AC 417 at 440, 443, 444, 455 and 486.

See also: *John Fairfax and Sons Pty Ltd v McRae* (1955) 93 CLR 351 at 364, [1955] HCA 12 and *Australian Consolidated Press Ltd v Morgan* (1965) 112 CLR 483, per Windeyer J at 497, [1965] HCA 21.

[190] See *Australian Building Construction Employees' and Builders Labourers' Federation v David Syme and Company Ltd* (1982) 59 FLR 48 at 49, [1982] FCA 43.

[191] See *Bhagat v Global Custodians Ltd* [2002] NSWCA 160, per Spigelman CJ.

[192] See:

- *Re Colina; ex parte Torney* (1999) 200 CLR 386, (1999) 73 ALJR 1576, (1999) 166 ALR 545 at 565, [1999] HCA 57; *Hinch and Macquarie Broadcasting Holdings Ltd v The Attorney-General for the State of Victoria* (1987) 164 CLR 15, [1987] HCA 56 and *International Union, United Mine Workers of America v Bagwell* (1994) 512 US 821 at 827 and 845, [1994] USSC 43; and
- United Kingdom Committee on Contempt of Court, 1974, 'Report of the Committee on Contempt of Court', HMSO, London, Cmnd 5794 which recommended that the distinction be abolished.

[193] See *Jennison v Baker* [1972] 2 QB 52, per Salmon LJ at 61 and *Attorney-General v Times Newspapers Ltd* [1991] 2 All ER 398, [1991] 2 WLR 994, [1992] 1 AC 191, per Oliver LJ at 217.

[194] See *Jennison v Baker* [1972] 2 QB 52, per Salmon LJ at 61 and *Attorney-General v Times Newspapers Ltd and another* [1991] 2 All ER 398, [1991] 2 WLR 994, [1992] 1 AC 191, per Oliver LJ at 217.

- academic[195];
- blurred[196];
- arbitrary[197];
- illusory[198];
- lost much of its significance[199];
- unsatisfactory[200]; and
- occasioning 'very great difficulty[201]'.

Notwithstanding such criticism the distinction still operates.[202]

---

195 See *Guildford Borough Council v Valler* [1993] Times LR 274, per Sedley J at 275.

196 See *Construction, Forestry, Mining and Energy Union v BHP Steel (AIS) Pty Ltd* [2001] FCA 1758.

197 See *Witham v Holloway* (1995) 183 CLR 525 at 534, (1995) 131 ALR 401, (1995) 69 ALJR 847, [1995] HCA 3.

198 See *Witham v Holloway* (1995) 183 CLR 525 at 534, (1995) 131 ALR 401, (1995) 69 ALJR 847, [1995] HCA 3; *Bhagat v Global Custodians Limited* [2002] NSWCA 160, per Spigelman CJ and *John Fairfax Publications Pty Ltd v Attorney-General (NSW)* (2000) 181 ALR 694, [2000] NSWCA 198, per Spigelman CJ.

199 See *Australian Prudential Regulation Authority v Siminton (No. 2)* [2006] FCA 397.

200 See *Australasian Meat Industry Employees' Union v Mudginberri Station Pty Ltd* (1986) 161 CLR 98 at 107, (1986) 66 ALR 577, [1986] HCA 46.

201 See *Australasian Meat Industry Employees' Union v Mudginberri Station Pty Ltd* (1986) 161 CLR 98 at 108, (1986) 66 ALR 577, [1986] HCA 46.

202 See *Witham v Holloway* (1995) 183 CLR 525 at 534, (1995) 131 ALR 401, (1995) 69 ALJR 847, [1995] HCA 3.

However, the distinction is now considered to be no longer of much importance.[203]

Historically, there was that absurd situation in which a contemnor who disobeyed an order committed a 'civil contempt'; whereas a person who aided and abeted the cottemnor was guilty of a 'criminal contempt'.[204]

Both kinds of proceedings must be seen as essentially:

- criminal in nature[205]; or

---

[203] See *Home Office v Harman* [1983] 1 AC 280, per Scarman LJ at 310, *Ansah v Ansah* [1977] Fam 130 at 144; *Australasian Meat Industry Employees' Union v Mudginberri Station Pty Ltd* (1986) 161 CLR 98 at 106, (1986) 66 ALR 577, [1986] HCA 46; *Gompers v Bucks Stove and Range Co* (1911) 221 US 418 at 441 and *Vidéotron Ltée v Industries Microlec Produits Électroniques Inc* [1992] 2 SCR 1065, [1992] SCC 29.

The distinction is not recognized in Scotland, see *Australasian Meat Industry Employees' Union v Mudginberri Station Pty Ltd* (1986) 161 CLR 98 at 106, (1986) 66 ALR 577, [1986] HCA 46.

See however: *United Nurses of Alberta v Alberta (Attorney-General)* [1992] 1 SCR 901, [1992] SCC 99.

[204] See *Seaward v Paterson* [1897] 1 Ch 545.

[205] See *In re Bramblevale Ltd* [1970] Ch. 128, per Lord Denning MR at 137; *Scott v Scott* [1913] AC 417 at 456 and the comments of Mathew J in *In re Maria Annie Davies* (1888) 21 QBD 236 at 238.

See also: *Hinch and Macquarie Broadcasting Holdings Ltd v The Attorney-General for the State of Victoria* (1987) 164 CLR 15, per Deane J at 49, [1987] HCA 56; *Witham v Holloway* (1995) 183 CLR 525 at 534, (1995) 131 ALR 401, (1995) 69 ALJR 847, [1995] HCA 3; *Poje v Attorney-General for British Columbia* [1953] 1 SCR 516, per Kellock J at 517, [1953] SCC 34; *Registrar of the Court of Appeal v Maniam (No. 2)* (1992) 26 NSWLR 309, per Kirby P at 314; *Director of Public Prosecutions v John Fairfax and Sons Ltd* (1987) 8 NSWLR 732 at 741; *Shell EP Ltd v McGrath and others* [2007] 1 IR 671; *Ross Company Ltd v Swan and others* [1981] ILRM 417; *Attorney-General v Kissane* 32 LR IR 220, per Chief Baron Palles; *Attorney-General v Whiley* (1993) 31 NSWLR 314 at 320; *Principal Registrar of the Supreme Court v Jando* (2001) 53 NSWLR 527, (2001) 125 A Crim R 473, [2001] NSWSC 969; *Hafele Australia Pty Ltd and another v Maggbury Pty Ltd and another* [2000] QCA 397 and *Scott and others v Evia Pty Ltd and others* [2007] VSC 15.

See however: *John Fairfax and Sons Pty Ltd v McRae* (1955) 93 CLR 351 at 364, [1955] HCA 12; *Australian Consolidated Press Ltd v Morgan* (1965) 112 CLR 483, [1965] HCA 21; *Australasian Meat Industry Employees' Union v Mudginberri Station Pty Ltd* (1986) 161 CLR 98 at 106, (1986) 66 ALR 577, [1986] HCA 46 and *Jendell Australia Pty Ltd v Kesby* [1983] 1 NSWLR 127.

- quasi-criminal[206],

although not necessarily a criminal prosecution[207].

Conduct designed to interfere with the proper administration of justice constitutes contempt of court which is said to be 'criminal' in that it transcends the limits of any dispute between particular litigants and constitutes an affront to the administration of justice as a whole.[208]

All proceedings for contempt which seek the imposition of punishment upon an alleged contemnor for a past or continuing breach of the law 'must realistically be seen as essentially criminal in nature'.[209]

Contempt in criminal proceedings has always been treated as a criminal matter.[210]

---

[206] See *In re Bramblevale Ltd* [1970] Ch. 128, per Lord Denning MR at 137.

See also: *Tankaria v Morgan* [2005] EWHC 3282; *Poje v Attorney-General for British Columbia* [1953] 1 SCR 516, per Kellock J at 517, [1953] SCC 34; *Australasian Meat Industry Employees' Union and others v Mudginberri Station Pty Ltd* (1986) 161 CLR 98 at 109, (1986) 66 ALR 577, [1986] HCA 46 and *Ambard v Attorney-General of Trinidad* (1936) 105 LJPC 72, per Atkin LJ at 74.

However, this description has been questioned, see *Director of Public Prosecutions v Chidiac* (1991) 25 NSWLR 372 at 376 and *Microsoft Corporation v Marks (No. 1)* (1996) 69 FCR 117, per Beaumont J at 137.

[207] See *Pelechowski v Registrar, Court of Appeal of New South Wales* (1999) 198 CLR 435, (1999) 162 ALR 336, (1999) 73 ALJR 687, [1999] HCA 19.

[208] See *Poje v Attorney-General for British Columbia* [1953] 1 SCR 516, per Kellock J at 517, [1953] SCC 34.

[209] See *Hinch and Macquarie Broadcasting Holdings Ltd v The Attorney-General for the State of Victoria* (1987) 164 CLR 15, per the observations of Deane J at 49, [1987] HCA 56; *Witham v Holloway* (1995) 183 CLR 525 at 534, (1995) 131 ALR 401, (1995) 69 ALJR 847, [1995] HCA 3; *Hearne v Street* (2008) 235 CLR 125 at 132, [2008] HCA 36 and *Australian Building Construction Employees' and Builders Labourers' Federation v David Syme and Co Ltd* (1982) 59 FLR 48, [1982] FCA 43.

[210] See *Connell v R (No. 5)* (1993) 10 WAR 424.

## DISTINCTION BETWEEN CRIMINAL AND CIVIL CONTEMPT OF COURT

Contempt of court at common law has also been described as a *sui generis offence*, ie., neither a civil action nor a prosecution for an offence, within the ordinary meaning of those terms.[211]

Contempt of court at common law is now treated 'in essence' as a criminal offence[212], but within the civil jurisidiction of the Court[213].

The offence of 'Contempt of Court' where it is alleged to have been committed against the Supreme Court or the National Court, is a common law offence that is part of the or underlying law[214].[215]

---

[211] See *Morris v The Crown Office* [1970] 1 All ER 1079, [1970] 2 QB 114 at 129 and *Petrie v Angus* (1889) 2 White 358.

See also: *HM Advocate v Airs* 1975 JC 64; *Re Colina, ex parte Torney* (1999) 200 CLR 386, (1999) 73 ALJR 1576, (1999) 166 ALR 545, per Kirby J at 550, [1999] HCA 57; *Australasian Meat Industry Employees' Union v Mudginberri Station Pty Ltd* (1986) 161 CLR 98 at 115, (1986) 66 ALR 577, [1986] HCA 46; *Myers v United States* (1924) 264 US 95 at 103, [1924] USSC 37; *In re Debs* (1895) 158 US 564, [1895] USSC 177; *Gompers v United States* (1914) 233 US 604, [1914] USSC 151; *Green v United States* (1958) 356 US 165, [1958] USSC 54 and *Ahnee v Director of Public Prosecutions* [1999] 2 WLR 1305 at 1314, [1999] 2 AC 294 at 306.

[212] See *Ian Augerea, Registrar of the National Court v David Tigavu* (2010) N4185, [2010] PGNC 182.

See also: *Mackenzie and Munro v Magistrates of Dingwall* (1839) 1 D 487, per Gillies LJ at 492; *HM Advocate v Robertson* (1842) 1 Broun 152, per Lord Justice Clerk Hope at 160; *Paterson v Kilgour* (1865) 3 M 1119, per Deas LJ at 1123; *MacLeod v Speirs* (1884) 5 Coup 387, per Young LJ at 403; *John Fairfax Publications Pty Ltd v Attorney-General (NSW)* (2000) 181 ALR 694, [2000] NSWCA 198; *Rich v Attorney-General* [1999] VSCA 14; *Attorney-General v Butterworth* [1963] 1 QB 696, per Lord Denning MR at 722; *Balogh v Crown Court at Saint Albans* [1974] 3 All ER 283, per Lord Denning MR at 289, [1975] QB 73; *Ahnee v Director of Public Prosecutions* [1999] 2 WLR 1305 at 1314, [1999] 2 AC 294; *Benham v United Kingdom* (1996) 22 EHRR 293, [1996] ECHR 22; *Wellesley v Duke of Beaufort* (1831) 2 Rus and My 639, [1831] EngR 809, (1831) 39 ER 538; *Re Colina; ex parte Torney* (1999) 200 CLR 386, per Kirby J at 411, (1999) 73 ALJR 1576, (1999) 166 ALR 545, [1999] HCA 57; *Registrar of the Court of Appeal v Maniam (No. 2)* (1992) 26 NSWLR 309, per Kirby P at 314 and *Attorney-General (NSW) v Whiley* (1993) 31 NSWLR 314 at 320.

[213] See *Hinch and Macquarie Broadcasting Holdings Ltd v The Attorney-General for the State of Victoria* (1987) 164 CLR 15, [1987] HCA 56; *R v Ogawa* [2011] 2 Qd R 350, [2009] QCA 307 and *Re Contempt of Court by CBD* [2002] ACTSC 87.

[214] Refer also to the chapter titled 'Sources Of Law' in the text titled 'Injia on Criminal Practice and Procedure in Papua New Guinea and the Pacific'.

[215] See *Agnes Okona Meten v William Seneka and Magisterial Services* (2011) N4462, [2011] PGNC 169.

## DISTINCTION BETWEEN CRIMINAL AND CIVIL CONTEMPT OF COURT

'Contempt of Court' has the following characteristics of an 'offence':

- it is an act against the State or society[216];
- it leads to criminal proceedings[217];
- it attracts a conviction[218]; and
- is subject to a penalty by way of fine or imprisonment[219],

notwithstanding that the usual criminal procedure prescribed by written law does not have to be followed[220].

All charges of contempt must be proven 'beyond reasonable doubt'.[221]

[216] See *Public Employees Association of Papua New Guinea v Public Services Commission* [1983] PNGLR 206, [1983] PGSC 18.

[217] See *Public Employees Association of Papua New Guinea v Public Services Commission* [1983] PNGLR 206, [1983] PGSC 18.

[218] See *Andrew Kwimberi of Paulus M Dowa Lawyers v The State* (1998) SC545, [1998] PGSC 9 and *Anderson Agiru v The Electoral Commission and The State* (2002) SC687, [2002] PGSC 5.

[219] See *Andrew Kwimberi of Paulus M Dowa Lawyers v The State* (1998) SC545, [1998] PGSC 9; *Public Employees Association of Papua New Guinea v Public Services Commission* [1983] PNGLR 206, [1983] PGSC 18 and *SCR No.1 of 1981 Re: Inter-Group Fighting Act 1977* [1981] PNGLR 151 at 154.

[220] See *Andrew Kwimberi of Paulus M Dowa Lawyers v The State* (1998) SC545, [1998] PGSC 9.

[221] Refer also to the chapter titled 'Determination of Guilt'.

## CONTEMPT IN THE FACE OF THE COURT

### [1.0] STATUTORY PROVISION

Order 14, Division 6, Subdivision B of the *National Court Rules 1983* ['Contempt in the Face Or Hearing of the Court'] states:

> '**38. Arrest.**
>
> Where it is alleged, or appears to the Court on its own view, that a person is guilty of contempt of Court, committed in the face of the Court or in the hearing of the Court, the Court may –
>
> (a) by oral order direct that the contemnor[222] be brought before the Court; or
>
> (b) issue a warrant for the arrest of the contemnor.
>
> **39. Charge, defence and determination.**
>
> Where a contemnor is brought before the Court, the Court shall --
>
> (a) cause him to be informed orally of the contempt with which he is charged; and
>
> (b) require him to make his defence to the charge; and
>
> (c) after hearing him, determine the matter of the charge; and
>
> (d) make an order for the punishment or discharge of the contemnor.
>
> **40. Interim custody.**
>
> (1) The Court may, pending disposal of the charge --
>
> (a) direct that the contemnor be kept in such custody as the Court may determine; or
>
> (b) direct that the contemnor be released.
>
> (2) The Court may make a direction under Sub-rule (1)(b) on terms, which may include a requirement that the contemnor give security, in such sum as the Court directs, for his appearance in person to answer the charge'.

---

[222] The term 'contemnor' is defined in Order 14, rule 37 of the *National Court Rules 1983* for the purpose of Division 6 as meaning:

'a person guilty or alleged to be guilty of contempt of the Court'.

## CONTEMPT IN THE FACE OF THE COURT

### [2.0] INTRODUCTION

As commented by Lord Denning MR in *Morris v The Crown Office*[223]:

> The phrase 'contempt in the face of the Court' has a quaint old-fashioned ring about it: but the importance of it, is this: of all places where law and order must be maintained, it is here, in these courts.

The term 'contempt in the face of the court' really means:

> Contempt in the cognizance of the Court.[224]

The essence of the test for whether conduct constitutes contempt in the face of the court at common law is broad:

> conduct, active or inactive, amounting to an interference with or obstruction to, or tendency to interfere with or obstruct, the due administration of justice.[225]

It is not necessary that the offending conduct be carried out with the actual purpose or intention of prejudicing the due administration of justice.[226]

---

[223] [1970] 1 All ER 1079 at 1081, [1970] 2 QB 114.

[224] See *Andrew Kwimberi of Paulus M Dowa Lawyers v The State* (1998) SC545, [1998] PGSC 9 and *Re: Contempt of Court; Re: Assistant Registrar, Philip Kaumba* (2004) N2763.

See also: *Balogh v Crown Court at Saint Albans* [1975] QB 73, [1974] 3 All ER 283, per Lord Denning MR at 287 and *State v Navunigasau* [1996] FJMC 4.

[225] See *Ex parte Bellanto; Re Prior* [1963] SR (NSW) 190 at 202.

See also: *John Fairfax and Sons Pty Ltd v McRae* (1955) 93 CLR 351, [1955] HCA 12.

[226] See *Hinch and Macquarie Broadcasting Holdings Ltd v The Attorney-General for the State of Victoria* (1987) 74 ALR 353, per Toohey J at 394, [1987] HCA 56.

## CONTEMPT IN THE FACE OF THE COURT

### [3.0] IN THE FACE AND OUTSIDE COURT

A 'Contempt of Court' may be committed:

- in the face of the Court ('*in facie curiae*')[227]; and
- outside Court[228] ('*ex facie curiae*[229]').[230]

  Contempt '*ex facie curiae*' consists of conduct so direct and immediate as to be deemed to be in the personal knowledge of the Court.[231]

  The elements of immediacy and necessity require that before the power is exercised there must be such proximity in time and space between the conduct and the trial of the proceedings that the conduct provides the present confrontation to the trial then in progress. Each case will require consideration of its own facts.[232]

---

227 See *Paul Metta v The State* [1992] PNGLR 176.

228 See *Paul Metta v The State* [1992] PNGLR 176 at 184; *David Gwaya Poka v The State* [1988-89] PNGLR 218 at 219, [1988] PGSC 27; *SCR No 3 of 1984; Ex parte Callick and Koroma* [1985] PNGLR 67 at 75, [1985] PGSC 20; *Re Passingan Taru and Contempt Proceedings* [1982] PNGLR 292 at 295; *Public Prosecutor v Nahau Rooney (No. 2)* [1979] PNGLR 448 at 473, [1979] PGSC 23; *The State v Lucas Sasoruo* [1997] PNGLR 676 and *Andrew Kwimberi of Paulus M Dowa Lawyers v The State* (1998) SC545, [1998] PGSC 9.

See also:

- *Registrar, Court of Appeal v Collins* [1982] 1 NSWLR 682; *Balogh v Crown Court at Saint Albans* [1974] 3 All ER 283, [1975] QB 73; *McKeown v R* [1971] SCR 446, [1971] SCC 194; *Re Dakin* [1887] VicLawRp 104, (1887) 13 VLR 522; *In re Johnson* (1887) 20 QBD 68, per Lord Esher MR at 72 and *Registrar v Unnamed Respondent* [1994] ACTSC 24; and
- 'Halsbury's Laws of England' 4th ed., Vol. 9, para. 7.

See however: *Fraser v R* [1984] 3 NSWLR 212 at 229 and *European Asian Bank AG v Wentworth* (1986) 5 NSWLR 445.

229 See Australian Law Reform Commission, 1986, 'Contempt: Disruption, Disobedience and Deliberate Interference', Discussion Paper No. 27.

230 However, the traditional view appears to have been that the contempt was only 'in the face of the court' where the judicial officer was able to personally observe all of the circumstances constituting the alleged contempt, see *European Asian Bank AG v Wentworth* (1986) 5 NSWLR 445, per Kirby P at 453.

231 See *Morris v The Crown Office* [1970] 1 All ER 1079, per Lord Denning MR at 1081, [1970] 2 QB 114.

See also: *Ex parte Tuckerman; Re Nash* [1970] 3 NSWR 23 at 27.

232 See *Registrar, Court of Appeal v Collins* [1982] 1 NSWLR 682, per Moffitt P at 108.

However, the contempt is not necessarily confined to something said or done:

- while proceedings are pending; or
- in the course of the proceedings being heard.[233]

The gravamen of the offence lies not in protecting the personal dignity of the presiding Judge, but of protecting the public from the mischief that will incur if the authority of the Courts is undermined or impaired.[234]

Actual physical disruption of the hearing is not an essential element in establishing contempt in the face of the Court. The essential element is that the conduct in question tends to cause an interference with the authority of the Courts in the sense that there may be:

- a detraction from the authority of the judicial process; and
- an impairment of confidence and respect in the courts.[235]

In determining whether a contempt of court has been committed a Court should not consider the state of mind of the alleged contemnor, but the inherent nature of the act itself.[236]

However, where the dominant motive is directly to interfere with the administration of justice, contempt is more easily made out and more serious; whereas where the dominant motive is not so direct, there is a greater need for close examination of whether the possibility of interference was:

- a matter of practical reality; or

---

[233] See *Re Johnson* (1887) 20 QBD 68, per Bowen LJ at 74 and *Attorney-General v Butterworth* [1963] 1 QB 696, per Donovan LJ at 723, Lord Denning MR at 719 and Pearson LJ at 728.

See also: *R v Wright (No. 1)* [1968] VicRp 15, [1968] VR 164 at 166; *Ex parte Tubman; Re Lucas* [1970] 3 NSWR 41, per Asprey J at 53; *Registrar, Court of Appeal v Collins* [1982] 1 NSWLR 682 and *In the matter of Samuel Goldman* (1968) 3 NSWR 325 at 328.

See however: See *Balli, Re Contempt of Court Act 1981 (Rev. 1)* [2011] EWHC 1736 (Ch).

[234] See *Re Johnson* (1887) 20 QBD 68.

See also: *Ex parte Bellanto re Prior* [1963] SR NSW 190 at 203; *Bell v Stewart* (1920) 28 CLR 413 at 428; *R v Dunbabim; ex parte Williams* (1935) 53 CLR 434 at 442; [1935] HCA 34 and *Ex parte Tuckerman re Nash* [1970] 3 NSWR 23.

[235] See *Ex parte Tuckerman; Re Nash* (1970) 3 NSWR 23 at 28.

[236] See *Attorney-General v Butterworth and others* [1963] 1 QB 696, per Donovan LJ at 725.

- more theoretical.[237]

## [4.0] CONTEMPTUOUS BEHAVIOUR

### [4.1] INTRODUCTION

It is not possible to particularise the acts which can or cannot constitute contempt 'in the face of the Court'.[238]

The categories of 'Contempt in the face of the Court' are never closed. It all depends on the circumstances of each case.[239]

General contemptuous behavior includes:

- any interference with the course of the administration of justice or impairment of the capacity of the Court to administer impartial justice[240];

---

[237] See *Registrar of the Supreme Court, Equity Division v McPherson and others* (1980) 1 NSWLR 688 at 700.

[238] See *Andrew Kwimberi of Paulus M Dowa Lawyers v The State* (1998) SC545, [1998] PGSC 9.

See also:
- *Izuora v R* [1953] AC 327 at 336; and
- M Chesterman, 'Disorder in the Court: The Judge's Response', [1987] UNSWLawJl 4, (1987) 10(1) University of New South Wales Law Journal 32.

[239] See *Re: Contempt of Court; Re: Assistant Registrar, Philip Kaumba* (2004) N2763.

[240] See *Clough v Leahy* (1904) 2 CLR 139, per Griffiths CJ at 161, [1904] HCA 38 and *Packer v Peacock* (1912) 13 CLR 577 at 581, [1912] HCA 8.

Refer also to the chapter titled 'Administration Of Justice Offences' in the text titled 'Injia on Criminal Offences in Papua New Guinea and the Pacific'.

However, section 5 of the *Criminal Code Act* (Ch. 262) states:

'(1) Subject to Subsection (2), this Act or the Code does not affect the authority of any court of record to punish a person summarily for the offence commonly known as "Contempt of Court".

(2) A person shall not be punished under Subsection (1) and under the Code for the same act or omission'.

Refer also to the chapter titled 'Double Jeopardy' in the text titled 'Injia on Criminal Practice and Procedure in Papua New Guinea and the Pacific'.

## CONTEMPT IN THE FACE OF THE COURT

The due administration of justice requires that all citizens should have unhindered access to the constitutionally established courts of criminal or civil jurisdiction for the determination of disputes as to their legal rights and liabilities[241];

- words used, or conduct engaged in, in the face of the Court, or in the course of proceedings, which are such as would interfere, or tend to interfere with the course of justice[242];

- acts that interfere with persons having duties to discharge in a court, including parties, witnesses and officers of the Court.[243]

  As stated by Bowen LJ in *In Re Johnson*[244]:

  > Those who have duties to discharge in a court of justice are protected by the law, and shielded on their way to the discharge of such duties, while discharging them, and on their return therefrom, in order that such persons may safely have resort to the courts of justice;

- distrupting court proceedings[245];

---

[241] As stated by Diplock LJ in *Attorney-General v Times Newspapers Ltd* [1973] 3 All ER 54, [1974] AC 273 at 308.

[242] See *Parashuram Detaram Shamdasani v King-Emperor* [1945] AC 264 at 268.

See also: *Anthony Radcliffe Lewis v His Honour Judge Ogden* (1984) 153 CLR 682 at 688, [1984] HCA 26.

Refer also to:
- the section titled 'Provoke A Breach Of The Peace' in the chapter titled 'Public Order Offences' in the text titled 'Injia on Criminal Offences in Papua New Guinea and the Pacific'; and
- the chapter titled 'Double Jeopardy' in the text titled 'Injia on Criminal Practice and Procedure in Papua New Guinea and the Pacific'.

[243] See G Borrie and N Lowe, 1983, 'The Law of Contempt' 2nd ed., Butterworths, London, p. 205 and CJ Miller, 1976, 'Contempt of Court' 1st ed., Clarendon Press, Oxford, p. 229.

[244] (1887) 20 QBD 68 at 74.

[245] See *Jesus Aquarius* (1974) 59 Cr App R 65.

Refer also to:
- the section titled 'Provoke A Breach Of The Peace' in the chapter titled 'Public Order Offences' in the text titled 'Injia on Criminal Offences in Papua New Guinea and the Pacific'; and
- the chapter titled 'Double Jeopardy' in the text titled 'Injia on Criminal Practice and Procedure in Papua New Guinea and the Pacific'.

- any conduct that is done in the knowledge of the presiding Judge's status and with the intent to interfere with the administration of justice[246];
- misusing the Court's processes, at least where other parties are thereby prejudiced[247];
- engaging in conduct designed to interfere with the fair trial of a particular case that is proceeding in a court[248];
- frustrating the due and orderly administration of criminal justice[249];
- refusing to stand up when the presiding Judge enters the courtroom[250];
- the ringing of a spectator's mobile telephone in court[251];
- conducting oneself disrespectfully to the Court during the sittings of the Court[252];

[246] As commented by Smith MR in *Birch v Walsh* (1846) 10 Ir Eq Rep 93 at 96.

[247] See *R v Gregory* (1843) 1 Cox CC 31.

See also: G Borrie and N Lowe, 1996, 'The Law of Contempt' 3rd ed., Butterworths, London, p. 459.

[248] See *Catalfamo v Hersfield Holdings Pty Ltd* (1981) 52 FLR 343 at 360, [1981] FCA 50.

[249] See *In re Dunn* [1906] VicLawRp 84, [1906] VLR 493, per Cussen J at 497 and *Allen v R* [2013] VSCA 44.

[250] See *R v Hume; ex parte Hawkins* (1965) 53 DLR (2d) 453.

[251] See *Williams v Clark* [2001] SCCR 505.

[252] See *Re Contempt of Court; Re Assistant Registrar, Philip Kaumba* (2004) N2763, [2004] PGNC 21.

See also: section 277(1)(b) of the *District Courts Act* (Ch. 40) ['Contempt of Court'].

- making a clenched fist salute in court[253];
- pretending to be a lawyer[254];
- misleading or otherwise misbehaving in the course of proceedings[255];
- conducting oneself disrespectfully to the Court during the sittings of the Court[256];

---

[253] See *Ex parte Tuckerman, re Nash* [1970] 3 NSWR 23.

Refer also to:
- the section titled 'Provoke A Breach Of The Peace' in the chapter titled 'Public Order Offences' in the text titled 'Injia on Criminal Offences in Papua New Guinea and the Pacific'; and
- the chapter titled 'Double Jeopardy' in the text titled 'Injia on Criminal Practice and Procedure in Papua New Guinea and the Pacific'.

[254] See *In the Marriage of Slender (Mr H and DM)* (1977) 29 FLR 267; *Legal Practice Board v Clohessy* [2006] WASC 21; *Legal Practice Board v Tee* [2009] WASC 5; *Legal Practice Board v Rogers* [1999] WASC 106 and *Legal Practice Board v Tilley and another* [2006] WASC 73.

Section 60(1) of the *Lawyers Act* (Ch. 91) states:

'It is an offence for a person who has not been admitted to practise as a lawyer –
(a) to practise, or purport to practise, as a lawyer; or
(b) to hold himself out or represent himself to be a lawyer; or
(c) to permit other persons to use his name as being admitted to practise as a lawyer.
Penalty: A fine not exceeding K1,000.00'.

This is not an indictable offence [see section 21(b) of the *Interpretation Act* (Ch. 2)] and therefore can be dealt with summarily [see section 22 of the *Interpretation Act* (Ch. 2)].

Refer also to:
- the chapter titled 'Classification Of Offences' in the text titled 'Injia on Criminal Practice and Procedure in Papua New Guinea and the Pacific';
- the text titled 'Injia on Sentencing in Papua New Guinea and the Pacific'; and
- the chapter titled 'Double Jeopardy' in the text titled 'Injia on Criminal Practice and Procedure in Papua New Guinea and the Pacific'.

[255] See *Markisic (Oliver) v The Commonwealth* [2006] NSWCA 150.

[256] See *Re Contempt of Court; Re Assistant Registrar, Philip Kaumba* (2004) N2763, [2004] PGNC 21.

See also: section 277(1)(b) of the *District Courts Act* (Ch. 40) ['Contempt of Court'].

- assaulting or threatening any person in court during court proceedings[257];
- wilfully interrupting[258] or disrupting a court proceedings, whether by words or other conduct[259], including by invading the court room and conducting a group protest[260];

---

[257] See *Andrew Kwimberi of Paulus M Dowa Lawyers v The State* (1998) SC545, [1998] PGSC 9.

See also:
- *Balogh v Crown Court at Saint Albans* [1975] QB 73, [1974] 3 All ER 283, per Lawton LCJ at 295; *Mitchell v Smyth* [1894] 2 IR 351 and *R v Hill* [1986] Crim LR 457; and
- section 277(1)(c) of the *District Courts Act* (Ch. 40) ['Contempt of Court'].

Refer also to:
- the section titled 'Provoke A Breach Of The Peace' in the chapter titled 'Public Order Offences'; and
- the chapter titled 'Offences Against The Person'

in the text titled 'Injia on Criminal Offences in Papua New Guinea and the Pacific'.

However, section 5 of the *Criminal Code Act* (Ch. 262) states:

'(1) Subject to Subsection (2), this Act or the Code does not affect the authority of any court of record to punish a person summarily for the offence commonly known as "Contempt of Court".

(2) A person shall not be punished under Subsection (1) and under the Code for the same act or omission'.

Refer also to the chapter titled 'Double Jeopardy' in the text titled 'Injia on Criminal Practice and Procedure in Papua New Guinea and the Pacific'.

[258] See *Balogh v Crown Court at Saint Albans* [1974] 3 All ER 283, per Lawton CJ at 295, [1975] QB 73.

[259] See *Andrew Kwimberi of Paulus M Dowa Lawyers v The State* (1998) SC545, [1998] PGSC 9.

See also:
- *Balogh v Crown Court at Saint Albans* [1975] QB 73, [1974] 3 All ER 283, per Lawton LCJ at 295; *Morris v The Crown Court* [1970] 1 All ER 1079, [1970] 2 QB 114 and *Re Rea* (1878) 2 LR Ir 429; and
- section 277(1)(a) of the *District Courts Act* (Ch. 40) ['Contempt of Court'].

[260] See *Morris v The Crown Office* [1970] 1 All ER 1079, [1970] 2 QB 114.

- where the accused person or a witness is drunk[261];
- offensive or insulting behaviour in Court[262];
- misrepresenting an order of the Court.[263]

  As stated by Hardwick LC in *In re Read and Huggonson (The St. James's Evening Post Case)*[264]:

  > Nothing is more incumbent upon courts of justice, than to preserve their proceedings from being misrepresented;

- conduct that is calculated to inhibit people from availing themselves of their constitutional right to have their legal rights and obligations ascertained and enforced in courts of law. Such conduct affects not only the particular interests of the parties to the case, but also the public interest in the due administration of justice.[265]

  Justice Wills in *R v Davies*[266] stated that Courts or the administration of justice exist for the benefit of the people and their independence must be protected from unauthorized interference;

---

261 See *Gillies v McClory* [1994] SCCR 886; *Elizabeth Yates* (1847) Ark 238 and *John Allan* [1826] Shaw 172.

Refer also to:
- the section titled 'Drunkenness' in the text titled 'Injia on Criminal Offences in Papua New Guinea and the Pacific'; and
- the chapter titled 'Double Jeopardy' in the text titled 'Injia on Criminal Practice and Procedure in Papua New Guinea and the Pacific'.

262 See *In re Dunn; In re Aspinall* [1906] VicLawRp 84, (1906) VLR 493 at 497 and *Director of Public Prosecutions v Johnson* [2002] VSC 583.

263 See *Tobacco Institute of Australia Ltd v Australian Federation of Consumer Organisations Inc (No. 2)* at 92, [1993] FCA 83.

264 [1742] EngR 142, (1742) 2 Atk 469, (1742) 26 ER 683.

265 See *Attorney-General v Times Newspapers Ltd* [1973] 3 All ER 54, [1974] AC 273, per Diplock LJ at 310.

266 [1906] 1 KB 32 at 41.

- conduct outside the courtroom deliberately frustrating the effect of an order made to enable a Court to act effectively within its jurisdiction[267];

- without lawful authority or justification, preventing or attempting to prevent not only parties, their legal representatives or witnesses, but also members of the public who are desirous of being present at those proceedings, from entering the court or its precincts.[268]

  Assuring unimpeded access to the courts is plainly an objective of sufficient importance to warrant overriding a constitutionally protected right or freedom, ie., section 47 of the *Constitution of the Independent State of Papua New Guinea* ['Freedom of Assembly and Association'][269] and relates to a concern which is pressing and substantial in a free and democratic society[270].

---

[267] See *John Fairfax and Sons Ltd v Police Tribunal* (NSW) (1986) 5 NSWLR 465, per McHugh JA at 477 and Glass JA agreeing at 467; *Attorney-General (NSW) v Mayas Pty Ltd* (1988) 14 NSWLR 342, per McHugh JA at 355-356 and Hope JA agreeing at 344; *Savvas* (1989) 43 A Crim R 331, per Hunt J at 334 and *United Telecasters Sydney Ltd v Hardy* (1991) 23 NSWLR 323 at 333-334.

[268] See *Re British Columbia Government Employees Union et al. and AGBC et al.* (1983) 2 DLR (4th) 705, (1984) 48 BCLR 5, [1984] BCSC 594; *Ex parte Tubman; Re Lucas* [1970] 3 NSWR 41, per Aspey JA at 51 and *Brambles Holdings Ltd v Trade Practices Commission* (1980) 44 FLR 182, [1980] FCA 120.

[269] See *R v Big M Drug Mart Ltd* [1985] 1 SCR 295 at 352, [1985] SCC 69.

As regards 'Unlawful Processions', see:
- section 78 of the *Criminal Code* (Ch. 262) ['Unlawful Processions']; and
- the *Peace and Good Order Act 1991*.

Refer also to the section titled 'Unlawful Assemblies: Breaches of the Peace' in the chapter titled 'Public Order Offences' in the text titled 'Injia on Criminal Offences in Papua New Guinea and the Pacific'.

However, section 5 of the *Criminal Code Act* (Ch. 262) states:

'(1) Subject to Subsection (2), this Act or the Code does not affect the authority of any court of record to punish a person summarily for the offence commonly known as "Contempt of Court".

(2) A person shall not be punished under Subsection (1) and under the Code for the same act or omission'.

Refer also to the chapter titled 'Double Jeopardy' in the text titled 'Injia on Criminal Practice and Procedure in Papua New Guinea and the Pacific'.

[270] See *R v Oakes* [1986] 1 SCR 103 at 138, [1986] SCC 46.

The due administration of justice requires that all citizens should have unhindered access to the constitutionally established courts of criminal or civil jurisdiction for the determination of disputes as to their legal rights and liabilities[271]; and

- non-compliance with an order of a Court and or an undertaking given to a Court, referred to as 'disobedience contempt[272]'.

## [4.2] THE PRESIDING JUDGE

Contemptuous behavior directed at the presiding Judge includes:

- threatening the presiding Judge[273], including sending a threatening letter[274];

- making insulting and blasphemous remarks[275];

---

[271] See *Attorney-General v Times Newspapers Ltd* [1973] 3 All ER 54, [1974] AC 273, per Diplock LJ at 309.

[272] See *Public Officers Superannuation Fund Board v Paul Paraka Trading as Paul Paraka Lawyers and Paul Paraka Trading as Paul Paraka Lawyers v Public Officers Superannuation Fund Board* (2005) N2791.

See also: Australian Law Reform Commission, 1987, 'Contempt', Report No. 35, Ch. 5.

[273] See *Balogh v Crown Court at St Albans* [1974] 3 All ER 283, per Lawton LCJ at 295, [1975] QB 73.

See also: *Brown v Putman* (1975) 6 ALR 307.

Refer also to the chapter titled 'Offences Against The Person' in the text titled 'Injia on Criminal Offences in Papua New Guinea and the Pacific'.

However, section 5 of the *Criminal Code Act* (Ch. 262) states:

'(1) Subject to Subsection (2), this Act or the Code does not affect the authority of any court of record to punish a person summarily for the offence commonly known as "Contempt of Court".

(2) A person shall not be punished under Subsection (1) and under the Code for the same act or omission'.

Refer also to the chapter titled 'Double Jeopardy' in the text titled 'Injia on Criminal Practice and Procedure in Papua New Guinea and the Pacific'.

[274] See *Re Ludlow's Charities; Mr Lechmere Charlton's case* [1837] EngR 524, (1837) 2 My and Cr 316, (1837) 40 ER 661; *Smith v Lakeman* (1857) 26 LJ Ch 305, per Lord Stuart VC at 306 and *Attorney-General v Butterworth* [1963] 1 QB 696.

[275] See *Dow v Attorney-General* [1980] Qd R 58.

- insulting the presiding Judge[276];
- assaulting the presiding Judge[277]; and
- privately communicating with the presiding Judge for the purpose of influencing his or her decision[278].

---

[276] See *Balogh v Crown Court at Saint Albans* [1974] 3 All ER 283, per Lawton LCJ at 295, [1975] QB 73.

See also:

- *R v Hill* [1986] Crim LR 457; *Anthony Radcliffe Lewis v His Honour Judge Ogden* (1984) 153 CLR 682 at 688, [1984] HCA 26 and *Bakir v Doueihi and others* [2001] QSC 414; and
- (1293) Coram Rege roll, P. 21 Edward I, par I, m 95 (Solly-Flood), William de Bereford J.

[277] See *Bakir v Doueihi and others* [2001] QSC 414 and *Prothonotary v Wilson* [1999] NSWSC 1148.

See also: (1348) YB 22 Edward III, p. 13, pl. 26.

Refer also to the chapter titled 'Offences Against The Person' in the text titled 'Injia on Criminal Offences in Papua New Guinea and the Pacific'.

However, section 5 of the *Criminal Code Act* (Ch. 262) states:

'(1) Subject to Subsection (2), this Act or the Code does not affect the authority of any court of record to punish a person summarily for the offence commonly known as "Contempt of Court".
(2) A person shall not be punished under Subsection (1) and under the Code for the same act or omission'.

Refer also to the chapter titled 'Double Jeopardy' in the text titled 'Injia on Criminal Practice and Procedure in Papua New Guinea and the Pacific'.

[278] See *Re Dyce Sombre* [1849] EngR 498, (1849) 1 Mac and G 116, (1849) 41 ER 1207, per Cottenham LC at 122 and 1209.

Refer also to the section titled 'Attempting To Pervert Justice' in the chapter titled 'Administration Of Justice Offences' in the text titled 'Injia on Criminal Offences in Papua New Guinea and the Pacific'.

However, section 5 of the *Criminal Code Act* (Ch. 262) states:

'(1) Subject to Subsection (2), this Act or the Code does not affect the authority of any court of record to punish a person summarily for the offence commonly known as "Contempt of Court".
(2) A person shall not be punished under Subsection (1) and under the Code for the same act or omission'.

Refer also to the chapter titled 'Double Jeopardy' in the text titled 'Injia on Criminal Practice and Procedure in Papua New Guinea and the Pacific'.

## [4.3] WITNESSES

Contemptuous behavior involving witnesses includes:

- a witness who wilfully disobeys an order of the Court issued under section 63 of the *District Courts Act* (Ch. 40) ['Ordering Witnesses Outside of Court'] to go and remain outside and beyond the hearing of the Court until required to give evidence[279];

- failure by a witness, including a police officer, to attend court to give evidence after being summonsed.[280]

  Police officers who are witnesses, or any witness for that matter, should be warned in no uncertain terms that they cannot flout the authority of the Court, nor can they display gross disrespect or cause undue delay and inconvenience to the Court.[281]

---

[279] Section 63 of the *District Court* (Ch. 40) states:

> 'At any time during the hearing, a Court may if it thinks fit, and shall if required by a party, order that all witnesses, other than the complainant and the defendant and the witnesses under examination, go and remain outside and beyond the hearing of the Court until required to give evidence, except in so far as in particular cases and in special circumstances it sees fit to do otherwise'.

See also: section 277(1)(d) of the *District Courts Act* (Ch. 40) ['Contempt of Court'].

[280] See *Andrew Kwimberi of Paulus M Dowa Lawyers v The State* (1998) SC545, [1998] PGSC 9; *The State v Foxy Kia Tala; Re Corney Winjan* (1994) N1192, [1994] PGNC 76 and *Re Passingan Taru and Contempt Proceedings* [1982] PNGLR 292.

See also: *Balogh v Crown Court at Saint Albans* [1975] QB 73, [1974] 3 All ER 283, per Lawton LCJ at 295 and *James v Cowan* (1929) 42 CLR 305, [1929] HCA 46.

Refer also to the section titled 'Prevent A Witness Attending Court' in the chapter titled 'Administration Of Justice Offences' in the text titled 'Injia on Criminal Offences in Papua New Guinea and the Pacific'.

However, section 5 of the *Criminal Code Act* (Ch. 262) states:

> '(1) Subject to Subsection (2), this Act or the Code does not affect the authority of any court of record to punish a person summarily for the offence commonly known as "Contempt of Court".
>
> (2) A person shall not be punished under Subsection (1) and under the Code for the same act or omission'.

Refer also to:

- the section titled 'Witness Attendance' in the chapter titled 'Witnesses'; and
- the chapter titled 'Double Jeopardy'

in the text titled 'Injia on Criminal Practice and Procedure in Papua New Guinea and the Pacific'.

[281] See *The State v Foxy Kia Tala; Re Corney Winjan* [1995] PNGLR 303, (1995) N1192.

If a police officer is required as a witness, that police officer should be released to attend as a witness. If the police officer is ordered or instructed to go elsewhere when he or she should be attending as witness, those responsible could be dealt with severely[282];

- a competent and compellable witness refusing to answer a question after being directed to do so by the Court, provided that the question is relevant and necessary to the proceedings.[283]

When a witness fails to give evidence it is a failure of law and order.[284]

---

[282] See *The State v Foxy Kia Tala; Re Corney Winjan* [1995] PNGLR 303, (1995) N1192.

As regards the duty of a police officer to a Court, see Pratt J's lengthy discussion in *Re Passingan Taru and Contempt Proceedings* [1982] PNGLR 292.

[283] See *Andrew Kwimberi of Paulus M Dowa Lawyers v The State* (1998) SC545, [1998] PGSC 9.

See also: *Balogh v Crown Court at Saint Albans* [1975] QB 73, [1974] 3 All ER 283, per Lawton LCJ at 295; *O'Brennan v Tully* (1933) 69 ILTR 115; *Keegan v de Burca* [1973] IR 223; *Re O'Kelly* (1974) 108 ILTR 97; *McGuinness v Attorney-General for Victoria* (1940) 63 CLR 73; *Secretary Of State for Defence v Guardian Newspapers* [1985] AC 339; *R v Jones* (1992) 58 A Crim R 471, per Hedigan J at 474; *R v Montgomery* [1995] 2 All ER 28 at 34; *Registrar of the Court of Appeal v Gilby* [1991] NSWCA 235; *R v Phillips* (1983) 78 Cr App R 88, per Watkins LJ at 94; *Smith v R* (1991) 25 NSWLR 1 at 9; *Registrar, Supreme Court v Zappia* (2003) 86 SASR 388 at 399, [2003] SASC 276; *R v Moran* (1985) 81 Cr App R 51 at 53; *The Honorable Mr Acting Justice Morris David Ireland v Renee Ann Russell* [2001] NSWSC 468; *Director of Public Prosecutions v Chidiac* (1991) 25 NSWLR 372; *R v Duncan* [2000] NSWSC 440; *Registrar of the Court of Appeal of New South Wales v Craven (No. 2)* (1995) 80 A Crim R 272; *Wood v Staunton (No. 5)* (1995) 86 A Crim R 183, per Dunford J at 185; *Principal Registrar of the Supreme Court v Jando* (2001) 53 NSWLR 527, (2001) 125 A Crim R 473, [2001] NSWSC 969; *Registrar, Criminal Division, Supreme Court v Glasby* [1999] NSWSC 846; *R v Garland* (1997) 95 A Crim R 264; *R v Mahir El Kholed* [2009] QSC 335; *Attorney-General v Mulholland* [1963] 2 QB 477; *Hennegall v Evance* [1806] EngR 118, (1806) 12 Ves 201, (1806) 33 ER 77; *Wylie v HM Advocate* 1966 SLT 149; *Smith v R* [1991] 25 NSWLR 1, per Kirby P at 8; *Attorney-General v Lundin* (1982) 75 Cr App R 90 and the observations of O' Dalaigh CJ in *Keegan v de Burca* [1973] IR 223 at 229.

Refer also to the section titled 'Compulsion' in the chapter titled 'Criminal Responsibility' in the text titled 'Injia on Criminal Offences in Papua New Guinea and the Pacific'.

See also: *R v Hurley* [1967] VicRp 57, [1967] VR 526, per Smith J at 543 and *Registrar of the Court of Appeal v Gilby* [1991] NSWCA 235 as regards the application of such a defence.

The District Court may adjourn the proceedings for any period not exceeding eight days, and may in the meantime by warrant commit the person to a correctional institution, police lock-up or other place of security, see section 70 of the *District Courts Act* (Ch. 40) ['Refusal of Witness to be Examined'].

[284] See *R v Montgomery* [1995] 2 All ER 28, per Potter LJ at 34.

The refusal to give evidence is a failure to discharge the obligation which the person owes as a member of the community or because he or she is within it.[285]

Where a person with relevant evidence to give declines to give evidence, it strikes at the heart of the system of the administration of justice.[286]

It is of the utmost importance that everyone called upon to testify recognises that he or she is under a duty to do so and that a refusal or neglect to perform that duty may have dire consequences for:

- the proper administration of justice; and
- that person.[287]

Refusal to give evidence may have serious consequences in the particular case: an innocent person may be convicted or a guilty one may escape punishment. Equally important, it may be thought in the community that the proper course of justice may be ignored or impeded; public confidence in the due administration of the law may be destroyed[288];

- a witness refusing to take the oath or affirm.[289]

  The refusal to be sworn is a failure to discharge the obligation which the person owes as a member of the community or because he or she is within it[290];

---

[285] See *Registrar of the Court of Appeal v Gilby* [1991] NSWCA 235.

[286] See *Principal Registrar of the Supreme Court v Jando* (2001) 53 NSWLR 527 at 533, (2001) 125 A Crim R 473, [2001] NSWSC 969.

[287] As stated by Watkins LJ in *R v Phillips* (1983) 78 Cr App R 88 at 94.

[288] As commented by Mahoney P in *C v Registrar, Court of Appeal No. Ca 40130/94 Contempt* [1996] NSWSC 103.

[289] See *Hennegall v Evance* [1806] EngR 118, (1806) 12 Ves 201, (1806) 33 ER 77.

See also: *Wylie v HM Advocate* [1966] SLT 149 and *Smith v R* [1991] 25 NSWLR 1, per Kirby P at 8.

The District Court may adjourn the proceedings for any period not exceeding eight days, and may in the meantime by warrant commit the person to a correctional institution, police lock-up or other place of security, see section 70 of the *District Courts Act* (Ch. 40) ['Refusal of Witness to be Examined'].

[290] See *Registrar of the Court of Appeal v Gilby* [1991] NSWCA 235.

- knowingly putting forward a falsehood in an attempt to deceive the Court and thereby interfere with the due and proper administration of justice[291];

- evasively answering questions.[292]

  Courts have recognized that testimony false and evasive on its face is the equivalent of refusing to testify at all. Refusal to disclose information known to a witness by evasive answers can be as obstructive of justice as an outright refusal to testify.[293]

  However, even if the prevarication does involve perjury, it may not be possible to bring a prosecution; for example, where the witness gives two contradictory accounts, but it is impossible to know which is untrue[294];

---

[291] See *Lord v Thornton* (1614) 2 Bulstr 67; *Re Elsam* (1824) 3 BandC 597; *Apted v Apted and Bliss* [1930] P 246 and *R v Weisz; ex parte Hector MacDonald Ltd* [1951] 2 KB 611.

See also: *Markisic and another v Keelty* [2005] NSWSC 1124.

Refer also to the sections titled 'Conspiracy To Bring False Accusation' and 'Corruption Of A Witness' in the chapter titled 'Administration Of Justice Offences' in the text titled 'Injia on Criminal Offences in Papua New Guinea and the Pacific'.

However, section 5 of the *Criminal Code Act* (Ch. 262) states:

'(1) Subject to Subsection (2), this Act or the Code does not affect the authority of any court of record to punish a person summarily for the offence commonly known as "Contempt of Court".

(2) A person shall not be punished under Subsection (1) and under the Code for the same act or omission'.

Refer also to the chapter titled 'Double Jeopardy' in the text titled 'Injia on Criminal Practice and Procedure in Papua New Guinea and the Pacific'.

[292] See *Valenti v McCloskey Sub. Nom People ex rel. Valenti v McCloskey* (1959) 6 NY 2d 390, per Desmond J at 406.

As regards a witness who speaks evasively whilst answering questions, see section 277(2) of the *District Courts Act* (Ch. 40) ['Contempt of Court'].

[293] See *Richardson v United States* (1959) 273 F 2d 144 at 147.

[294] See *Logan v McGlennan* [1999] SCCR 584 at 586.

- the victimization[295] of a witness before or after giving evidence[296]; including:
    - frightening a witness[297];

---

[295] As stated by Denning LJ in *Attorney-General v Butterworth* [1963] 1 QB 696 at 719.

[296] See *Andrew Kwimberi of Paulus M Dowa Lawyers v The State* (1998) SC545, [1998] PGSC 9 and *Ian Augerea, Registrar of the National Court v David Tigavu* (2010) N4185, [2010] PGNC 182.

See also: *Balogh v Crown Court at Saint Albans* [1975] QB 73, [1974] 3 All ER 283, per Lawton LCJ at 295; *Moore v Clerk of Assize, Bristol* [1972] 1 All ER 58, per Denning LJ at 59; *R v Martin* (1848) 5 Cox 356, per Pigot CB at 359; *Morris v Wellington City Corporation* [1969] NZLR 1038; *Moore v Clerk of Assize, Bristol* [1972] 1 All ER 58, per Denning LJ at 59; *Clarkson v Mandarin Club* (1998) 90 FCR 356; *Lawley's case* (1731) 2 Strange 904, (1731) 93 ER 930; *R v Rafique* [1993] QB 843 at 846; *R v Carrol* (1744) 1 Wils 75; *Smith v Lakeman* (1856) 26 LJ Ch 305; *In re Mulock* (1864) 3 Sw and Tr 599, (1864) 164 ER 1407; *Attorney-General v Times Newspapers Ltd* [1973] 3 All ER 54, [1974] AC 273, per Simon LJ at 318; *R v Wright (No. 1)* [1968] VicRp 15, [1968] VR 164 and *Re Ludlow Charities; Mr Lechmere Charlton's Case* [1837] EngR 524, (1837) 2 My and Cr 316 at 339, (1837) 40 ER 661 at 670.

Refer also to:
- the section titled 'Prevent A Witness Attending Court' in the chapter titled 'Administration Of Justice Offences';
- the section titled 'Provoke A Breach Of The Peace' in the chapter titled 'Public Order Offences'; and
- the chapter titled 'Offences Against The Person'

in the text titled 'Injia on Criminal Offences in Papua New Guinea and the Pacific'.

However, section 5 of the *Criminal Code Act* (Ch. 262) states:
'(1) Subject to Subsection (2), this Act or the Code does not affect the authority of any court of record to punish a person summarily for the offence commonly known as "Contempt of Court".
(2) A person shall not be punished under Subsection (1) and under the Code for the same act or omission'.

Refer also to the chapter titled 'Double Jeopardy' in the text titled 'Injia on Criminal Practice and Procedure in Papua New Guinea and the Pacific'.

[297] See *Moore v Clerk of Bristol Assize* [1971] 1 WLR 1669, per Denning LJ at 1670 and as commented by Donovan LJ in *Attorney-General v Butterworth* [1963] 1 QB 696 at 723.

Refer also to:
- the section titled 'Provoke A Breach Of The Peace' in the chapter titled 'Public Order Offences' in the text titled 'Injia on Criminal Offences in Papua New Guinea and the Pacific'; and
- the chapter titled 'Double Jeopardy' in the text titled 'Injia on Criminal Practice and Procedure in Papua New Guinea and the Pacific'.

- assaulting or punishing a witness[298]; and
- insulting a witness[299].

A witness must be able to come freely and voluntarily to court to give their evidence without the fear of threats or violence.[300]

Otherwise, they may not come at all, or if they are forced to come, they may end or twist their evidence[301] and potential witnesses may be deterred in future cases from risking a like vengeance[302].

The Court will always preserve the freedom and integrity of witnesses and not allow them to be intimidated in any way, either before the trial, pending it or after it[303]; and

---

298 See *Davis's Case* (1461) 2 Dyer 188, (1461) 73 ER 415 and *Attorney-General v Butterworth* [1963] 1 QB 696.

See also: *Simon Runting* (1989) 89 Cr App R 243 at 245; *Bakir v Doueihi and others* [2001] QSC 414 and *R v Wright (No. 1)* [1968] VicRp 15, [1968] VR 164.

Refer also to:
- the section titled 'Corruption Of A Witness' in the chapter titled 'Administration Of Justice Offences'; and
- the chapter titled 'Offences Against The Person'

in the text titled 'Injia on Criminal Offences in Papua New Guinea and the Pacific'.

However, section 5 of the *Criminal Code Act* (Ch. 262) states:

'(1) Subject to Subsection (2), this Act or the Code does not affect the authority of any court of record to punish a person summarily for the offence commonly known as "Contempt of Court".

(2) A person shall not be punished under Subsection (1) and under the Code for the same act or omission'.

Refer also to the chapter titled 'Double Jeopardy' in the text titled 'Injia on Criminal Practice and Procedure in Papua New Guinea and the Pacific'.

299 See *Re: Johnson* (1887) 20 QBD 68, per Bowen LJ.

300 As stated by Starke J in *R v Wright (No. 1)* [1968] VicRp 15, [1968] VR 164 at 166.

301 As stated by Starke J in *R v Wright (No. 1)* [1968] VicRp 15, [1968] VR 164 at 166.

302 As commented by Donovan LJ in *Attorney-General v Butterworth* [1963] 1 QB 696 at 723.

303 See *Attorney-General v Butterworth* [1963] 1 QB 696 and *Moore v Clerk of Bristol Assize* [1971] 1 WLR 1669, per Denning LJ at 1670.

- intimidating a potential witness to not give evidence[304].

## [4.4] OFFICERS OF THE COURT

Contemptuous behavior involving officers of the court includes:

- assaulting an officer of the Court while he or she is carrying out his or her official functions[305];

---

[304] See *Simon Runting* (1989) 89 Cr App R 243 at 245.

See also: *Gregory v Philip Morris Ltd* (1987) 74 ALR 300, per Gray J at 308.

Refer also to the section titled 'Corruption Of A Witness' in the chapter titled 'Administration Of Justice Offences' in the text titled 'Injia on Criminal Offences in Papua New Guinea and the Pacific'.

However, section 5 of the *Criminal Code Act* (Ch. 262) states:

'(1) Subject to Subsection (2), this Act or the Code does not affect the authority of any court of record to punish a person summarily for the offence commonly known as "Contempt of Court".

(2) A person shall not be punished under Subsection (1) and under the Code for the same act or omission'.

Refer also to the chapter titled 'Double Jeopardy' in the text titled 'Injia on Criminal Practice and Procedure in Papua New Guinea and the Pacific'.

[305] See *Anon* [1631] Dyer 1886n, (1631) 73 ER 416; *Re Johnson* (1887) 20 QBD 68 and *Balogh v Crown Court at St Albans* [1974] 3 All ER 283, per Lawton LCJ at 295, [1975] QB 73.

See also:

- *Bakir v Doueihi and others* [2001] QSC 414;
- (1317) Coram Rege roll, T. 11 Edward II, m 48;
- The Law Reform Commission of Ireland, 1991, 'Contempt of Court', Consultation Paper, p. 128; and
- section 277(1)(c) of the *District Courts Act* (Ch. 40) ['Contempt of Court'].

Refer also to the chapter titled 'Offences Against The Person' in the text titled 'Injia on Criminal Offences in Papua New Guinea and the Pacific'

However, section 5 of the *Criminal Code Act* (Ch. 262) states:

'(1) Subject to Subsection (2), this Act or the Code does not affect the authority of any court of record to punish a person summarily for the offence commonly known as "Contempt of Court".

(2) A person shall not be punished under Subsection (1) and under the Code for the same act or omission'.

Refer also to the chapter titled 'Double Jeopardy' in the text titled 'Injia on Criminal Practice and Procedure in Papua New Guinea and the Pacific'.

- shouting abuse at an officer of the Court[306];
- delaying the processing of appeal documents[307];
- threatening an officer of the Court[308];
- making allegations in court against officers of the Court tending to bring the administration of justice into disrepute[309]; and

306 See *Young v Lees* [1998] SCCR 558.

Refer also to:
- the section titled 'Provoke A Breach Of The Peace' in the chapter titled 'Public Order Offences' in the text titled 'Injia on Criminal Offences in Papua New Guinea and the Pacific'; and
- the chapter titled 'Double Jeopardy' in the text titled 'Injia on Criminal Practice and Procedure in Papua New Guinea and the Pacific'.

307 See *Pupu v Mara* [1996] PNGLR 226, [1996] PGNC 161.

308 See *Ian Augerea, Registrar of the National Court v David Tigavu* (2010) N4185, [2010] PGNC 182.

See also: *Brown v Putman* (1975) 6 ALR 307 and *Balogh v Crown Court at St Albans* [1974] 3 All ER 283, per Lawton LCJ at 295, [1975] QB 73.

Refer also to:
- the section titled 'Provoke A Breach Of The Peace' in the chapter titled 'Public Order Offences'; and
- the chapter titled 'Offences Against The Person'

in the text titled 'Injia on Criminal Offences in Papua New Guinea and the Pacific'.

However, section 5 of the *Criminal Code Act* (Ch. 262) states:

'(1) Subject to Subsection (2), this Act or the Code does not affect the authority of any court of record to punish a person summarily for the offence commonly known as "Contempt of Court".

(2) A person shall not be punished under Subsection (1) and under the Code for the same act or omission'.

Refer also to the chapter titled 'Double Jeopardy' in the text titled 'Injia on Criminal Practice and Procedure in Papua New Guinea and the Pacific'.

309 See *Re Johnson* (1887) 20 QBD 68 at 75 and *Parashuram Detaram Shamdasani v King-Emperor* [1945] AC 264 at 269.

Refer also to the section titled 'Right To An Independent and Impartial Court' in the chapter titled 'Rights Of An Accused Person' in the text titled 'Injia on Criminal Practice and Procedure in Papua New Guinea and the Pacific'.

- the victimization of a legal representative, including:
    - abuse[310];
    - an unlawful assault[311]; and
    - a threat[312].[313]

Lawyers are officers of the court, so any interference with the discharge of their duty to the Court to represent their clients' interests fully and freely is an interference in the due administration of justice.[314]

---

310 See *Re Goldman* [1968] 3 NSWR 325 at 328.

311 See *Principal Registrar, Supreme Court v Katelaris* [2001] NSWSC 506.

312 See *Ian Augerea, Registrar of the National Court v David Tigavu* (2010) N4185, [2010] PGNC 182.

See also: *Re Johnson* (1887) 20 QBD 68 and *Re Samuel Goldman* [1968] 3 NSWR 325.

313 Refer also to:

- the section titled 'Provoke A Breach Of The Peace' in the chapter titled 'Public Order Offences'; and
- the chapter titled 'Offences Against The Person'

in the text titled 'Injia on Criminal Offences in Papua New Guinea and the Pacific'.

However, section 5 of the *Criminal Code Act* (Ch. 262) states:

'(1) Subject to Subsection (2), this Act or the Code does not affect the authority of any court of record to punish a person summarily for the offence commonly known as "Contempt of Court".

(2) A person shall not be punished under Subsection (1) and under the Code for the same act or omission'.

Refer also to the chapter titled 'Double Jeopardy' in the text titled 'Injia on Criminal Practice and Procedure in Papua New Guinea and the Pacific'.

314 See *Ian Augerea, Registrar of the National Court v David Tigavu* (2010) N4185, [2010] PGNC 182.

## [4.5] THE OPPOSING PARTY

Contemptuous behavior involving the opposing party includes:

- threatening harm to the party's reputation or contractual, commercial or industrial relations[315];
- inducing the party to suppress evidence[316];
- assaulting the party[317];

---

[315] See *Re Mulock* (1865) 3 Sw and Tr 599 and *Webster v Bakewell RDC* [1916] 1 Ch 300.

See also: *Australian Building Construction Employees' and Builders Labourers' Federation and others v Viner and others* (1982) 63 FLR 253, [1982] FCA 131.

[316] See Australian Law Reform Commission, 1987, 'Contempt', Report No. 35, p. 105.

Refer also to the sections titled 'Attempting To Pervert Justice', 'Conspiring To Defeat Justice' and 'Compounding Crimes' in the chapter titled 'Administration Of Justice Offences' in the text titled 'Injia on Criminal Offences in Papua New Guinea and the Pacific'.

However, section 5 of the *Criminal Code Act* (Ch. 262) states:

'(1) Subject to Subsection (2), this Act or the Code does not affect the authority of any court of record to punish a person summarily for the offence commonly known as "Contempt of Court".

(2) A person shall not be punished under Subsection (1) and under the Code for the same act or omission'.

Refer also to the chapter titled 'Double Jeopardy' in the text titled 'Injia on Criminal Practice and Procedure in Papua New Guinea and the Pacific'.

[317] See *Bakir v Doueihi and others* [2001] QSC 414.

See also: Coram Rege roll, T 30 Edward I, m 9d. (1323) Coram Rege roll, M. 17 Edward II, m 16d; (1398) Cal Pat Rolls, 22 Richard II, 427.

Refer also to the chapter titled 'Offences Against The Person' in the text titled 'Injia on Criminal Offences in Papua New Guinea and the Pacific'.

However, section 5 of the *Criminal Code Act* (Ch. 262) states:

'(1) Subject to Subsection (2), this Act or the Code does not affect the authority of any court of record to punish a person summarily for the offence commonly known as "Contempt of Court".

(2) A person shall not be punished under Subsection (1) and under the Code for the same act or omission'.

Refer also to the chapter titled 'Double Jeopardy' in the text titled 'Injia on Criminal Practice and Procedure in Papua New Guinea and the Pacific'.

- threatening the party with criminal proceedings[318];

- the bringing of improper pressure on a party to collateral proceedings, irrespective of whether or not the pressured party is, in fact, deterred from litigating[319];

- deterring the party from bringing or continuing proceedings[320], including by threats of unlawful action, by abuse, by misrepresentation of the nature of the proceedings or the circumstances out of which they arose and such like[321].

  However, the Court must determine whether the conduct complained of amounted to improper pressure to induce a litigant to withdraw from proceedings or to settle them on terms that he or she regarded as inadequate[322]; and

---

318 See *Smith v Lakeman* (1856) 26 LJ Ch 305.

319 See *Smith v Lakeman* (1856) 26 LJ Ch 305, per Lord Stuart VC at 306.

See also: *Harkianakis v Skalkos* (1997) 42 NSWLR 22 and *Resolute Ltd and another v Warnes* [2000] WASCA 359.

320 See *Harkianakis v Skalkos* (1987) 42 NSWLR 22 and *Harrison v Schipp* [1999] NSWCA 443.

See also: Australian Law Reform Commission, 1987, 'Contempt', Report No. 35, p. 105.

Refer also to the section titled 'Compounding Crimes' in the chapter titled 'Administration Of Justice Offences' in the text titled 'Injia on Criminal Offences in Papua New Guinea and the Pacific'.

However, section 5 of the *Criminal Code Act* (Ch. 262) states:

'(1) Subject to Subsection (2), this Act or the Code does not affect the authority of any court of record to punish a person summarily for the offence commonly known as "Contempt of Court".

(2) A person shall not be punished under Subsection (1) and under the Code for the same act or omission'.

Refer also to the chapter titled 'Double Jeopardy' in the text titled 'Injia on Criminal Practice and Procedure in Papua New Guinea and the Pacific'.

321 See *Attorney-General v Times Newspapers Ltd* [1973] 3 All ER 54, [1974] AC 273, per Cross LJ at 326.

322 See *Willshire-Smith v Votino Bros Pty Ltd* (1993) 41 FCR 496, per O'Loughlin J at 505, [1993] FCA 138.

- inducing the party to give false evidence[323].

## [4.6] LEGAL REPRESENTATIVES AS CONTEMNORS

### [4.6.1] INTRODUCTION

The primary responsibility of the Courts and lawyers of the State are to administer justice.[324]

Lawyers should know very well that, they personally owe a duty to the court as 'Officers of the Courts'.[325]

It is their obligation, both professional and ethical, towards the courts they are to appear before.[326]

---

[323] See Australian Law Reform Commission, 1987, 'Contempt', Report No. 35, p. 105.

Refer also to the sections titled 'Conspiring To Bring False Accusation' in the chapter titled 'Administration Of Justice Offences' in the text titled 'Injia on Criminal Offences in Papua New Guinea and the Pacific'.

However, section 5 of the *Criminal Code Act* (Ch. 262) states:

'(1) Subject to Subsection (2), this Act or the Code does not affect the authority of any court of record to punish a person summarily for the offence commonly known as "Contempt of Court".

(2) A person shall not be punished under Subsection (1) and under the Code for the same act or omission'.

Refer also to the chapter titled 'Double Jeopardy' in the text titled 'Injia on Criminal Practice and Procedure in Papua New Guinea and the Pacific'.

[324] See *The State v Lucas Sasoruo* [1997] PNGLR 676 and *Re: Paul Luben and David Poka* (1987) N612.

[325] See *Beecraft No 20 Limited v Dr Fabian Pok as Minister for Lands and The State* (2001) N2125.

[326] See *The State v Lucas Sasoruo* [1997] PNGLR 676 and *Re: Paul Luben and David Poka* (1987) N612.

## CONTEMPT IN THE FACE OF THE COURT

Most people in the country are illiterate. Their level of knowledge and understanding of the law is very limited except for lawyers. This is even the case for some well to do Papua New Guineans but not trained in the law. There is hence, a case of total dependence on lawyers for proper legal advice and representation of their client's interest in the Courts or in any transaction that involves a lawyer. A lawyer is always under a duty to conduct his or her client's case to the best of his or her abilities based on his or her instructions and anything falling short of that would amount to professional negligence.[327]

For any breach of his or her duty to the Court, a lawyer may be dealt with by the Court either:

- for contempt of Court; or
- referred to the Lawyers Statutory Committee.[328]

### [4.6.2] LAWYERS STATUTORY COMMITTEE

The function of the Lawyers Statutory Committee[329] is to enquire into complaints against a lawyer of improper conduct as a lawyer[330] and has the power to impose penalties[331].

### [4.6.3] PROFESSIONAL CONDUCT RULES

Section 3 of the *Professional Conduct Rules 1989* ['Duty of Every Lawyer'] states:

> 'It is the duty of a lawyer –
>
> (a) not to engage in conduct (whether in pursuit of his profession or otherwise) which –
>
> (i) is illegal; or
>
> (ii) is dishonest; or

---

[327] See *Takai Kapi also known as "Tataki Kapi" v George James Sheppard and Harvey Maldina trading as Maladinas Lawyers and another* (2003) N2323.

[328] See *Takai Kapi also known as "Tataki Kapi" v George James Sheppard and Harvey Maldina trading as Maladinas Lawyers and another* (2003) N2323.

[329] As established under section 48 of the *Lawyers Act* (Ch. 91).

[330] See section 52(1) of the *Lawyers Act* (Ch. 91).

[331] See section 54 of the *Lawyers Act* (Ch. 91).

(iii) is unprofessional; or

(iv) is prejudicial to the administration of justice; or

(v) may otherwise bring the legal profession into disrepute; and

(b) to observe the ethics and etiquette of the legal profession; and

(c) to be competent in all his professional activities; and

(d) to respond within a reasonable time and in any event within 21 days (or such extended time of the Committee may allow) to any requirement of the Committee for comments or information on a complaint and in doing so he shall furnish in writing a full and accurate account of his conduct –

(i) in relation to the matter the subject of the complaint; or

(ii) in relation to any other matter the subject of an investigation or enquiry by the Committee; and

(e) to respond within the time and in the matter required by the Committee to any requirement of the Committee for comments or information on a complaint; and

(f) to comply with the Act and these Rules and the common law'.

## [4.6.4] CONTEMPTUOUS BEHAVIOUR

Whilst a Court may tolerate some level of discourtesy and conflict by a legal representative[332] at its sole discretion contemptuous behavior would include:

- conduct that is done in the knowledge of the presiding Judge's status and with the intent to interfere with the administration of justice[333];

[332] See *David Toll v The State* (1989) SC378, [1989] PGSC 1 and *The State v Re Awaita; Contempt Proceedings* [1985] PNGLR 179, [1985] PGNC 29, (1985) N508.

See also: *Parashuram Detaram Shamdasani v King-Emperor* [1945] AC 264 at 270; *Izuora v R* [1953] AC 327 at 336; *R v O'Neill* (1885) 6 NSWLR 43, per Marton CJ at 45 and *R v Mathews* (1887) 8 NSWLR 45, per Darley CJ at 50.

[333] As commented by Lord Smith MR in *Birch v Walsh* (1846) 10 Ir Eq Rep 93 at 96.

Section 15(4)(a) ['Court Proceedings'] states:
'A lawyer should act with due courtesy to the Court before which he is appearing'.

- the use of critical language[334];
- making an insulting remark[335];
- coming into court intoxicated[336];
- persistently refusing to obey a ruling of the presiding Judge[337];
- refusing to abandon a line of questioning deemed by the Court to be damaging to a trial[338];

---

334 See *Alan Robinson v The State* [1986] PNGLR 307.

Section 15(4)(a) ['Court Proceedings'] states:
'A lawyer shall act with due courtesy to the Court before which he is appearing'.

335 See *David Toll v The State* (1989) SC378, [1989] PGSC 1.

See also:
- *Re Rea* (1878) 2 LR Ir 429; and
- section 277(1)(a) of the *District Courts Act* (Ch. 40) ['Contempt of Court'].

Section 15(4)(a) ['Court Proceedings'] states:
'A lawyer shall act with due courtesy to the Court before which he is appearing'.

Refer also to:
- the section titled 'Provoke A Breach Of The Peace' in the chapter titled 'Public Order Offences' in the text titled 'Injia on Criminal Offences in Papua New Guinea and the Pacific'; and
- the chapter titled 'Double Jeopardy' in the text titled 'Injia on Criminal Practice and Procedure in Papua New Guinea and the Pacific'.

336 See *David Toll v The State* (1989) SC378, [1989] PGSC 1.

See also: *R v O'Neill* (1885) 6 NSWLR 43, per Marton CJ at 45 and *R v Mathews* (1887) 8 NSWLR 45, per Darley CJ at 50.

337 See *David Toll v The State* (1989) SC378, [1989] PGSC 1.

See also: *R v O'Neill* (1885) 6 NSWLR 43, per Marton CJ at 45 and *R v Mathews* (1887) 8 NSWLR 45, per Darley CJ at 50.

Section 15(4)(a) ['Court Proceedings'] states:
'A lawyer shall act with due courtesy to the Court before which he is appearing'.

338 See *Ex parte Ballanto, re Prior* (1963) 63 SR (NSW) 190.

Section 15(4)(a) ['Court Proceedings'] states:
'A lawyer shall act with due courtesy to the Court before which he is appearing'.

- wearing improper court dress[339];

- making a threat of violence[340];

- using provocative language likely to lead to a brawl[341];

- doing an act of defiance of the authority of the Court, such as burning a document in disobedience of an order of the Court[342];

339 See *David Toll v The State* (1989) SC378, [1989] PGSC 1.

Section 15(4)(g) of the *Professional Conduct Rules 1989* ['Court Proceedings'] states:

'A lawyer shall appear in court wearing a long-sleeved clean ironed opaque white shirt or blouse with collar closed at the throat and dark trousers or rami, laplap or a skirt and business shoes and –

(i) if appearing as Counsel, properly gowned with bib (tabs) and wig; and

(ii) if appearing as instructing lawyer, a tie in the case of a male'.

340 See *Parashuram Detaram Shamdasani v King-Emperor* [1945] AC 264 at 269.

Refer also to:

- the section titled 'Provoke A Breach Of The Peace' in the chapter titled 'Public Order Offences'; and
- the section titled 'Common Assault' in the chapter titled 'Offences Against The Person'

in the text titled 'Injia on Criminal Offences in Papua New Guinea and the Pacific'.

However, section 5 of the *Criminal Code Act* (Ch. 262) states:

'(1) Subject to Subsection (2), this Act or the Code does not affect the authority of any court of record to punish a person summarily for the offence commonly known as "Contempt of Court".

(2) A person shall not be punished under Subsection (1) and under the Code for the same act or omission'.

Refer also to the chapter titled 'Double Jeopardy' in the text titled 'Injia on Criminal Practice and Procedure in Papua New Guinea and the Pacific'.

341 See *Parashuram Detaram Shamdasani v King-Emperor* [1945] AC 264 at 269.

Refer also to:

- the section titled 'Provoke A Breach Of The Peace' in the chapter titled 'Public Order Offences' in the text titled 'Injia on Criminal Offences in Papua New Guinea and the Pacific'; and
- the chapter titled 'Double Jeopardy' in the text titled 'Injia on Criminal Practice and Procedure in Papua New Guinea and the Pacific'.

342 See *Linwood v Andrews and Moore* (1888) 58 LT 612.

- generally misconducting himself or herself[343];
- knowingly deceiving or misleading the Court[344];
- arriving late for court.[345]

One of the professional and ethical obligations of lawyers towards the Courts is to appear on the dates their clients' cases are set for hearing. Apart from their duty to their clients, they also have a duty to the Court. Their obligation to appear in Court is owed to both the Court and their clients[346];

---

[343] See *R v O'Neill* (1885) 6 NSWLR 43, per Marton CJ at 45 and *R v Mathews* (1887) 8 NSWLR 45, per Darley CJ at 50.

Section 15(4)(a) ['Court Proceedings'] states (in part):
'A lawyer shall act with due courtesy to the Court before which he is appearing'.

[344] See *David Toll v The State* (1989) SC378, [1989] PGSC 1.

See also:
- *Ditfort v Brown* (1990) 19 NSWLR 49; *Linwood v Andrews and Moore* (1988) 58 LT 612 and *R v Weisz; ex parte Hector MacDonald* [1951] 2 KB 611; and
- G Borrie and N Lowe, 1983, 'The Law of Contempt' 2nd ed., Butterworths, London, p. 250.

Section 15(2) ['Court Proceedings'] states:
'A lawyer shall not knowingly deceive or mislead the Court'.

[345] See *Koang No. 47 Limited v Monodo Merchants Limited and Melpa Properties Limited* (2001) SC675; *Andrew Kwimberi of Paulus M Dowa Lawyers v The State* (1998) SC545, [1998] PGSC 9; *Beecraft No 20 Limited v Dr Fabian Pok as Minister for Lands and The State* (2001) N2125 and *The State v Joseph Waine, Jack B'sour and Matilda Kupul* (2002) N2276.

Section 15(4) ['Court Proceedings'] states (in part):
'A lawyer shall –
(a) act with due courtesy to the Court before which he is appearing; and
(b) use his best endeavours to avoid unnecessary expenses and waste of the Court's time;
(f) not delay proceedings that have been set down for trial only for the reason that he does not hold money on account of his costs'.

Section 20(1) ['Professional Courtesy'] states:
'A lawyer shall treat his professional colleagues with the utmost courtesy and fairness'.

[346] See *The State v Lucas Sasoruo* [1997] PNGLR 676.

- interfering in the any way with the administration of justice[347];
- wilfully interrupting the Court[348]; and
- failing to attend court[349]:
    - with a deliberate intent to interfere with or obstruct the fair administration of justice[350];
    - due to gross carelessness[351]; or

---

[347] See *R v O'Neill* (1885) 6 NSWLR 43, per Marton CJ at 45 and *R v Mathews* (1887) 8 NSWLR 45, per Darley CJ at 50.

Section 3(a)(iv) of the *Professional Conduct Rules 1989* ['Duty of Every Lawyer'] states:
'It is the duty of a lawyer not to engage in conduct (whether in pursuit of his profession or otherwise) which is prejudicial to the administration of justice'.

[348] See *Re Rea* (1878) 2 LR Ir 429.

See also: section 277(1)(a) of the *District Courts Act* (Ch. 40) ['Contempt of Court'].

Section 15(4) of the *Professional Conduct Rules 1989* ['Court Proceedings'] states (in part):
'A lawyer shall act --
(a) with due courtesy to the Court before which he is appearing; and
(b) use his best endeavours to avoid unnecessary expenses and waste of the Court's time'.

Section 20(1) ['Professional Courtesy'] states:
'A lawyer shall treat his professional colleagues with the utmost courtesy and fairness'.

[349] Non-attendance by a prosecutor may result in a charge being dismissed, see sections 124 ['Absence of Complainant'] and 130 ['Hearing in Absence of Both or Either of the Parties'] of the *District Courts Act* (Ch. 40).

See also: *The State v Raymond Tupundu* (1996) N1536, [1996] PGNC 10; *McKeown v R* (1971) 16 DLR (3d) 390 and *Weston v Central Criminal Courts' Administrator* [1977] QB 32, per Denning LJ.

See however: *Behn v The President and Members of the Court of Arbitration* (1929) 32 WALR 28 at 30.

[350] See *David Gwaya Poka v The State* [1988-89] PNGLR 218, [1988] PGSC 27; *The State v Lucas Sasoruo* [1997] PNGLR 676 and *The State v Joseph Waine and others* (2002) N2276.

[351] See *Andrew Kwimberi of Paulus M Dowa Lawyers v The State* (1998) SC545, [1998] PGSC 9; *Ian Augerea in his Capacity as Registrar of The National and Supreme Courts v Jack Pambel as the Acting Public Prosecutor and others* (2008) N3332 and *The State v Joel Donne and others* (2007) N3133, [2007] PGNC 47.

- due to negligence or recklessness[352].

However, it is never possible to exhaustively particularise the acts which may or may not amount to contempt 'in the face of Court' when a lawyer fails to attend court on a fixed date.[353]

But the failure to attend Court due to:

- carelessness and inadequate arrangements[354]; or
- circumstances that are unavoidable and beyond their control[355]

do not necessarily amount to 'Contempt of Court'.

The Courts will not tolerate delays or non-appearances by lawyers that are not reasonable in the circumstances.[356]

---

[352] See *Agnes Okona Meten v William Seneka and Magisterial Services* (2011) N4462, [2011] PGNC 169.

[353] See *Andrew Kwimberi of Paulus M Dowa Lawyers v The State* (1998) SC545, [1998] PGSC 9.

[354] See *David Gwaya Poka v The State* [1988-89] PNGLR 218 at 221, [1988] PGSC 27.

[355] See *The State v Lucas Sasoruo* [1997] PNGLR 676 and *Re: Paul Luben and David Poka* (1987) N612.

[356] See *The State v Lucas Sasoruo* [1997] PNGLR 676 and *Re: Paul Luben and David Poka* (1987) N612.

Section 15(4) ['Court Proceedings'] states (in part):

'A lawyer shall –
(a) act with due courtesy to the Court before which he is appearing; and
(b) use his best endeavours to avoid unnecessary expenses and waste of the Court's time;
(f) not delay proceedings that have been set down for trial only for the reason that he does not hold money on account of his costs'.

Section 20(1) ['Professional Courtesy'] states:

'A lawyer shall treat his professional colleagues with the utmost courtesy and fairness'.

## CONTEMPT IN THE FACE OF THE COURT

Lawyers are, apart from representing their clients, 'Officers of the Court'. They should therefore, be at the convenience of the Court more than themselves. That means, if for whatever reason they are not ready in a matter that has been fixed for hearing, they should appear in Court on the date and time appointed and apply for an adjournment or a delay of the hearing. Then unless, the Court grants such an application, they should not on their own accord and without notice to the other counsel(s) involved, delay hearings.[357]

Lawyers in Papua New Guinea know that it is quite easy to approach the Court when there may be difficulty with circuits and, so long as adequate warnings are given, the Court can usually adjust its arrangements.[358]

A lawyer who fails to attend Court on time when the lawyer knows that he or she is required to do so as Counsel without a reasonable excuse is guilty of 'Contempt of Court'.[359]

The Courts must act sternly and decisively to deter unreasonable conduct and unacceptable behaviour of lawyers.[360]

---

[357] See *Koang No 47 Ltd v Mondo Merchants Ltd and another* (2001) SC675.

[358] See *The State v Re Awaita; Contempt Proceedings* [1985] PNGLR 179, [1985] PGNC 29.

[359] See *Re Paul Luben and David Poka* [1987] PGNC 6, (1987) N612.

[360] See *The State v Lucas Sasoruo* [1997] PNGLR 676.

## DISOBEDIENCE CONTEMPT

### [1.0] CONSTITUTIONAL PROVISION[361]

Section 155(6) of the *Constitution of the Independent State of Papua New Guinea* ['The National Judicial System'] states:

> 'Subject to any right of appeal or power of review of a decision, it is the duty of all persons (including the Law Officers of Papua New Guinea and other public officers in their respective official capacities), and of all bodies and institutions, to comply with and, so far as is within their respective lawful powers, to put into effect all decisions of the National Judicial System'.

### [2.0] CRIMINAL CODE ACT

Section 206 of the *Criminal Code* (Ch. 262) ['Disobedience to Lawful Order Issued by Statutory Authority'] states:

> '(1) Subject to Subsection (2), a person who without lawful excuse (proof of which is on him), disobeys a lawful order issued by any court, *or by any person authorized by any law to make the order*[362], is guilty of a misdemeanour.
>
> Penalty[363]: Imprisonment for a term not exceeding one year[364].
>
> (2) Subsection (1) does not apply if some other mode of proceeding against the defaulter is expressly provided for by any law, and intended to be exclusive of all other punishment'. (emphasis added)

---

[361] See also: section 178 of the *Constitution of the Autonomous Region of Bougainville* ['Basic Rights'].

[362] As regards the legality of those words, see *The State v John Rumet Kaputin* [1979] PNGLR 544.

[363] This indictable offence [see section 3(2) of the *Criminal Code* (Ch. 262)] cannot be dealt with summarily [see section 420(1) of the *Criminal Code* (Ch. 262)].

Refer also to the chapter titled 'Classification Of Offences' in the text titled 'Injia on Criminal Practice and Procedure in Papua New Guinea and the Pacific'.

[364] As regards the law in relation to 'Sentencing', refer to the text titled 'Injia on Sentencing in Papua New Guinea and the Pacific'.

# DISOBEDIENCE CONTEMPT

Section 5 of the *Criminal Code Act* (Ch. 262) ['Contempt of Court'] states:

> '(1) Subject to Subsection (2), this Act or the Code does not affect the authority of any court of record to punish a person summarily for the offence commonly known as "Contempt of Court".
>
> (2) A person shall not be punished under Subsection (1) and under the Code for the same act or omission'.

## [3.0] GENERAL PRINCIPLES

Any system of dispute settlement is effective only to the extent that its orders are complied with:

- voluntarily; or
- in the absence of voluntary compliance, by means of enforcement.[365]

Proceedings for 'Contempt of Court' may be regarded as the ultimate enforcement mechanism.[366]

Non-compliance with:

- an order of a Court[367], including an injunction, whether interim or permanent; and
- an undertaking given to a Court[368],

---

365 See Australian Law Reform Commission, 1987, 'Contempt', Report No. 35, p. 291.

366 See Australian Law Reform Commission, 1987, 'Contempt', Report No. 35, p. 291.

367 See also: Law Reform Commission of Canada, 1977, 'Criminal Law: Contempt of Court -- Offences Against the Administration of Justice', Working Paper No. 22, p. 12 and New South Wales Law Reform Commission, 2000, 'Contempt by Publication', Discussion Paper No. 43.

368 See also: D Eady and ATH Smith, 1999, 'Arlidge, Eady and Smith on Contempt' 2nd ed., Sweet and Maxwell, London, para. 3-1 and New South Wales Law Reform Commission, 2000, 'Contempt by Publication', Discussion Paper No. 43.

Those who give undertakings to a Court are bound by the language they use, see *McNair Anderson and Associates v Hinch* [1985] VicRp 30, [1985] VR 309, per Southwell J at 311 and *Australian Consolidated Press Ltd v Morgan* (1965) 112 CLR 483, per Windeyer J at 503, [1965] HCA 21.

As regards the enforcement of an implied undertaking as a 'Contempt of Court', see *Temwood Holdings v Oliver* [1999] WASC 212 and *Naidoo v Naidoo* [2002] WASC 289.

involves an interference with the due administration of justice[369] and constitutes a 'Contempt of Court'[370] and is referred to as 'disobedience contempt[371]'.

Proceedings for the 'disobedience contempt' most commonly arise out of failure to comply with an order (s) which is (are) of such a nature that it (they) can only be obeyed (or, indeed, disobeyed) by the person (s) to whom it is (they are) directed.[372]

In the law in relation to disobedience contempt the principles relating to a court order equally apply to an undertaking.[373]

An undertaking in a civil action has the same force as an injunction made by the Court. Its breach is misconduct amounting to contempt.[374]

---

[369] See *Australasian Meat Industry Employees' Union v Mudginberri Station Pty Ltd* (1986) 161 CLR 98 at 107, (1986) 66 ALR 577, [1986] HCA 46 and *Witham v Holloway* (1995) 183 CLR 525 at 530, (1995) 131 ALR 401, (1995) 69 ALJR 847, [1995] HCA 3.

[370] See *Stephen John Rose and John Charles Harrison v Neville Devete, Acting Solicitor-General and The State* (2007) N3327; *Sr Dianne Liriope v Dr Jethro Usurup, Chief Executive Officer, Modilon General Hospital and others* (2009) N3572, [2009] PGNC 2; *Madang Development Corporation Ltd v Rabtrad Niugini* [2013] PGNC 113, (2013) N5259 and *Bank of South Pacific Ltd v Sekum* [2011] PGNC 176, (2011) N4588.

See also: *Trade Practices Commission v CG Smith Pty Ltd* (1978) 30 FLR 368, [1978] FCA 2; *Spindler v Balog* (1959) 76 WN (NSW) 391 and *Circuit Finance Australia v Sobbi* [2010] NSWSC 789.

[371] See *Stephen John Rose and another v Neville Devete, Acting Solicitor-General and The State* (2007) N3327 and *Public Officers Superannuation Fund Board v Paul Paraka Trading as Paul Paraka Lawyers and Paul Paraka Trading as Paul Paraka Lawyers v Public Officers Superannuation Fund Board* (2005) N2791.

See also: Australian Law Reform Commission, 1987, 'Contempt', Report No. 35, Ch. 5.

[372] See *Stephen John Rose and another v Neville Devete, Acting Solicitor-General and The State* (2007) N3327.

[373] See also: *R and I Bank of Western Australia v Anchorage Investments Pty Ltd* (1992) 10 WAR 59, per Ipp J at 69.

[374] See *Williams v Fawcett* [1986] 1 QB 604 at 607.

See also:

- *Midland Marts Ltd v Hobday* [1989] 1 WLR 1143 and *Capel v Caram Finance Aust Ltd* [1998] QSC 110; and
- 'Halsbury's Laws of England' 4th ed., para. 75.

## DISOBEDIENCE CONTEMPT

This class of contempt is reserved to cases where the behaviour of the alleged contemnor has been shown to be:

- aimed at the integrity of the Courts; and
- designed to degrade the administration of justice,

as distinguished from a simple interference with property rights manifested by a court order.[375]

This class of contempt protects the effective administration of justice by demonstrating that the Court's orders will be enforced[376] and shows the consequences of a breach of those orders[377].

As Lindley LJ stated in *Seward v Patterson*[378]:

> A court will not allow its process to be set at nought and treated with contempt.

The public interest in the administration of justice requires compliance with all orders[379] and undertakings, whether or not compliance also serves individual or private interests.[380]

---

375 See *Root v MacDonald* (1927) 157 NE 684 at 688, (1927) 54 Am LR 1422 (1927) and *Registrar of the Court of Appeal v Maniam (No. 2)* (1992) 26 NSWLR 309, per Kirby P at 315.

376 See *Australasian Meat Industry Employees Union v Mudginberri Station Pty Ltd* (1986) 161 CLR 98 at 107, (1986) 66 ALR 577 at 584, (1986) 66 ALR 577, [1986] HCA 46.

377 See *Papua New Guinea Forest Authority v Vele Iamo and another* (2003) N2490; *Kalip Salo and others on behalf of Lawful Landowners and another v Peter Terry Gerari and others* (2005) N2923; *Re Contempt Charges against Valentine Kambori (No. 2)* (2003) N2489 and *Pioneers Health Services Limited v Gabriel Yer, Secretary of Department of Finance and The State* (2008) N3326.

See also: *Australia Meat Industry Employees Union v Mudginberri Station Pty Ltd* (1986) 161 CLR 98, (1986) 66 ALR 577, [1986] HCA 46.

378 [1897] 1 Ch 545 at 556.

379 See *Australasian Meat Industry Employees Union and others v Mudginberri Station Pty Ltd* (1986) 161 CLR 98 at 108, (1986) 66 ALR 577, [1986] HCA 46; *Witham v Holloway* (1995) 183 CLR 525 at 532, (1995) 131 ALR 401, (1995) 69 ALJR 847, [1995] HCA 3 and *Primelife Corporation Limited by New Park Pty Ltd and another* [2003] VSC 106.

380 As stated by Salmon LJ in *Jennison v Baker* [1972] 2 QB 52 at 61.

See also: *Witham v Holloway* (1995) 183 CLR 525 at 532, (1995) 131 ALR 401, (1995) 69 ALJR 847, [1995] HCA 3; *Australasian Meat Industry Employees Union v Mudginberri Station Pty Ltd* (1986) 161 CLR 98 at 107, (1986) 66 ALR 577 at 584, [1986] HCA 46 and *Geoff Penney (Aust) Pty Ltd v Skyjack Computer and Office Supplies Pty Ltd* (1990) ATPR 41-013.

## DISOBEDIENCE CONTEMPT

It is the duty of the Courts to protect the administration of justice by demonstrating that its orders will be enforced.[381]

The administration of justice would be undermined if the order of any Court could be disregarded with impunity.[382]

The actual offence is interference, with knowledge of the Court's proceedings, with the course or administration of justice.[383]

The test to be applied for determining whether there has been a 'Contempt of Court' in disobeying an order or not conforming to an undertaking is 'objective'.

It is not necessary to prove any subjective intent to deliberately disobey the order.[384]

Non-compliance necessarily constitutes an interference with the administration of justice even if the position can be remedied as between the parties.[385]

Such interference offends the public good by weakening the authority of the Court and its task of doing justice between members of the public or, in the criminal process, between the State and the accused person.[386]

---

[381] See *Yap v Tin Siew Tan, B and T Engineering Pty Ltd, Robert L Wong, William Baptiste and David F Tau* [1987] PNGLR 227, [1987] PGSC 21 and *Pius Mark for and on behalf of the Council of the Mount Hagen Technical College v Korali Iki* [1995] PNGLR 116, [1995] PGNC 134.

See also: *Hadkinson v Hadkinson* [1952] 2 All ER 567, Romer LJ at 569.

[382] As observed by Diplock LJ in *Attorney-General v Times Newspapers Ltd* [1973] 3 All ER 54, [1974] AC 273 at 308.

See also:

- *Canada Metal Co Ltd v Canadian Broadcasting Corporation (No. 2)* (1975) 48 DLR (3d) 641 at 669 and *Heatons Transport (St. Helens) Ltd v Transport and General Workers' Union* [1973] AC 15, per Wilberforce LJ at 109; and
- G Borrie and N Lowe, 1983, 'The Law of Contempt' 2nd ed., Butterworths, London, p. 3.

[383] See *Attorney-General v Leveller Magazine Ltd and others* [1979] AC 440, per Scarman LJ at 471.

[384] See *Stancomb v Trowbridge Urban District Council* [1910] 2 Ch Div 190 at 194.

See also: *Australian Competition and Consumer Commission v Hughes* (2001) AT PR 41-807, [2001] FCA 38.

[385] See *Witham v Holloway* (1995) 183 CLR 525 at 532, (1995) 131 ALR 401, (1995) 69 ALJR 847, [1995] HCA 3.

[386] See *BHP v Dagi* [1996] VicRp 62, [1996] 2 VR 117, per Tadgell JA at 154 and Hayne JA at 193.

## DISOBEDIENCE CONTEMPT

A party in whose favour an order has been made is entitled to have it enforced, and also the effective administration of justice normally requires some penalty for disobedience of an order of a Court.[387]

Traditionally, contempt proceedings for non-compliance with an order made in the course of civil proceedings have been classified as 'civil contempt'[388] which was developed in England in the Court of Chancery.[389]

The National and Supreme Courts have undoubted power to compel:

- observance of their processes; and
- obedience of and compliance with their orders and directions.[390]

These powers are inherent in the sense that they are necessary attributes to render the judicial function effective in the administration of justice.[391]

It is the duty of all persons and all bodies and institutions, to comply with and, so far as is within their respective lawful powers, to put into effect all decisions of the National Judicial System[392], including the District Court[393] and Village Court[394].

---

387 See *Director General of Fair Trading v Pioneer Concrete (UK) Ltd* [1995] 1 AC 456, per Nolan LJ at 479.

388 Refer also to the chapter titled 'Distinction Between Criminal And Civil Contempt Of Court'.

389 See Australian Law Reform Commission, 1987, 'Contempt', Report No. 35, p. 291.

390 See *Peter Luga v Richard Sikani Commissioner, Correctional Services and The State* (2001) N2285; *Review Pursuant to Constitution, Section 155(2)(B); Application by Herman Joseph Leahy* (2006) SC855 and *Stephen John Rose and John Charles Harrison v Neville Devete, Acting Solicitor-General and The State* (2007) N3327.

391 See *Stephen John Rose and John Charles Harrison v Neville Devete, Acting Solicitor-General and The State* (2007) N3327.

392 See *Pius Mark for and on behalf of the Council of the Mt. Hagen Technical College v Korali Iki* [1995] PNGLR 116, [1995] PGNC 134.

Refer also to the section titled 'National Judicial System' in the chapter titled 'Criminal Jurisdiction Of The Courts' in the text titled 'Injia on Criminal Practice and Procedure in Papua New Guinea and the Pacific'.

393 See *Pius Mark for and on behalf of the Council of the Mt. Hagen Technical College v Korali Iki* [1995] PNGLR 116, [1995] PGNC 134; *Kimbe Bakery Pty Ltd v Ben Jalatang* (1993) N1274 and *In the Matter of an Application by Linah Edward* (2005) N2804.

394 See *The State v Charles Maniwa and Joseph Utura Maniwa* (2004) N2674.

## DISOBEDIENCE CONTEMPT

It should not need to be stated that all citizens of Papua New Guinea are:

- equal in the eyes of the law; and
- equally required to abide by the law by complying with orders of the Court.[395]

The duty is imposed on every human person (citizen or non-citizen) and every body or institution in the country to comply with lawful orders under section 155(6) of the *Constitution of the Independent State of Papua New Guinea* is all encompassing. No one is immune.[396]

Court orders are made for those against whom they are directed to take or not to take the actions that might be specified.[397]

However, a non-party will be in 'Contempt of Court' by:

- assisting the person to whom an order of a Court is directed to disobey it[398]; or

---

[395] See *John Rumet Kaputin v The State* [1979] PNGLR 559 at 563 and *Luga v Sikani, Commissioner of Correctional Services (No. 2)* [2002] PGNC 60, (2002) N2286.

[396] See *Review Pursuant to Constitution, Section 155(2)(B); Application by Herman Joseph Leahy* (2006) SC855.

[397] See *The State v Charles Maniwa and Joseph Utura Maniwa* (2004) N2674.

[398] See *Seaward v Paterson* [1897] 1 Ch 545, per Lindley LJ at 554; *Lord Wellesley v Earl of Mornington* [1848] EngR 457, (1848) 11 Beav 180 at 183, (1848) 50 ER 785 at 787 and *Marengo v Daily Sketch and Sunday Graphic Ltd* [1948] 1 All ER 406 at 407.

See also: *Z Ltd v A-Z and AA-LL* [1982] 1 QB 558, per Eveleigh LJ at 578; *Cardile v LED Builders Pty Ltd* (1999) 198 CLR 380 at 395; *Zhu v Treasurer of New South Wales* (2004) 218 CLR 530 at 571, [2004] HCA 56; *Chan and others v Chen and others (No. 2)* [2007] VSC 24; *Deputy Commissioner of Taxation v Gashi and another (No. 2)* [2011] VSC 351; *Attorney-General v Newspaper Publishing plc* [1988] Ch 333 at 366; *CCOM Pty Ltd v Jiejing Pty Ltd* (1992) 36 FCR 524 at 530, [1992] FCA 325; *Reid v Howard* (1993) 31 NSWLR 298 at 309; *Marron v Salvemini; Re Scardigno* [1969] WAR 178 at 180 and *Cardile v LED Builders Pty Ltd* (1999) 198 CLR 380 at 395.

- knowingly doing an act that subverts the purpose of an order of a Court[399] even though the non-party may be acting independently of the party against whom the order was made[400],[401]

thereby interfering with the administration of justice.[402]

Court orders are made for good order in society and to enable peaceful co-existence.[403]

If people do not obey orders given by Courts, there will be chaos where people will take the law into their own hands.[404]

A breach of an order of a Court amounts to a serious misconduct as it operates against the entire system of justice.[405]

Non-compliance with an order of a Court can be exhibited either by:

- refusing[406] or neglecting to do an act required by an order of a Court; or

---

[399] See *Ome Ome Forests Ltd v Ray Cheong and others* (2002) N2289.

See also: *Attorney-General v Times Newspapers Ltd and another* [1991] 2 All ER 398, [1992] 1 AC 191, [1991] 2 WLR 994; *M v Home Office* [1994] 1 AC 377, [1993] 3 WLR 433, [1993] 3 All ER 537, [1994] AC 377, [1993] UKHL 5; *Attorney-General v Newspaper Publishing plc* [1997] 1 WLR 927, per Bingham LCJ at 936 and *Bartle and Gibson Co v Retail, Wholesale and Department Store Union, Local 580* [1971] 2 WWR 449, per Tysoe JA at 455.

[400] See *Attorney-General v Punch Ltd* [2003] 1 All ER 289, [2003] HRLR 14, [2003] 2 WLR 49, [2002] UKHL 50, [2003] AC 1046, [2003] 1 AC 1046, [2003] EMLR 7.

[401] See *Attorney-General v Times Newspapers Ltd and another* [1991] 2 All ER 398, [1992] 1 AC 191, [1991] 2 WLR 994 and *In re Supply of Ready Mixed Concrete* [1991] 3 WLR 707 at 718.

[402] See also: Order 13, rule 9 of the *National Court Rules 1983* ['Enforcement By or Against Non-party'].

[403] See *The State v Charles Maniwa and Joseph Utura Maniwa* (2004) N2674.

[404] See *Pius Mark for and on behalf of the Council of the Mount Hagen Technical College v Korali Iki* [1995] PNGLR 116, [1995] PGNC 134.

[405] See *The State v Charles Maniwa and Joseph Utura Maniwa* (2004) N2674.

[406] See *The State v Charles Maniwa and Joseph Utura Maniwa* (2004) N2674.

See also: *James v Cowan* (1929) 42 CLR 305, per Starke J at 310.

- disobeying an order of a Court requiring him or her to abstain from doing a specified act.[407]

The obligation of every person against, or in respect of, whom an order is made, is to strictly observe the terms of the order[408] unless and until it is:

- discharged; or
- set aside[409]

---

[407] See *Yap v Tin Siew Tan, B and T Engineering Pty Ltd, Robert L Wong, William Baptiste and David F Tau* [1987] PNGLR 227, [1987] PGSC 21 and *Milupol Development Corporation Ltd v Garai* [2012] PGNC 29, (2012) N4635.

See also: *Helmore v Smith* (1887) 35 Ch D 436 and *Miller v Knox* [1838] EngR 648, (1838) 4 Bing (NC) 574, (1838) 132 ER 910, (1838) Scott 1, per Patterson LJ.

[408] See *Honourable Bire Kimisopa MP, Minister for Justice and others v Paul Paraka trading as Paul Paraka Lawyers* (2009) SC1008; *Central Provincial Government v National Capital District Interim Commission* [1987] PNGLR 249 and *The State v Charles Maniwa and Joseph Utura Maniwa* (2004) N2674.

See also: *Spokes v Banbury Board of Health* (1865) LR 1 Eq 42 at 48; *Canada (Human Rights Commission) v Taylor* [1990] 3 SCR 892, per Dickson CJ at 942 and McLachlin J at 972; *Canada Metal Co v Canadian Broadcasting Corp (No 2)* (1974) 4 OR (2d) 584; *R v Litchfield* [1993] 4 SCR 333, per Iacobucci J at 347 and *Australian Competition and Consumer Commission v INFO4PC.com Pty Ltd* [2002] FCA 949.

See also: G Borrie and N Lowe, 1996, 'The Law of Contempt' 3rd ed., Butterworths, London, p. 559 and D Eady and ATH Smith, 1999, 'Arlidge, Eady and Smith on Contempt' 2nd ed., Sweet and Maxwell, London, p. 189.

[409] See *Concord Pacific Ltd and Paiso Company Ltd v Thomas Nen – Managing Director, Papua New Guinea Forest Authority and the State* [2000] PNGLR 47 and *Ome Ome Forests Limited v Ray Cheong and others* (2002) N2289.

See also: *Chuck v Cremer* [1846] Eng R 924, (1846) 47 ER 820; *Hadkinson v Hadkinson* [1952] P 285, per Romer LJ at 288; *Scott v Bennett* (1871) LR 5HL 234 at 245; *Revell v Blake* (1873) LR 8CP 533 at 544; *Isaacs v Robertson* [1985] AC 97 at 101; *In re A Company* [1981] AC 374, per Diplock LJ at 384; *M v Home Office* [1993] UKHL 5; *Smith v East Elloe Rural District Council* [1956] AC 736, per Radcliffe LJ at 769, [1956] UKHL 2; *Wilson v R* [1983] 2 SCR 594, per McIntyre J at 599; *Jackson v Sterling Industries Ltd* (1987) 162 CLR 612 at 620, [1987] HCA 23; *Russell v East Anglian Railway Co* [1850] EngR 870, (1850) 3 Mac & G 104, (1850) 42 ER 201 (Ch); *Cameron v Cole* (1944) 68 CLR 571 at 585, 590, 598 and 607, [1944] HCA 5; *Re Macks: Ex parte Saint* (2000) 204 CLR 158, per Gaudron J at 177, [2000] HCA 62; *Hillig v Darkinjung Pty Ltd* [2008] NSWCA 75, per McColl JA; *Mathews v Australian Securities and Investments Commission* (2000) 170 ALR 149, [2000] FCA 288 and *Little v Lewis* [1987] VicRp 64, [1987] VR 798.

even when the person affected by it believes it to be:

- irregular; or
- void.[410]

It is a good law that maintains and upholds the integrity of the courts so that court orders are obeyed without question.[411]

An order made by a superior court of record, ie., the Supreme and National Court:

- erroneously; or
- in excess of jurisdiction

is merely voidable and remains valid and enforceable until set aside.[412]

---

[410] See *Review Pursuant to Constitution, Section 155(2)(B); Application by Herman Joseph Leahy* (2006) SC855; *Jack Livinai Patterson v Lawyers Statutory Committee and Papua New Guinea Law Society* (2005) SC822; *Philip Soon Kiat Yap v Tin Siew Tan, B and T Engineering Pty Ltd, Robert L Wong, William Baptiste and David F Tau* [1987] PNGLR 227, [1987] PGSC 21; *Concord Pacific Limited and Paiso Company Limited Thomas Nen – Managing Director – Papua New Guinea Forest Authority and The State* (2000) N1981; *latinata v Toiwat and Valaun* [1994] PNGLR 568, [1994] PGNC 107; *Soso Tomu and others v The State and others* (2002) N2190; *Stephen John Rose and another v Neville Devete, Acting Solicitor-General and The State* (2007) N3327; *21 ILGS Gobe Project Area Inc Land Groups v Pawih* [2006] PGNC 10, (2006) N3066; *John Siune v Rendle Rimua, Secretary, Department of Petroleum and Energy and The State* (2013) N5110, [2013] PGNC 83 and *Joel Ivat v Department of Health and Department of Personnel Management* (2002) N2230, [2002] PGNC 108.

See also: *Hadkinson v Hadkinson* [1952] 2 All ER 567, per Lomer LJ at 569; *Chuck v Cremer* [1846] 1 Coop T Cott 205, (1846) 47 ER 820, per Cottenham LC; *Spokes v Banbury Board of Health* [1865] LR 1 Eq 42, per Lord Wood VC at 48; *Harding v Tingey* (1864) 12 WR 684, per Lord Kindersley VC; *Howitt Transport v Transport and General Workers Union* [1973] ICR 1, per Sir John Donaldson MR at 10; *Re Swan River - The Pas Transfer Ltd* (1975) 51 DLR (3d) 292 at 308; *Northwest Territories Public Service Association v Commissioner of the Northwest Territories* (1980) 97 DLR (3d) 202 at 233 and *Stancomb v Trowbudge District Council* [1910] Ch Div 190.

[411] See *Jack Livinai Patterson v Lawyers Statutory Committee and Papua New Guinea Law Society* (2005) SC822.

[412] See *Cameron v Cole* (1944) 68 CLR 571, [1944] HCA 5; *Re Wakim; Ex parte McNally* (1999) 198 CLR 511, [1999] HCA 27; *Jackson v Sterling Industries Ltd* (1987) 162 CLR 612 at 620, [1987] HCA 23; *Matthews v Australian Securities and Investments Commission* (2000) 97 FCR 396 at 401, [2000] FCA 288; *Australia and New Zealand Banking Group Ltd v Merribee Pastoral Industries Pty Ltd* (1998) 84 FCR 367 at 380 and *Australian Competition and Consumer Commission v Purple Harmony Plates Pty Limited (No. 3)* [2002] FCA 1487.

However, if an inferior court, such as the other courts of Papua New Guinea, exercising judicial power has no authority to make an order of the kind in question, the failure to obey it cannot be a contempt. Such an order is a nullity.[413] That principle equally applies to undertakings.[414]

Irrespective, the orderly and functional administration of justice requires that court orders and undertakings be considered final[415] and binding, unless they are reversed on appeal.[416]

A court order is not mere empty words.[417]

A court order cannot be ignored, or treated as a nullity, whatever defects there might be in it. Even if the judgment is beyond the jurisdiction of the Court giving it, this does not deprive it of its binding effect, and it must be obeyed unless and until properly set aside, eg., on appeal.[418]

So long as a court order exists it must be obeyed and obeyed to the letter[419], in strict in compliance with its terms[420].

As stated by Chief Justice McKean of the Supreme Court of the United States in 1778:

> Since, however, the question seems to resolve itself into this, whether you shall bend to the law, or the law shall bend to you, it is our duty to determine that the former shall be the case.[421]

---

[413] See *United Telecasters Sydney Ltd v Hardy* (1991) 23 NSWLR 323 at 335 and *Attorney-General for New South Wales v Mayas Pty Ltd* (1988) 14 NSWLR 342 at 357.

[414] See *United Telecasters Sydney Ltd v Hardy* (1991) 23 NSWLR 323 at 335 and *Thomson Australian Holdings Pty Ltd v Trade Practices Commission* (1981) 148 CLR 150 at 165, [1981] HCA 48.

[415] See *Stambulich v Ekamper (No. 4)* [2008] WASCA 189, per Pullin JA; *Leslie v GE Commercial Corporation (Australia) Pty Ltd (No. 2)* [2009] WASCA 28, per Steytler P and *Matta v R* [2011] WASCA 2, per Buss JA.

[416] See *R v Pastro* (1988) 42 CCC (3d) 485 at 497, [1988] SCC 214 and *R v Litchfield* [1993] 4 SCR 333, per Iacobucci J at 349, [1993] SCC 44.

[417] See *Pioneers Health Services Limited v Gabriel Yer, Secretary of Department of Finance and The State* (2008) N3326.

[418] See *Cameron v Cole* (1944) 68 CLR 571, per Rich J at 590, McTiernan J at 598 and Williams J at 607, [1944] HCA 5; *Re Macks; ex Parte Saint* (2000) 204 CLR 158, [2000] HCA 62 and *Eastman v R* [2008] FCAFC 62.

[419] See *Spokes v Banbury Board of Health* (1865) LR 1 Eq 42, per Lord Wood VC at 48.

[420] See *Howitt Transport v Transport and General Workers' Union* [1973] ICR 1, per Sir John Donaldson MR at 10.

[421] See J Fox, 1927, 'The History of Contempt fo Court', p. 47.

## DISOBEDIENCE CONTEMPT

As stated by Lord Vice Chancellor, Sir William Page Wood in *Spokes v Banbury Board of Health*[422]:

> [T]he simple and only view is, that an order must be obeyed, and that those who wish to get rid of that order must do so by the proper course, on appeal. So long as it exists, the order must be obeyed, and obeyed to the letter; and anyone who does not obey it to the letter is guilty of committing a wilful breach of it.

However, mere non-production of documents that are called for by a subpoena, or other court order to produce documents, is insufficient to establish that there has been a contempt. There needs to be established that, at the date on which the documents were required to be produced, the alleged contemnor had documents that met the description of the documents called for by the subpoena or other order to produce.[423]

It is not open to any party to question the orders of a Court, or any process issued under the authority of a Court, by disobedience. The parties must take a proper course to question their validity, but while they exist they must be obeyed.[424]

Therefore, the party who is required to comply has no choice but to comply. Even if such a person:

- wishes not to comply; or
- is in doubt as to what is required of him or her,

he or she is at no liberty to ignore it.[425]

By the same token, the party is not at any liberty to engage in conduct that runs contrary to the direction, order or judgement of the Court.[426]

---

[422] (1865) LR 1 Eq 42 at 48.

[423] See *In re Bramblevale Ltd* [1970] 1 Ch 128 at 137.

See also: *Thorpe v Marr's Furniture Removals Pty Ltd* [2000] QSC 279 and *Wyszynski v Bill* [2005] NSWSC 110.

[424] See *Russell v East Anglican Railway Co* [1850] Eng R 870, (1850) 42 ER 201, per Truro LJ at 206 and *Spokes v Banbury Board of Health* (1865) LR 1 Eq 42 at 48.

[425] See *Ome Ome Forests Ltd v Ray Cheong, Jackson Whong and Bill Garey* (2002) N2289.

[426] See *Ome Ome Forests Ltd v Ray Cheong, Jackson Whong and Bill Garey* (2002) N2289.

If a party is legally advised that an order has been made invalidly, delay in complying with the order is legitimate only pending application to the Court to discharge the order. However, this course can only be justified if:

- the application is made at the first practicable opportunity; and
- in the meantime all appropriate steps have been taken to ensure that the person in whose favour the order was made will not be disadvantaged pending the hearing of the application.[427]

A court order may not be attacked collaterally.[428] A collateral attack may be described as an attack made in proceedings other than those whose specific object is the reversal, variation, or nullification of the order or judgment.[429]

A Court may act on its own to commence proceedings for disobedience.[430]

[427] See *M v Home Office* [1994] 1 AC 377, per Woolf LJ at 424.

[428] See *Wilson v R* [1983] 2 SCR 594, per McIntyre J at 599; *Re Macks; ex parte Saint* (2000) 204 CLR 158, (2000) 176 ALR 545, (2000) 75 ALJR 203, [2000] HCA 62; *Merribee Pastoral Industries Pty Ltd v ANZ Banking Group Ltd* (1998) 193 CLR 502 at 516, [1998] HCA 41; *DJL v Central Authority* (2000) 201 CLR 226 at 263, [2000] HCA 17 and *Vincent Ross Siemer v The Solicitor-General* [2013] NZSC 68.

[429] See *Wilson v R* [1983] 2 SCR 594, per McIntyre J at 599.

[430] See Order 14, Division 6, rule 47(1) of the *National Court Rules 1983* ['Motion or Proceedings by Registrar'] states:

> Where it is alleged, or appears to the Court on its own view, that a person is guilty of contempt of the court or of any other court, the Court may, by order, direct the Registrar to apply by motion for, or to commence proceedings for, punishment of the contempt.

See also: *Foothills Provincial General Hospital Board v Broad* (1975) 57 DLR (3d) 758; *Churchman v Joint Shop Stewards' Committee of the Workers of the Port of London* [1972] 3 All ER 603; *Con-Mech (Engineers) Ltd v Amalgamated Union of Engineering Workers* [1973] ICR 620 and *R v United Fishermen and Allied Workers' Union* (1967) 63 DLR (2d) 356.

## DISOBEDIENCE CONTEMPT

### [4.0] MUST BE CLEAR

The order of the Court must be clear.[431]

The proper construction of an order is not a matter of fact, but a question of law.[432]

---

[431] See *Ross Bishop and others v Bishop Brothers Engineering and Pty Ltd* [1998-89] PNGLR 533, [1988] PGSC 8; *Stephen John Rose and another v Neville Devete, Acting Solicitor-General and The State* (2007) N3327; *21 ILGS Gobe Project Area Inc Land Groups v Pawih* [2006] PGNC 10, (2006) N3066; *Moses Vua and others v Francis Mavu and another* (2008) N3294; *Keven Manase v Thomas Opa* (2013) N5280, [2013] PGNC 94; *Joel Ivat and Department of Health v Department of Personnel Management* (2002) N2230; *Aisi Iuma Bore on behalf of Behori Clan of Furimuti Village v Clement Malaisa, Land Titles Commission* (2013) N5273, [2013] PGNC 92; *Luchya Mussa Tikuye v Patrick Haines* (2009) N4434, [2009] PGNC 259; *Mathew Michael, on behalf of himself and 147 other teachers v John Glengme, Provincial Education Adviser and others* (2008) N3429, [2008] PGNC 114; *John Siune v Rendle Rimua, Secretary, Department of Petroleum and Energy and The State* (2013) N5110, [2013] PGNC 83; *Martin Kenehe and others v Michael Pearson, Chairman, Teaching Service Commission and others* (2009) N3763, [2009] PGNC 158; *Newsat Ltd v Telikom PNG Ltd, ICCC and The State* (2007) N3447, [2007] PGNC 157 and *Sr Dianne Liriope v Dr Jethro Usurup, Chief Executive Officer, Modilon General Hospital and others* (2009) N3572, [2009] PGNC 2.

See also:

- *Australian Consolidated Press Ltd v Morgan* (1965) 112 CLR 483 at 503, 506 and 515, [1965] HCA 21; *Metcash Trading Ltd v Bunn (No. 5)* [2009] FCA 16; *Iberian Trust Ltd v Founders Trust and Investment Co Ltd* [1932] 2 KB 87 at 95; *Australian Industry Group v Automotive, Food, Metals, Engineering, Printed and Kindred Industries Union* [2000] FCA 629; *ICI Australia Operations Pty Ltd v Trade Practices Commission* (1992) 38 FCR 248, per Lockhart J at 259, [1992] FCA 474; *Randl Bank of Western Australia Ltd v Anchorage Investments Pty Ltd* (1993) 10 WAR 59 at 60; *Commissioner of Water Resources v Federated Engine Drivers and Fireman's Association of Australasia Queensland Branch and others* [1988] 2 Qd R 385, per McPherson J at 390; *Evenco Pty Ltd v ABCE and BLF (Qld Branch)* [2001] 2 Qd R 118 at 133; *Commissioner of Water Resources v FED and FA* [1988] 2 Qd R 385 at 390; *Advan Investments Pty Ltd v Dean Gleeson Motor Sales Pty Ltd* [2003] VSC 201; *Scott and others v Evia Pty Ltd and others* [2007] VSC 15; *National Australia Bank v Juric* [2001] VSC 375; *Chan and others v Chen and others (No. 2)* [2007] VSC 24; *Deputy Commissioner of Taxation v Gashi and another (No. 2)* [2011] VSC 351; *Collins v Wayne Iron Works* (1910) 227 Pa 326, (1910) 76 A 24 at 25; *National Australia Bank v Juric* [2001] VSC 375 and *Law Institute of Victoria v Nagle* [2005] VSC 35; and
- G Borrie and N Lowe, 1983, 'The Law of Contempt' 2nd ed., Butterworths, London, p. 379.

[432] See *Universal Music Australia Pty Ltd v Sharman Networks Ltd* (2006) 150 FCR 110, [2006] FCAFC 41 and *Metcash Trading Ltd v Bunn (No. 5)* [2009] FCA 16.

Nonetheless it may be highly relevant to the question of penalty that the alleged contemnor disobeyed an order because he or she placed a construction on it that was not its true construction.[433]

This requirement involves the following issues:

- what is the true construction of the order; and

- was the true construction of the order sufficiently clear to the person bound by the order to warrant enforcement of the order against that person.[434]

However, the principle that an order ought to make clear what is that the party is required to do or not do is a counsel of perfection, rather than a mandatory standard, and there are limits to its application.[435]

An undertaking does not fall foul of the principle that its terms must be clear and ascertainable on its face simply because someone can contend for an unlikely construction thereof.[436]

It is not necessary for a Court to prescribe the manner in which the required result is to be achieved and it is sufficient if the Court clearly specifies that a party is to carry out a particular course of conduct.[437]

---

433 See *Universal Music Australia Pty Ltd v Sharman Networks Ltd* (2006) 150 FCR 110, [2006] FCAFC 41 and *Metcash Trading Ltd v Bunn (No. 5)* [2009] FCA 16.

434 See *Athens and another v Randwick City Council* (2005) 64 NSWLR 58, per Hodgson JA at 69, [2005] NSWCA 317.

435 See *Curro v Beyond Productions Pty Ltd* (1993) 30 NSWLR 337 at 349.

436 See *Evenco Pty Ltd v Australian Building Construction Employees and Builders Labourers Federation (Qld Branch)* [2001] 2 Qd R 118, per Williams J at 136 and *Australian Consolidated Press Ltd v Morgan* (1965) 112 CLR 483, per Barwick CJ at 492, [1965] HCA 21.

437 See *Concrete Constructions Pty Ltd v Plumbers and Gasfitters Employees Union (No. 2)* (1987) 15 FCR 64, per Wilcox J at 72, [1987] FCA 117 and *Australian Competition and Consumer Commission v INFO4PC.com Pty Ltd* [2002] FCA 949.

| **DISOBEDIENCE CONTEMPT** |
|---|

It is not for a party to suggest, or for the Court to prescribe, a particular method of compliance.[438]

An order requiring an act to be done must state the time within which the act is to be done before it can be enforced.[439]

An order requiring the doing of an act which does not specify:

- a period; or
- date

by which the act is to be done is generally unenforceable.[440]

There are exceptions to this proposition, such as where the person to perform the terms of the order deliberately puts it beyond his or her power to comply with the order after it is made.[441]

Where the Rules require time to be specified for doing an act and the order does not so specify, this is a ground on which the subject of the order might apply to have the order set aside.[442]

---

438 See *Australian Competition and Consumer Commission v Hughes* [2001] FCA 38.

439 See *Steven Kambu Tandawi v Lucas Lau Kore and others* (1997) N1510 and *21 ILGS Gobe Project Area Inc Land Groups v Pawih* [2006] PGNC 10, (2006) N3066.

See also: Order 13 rule 5 of the *National Court Rules 1983*.

440 See *21 ILGS Gobe Project Area Inc Land Groups v Pawih* [2006] PGNC 10, (2006) N3066.

441 See *21 ILGS Gobe Project Area Inc Land Groups v Pawih* [2006] PGNC 10, (2006) N3066.

See also: *Gilbert v Endean* (1878) 9 Ch D 259, per Lord Jessel MR at 266 and *Carter v Roberts* [1903] 2 Ch 312, per Bryne J at 320.

442 See *21 ILGS Gobe Project Area Inc Land Groups v Pawih* [2006] PGNC 10, (2006) N3066.

See also: *Hitachi Sales (UK) v Mitsui Lines* [1986] 2 Lloyd's Rep 574.

## DISOBEDIENCE CONTEMPT

### [5.0] MUST BE UNAMBIGUOUS

The order of the Court must be unambiguous.[443]

The ambiguity must be such that it cannot be said what it was that required compliance.[444]

The context in which an undertaking is given is relevant in understanding it, and giving it meaning.[445]

---

[443] See *Ross Bishop v Bishop Bros Engineering Pty Ltd* [1988-89] PNGLR 533, [1988] PGSC 8; *Sr Dianne Liriope v Dr Jethro Usurup, Chief Executive Officer, Modilon General Hospital and others* (2009) N3572, [2009] PGNC 2; *In re Section 57 of the Constitution of Papua New Guinea, Application by John Bosco* [2007] PGNC 195, (2007) N4999; *Luchya Mussa Tikuye v Patrick Haines* (2009) N4434, [2009] PGNC 259; *Madang Cocoa Growers Export Co Ltd v Gumar* [2012] PGNC 177, (2012) N4881; *Peter Luga v Richard Sikani and The State* (2002) N2286; *Stephen John Rose and another v Neville Devete, Acting Solicitor-General and The State* (2007) N3327; *21 ILGS Gobe Project Area Inc Land Groups v Pawih* [2006] PGNC 10, (2006) N3066; *Newsat Ltd v Telikom PNG Ltd, ICCC and The State* (2007) N3447, [2007] PGNC 157; *Martin Kenehe and others v Michael Pearson, Chairman, Teaching Service Commission and others* (2009) N3763, [2009] PGNC 158; *Aisi Iuma Bore on behalf of Behori Clan of Furimuti Village v Clement Malaisa, Land Titles Commission* (2013) N5273, [2013] PGNC 92; *Moses Vua and others v Francis Mavu and another* (2008) N3294, [2008] PGNC 20; *Keven Manase v Thomas Opa* (2013) N5280, [2013] PGNC 94; *Mathew Michael, on behalf of himself and 147 other teachers v John Glengme, Provincial Education Adviser and others* (2008) N3429, [2008] PGNC 114 and *Raina No. 1 Ltd v Elisha* [2013] PGNC 63, (2013) N5234.

See also:

- *Iberian Trust Ltd v Founders Trust and Investment Co Ltd* [1982] 2 KB 87, per Luxmore LJ at 95; *Australian Consolidated Press Ltd v Morgan* (1965) 112 CLR 483, per Owen J at 515, [1965] HCA 21; *Metcash Trading Ltd v Bunn (No. 5)* [2009] FCA 16; *Spokes v Banbury Board of Health* (1865) LR 1 Eq 42 at 58; *Kirkpatrick v Kotis* (2004) 62 NSWLR 567, [2004] NSWSC 1265, per Campbell J; *Australian Industry Group v Automotive, Food, Metals, Engineering, Printed and Kindred Industries Union* [2000] FCA 629; *ICI Australia Operations Pty Ltd v Trade Practices Commission* (1992) 38 FCR 248, per Lockhart J at 259, [1992] FCA 474; *Commissioner of Water Resources v Federated Engine Drivers and Fireman's Association of Australasia Queensland Branch and others* [1988] 2 Qd R 385, per McPherson J at 390; *Randl Bank of Western Australia Ltd v Anchorage Investments Pty Ltd* (1993) 10 WAR 59 at 60; *Advan Investments Pty Ltd v Dean Gleeson Motor Sales Pty Ltd* [2003] VSC 201; *Scott and others v Evia Pty Ltd and others* [2007] VSC 15; *Deputy Commissioner of Taxation v Gashi and another (No. 2)* [2011] VSC 351; *National Australia Bank v Juric* [2001] VSC 375; *Law Institute of Victoria v Nagle* [2005] VSC 35; *Animal Liberation (Vic) Inc v Gasser* [1991] VicRp 5, [1991] VR 51 at 56 and *Tovehead Pty Ltd and another v Owston Nominees No. 2 Pty Ltd and another* [2002] NTSC 64; and
- G Borrie and N Lowe, 1983, 'The Law of Contempt' 2nd ed., Buterworths, London, p. 379 and Spry, 1990, 'Principles of Equitable Remedies' 5th ed., p. 374.

[444] See *Pang v Bydand Holdings Pty Ltd* [2011] NSWCA 69, per Beazley JA.

[445] See *Pang v Bydand Holdings Pty Ltd* [2011] NSWCA 69, per Beazley JA.

## DISOBEDIENCE CONTEMPT

Whoever gives an undertaking to a Court is bound by the language they use. If its true meaning, although not immediately plain, can be ascertained according to ordinary rules of construction, then the person giving the undertaking is bound by it and in that sense.[446]

But a person cannot be committed for contempt on the ground that upon one of two possible constructions, the person had breached the undertaking.[447]

However, there is a distinction between terms which are ambiguous and the situation where there are difficulties of construction.[448]

### [6.0] MUST BE CAPABLE OF COMPLIANCE

An order[449] and undertaking[450] must be capable of being complied with.

---

[446] As stated by Windeyer J in *Australian Consolidated Press Ltd v Morgan* (1965) 112 CLR 483 at 503, [1965] HCA 21.

[447] See *Iberian Trust Ltd v Founders Trust and Investments Co* [1932] 2 KB 87 at 95 and *Re Bramblevale Ltd* (1969) 3 All ER 1062 at 1064.

See also: *Australian Consolidated Press Ltd v Morgan* (1965) 112 CLR 483, per Owen J at 515, [1965] HCA 21; *Redwing Ltd v Redwing Forest Products Ltd* (1947) 177 LT 387, per Jenkins J; *John Fairfax and Sons Pty Ltd v Australian Consolidated Press Ltd* (1960) SR (NSW) 413 at 416; *Concrete Constructions Pty Ltd v Plumbers and Gasfitters Employees' Union (No. 2)* (1987) 15 FCR 64 at 71, [1987] FCA 117 and *Nexus Mortgage Securities Pty Ltd v Ecto Pty Ltd* (1998) 4 VR 220.

[448] See *Redwing Ltd v Redwing Forest Products Ltd* (1947) 177 LT 387.

[449] See *Iberian Trust Ltd v Founders Trust and Investment Co Ltd* [1932] 2 KB 87 at 95.

See also:

- *Hicks v Feiock* (1988) 485 US 624 at 638; *Turner v Rogers* 564 US 10-10 2011, per Breyer J at 8; *Concorde Construction Co. Ltd v Colgan Co Ltd (No. 2)* [1984] HKC 253; *Australian Consolidated Press Ltd v Morgan* (1965) 112 CLR 483 at 515, [1965] HCA 21; *Metcash Trading Ltd v Bunn (No. 5)* [2009] FCA 16; *National Australia Bank v Juric* [2001] VSC 375; *Advan Investments Pty Ltd v Dean Gleeson Motor Sales Pty Ltd* [2003] VSC 201; *Scott and others v Evia Pty Ltd and others* [2007] VSC 15; *Chan and others v Chen and others (No. 2)* [2007] VSC 24; *Deputy Commissioner of Taxation v Gashi and another (No. 2)* [2011] VSC 351 and *Law Institute of Victoria v Nagle* [2005] VSC 35; and
- G Borrie and N Lowe, 1983, 'The Law of Contempt' 2$^{nd}$ ed., Butterworths, London, p. 379.

[450] See *Australia Prudential Regulation Authority v No.7)* [2007] FCA 1609 and *Matthews v Australian Securities Investment Commission* [2009] NSWCA 155, per Tobias JA.

## [7.0] AWARENESS OF THE ORDER

Awareness of an order can be proved by either:

- proof of service[451] in accordance with Order 6 of the *National Court Rules 1983* ['Service of Documents'][452]; or

- proof that the alleged contemnor was present in Court when the order was made[453].

---

451 See also: Order 6 of the *National Court Rules 1983* ['Service of Documents'].

As started by Greene LJ in *Gordon v Gordon* [1946] P 99 at 105:

> 'Where a definite time is mentioned in the order for doing something, service of the order after the expiration of that time is not sufficient to found proceedings for contempt is well established'.

452 See *Ross Bishop v Bishop Bros Engineering Pty Ltd* [1988-89] PNGLR 533, [1988] PGSC 8; *Sr Dianne Liriope v Dr Jethro Usurup, Chief Executive Officer, Modilon General Hospital and others* (2009) N3572, [2009] PGNC 2; *In re Section 57 of the Constitution of Papua New Guinea, Application by John Bosco* [2007] PGNC 195, (2007) N4999; *Madang Cocoa Growers Export Co Ltd v Gumar* [2012] PGNC 177, (2012) N4881; *Peter Luga v Richard Sikani and The State* (2002) N2286; *Newsat Ltd v Telikom PNG Ltd, ICCC and The State* (2007) N3447, [2007] PGNC 157; *Martin Kenehe and others v Michael Pearson, Chairman, Teaching Service Commission and others* (2009) N3763, [2009] PGNC 158; *Stephen John Rose and another v Neville Devete, Acting Solicitor-General and The State* (2007) N3327; *John Siune v Rendle Rimua, Secretary, Department of Petroleum and Energy and The State* (2013) N5110, [2013] PGNC 83; *Aisi Iuma Bore on behalf of Behori Clan of Furimuti Village v Clement Malaisa, Land Titles Commission* (2013) N5273, [2013] PGNC 92; *Mathew Michael, on behalf of himself and 147 other teachers v John Glengme, Provincial Education Adviser and others* (2008) N3429, [2008] PGNC 114; *Keven Manase v Thomas Opa* (2013) N5280, [2013] PGNC 94; *Joel Ivat and Department of Health v Department of Personnel Management* (2002) N2230; *Moses Vua and others v Francis Mavu and another* (2008) N3294, [2008] PGNC 20; *21 ILGS Gobe Project Area Inc Land Groups v Pawih* [2006] PGNC 10, (2006) N3066 and *Raina No. 1 Ltd v Elisha* [2013] PGNC 63, (2013) N5234.

See also: *Ex parte Langley* (1879) 13 Ch D 110, per Thesiger LJ at 119; *Attorney-General v Times Newspapers Ltd and another* [1991] 2 All ER 398, [1991] 2 WLR 994, [1992] 1 AC 191, per Oliver LJ at 217; *Cartier International BV and others v Kaybee International Ltd* [1985] HKLR 127, per Huggins VP at 129; *Nicolas Pappadiis and another v Chan Shing-sheung, Barry and others* [1989] 2 HKLR 511, per Hunter JA at 519; *Abu Dhabi National Tanker Co v Lam Ming Chi and another* [1998] 4 HKC 320, per Stone J; *National Australia Bank v Juric* [2001] VSC 375; *Advan Investments Pty Ltd v Dean Gleeson Motor Sales Pty Ltd* [2003] VSC 201; *Scott and others v Evia Pty Ltd and others* [2007] VSC 15; *Chan and others v Chen and others (No. 2)* [2007] VSC 24 and *Deputy Commissioner of Taxation v Gashi and another (No. 2)* [2011] VSC 351.

453 See *Hearn v Tennant* [1807] EngR 331, (1807) 14 Ves Jun 137, (1807) 33 ER 473; *M'Niel v Garratt* [1841] EngR 317, (1841) Cr and Ph 98, (1841) 41 ER 427; *United Telephone Co v Dale* (1884) 25 Ch D 778 at 784; *Hall and Co v Trigg* [1897] 2 Ch 219 at 222 and *Husson v Husson* [1962] 1 WLR 1434.

## [8.0] AWARENESS OF THE TERMS

The alleged contemnor must have knowledge of:

- the terms of the order[454]; or
- at least the substance of the order[455],

but not necessarily understand full or true meaning of the terms[456].

A person bound by an order is expected to try to understand and obey it.[457]

---

[454] See *Kimpton v Eve* (1813) 2 V and B 349, (1813) 35 ER 352, per Baxter LC and *Ex parte Langley* (1879) 13 Ch D 110, per Thesiger LJ at 119.

See also: *Sun Newspapers Pty Ltd v Brisbane TV Limited and others* (1989) 92 ALR 535, per Pincus J at 538, [1989] FCA 534; *Amalgamated Television Services Pty Ltd v Marsden* (2001) 122 A Crim R 166, [2001] NSWCA 32; *Advan Investments Pty Ltd v Dean Gleeson Motor Sales Pty Ltd* [2003] VSC 201; *Deckers Outdoor Corporation Pty Ltd v Farley (No. 6)* [2010] FCA 391; *Travenol Laboratories of Canada Ltd v Cutter (Canada) Ltd* [1983] 2 SCR 388, per Dickson J at 396, [1983] SCC 30; *Masri v Consolidated Contractors Intl Co SARL* [2011] EWHC 1024 (Comm), per Clarke J; *Marketmaker Technology (Beijing) Co Ltd v Obair Group International Corporation and others* [2009] EWHC 1445; *Re L (a Ward) (Publication of Information)* [1988] 1 FLR 255 at 259; *Scott and others v Evia Pty Ltd and others* [2007] VSC 15; *Madeira v Roggette Pty Ltd (No. 2)* [1992] 1 Qd R 394, per Thomas J at 403; *National Australia Bank v Juric* [2001] VSC 375; *Chan and others v Chen and others (No. 2)* [2007] VSC 24 and *Deputy Commissioner of Taxation v Gashi and another (No. 2)* [2011] VSC 351.

[455] See *Sun Newspapers Pty Ltd v Brisbane TV Limited and others* (1989) 92 ALR 535, per Pincus J at 538, [1989] FCA 534; *Amalgamated Television Services Pty Ltd v Marsden* (2001) 122 A Crim R 166, [2001] NSWCA 32; *Advan Investments Pty Ltd v Dean Gleeson Motor Sales Pty Ltd* [2003] VSC 201; *Deckers Outdoor Corporation Pty Ltd v Farley (No. 6)* [2010] FCA 391 and *Madeira v Roggette Pty Ltd (No. 2)* [1992] 1 Qd R 394, per Thomas J at 403.

[456] See *Redwing Ltd v Redwing Forest Products Ltd* (1947) 177 LT 387.

See also: *Sun Newspapers Pty Ltd v Brisbane TV Limited and others* (1989) 92 ALR 535, per Pincus J at 538, [1989] FCA 534; *Microsoft Corporation v Marks (No. 1)* (1996) 69 FCR 117, (1996) 139 ALR 99, per Lindgren J at 143 and 121 and *Metcash Trading Ltd v Bunn (No. 5)* [2009] FCA 16.

[457] See *Athens and another v Randwick City Council* (2005) 64 NSWLR 58, per Hodgson JA at 69, [2005] NSWCA 317 and *Kirkpatrick v Kotis* (2004) 62 NSWLR 567, [2004] NSWSC 1265, per Campbell J.

It is sufficient if the alleged contemnor has knowledge at a level that would induce an honest, reasonable, and responsible person to check the precise terms of the order.[458]

The inference of knowledge will always be available where facts capable of supporting the inference are proved.[459]

It would not be a casual, accidental or unintentional default where the party bound by an order (or an undertaking) misconstrued the terms of the undertaking.[460]

## [9.0] KNOWLEDGE OF FACTS OF BREACH

The alleged contemnor must know all the facts which made it a breach of the order.[461]

However, it is not necessary to prove that the alleged contemnor appreciated or was aware that he or she did breach the order.[462]

---

458 See *United Telephone Company v Dale* (1884) 25 Ch D 778 at 787.

See also: *Madeira v Roggette Pty Ltd* [1990] 2 Qd R 357 at 365 (affirmed in *Madeira v Roggette Pty Ltd (No. 2)* [1992] 1 Qd R 394); *Foley v Herald Sun TV Pty Ltd* [1981] VicRp 34, [1981] VR 315 and *Sun Newspapers Ltd v Brisbane TV Ltd* (1989) 92 ALR 535 at 538, [1989] FCA 534.

459 See *Avery v Andrews* (1882) 51 LJ Ch 414.

See also: *Baxter Travenol Laboratories of Canada Ltd v Cutter (Canada) Ltd* [1983] 2 SCR 388, per Dickson J at 396, [1983] SCC 30.

460 See *Athens v Randwick City Council* (2005) 64 NSWLR 58, per Hodgson JA at 36, [2005] NSWCA 317.

461 See *Spectravest Inc. v Aperknit Ltd* [1988] FSR 161, per Millett J at 173; *Citybase Property Management Ltd v Kam Kyun Tak (No. 1)* [2003] 2 HKC 98, per Ma J at 103; *International Land Developments Pty Ltd v Diamo Nominees Pty Ltd* (2007) 34 WAR 201, [2007] WASC 96 and *Chief Executive Officer, Department of Environment and Conservation v Szulc* [2010] WASC 195.

462 See *Heatons Transport (St. Helen's) Ltd v Transport and General Workers' Union* [1972] 3 All ER 101, [1973] AC 15; *Mileage Conference Group of the Tyre Manufacturers' Conference Ltd's Agreement* [1966] 2 All ER 849, [1966] 1 WLR 1137 and *Redwing Ltd v Redwing Forest Products Ltd* (1947) 177 LT 387.

See also: *Microsoft Corporation v Marks (No. 1)* (1996) 69 FCR 117, (1996) 139 ALR 99, per Lindgren J at 143 and 121; *Metcash Trading Ltd v Bunn (No. 5)* (2009) FCA 16, per Finn J; *Anderson v Hassett* [2007] NSWSC 1310, per Brereton J; *McNair Anderson and Associates Pty Ltd v Hinch* [1985] VicRp 30, [1985] VR 309 at 313; *Foley v Herald-Sun TV Pty Ltd* [1981] VicRp 34, [1981] VR 315 at 318 and *Spectravest Inc v Aperknit Ltd* [1988] FSR 161, per Millett J at 173.

An honest belief that a failure to act does not constitute a breach of an injunction is not a defence.[463]

## [10.0] MUST BE WILFUL

The failure to obey the terms of the order must be a wilful[464], as meaning a deliberate[465] or intentional[466], act or omission.

---

[463] See *McNair Anderson Associates Pty Ltd v Hinch* [1985] VicRp 30, [1985] VR 309 at 313 and *Australian Competition and Consumer Commission v Hughes* (2001) AT PR 41-807, [2001] FCA 38.

[464] See *Ross Bishop v Bishop Bros Engineering Pty Ltd* [1988-89] PNGLR 533, [1988] PGSC 8; *In re Section 57 of the Constitution of Papua New Guinea, Application by John Bosco* [2007] PGNC 195, (2007) N4999; *Stephen John Rose and another v Neville Devete, Acting Solicitor-General and The State* (2007) N3327; *Madang Cocoa Growers Export Co Ltd v Gumar* [2012] PGNC 177, (2012) N4881; *Peter Luga v Richard Sikani and The State* (2002) N2286; *21 ILGS Gobe Project Area Inc Land Groups v Pawih* [2006] PGNC 10, (2006) N3066 and *Raina No 1 Ltd v Elisha* [2013] PGNC 63, (2013) N5234.

See also: *Iberian Trust Limited v Founders Trust and Investment Company Limited* [1932] 2 KB 87, per Luxmore J at 95; *Multiform Displays Ltd v Whitmarley Displays Ltd* (1957) RPC 137; *Steiner Products Ltd v Willy Steiner Ltd* (1966) 1 WLR 986, [1966] 2 All ER 387; *In re Mileage Conference Group of the Tyre Manufacturers' Conference Ltd's Agreement* [1966] 1 WLR 1137, [1966] 2 All ER 849; *Heatons Transport (St Helens) Ltd v Transport and General Workers' Union* [1973] AC 15; *Coonan and Denlay Pty Ltd v Superstar Australia Pty Ltd (No. 2)* (1981) 57 FLR 118, [1981] FCA 197; *Putnin (as Liquidator of Maff Investments Pty Ltd (in Liquidation) v Fuller* (1991) 3 WAR 546; *Flamingo Park Pty Ltd v Dolly Dolly Creation Pty Ltd* (1985) 59 ALR 247, [1985] FCA 123; *Steiner Products Ltd v Willy Steiner Ltd* [1966] 1 WLR 986; *Director General of Fair Trading v Pioneer Concrete Ltd (UK)* [1995] 1 AC 456, per Nolan LJ at 479 and *Bakir v Doueihi and others* [2002] QSC 19.

[465] See *Moses Vua and others v Francis Mavu and another* (2008) N3294, [2008] PGNC 20; *Newsat Ltd v Telikom PNG Ltd, ICCC and The State* (2007) N3447, [2007] PGNC 157; *Mathew Michael, on behalf of himself and 147 other teachers v John Glengme, Provincial Education Adviser and others* (2008) N3429, [2008] PGNC 114; *Sr Dianne Liriope v Dr Jethro Usurup, Chief Executive Officer, Modilon General Hospital and others* (2009) N3572, [2009] PGNC 2; *Martin Kenehe and others v Michael Pearson, Chairman, Teaching Service Commission and others* (2009) N3763, [2009] PGNC 158; *John Siune v Rendle Rimua, Secretary, Department of Petroleum and Energy and The State* (2013) N5110, [2013] PGNC 83; *Keven Manase v Thomas Opa* (2013) N5280, [2013] PGNC 94 and *Aisi Iuma Bore on behalf of Behori Clan of Furimuti Village v Clement Malaisa, Land Titles Commission* (2013) N5273, [2013] PGNC 92.

See also: *Australasian Meat Industry Employees' Union v Mudginberri Station Pty Ltd* (1986) 161 CLR 98 at 113, (1986) 66 ALR 577, [1986] HCA 46; *Anthony Radcliffe Lewis v His Honour Judge Ogden* (1984) 153 CLR 682, [1984] HCA 26 and *Gliosca v Ninyett* (1992) 10 WAR 562 at 567.

[466] See *Anthony Radcliffe Lewis v His Honour Judge Ogden* (1984) 153 CLR 682, [1984] HCA 26 and *Gliosca v Ninyett* (1992) 10 WAR 562 at 567.

## DISOBEDIENCE CONTEMPT

Wilful disobedience of a Court order is determined from the conduct of the alleged contemnor.[467]

There must be some degree of:

- fault[468]; or
- misconduct[469].[470]

The actions of a party will not be wilful:

- if the party honestly trys to obey an order, but does not do so by mistake[471]; or
- if the party acts in a way that may reasonably be regarded as a means of satisfying the order if there is a reasonable doubt as to what is required by the terms of the order.[472]

The disobedience must not be:

- casual;
- accidental; or
- unintentional

in order to be regarded as 'wilful' so as to constitute a contempt.[473]

---

[467] See *Ome Ome Forests Limited v Ray Cheong and others* (2002) N2289.

[468] See *Ome Ome Forests Ltd v Ray Cheong, Jackson Whong and Bill Garey* (2002) N2289.

[469] See *Ome Ome Forests Ltd v Ray Cheong, Jackson Whong and Bill Garey* (2002) N2289.

[470] See *Ome Ome Forests Ltd v Ray Cheong and others* (2002) N2289.

See however: *21 ILGS Gobe Project Area Inc Land Groups v Pawih* [2006] PGNC 10, (2006) N3066 and *In re Mileage Conference Group of the Tyre Manufacturers Conference Ltd's Agreement* [1966] 2 All ER 849, [1966] 1 WLR 1137 at 1162.

[471] See *Adam Phones Ltd v Goldschmidt* [1999] 4 All ER 486 at 494 and the observation of Millett J in *Spectravest Inc v Aperknit Ltd* [1988] FSR 161 at 173.

[472] See *R and I Bank of WA Ltd v Anchorage Investments Pty Ltd* (1992) 10 WAR 59 at 68 and 78.

[473] The origin of this principle was the obiter dictum, per Russell LCJ in *Fairclough v Manchester Ship Canal Co* [1897] WN 7, (1897) 41 Sol Jo 225.

| DISOBEDIENCE CONTEMPT |
| --- |

## [11.0] CASUAL DISOBEDIENCE

There must not be casual obedience.[474]

---

[474] See *Peter Luga v Richard Sikani, Commissioner, Correctional Services and The State* (2002) N2285 and *Stephen John Rose and John Charles Harrison v Neville Devete, Acting Solicitor-General and The State* (2007) N3327.

See also: *Fairclough v Manchester Ship Canal Co* [1897] WN 7, (1897) 41 Sol Jo 225, per Russell LCJ; *Stancomb v Trowbridge Urban District Council* [1910] 2 Ch Div 100, per Warrington LJ at 194; *Putnin (as Liquidator of Maff Investments Pty Ltd in Liquidation) v Fuller* (1991) 3 WAR 546; *Director of Fair Trading v Pioneer Concrete (UK) Ltd* [1995] 1 AC 456, per Nolan LJ at 479; *Heatons Transport (St. Helen's) Ltd v Transport and General Workers' Union* [1972] 3 All ER 101 at 116, [1973] AC 15; *Steiner Products Ltd v Willy Steiner Ltd* [1966] 1 WLR 986, per Stamp LJ at 991; *Australasian Meat Industry Employees' Union v Mudginberri Station Pty Ltd* (1986) 161 CLR 98 at 111, (1986) 66 ALR 577, [1986] HCA 46; *Attorney-General; ex rel Leyton (Essex) Urban District Council v Walthamstow Urban District Council* (1895) 11 TLR 533; *The Walthamstow Sewage Question* (1895) 11 Times LR 533, per Chitty LJ; *Bakir v Doueihi and others* [2002] QSC 19; *Louis Vuitton Malletier SA v Design Elegance Pty Ltd* (2006) 149 FCR 494, [2006] FCA 83; *Metcash Trading Ltd v Bunn (No. 5)* [2009] FCA 16; *Madeira v Roggette Pty Ltd* [1990] 2 QdR 357 at 363 and 366; *Stewart v Gymboree Pty Ltd* [2001] QCA 307 and *Evenco Pty Ltd v Australian Building Construction Employees' and Builders Labourers Federation (Qld Branch) and other* [2000] QCA 108.

## DISOBEDIENCE CONTEMPT

### [12.0] ACCIDENTAL DISOBEDIENCE

There must not be accidental obedience.[475]

---

[475] See *Ome Ome Forests Ltd v Ray Cheong, Jackson Whong and Bill Garey* (2002) N2289; *Peter Luga v Richard Sikani, Commissioner, Correctional Services and The State* (2002) N2285; *Stephen John Rose and John Charles Harrison v Neville Devete, Acting Solicitor-General and The State* (2007) N3327 and *Pioneers Health Services Limited v Gabriel Yer, Secretary of Department of Finance and The State* (2008) N3326.

See also: *Fairclough v Manchester Ship Canal Co.* [1897] WN 7, (1897) 41 Sol Jo 225, per Russell LCJ; *Stancomb v Trowbridge Urban District Council* [1910] 2 Ch Div 100, per Warrington LJ at 194; *Putnin (as Liquidator of Maff Investments Pty Ltd in Liquidation) v Fuller* (1991) 3 WAR 546; *Witham v Holloway* (1995) 131 ALR 401, (1995) 183 CLR 525, (1995) 69 ALJR 847, [1995] HCA 3; *Director of Fair Trading v Pioneer Concrete (UK) Ltd* [1995] 1 AC 456, per Nolan LJ at 479; *Heatons Transport (St. Helen's) Ltd v Transport and General Workers' Union* [1972] 3 All ER 101 at 116, [1973] AC 15; *Citybase Property Management Ltd v Kam Kyun Tak (No. 1)* [2003] 2 HKC 98, per Ma J at 103; *Steiner Products Ltd v Willy Steiner Ltd* [1966] 1 WLR 986, per Stamp LJ at 991; *Australasian Meat Industry Employees' Union v Mudginberri Station Pty Ltd* (1986) 161 CLR 98 at 111, (1986) 66 ALR 577, [1986] HCA 46; *Attorney-General; ex rel Leyton (Essex) Urban District Council v Walthamstow Urban District Council* (1895) 11 TLR 533; *The Walthamstow Sewage Question* (1895) 11 Times LR 533, per Chitty LJ; *Bakir v Doueihi and others* [2002] QSC 19; *Madeira v Roggette Pty Ltd* [1990] 2 QdR 357 at 363 and 366; *Louis Vuitton Malletier SA v Design Elegance Pty Ltd* (2006) 149 FCR 494, [2006] FCA 83; *Metcash Trading Ltd v Bunn (No. 5)* [2009] FCA 16; *Stewart v Gymboree Pty Ltd* [2001] QCA 307 and *Evenco Pty Ltd v Australian Building Construction Employees' and Builders Labourers Federation (Qld Branch) and other* [2000] QCA 108.

## DISOBEDIENCE CONTEMPT

### [13.0] UNINTENTIONAL DISOBEDIENCE

There must not be unintentional disobedience.[476]

[476] See *Stephen John Rose and another v Neville Devete, Acting Solicitor-General and The State* (2007) N3327 and *Ome Ome Forests Limited v Ray Cheong and others* (2002) N2289.

See also: *Fairclough v Manchester Ship Canal Co.* [1897] WN 7, (1897) 41 Sol Jo 225, per Russell LCJ; *Stancomb v Trowbridge Urban District Council* [1910] 2 Ch Div 100, per Warrington LJ at 194; *Steiner Products Ltd v Willy Steiner Ltd* [1966] 1 WLR 986, per Stamp LJ at 991; *Attorney-General; ex rel Leyton (Essex) Urban District Council v Walthamstow Urban District Council* (1895) 11 TLR 533; *The Walthamstow Sewage Question* (1895) 11 Times LR 533, per Chitty J; *Director of Fair Trading v Pioneer Concrete (UK) Ltd* [1995] 1 AC 456, per Nolan LJ at 479; *Heatons Transport (St. Helen's) Ltd v Transport and General Workers' Union* [1972] 3 All ER 101 at 116, [1973] AC 15; *Australasian Meat Industry Employees' Union v Mudginberri Station Pty Ltd* (1986) 161 CLR 98 at 111, (1986) 66 ALR 577, [1986] HCA 46; *Bakir v Doueihi and others* [2002] QSC 19; *Madeira v Roggette Pty Ltd* [1990] 2 QdR 357 at 363 and 366; *Louis Vuitton Malletier SA v Design Elegance Pty Ltd* (2006) 149 FCR 494, [2006] FCA 83; *Metcash Trading Ltd v Bunn (No. 5)* [2009] FCA 16; *Putnin (as Liquidator of Maff Investments Pty Ltd (in Liquidation) v Fuller* (1991) 3 WAR 546; *Spectravest Inc v Aperknit Ltd* [1988] FSR 161, per Millett J at 173; *Attorney-General v Times Newspapers Ltd and another* [1991] 2 All ER 398, [1991] 2 WLR 994, [1992] 1 AC 191, per Oliver LJ at 217; *Stewart v Gymboree Pty Ltd* [2001] QCA 307 and *Evenco Pty Ltd v Australian Building Construction Employees' and Builders Labourers Federation (Qld Branch) and other* [2000] QCA 108.

## DISOBEDIENCE CONTEMPT

### [14.0] CONTEMPTUOUS DISOBEDIENCE

It is not necessary to prove beyond reasonable doubt a subjective intent to deliberately disobey or flout an order of the Court, ie., being contumacious.[477]

The mental element necessary for this category of contempt is simply that the disobeying party intended the conduct constituting the disobedience. There is, therefore, no need or obligation to demonstrate that the disobeying party intended to:

- disobey;
- refuse to obey; or
- make no reasonable attempt to obey.[478]

---

[477] See *Concord Pacific Ltd and Paiso Company Ltd v Thomas Nen – Managing Director, Papua New Guinea Forest Authority and the State* [2000] PNGLR 47.

See also: *Stancomb v Trowbridge Urban District Council* [1910] 2 Ch Div 190, per Warrington LJ at 194; *Heatons Transport (St Helens) Ltd v Transport and General Workers' Union* [1973] AC 15; *Steiner Products Ltd v Willy Steiner Ltd* [1966] 1 WLR 986 at 992; *Attorney-General; ex rel Leyton (Essex) Urban District Council v Walthamstow Urban District Council* (1895) 11 TLR 533; *In re Mileage Conference Group of the Tyre Manufacturers' Conference Ltd's Agreement* [1966] 1 WLR 1137 at 1162, [1966] 2 All ER 849 at 861; *Australasian Meat Industry Employees' Union v Mudginberri Station Pty Ltd* (1986) 161 CLR 98 at 111, (1986) 66 ALR 577, [1986] HCA 46; *Director General of Fair Trading v Pioneer Concrete (UK) Ltd* [1995] 1 AC 456 at 479; *Citybase Property Management Ltd v Kam Kyun Tak (No. 1)* [2003] 2 HKC 98, per Ma J at 103; *Universal Music Australia Pty Ltd v Sharman Networks Ltd* (2006) 150 FCR 110, [2006] FCAFC 41; *Metcash Trading Ltd v Bunn (No. 5)* [2009] FCA 16; *Pelechowski v Registrar, Court of Appeal of New South Wales* (1999) 198 CLR 435, per Kirby J at 484, (1999) 162 ALR 336, (1999) 73 ALJR 687, [1999] HCA 19; *Advan Investments Pty Ltd v Dean Gleeson Motor Sales Pty Ltd* [2003] VSC 2012; *Scott and others v Evia Pty Ltd* [2007] VSC 15, per Dodds-Streeton J; *Rothmans of Pall Mall v Australian Broadcasting Tribunal* (1985) 5 FCR 330, [1985] FCA 91; *Deputy Commissioner of Taxation v Rotary Offset Press* (1971) 45 ALJR 518; *Anderson v Hassett* [2007] NSWSC 1310 and *Matthews v Australian Securities Investment Commission* [2009] NSWCA 155, per Tobias JA.

See however: *Tikuye v Haines* [2009] PGNC 259, (2009) N4434; *Fairclough v Manchester Ship Canal Co* [1897] WN 7, (1897) 41 Sol Jo 225, per Russell LCJ; *Re Sheppard and Sheppard* [1976] DLR (3d) 592 and *Australian Consolidated Press Ltd v Morgan* (1965) 112 CLR 483, [1965] HCA 21.

[478] See *Stephen John Rose and another v Neville Devete, Acting Solicitor-General and The State* (2007) N3327.

## [15.0] LEGAL ADVICE OR OTHER GROUNDS

It is not a defence that the alleged contemnor honestly believed that the contemplated act did not constitute an act of disobedience, even if such a belief was:

- bona fide based on legal advice[479]; or
- reasonable on other grounds[480].[481]

A lawyer's negligence or failure to take the appropriate steps in any proceedings, does not form any good basis to excuse the need to comply with any rule or requirement in any proceedings before the Court. Proceeding on that basis, claims have been successfully lodged against negligent lawyers[482].[483]

---

[479] See *In re Mileage Conference Group of the Tyre Manufacturers Conference Ltd's Agreement* [1966] 1 WLR 1137, per Megaw LJ at 1162, [1966] 2 All ER 849.

See also: *McNair Anderson and Associates Pty Ltd v Hinch* [1985] VicRp 30, [1985] VR 309 at 313; *Foley v Herald-Sun TV Pty Ltd* [1981] VicRp 34, [1981] VR 315 at 318 and *Buckby and another v Wharton and another* [2012] QSC 416.

See however: *Ome Ome Forests Ltd v Ray Cheong, Jackson Whong and Bill Garey* (2002) N2289.

[480] See *In re Mileage Conference Group of the Tyre Manufacturers Conference Ltd's Agreement* [1966] 1 WLR 1137, per Megaw LJ at 1162, [1966] 2 All ER 849.

[481] See *21 ILGS Gobe Project Area Inc Land Groups v Pawih* [2006] PGNC 10, (2006) N3066.

[482] See *Martha Limitopa v The State and another* [1988-89] PNGLR 364.

[483] See *Benard Juali v The State* (2001) SC667.

See also: *Danny Sunu v The State* [1984] PNGLR 305 at 308.

## [16.0] CORPORATE DISOBEDIENCE

A corporate contemnor will ordinarily be responsible for the wilful disobedience of an order:

- even if it were not aware of the breach[484];
- even if it did not actively bring about the contemptuous conduct[485];
- even if a servant or agent did disobey the order through carelessness, neglect or even in dereliction of duty[486];
- even if the contemptuous conduct was a result of a deliberate act by the servant or agent on its behalf[487]; or
- if it wilfully failed to take steps to ensure that the order was obeyed.[488]

However, a corporate contemnor is not liable for the acts of its employees where it did not authorise the acts, but on the contrary expressly forbade them and foresaw the possibility of such acts but took reasonable steps to prevent them.[489]

---

[484] See *Pioneers Health Services Ltd v Gabriel Yer, Secretary of Department of Finance and The State* (2008) N3326.

See also:
- *Stancomb v Trowbridge Urban District Council* [1910] 2 Ch Div 190 and *Re Garage Equipment Association's Agreement* (1964) LR 4 RP 491; and
- CJ Miller, 2000, 'Contempt of Court' 3rd ed., Clarendon Press, Oxford, p. 672.

[485] See *Biba Ltd v Stratford Investments Ltd* [1973] Ch 281, per Brightman LJ at 287.

See also: *Madeira v Rogette Pty Ltd* [1990] 2 Qd R 357.

[486] See *Stancomb v Trowbridge Urban District Council* [1910] 2 Ch Div 190, per Warrington LJ at 194.

See also: *In re Supply of Ready Mixed Concrete (No. 2)* [1995] 1 AC 456; *Australasian Meat Industry Employees' Union v Mudginberri Station Pty Ltd* (1986) 161 CLR 98 at 112, (1986) 66 ALR 577, [1986] HCA 46 and *Madeira v Roggette Pty Ltd* [1990] 2 QdR 357 at 366.

[487] See *In re Supply of Ready Mixed Concrete (No. 2)* [1995] 1 AC 456, per Nolan LJ at 481.

[488] See *Attorney-General for Tuvalu and another v Philatelic Distribution Corporation Ltd and others* [1990] 1 WLR 926 and *R v David Syme and Co Ltd* [1982] VicRp 16, [1982] VR 173 at 180.

[489] See *In re Supply of Ready Mixed Concrete* [1992] QB 213, [1992] ICR 229, per Lord Donaldson MR.

## SCANDALISING THE COURT

### [1.0] INTRODUCTION

The term 'scandalising the Court is an 'archaic description'[490] that can be traced back to Hardwicke LJ in 1742[491].

Scandalising a court involves despising the authority, justice or dignity of a Court.[492]

The policy of the common law in this area has been the subject of controversy.[493]

The essence of the offence of 'scandalising the court' is:

> Any matter is a contempt which had a tendency to deflect the Court from the strict and unhesitating application of the letter of the law.[494]

Wilmot LJ in *R v Almon*[495] made the following remark:

> But the principle upon which attachments issue for libels upon Courts is to keep a blaze of glory around them, and to deter people from attempting to render them contemptible in the eyes of the public.

Grose LJ in *R v White and another*[496] held that the writers of an article were guilty of 'Contempt of Court' if the published material contained no reasoning or discussion, but only declamation and invective, and were written not with a view to elucidate the truth, but to injure the characters of individuals, and to bring into hatred and contempt the administration of justice.

---

490 See *The State (Director of Public Prosecutions) v Walsh* [1981] IR 412, per O'Higgins CJ at 421 and Brennan J in *Nationwide News Pty Limited v Wills* (1991-1992) 177 CLR 1, [1992] HCA 46.

491 See *In re Read and Huggonson (The St. James's Evening Post Case)* (1742) 2 Atk 469, (1742) 26 ER 683 at 684, [1742] EngR 142.

492 As commented by Patteson J in *Miller v Knox* [1838] EngR 648, (1838) 4 Bing (NC) 574 at 593, (1838) 132 ER 910 at 918, (1838) Scott 1.

493 See *R v Kopyto* (1987) 39 CCC (3d) 1 and *Attorney-General for New South Wales v Mundey* [1972] 2 NSWLR 887 at 908.

See also: Australian Law Reform Commission,1987, 'Contempt', Report No. 35, para. 67.

494 See *R v Dunbabin; ex parte Williams* (1935) 53 CLR 434, per Rich J at 442, [1935] HCA 34 and *Re Colina; ex parte Torney* (1999) 200 CLR 386, per Gleeson CJ and Gummow J at 390, (1999) 73 ALJR 1576, (1999) 166 ALR 545, [1999] HCA 57.

495 [1765] EngR 25, (1765) 97 ER 94, (1765) Wilm 243 at 270.

496 (1808) 1 Camp 360.

## SCANDALISING THE COURT

The contempt of 'scandalising the court' is designed to prevent public confidence in the courts from being shaken by attacks that are baseless and unwarrantable.[497]

The rationale for contempt by 'scandalising the Court' is that it has always been regarded as vital to the 'Rule of Law' for:

- respect for the judiciary to be maintained; and
- their dignity to be upheld.[498]

It is contrary to the public interest that public confidence in the administration of justice should be undermined.[499]

It is the duty of the Court to protect the public against every attempt to:

- overawe or intimidate the Court by insult or defamation; or
- deter actual and prospective litigants from complete reliance upon the Court's administration of justice.[500]

---

[497] See *Gallagher v Durack* (1983) 152 CLR 238 at 243, (1982) 44 ALR 272, [1983] HCA 2.

[498] See *Secretary for Justice v The Oriental Press Group Ltd and others* (1998) 2 HKLRD 123, [1998] 2 HKC 627.

See also: L Oyiela, 'Does the "Offence" of Contempt by Scandalising the Court Have a Valid Place in the Law of Modern Day Australia?' [2003] Deakin Law Review 6, (2003) 8(1) Deakin Law Review 113 and R Sackville, 'How Fragile are the Courts? Freedom of Speech and Criticism of the Judiciary', [2005] Monash University Law Review 8, (2005) 31(2) Monash University Law Review 191.

[499] See *State v Morrill* (1855) 16 Ark 384 at 399 and *Re Shepherd* (1903) 177 Mo 205, per Marshall LJ at 261.

See also: *Solicitor-General v Radio Avon Ltd* [1978] 1 NZLR 225, per Richmond P at 230.

[500] See *R v Gray* [1900] 2 QB 36, per Russell LCJ at 40; *In re Sarbadhicary* (1906) 23 Times LR 180 at 182 and *R v Editor of the New Statesman; ex parte Director of Public Prosecutions* (1928) 44 Times LR 301.

See also: *Attorney-General of the Irish Free State v O'Kelly* [1928] IR 308 at 315 and *R v Fletcher; ex parte Kisch* (1935) 52 CLR 248, per Evatt J at 257, [1935] HCA 1.

## SCANDALISING THE COURT

Contempt by 'scandalising the Court' does not exist simply to protect the the dignity of the Court or the person of the Judge.[501]

It was not intended to protect judges personally from imputations to which they may be exposed as individuals.[502]

It exists to maintain public confidence in the courts and the judges[503] and therefore, the administration of justice.[504]

However, in the context of this offence scandalising of a Court must be committed only so far as it relates to conduct in the Judge's official capacity.[505]

It is essential to the proper administration of justice that unwarranted attacks should not be made with impunity upon Judges in their public capacity.[506]

A person's language in his or her everyday speech may be colourful, forceful, vulgar or otherwise, be it in good or bad taste and a matter of his or her own choosing. It is, however, an entirely different matter when directed against the Court.[507]

---

[501] See *Helmore v Smith (No. 2)* (1886) 35 Ch D 449, per Bowen LJ.

[502] See *R v Dunbabin; ex parte Williams* (1935) 53 CLR 434, per Rich J at 442, [1935] HCA 34 and *R v Fowler* (1905) 1 Tas LR 53, per Dodds CJ at 56.

See however: *Bridges v State of California* (1941) 62 S Ct 190 at 217, (1941) 314 US 252.

[503] This area of the law of contempt however applies equally to magaistrates.

[504] See *Ambard v Attorney-General for Trinidad and Tobago* [1936] AC 322 and *R v Commissioner of Police for the Metropolis; ex parte Blackburn (No. 2)* [1968] 2 QB 150.

See also: *Secretary for Justice v The Oriental Press Group Ltd and others* (1998) 2 HKLRD 123, [1998] 2 HKC 627 and *Solicitor-General v Radio Avon Ltd* [1978] 1 NZLR 225.

[505] See *In the Matter of a Special Reference from the Bahama Islands* [1893] AC 138 and *R v Gray* [1900] 2 QB 36, per Russell LCJ at 40.

See also: *R v McHugh* [1901] 2 IR 569 at 579 and *Attorney-General v Kelly* [1928] IR 308 at 327.

[506] See *Re SB Sarbadhicary* (1907) 95 LT 894 at 895.

[507] See *Re Borowski* (1971) 19 DLR (3d) 537 at 547.

## SCANDALISING THE COURT

No criticism of a judgement, however vigorous, can amount to 'Contempt of Court', provided it keeps within the limits of reasonable courtesy and good faith.[508]

No wrong is committed by any member of the public who exercises the ordinary right of criticising, in good faith, in private or public, the public act done in the seat of justice.[509]

To the contrary, a public comment fairly made on judicial conduct that is truly disreputable (in the sense that it would impair the confidence of the public in the competence or integrity of the court) is for the public benefit.[510]

The jurisdiction to punish for contempt by scandalising the court should be exercised 'sparingly'[511] and only when warrantable[512].

There should be a real risk of the administration of justice being undermined.[513]

---

[508] See *R v Commissioner of Police of the Metropolis; ex parte Blackburn (No. 2)* [1968] 2 QB 150, per Salmon LJ at 155.

[509] See *R v Gray* [1900] 2 QB 36, per Russell LCJ at 40 and *Ambard v Attorney-General for Trinidad and Tobago* [1936] AC 322, per Atkin LJ at 335.

See also: *Nationwide News Pty Limited v Wills* (1991-1992) 177 CLR 1, [1992] HCA 46; *Badry v Director of Public Prosecutions* [1983] 2 AC 297 and *Ahnee v Director of Public Prosecutions* [1999] 2 AC 294.

[510] See *R v Nicholls* (1911) 12 CLR 280 at 286, [1911] HCA 22.

[511] See *MacLeod v St Aubyn* [1899] AC 549, per Morris LJ at 561.

See also: *Re Colina and another; ex parte Torney* (1999) 200 CLR 386, per Gleeson CJ and Gummow J at 391 and Hayne J at 428, (1999) 166 ALR 545, (1999) 73 ALJR 1576, [1999] HCA 57.

[512] See *R v Fletcher; ex parte Kisch* (1935) 52 CLR 248, per Evatt J at 257 and *Gallagher v Durack* (1983) 152 CLR 238 at 243, (1982) 44 ALR 272, [1983] HCA 2.

[513] See *Ahnee v Director of Public Prosecutions* [1999] 2 WLR 1305, [1999] 2 AC 294, per Steyne LJ at 304.

## [2.0] DEFINITION

'Contempt by Scandalising the Court' means:

- any act done[514]; or
- any writing published[515]

that is calculated[516] to:

[514] See *The Attorney-General, Mr Michael Gene; The State and Internal Revenue Commissioner, Mr David Sode v Dr Pirouz Hamidian-Rad* [1999] PNGLR 278 and *Ian Augerea, Registrar of the National Court v David Tigavu* (2010) N4185, [2010] PGNC 182.

See also: *R v Gray* [1900] 2 QB 36, per Russell LCJ at 40; *Ambard v Attorney-General for Trinidad & Tobago* [1936] AC 322 at 334; *Arthur Reginald Perera v R* [1951] AC 482 at 488 and *Nationwide News Pty Limited v Wills* (1991-1992) 177 CLR 1, [1992] HCA 46.

[515] See *The Attorney-General, Mr Michael Gene; The State and Internal Revenue Commissioner, Mr David Sode v Dr Pirouz Hamidian-Rad* [1999] PNGLR 278 and *Ian Augerea, Registrar of the National Court v David Tigavu* (2010) N4185, [2010] PGNC 182.

See also:
- *R v Gray* [1900] 2 QB 36, per Russell LCJ at 40; *Ambard v Attorney-General for Trinidad and Tobago* [1936] AC 322 at 334; *Arthur Reginald Perera v R* [1951] AC 482 at 488; *Nationwide News Pty Limited v Wills* (1991-1992) 177 CLR 1, [1992] HCA 46; *R v Collins* [1954] VicLawRp 7, [1954] VLR 46 at 56 and *Ex parte Attorney-General; Re Goodwin* [1969] 2 NSWR 360 at 362; and
- S Walker, 1989, 'The Law of Journalism in Australia', Law Book Company, Sydney, para. 1.3.04.

The common law of contempt treats as a 'publication' any material disseminated by recognized institutions of the media, such as newspapers, radio stations or television stations, see Australian Law Reform Commission, 1987, 'Contempt', Report 35, p. 135.

Refer also to the section titled 'Material Is Published' in the chapter titled 'Sub-judice Contempt'.

[516] The question as to whether an alleged contemnor's action was calculated involves a consideration not of their state of mind on this particular point but of the inherent nature of their act, see *Attorney-General v Butterworth* [1963] 1 QB 696, per Donovan LJ at 725 and *Secretary for Justice v The Oriental Press Group Ltd and others* (1998) 2 HKLRD 123 at 155, [1998] 2 HKC 627.

In this context, 'calculated' does not mean 'intended'. It means that, when viewed 'objectively', the relevant conduct is likely or has a tendency to, see *R v Hoser and Kotabi Pty Ltd* [2001] VSC 443; *Hoser and Kotabi Pty Ltd v R (ex parte The Attorney-General for the State of Victoria); R (ex parte The Attorney-General for the State of Victoria) v Hoser and Kotabi Pty Ltd* [2003] VSCA 194 and *McGuirk v University of NSW* [2009] NSWSC 1058.

- bring a Court or a judge[517] into contempt[518];
- lower the authority of the Court[519];
- lower the authority of the judge[520];
- undermine the confidence of the public in the administration of justice[521];
- interfere with the due course of justice;

---

517 This area of the law of contempt however applies equally to magistrates.

518 See *The Attorney-General, Mr Michael Gene; The State and Internal Revenue Commissioner, Mr David Sode v Dr Pirouz Hamidian-Rad* [1999] PNGLR 278 and *Ian Augerea, Registrar of the National Court v David Tigavu* (2010) N4185, [2010] PGNC 182.

See also: *R v Gray* [1900] 2 QB 36, per Russell LCJ at 40; *Ambard v Attorney-General for Trinidad & Tobago* [1936] AC 322 at 334; *Nationwide News Pty Ltd v Wills* (1991-1992) 177 CLR 1, per Mason CJ at 31, [1992] HCA 46; *Hoser and Kotabi Pty Ltd v R (ex parte The Attorney-General for the State of Victoria); R (ex parte The Attorney-General for the State of Victoria) v Hoser and Kotabi Pty Ltd* [2003] VSCA 194 and *Arthur Reginald Perera v R* [1951] AC 482 at 488.

519 See *Public Prosecutor v Nahau Rooney (No. 2)* [1979] PNGLR 448, [1979] PGSC 23 and *SCR No. 3 of 1984; Ex parte Callick and Koroma* [1985] PNGLR 67, [1985] PGSC 20.

See also: *Re Application by the Attorney-General of Fiji* [2009] FJHC 8.

520 See *Public Prosecutor v Nahau Rooney (No. 2)* [1979] PNGLR 448, [1979] PGSC 23; *SCR No. 3 of 1984; Ex parte Callick and Koroma* [1985] PNGLR 67, [1985] PGSC 20; *The Attorney-General, Mr Michael Gene; The State and Internal Revenue Commissioner, Mr David Sode v Dr Pirouz Hamidian-Rad* [1999] PNGLR 278 and *Ian Augerea, Registrar of the National Court v David Tigavu* (2010) N4185, [2010] PGNC 182.

See also: *R v Gray* [1900] 2 QB 36, per Russell LCJ at 40; *Ambard v Attorney-General for Trinidad and Tobago* [1936] AC 322 at 334; *Nationwide News Pty Ltd v Wills* (1991-1992) 177 CLR 1, per Mason CJ at 31, [1992] HCA 46; *Hoser and Kotabi Pty Ltd v R (ex parte The Attorney-General for the State of Victoria); R (ex parte The Attorney-General for the State of Victoria) v Hoser and Kotabi Pty Ltd* [2003] VSCA 194; *Re Application by the Attorney-General of Fiji* [2009] FJHC 8 and *Arthur Reginald Perera v R* [1951] AC 482.

521 See *Hoser and Kotabi Pty Ltd v R (ex parte The Attorney-General for the State of Victoria); R (ex parte The Attorney-General for the State of Victoria) v Hoser and Kotabi Pty Ltd* [2003] VSCA 194 and *Ahnee v Director of Public Prosecutions* [1999] 2 WLR 1305 at 1314, [1999] 2 AC 294, per Steyne LJ at 306.

- interfere with the lawful process of the Court[522]; or
- endanger public confidence in the Court[523].

Truth or falsity is irrelevant.[524]

## [3.0] FREEDOM OF EXPRESSION

## [3.1] CONSTITUTIONAL PROVISION[525]

Section 46(1) of the *Constitution of the Independent State of Papua New Guinea* states (in part):

> 'Every person has the right to freedom of expression and publication, except to the extent that the exercise of that right is regulated or restricted by a law'.

## [3.2] GENERAL PRINCIPLES

Historically, freedom of speech and of the press has been viewed as indispensable to a free society and its government.[526]

Every person has the right to make fair comment, even outspoken comment, on matters of public interest.[527]

---

[522] See *Public Prosecutor v Nahau Rooney (No. 2)* [1979] PNGLR 448, [1979] PGSC 23 and *The Attorney-General, Mr Michael Gene; The State and Internal Revenue Commissioner, Mr David Sode v Dr Pirouz Hamidian-Rad* [1999] PNGLR 278.

See also: *Ambard v Attorney-General for Trinidad and Tobago* [1936] AC 322 at 334 and *R v Gray* [1900] 2 QB 36.

[523] See *New Statesman (Editor); ex parte Director of Public Prosecutions* (1928) 44 Times LR 301.

[524] See *Attorney-General v Blomfield* (1913) 33 NZLR 545 and *Viner v BLF* [1982] 2 IR 177 at 183.

[525] See also: section 178 of the *Constitution of the Autonomous Region of Bougainville* ['Basic Rights'].

[526] See *Smith v Daily Mail Publishing Co* (1979) 443 US 97, per Rehnquist J at 106 and *Hector v Attorney-General of Antigua* [1990] 2 AC 312, per Bridge LJ at 318.

[527] See *R v Metropolitan Police Commissioner; ex parte Blackburn (No. 2)* [1968] 2 QB 150, per Lord Denning MR at 155.

## SCANDALISING THE COURT

Even the Courts and judges are open to criticism.[528]

Justice is not a cloistered virtue: it must be allowed to suffer the scrutiny and the respectful, even though outspoken, comments of ordinary people.[529]

Judges, magistrates and courts are alike open to criticism, and if reasonable argument or expostulation is offered against any judicial act as contrary to law or the public good, no Court could or would treat that as 'Contempt of Court'.[530]

Not everthing that is said of a Judge is calculated to bring him or her into contempt.[531]

However, it the duty of the Court to:

- protect the public against every attempt to overawe or intimidate the Court by insult or defamation[532]; and
- ensure that public confidence in the administration of justice is not undermined[533].

The contempt powers of the Court do not exist to protect the personal feelings or dignity of the presiding Judge.[534]

---

528 See *R v Gray* [1900] 2 QB 36, per Russell LCJ at 40.

See also: *Landmark Communications Inc v Virginia* (1978) 435 US 829 at 842, [1978] USSC 70; the observation of Brennan J in *Nationwide News Pty Limited v Wills* (1991-1992) 177 CLR 1, [1992] HCA 46 and the observation of Black J in *Bridges v California* (1941) 314 US 252 at 270, [1941] USSC 148.

529 See *Ambard v Attorney-General for Trinidad and Tobago* [1936] AC 322, per Atkin LJ at 335.

530 See *R v Gray* [1900] 2 QB 36, per Russell LCJ at 40.

531 As observed by Griffiths CJ in *R v Nicholls* (1911) 12 CLR 280 at 285, [1911] HCA 22.

532 See *R v Fletcher and another* (1935) 52 CLR 248, per Evatt J at 257, [1935] HCA 1.

533 See *Solicitor-General v Radio Avon Ltd and another* (1978) 1 NZLR 225, per Richard P at 230.

534 See *In re Section 57 of the Constitution of Papua New Guinea, Application by John Bosco* [2007] PGNC 195, (2007) N4999.

See also: *R v Fowler* (1905) 1 Tas LR 53, per Dodds CJ at 56; *Helmore v Smith (No. 2)* (1886) 35 Ch D 449, per Bowen LJ; *R v Dunbabin; ex parte Williams* (1935) 53 CLR 434, per Rich J at 442; [1935] HCA 34; *Anthony Radcliffe Lewis v His Honour Judge Ogden* (1984) 153 CLR 682, [1984] HCA 26; *Ex parte Ferandez* [1861] EngR 556, [1861] 30 LJCP 321 at 332; *Skipworth's case* (1873) LR 9 QB 219 at 232 and *Balanto* [1963] SRNSW 200 at 202.

It is justice itself[535] and the fundamental supremacy of the law[536] that is flouted by the 'Contempt of Court'.

The dignity of an individual judicial officer is of very subordinate importance compared with the dignity of the Court.[537]

Judges must rely upon merited good reputation for protection against *bona fide* censure even if it is fierce and misguided.[538]

Judges, by virtue of their office, cannot reply to criticisms.[539]

## [4.0] CONTEMPTUOUS BEHAVIOUR

Notwithstanding the right in a member of the public to criticise the conduct of courts or judges:

- criticism will constitute contempt if it is merely scurrilous abuse.[540]

  Scurrilous abuse means personal attacks on a judge in abusive language which vilifies the judge, rather than pointing out his or her errors[541]; and

[535] See *The State v Foxy Kia Tala, Re Detective Constable Corney Winjan* [1995] PNGLR 303.

See also: *Attorney-General v Leveller Magazine Ltd and others* [1979] AC 440, per Diplock LJ at 449; *Jennison v Baker* [1972] 2 QB 52 at 61; *Anthony Radcliffe Lewis v His Honour Judge Ogden* (1984) 153 CLR 682 at 693, [1984] HCA 26 and *Attorney-General (NSW) v Willesee* [1980] 2 NSWLR 143 at 161.

[536] See *Johnson v Grant* [1923] SC 789, per Lord President Clyde at 790.

[537] See *Davenport v Vose* [2003] WASCA 44, per Pullin J.

[538] See *Wong Yeung Ng v Secretary for Justice* [1999] 2 HKC 24.

[539] See *R v Metropolitan Police Commissioner; ex parte Blackburn (No. 2)* [1968] 2 QB 150, per Lord Denning MR at 155.

[540] See *R v Dunbabin; ex parte Williams* (1935) 53 CLR 434, per Rich J at 442; [1935] HCA 34; *Attorney-General (NSW) v Mundey* (1972) 2 NSWLR 887, per Hope JA at 910 and *R v Hoser and Kotabi Pty Ltd* (2001) VSC 443.

[541] See *Secretary for Justice v The Oriental Press Group Ltd and others* (1998) 2 HKLRD 123, [1998] 2 HKC 627.

- criticism may constitute contempt if it excites misgivings as to the integrity, propriety and impartiality brought to the exercise of the judicial office.[542]

  However, the mere fact that a criticism involved the imputation of improper motives to a Judge or magistrate does not, in itself, determine that contempt had been committed.[543]

As a consequence of such contemptuous behavior the administration of justice is:

- obstructed[544];
- unduly interfered with[545]; and
- undermined[546].

Such contemptuous behavior includes:

- calling a Judge or magistrate a liar[547] or an imbecile[548];
- making an application for a judge to disqualify himself or herself without any proper factual and/or legal foundation.[549]

---

542 See *R v Dunbabin; ex parte Williams* (1935) 53 CLR 434, per Rich J at 442; [1935] HCA 34; *Attorney-General (NSW) v Mundey* (1972) 2 NSWLR 887, per Hope JA at 910 and *R v Hoser and Kotabi Pty Ltd* (2001) VSC 443.

543 See *Solicitor General v Radio Avon Ltd and another* [1978] 1 NZLR 225 at 231.

544 See *The State (Director of Public Prosecutions) v Walsh* [1981] 412, per O'Higgins CJ at 421.

545 See *Helmore v Smith (No. 2)* (1886) 35 Ch D 449, per Bowen LJ.

See also: *The State (Director of Public Prosecutions) v Walsh* [1981] 412, per O'Higgins CJ at 421 and *Attorney-General for New South Wales v Mundey* [1972] 2 NSWLR 887, per Hope JA at 911.

546 See *Secretary for Justice v The Oriental Press Group Ltd and others* (1998) 2 HKLRD 123, [1998] 2 HKC 627.

547 See G Borrie and N Lowe, 1996, 'The Law of Contempt' 3rd ed., Butterworths, London, p. 343.

548 See *Re Quellet* (1976) 72 DLR (3rd) 95, per Tremblay CJ at 97.

549 See *In the Matter of the Organic Law on National and Local Level Government Elections And in the Matter of a Disputed Return for the Wapenamanda Open Electorate between Rimbink Pato v Reuben Kaiulo, Electoral Commissioner of Papua New Guinea and another and In the Matter of the Organic Law on National and Local Level Government Elections And in the Matter of a Disputed Return for the Wapenamanda Open Electorate between Masket Iangalio v Yangakun Miki Kaeok and another* (2003) N2455.

It is a very serious matter when a party applies for a judge to disqualify himself or herself[550];

- making a baseless and scandalous attack on the integrity and reputation of a judge[551];
- casting unjustified allegations of corruption or impropriety[552];
- casting adverse imputations upon the courts of justice, which if continued, are likely to impair their authority[553]; and

---

[550] See *In the Matter of the Organic Law on National and Local Level Government Elections And in the Matter of a Disputed Return for the Wapenamanda Open Electorate between Rimbink Pato v Reuben Kaiulo, Electoral Commissioner of Papua New Guinea and another and In the Matter of the Organic Law on National and Local Level Government Elections And in the Matter of a Disputed Return for the Wapenamanda Open Electorate between Masket Iangalio v Yangakun Miki Kaeok and another* (2003) N2455 and *Coecon Limited (Receiver/Manager Appointed) v The National Fisheries Authority of Papua New Guinea and another* (2002) N2182.

Refer also to the section titled 'Right To An Independent And Impartial Court' in the chapter titled 'Rights Of An Accused Person' in the text titled 'Injia on Criminal Practice and Procedure in Papua New Guinea and the Pacific'.

[551] See *In the Matter of the Organic Law on National and Local Level Government Elections And in the Matter of a Disputed Return for the Wapenamanda Open Electorate between Rimbink Pato v Reuben Kaiulo, Electoral Commissioner of Papua New Guinea and another and In the Matter of the Organic Law on National and Local Level Government Elections And in the Matter of a Disputed Return for the Wapenamanda Open Electorate between Masket Iangalio v Yangakun Miki Kaeok and another* (2003) N2455.

Section 15(10) of the *Professional Conduct Rules 1989* ['Court Procedings'] states:

> 'In all cases, it is the duty of a lawyer --
> (a) to guard against being made the channel for questions or statements which are only intended to insult or annoy either the witness or any other person or otherwise are an abuse of a lawyer's function; and
> (b) to exercise his own judgement both as to the substance and the form of the questions put or statements made'.

[552] See *New Statesman (Editor); ex parte Director of Public Prosecutions* (1928) 44 Times LR 301.

[553] See *R v Dunbabin, ex parte Williams* (1935) 53 CLR 434, per Rich J at 447, [1935] HCA 34 and *Gallagher v Durack* (1983) 152 CLR 238 at 283, (1982) 44 ALR 272, [1983] HCA 2.

- casting unjustified allegations that the presiding Judge has:
    - been affected by some personal bias against a party;
    - acted mala fide; or
    - failed to act with the impartiality required of his or her judicial office[554].

Attacks based on lack of impartiality might have a tendency to embarrass a Court itself in arriving at its decision[555] and are regarded as a particularly serious form of contempt[556].

The authority of the law rests on public confidence, and it is important for the stability of society that the confidence of the public should not be shaken by baseless attacks on the integrity or impartiality of courts or judges.[557]

Proof that the comments actually did undermine the standing of the Court or its officers is unnecessary.[558]

---

[554] See *New Statesman (Editor); ex parte Director of Public Prosecutions* (1928) 44 Times LR 301.

See also: *Attorney-General (NSW) v Mundey* (1972) 2 NSWLR 887, per Hope JA at 910; *Ahnee v Director of Public Prosecutions* [1999] 2 WLR 1305, [1999] 2 AC 294, per Steyne LJ at 304; *Nationwide News Pty Ltd v Wills* (1991-1992) 177 CLR 1, [1992] HCA 46, per McHugh J and *R v Nicholls* (1911) 12 CLR 280, per Griffiths CJ at 286, [1911] HCA 22.

Refer also to the section titled 'Right To An Independent And Impartial Court' in the chapter titled 'Rights Of An Accused Person' in the text titled 'Injia on Criminal Practice and Procedure in Papua New Guinea and the Pacific'.

[555] See *R v Collins* [1954] VicLawRp 7, [1954] VLR 46 at 49.

[556] See *R v Editor of New Statesman* (1928) 44 TLR 301.

[557] See *Gallagher v Durack* (1983) 152 CLR 238 at 238, (1982) 44 ALR 272, [1983] HCA 2 and *R v Fletcher; ex parte Kisch* (1935) 52 CLR 248, per Evatt J at 257, [1935] HCA 1.

[558] See *R v Hoser and Kotabi Pty Ltd* [2001] VSC 443 and *McGuirk v University of NSW* [2009] NSWSC 1058

Nor is it necessary to prove that the contemnor had the intention[559] to:

- bring a Court or a judge[560] into contempt[561];
- lower the authority of the Court[562];
- lower the authority of the judge[563];
- undermine the confidence of the public in the administration of justice;
- interfere with the due course of justice;
- interfere with the lawful process of the Court; or
- endanger public confidence in the Court.

It is sufficient if the Court is satisfied, 'objectively', that was a real risk as a matter of practical reality that the contemptuous behaviour had the tendency to do so.[564]

---

[559] See *Attorney General (NSW) v Mundey* [1972] 2 NSWLR 887 at 911.

[560] This area of the law of contempt however applies equally to magistrates.

[561] See *The Attorney-General, Mr Michael Gene; The State and Internal Revenue Commissioner, Mr David Sode v Dr Pirouz Hamidian-Rad* [1999] PNGLR 278 and *Ian Augerea, Registrar of the National Court v David Tigavu* (2010) N4185, [2010] PGNC 182.

See also: *R v Gray* [1900] 2 QB 36, per Russell LCJ at 40; *Ambard v Attorney-General for Trinidad & Tobago* [1936] AC 322 at 334; *Nationwide News Pty Ltd v Wills* (1991-1992) 177 CLR 1, per Mason CJ at 31, [1992] HCA 46; *Hoser and Kotabi Pty Ltd v R (ex parte The Attorney-General for the State of Victoria); R (ex parte The Attorney-General for the State of Victoria) v Hoser and Kotabi Pty Ltd* [2003] VSCA 194 and *Arthur Reginald Perera v R* [1951] AC 482 at 488.

[562] See G Borrie and N Lowe, 1996, 'The Law of Contempt' 3rd ed., Butterworths, London, p. 359.

[563] See G Borrie and N Lowe, 1996, 'The Law of Contempt' 3rd ed., Butterworths, London, p. 359.

[564] See *Saltalamacchia v Parsons* [2000] VSCA 83; *R v Hoser and Kotabi Pty Ltd* (2001) VSC 443; *Hoser and Kotabi Pty Ltd v R; ex parte The Attorney-General for the State of Victoria; R; ex parte The Attorney-General for the State of Victoria v Hoser and Kotabi Pty Ltd* [2003] VSCA 194 and *McGuirk v University of NSW* [2009] NSWSC 1058.

See also: *Solicitor-General v Radio Avon Ltd* [1978] 1 NZLR 225 at 233 and *Ahnee v Director of Public Prosecutions* [1999] 2 WLR 1305 at 1314, [1999] 2 AC 294, per Steyne LJ at 306.

In determining whether the material has that tendency, it is to be judged by reference to its impact upon:

- the ordinary reader[565]; or
- a reasonable person[566].[567]

Matters relevant to the determination of whether published material tends to lower the authority of the Court, include:

- the legitimate exercise of the right to freedom of expression[568];
- the nature of the material and the manner and time of publication; and
- the balancing of:
    - the private right to criticise in good faith public acts done in the seat of justice; and
    - the rights of those before the Courts to have their cases heard free from matters of prejudice.[569]

---

[565] See *R v Brett* [1950] VicLawRp 42, [1950] VLR 226, per O'Bryan J at 232.

[566] See *Bell v Stewart* (1920) 28 CLR 419 at 425.

[567] See *R v Hoser and Kotabi Pty Ltd* [2001] VSC 443 and *McGuirk v University of NSW* [2009] NSWSC 1058.

[568] See *Public Prosecutor v Nahau Rooney (No. 2)* [1979] PNGLR 448, [1979] PGSC 23.

See also: section 46 of the *Constitution of the Independent State of Papua New Guinea* ['Freedom Of Expression']

[569] See *Public Prosecutor v Nahau Rooney (No. 2)* [1979] PNGLR 448, [1979] PGSC 23 and *SCR No. 3 of 1984; Ex parte Callick and Koroma* [1985] PNGLR 67, [1985] PGSC 20.

## [5.0] DEFENCE OF FAIR COMMENT

The contempt of 'scandalising the court' is not to restrict honest criticism based on rational grounds of the manner in which the Court performs its functions. The law permits in respect of courts, as of other institutions, the fullest discussion of their doings so long as that discussion is:

- fairly conducted; and
- honestly directed to some definite public purpose.[570]

Fair criticism of the decisions of the Court is not only lawful, but regarded as being for the public good[571]; but:

- the facts forming the basis of the criticism must be accurately stated; and
- the criticism must be fair, and not distorted by:
  - malice[572]; or
  - improper motives[573].

So long as the party is genuinely exercising a right of criticism and not acting in malice or attempting to impair the administration of justice, the party is immune.[574]

---

[570] See *R v Dunbabin, ex parte Williams* (1935) 53 CLR 434, per Rich J at 442, [1935] HCA 34.

[571] See *R v Fletcher; ex parte Kisch* (1935) 52 CLR 248, per Evatt J at 257.

[572] See *R v Nicholls* (1911) 12 CLR 280 at 286, [1911] HCA 22; *R v Fletcher; ex parte Kisch* (1935) 52 CLR 248, per Evatt J at 257 and *Nationwide News Pty Limited v Wills* (1991-1992) 177 CLR 1, [1992] HCA 46.

[573] See *Ambard v Attorney-General for Trinidad and Tobago* [1936] AC 322, per Aitkin LJ at 335.

[574] See *R v Dunbabin, ex parte Williams* (1935) 53 CLR 434, per Rich J at 442, [1935] HCA 34; *Nationwide News Pty Limited v Wills* (1991-1992) 177 CLR 1, [1992] HCA 46, per Mason CJ at 31 and *Gallagher v Durack* (1983) 152 CLR 238 at 243, (1982) 44 ALR 272, [1983] HCA 2.

See also: *Solicitor General v Radio Avon Ltd and another* [1978] 1 NZLR 225 at 231.

## SUB-JUDICE RULE

### [1.0] CONSTITUTIONAL PROVISION[575]

Section 46(1) of the *Constitution of the Independent State of Papua New Guinea* ['Freedom of Expression'] states:

> 'Every person has the right to freedom of expression and publication, except to the extent that the exercise of that right is regulated or restricted by a law'.

### [2.0] INTRODUCTION

Unnecessary public comments on issues that are before the courts should not be made. If such comments are made in a careless or ill-considered way the person making the statement and the media organisation which publishes the statement run a real risk of being in contempt of court. Lawyers have a duty to advise their clients on these matters. The place for litigating disputes is in the courtroom, not in the pages of the newspapers.[576]

The 'sub-judice rule' refers to the restrictions imposed on publications that have a tendency to influence the conduct of particular legal proceedings or that prejudge the issues at stake in those proceedings.[577]

The phrase '*sub-judice*' means 'under or before a judge or court'.[578]

---

[575] See also: section 178 of the *Constitution of the Autonomous Region of Bougainville* ['Basic Rights'].

[576] As warned and commented in *Gabriel Yer, Secretary, Department of Finance and others v Peter Yama* (2009) SC996.

[577] See New South Wales Law Reform Commission, 2000, 'Contempt by Publication', Discussion Paper No. 43, Ch. 1 'Introduction'.

[578] See New South Wales Law Reform Commission, 2000, 'Contempt by Publication', Discussion Paper No. 43, Ch. 1 'Introduction'.

## SUB-JUDICE RULE

A 'suppression' or 'non-publication' order issued by a Court directed at preventing prejudicial media comment is akin to an anticipatory exercise of the Court's power to deal with contempt of court. The same objective informs the Court's power to grant an injunction to restrain a threatened contempt.[579]

It is, however, a power to be exercised sparingly.[580]

The Courts have always recognised that their ability to control pre-trial publicity prejudicial to an accused person is limited. Nevertheless, the trial judge should do what he or she can in order to protect the rights of the accused person to a fair trial and thereby protect the integrity of its process.[581]

---

[579] See:

- Order 4, Division 4 of the *Criminal Practice Rules 1987* ['Prohibition of Publication'];
- section 19 of the *HIV/AIDS Management and Prevention Act 2003* ['Privacy of Proceedings'];
- section 28 of the *Juvenile Courts Act 1991* ['Restriction of Publication of Proceedings']; and
- section 30 of the *Coroners Court Act* (Ch. 32) ['Power of Exclusion'].

As regards the issuance of such an order at common law, see *State of Victoria and Commonwealth of Australia v Australian Building Construction Employees and Builders Labourers Federation* (1982) 152 CLR 25 at 42, [1982] HCA 31; *Critchley v Australian Urban Investment Ltd* [1979] VicRp 39, [1979] VR 374 at 377; *Attorney-General v Times Newspapers Ltd* [1973] 3 All ER 54, [1974] AC 273; *P v Liverpool Post and Echo Newspapers Plc* [1991] 2 AC 370; *National Mutual Life Association of Australiasia Ltd v GTV Corporation Pty Ltd* [1989] VicRp 66, [1989] VR 747; *Watts v Hawke and David Syme Co Ltd* [1976] VicRp 77, [1976] VR 707; *Brych v The Herald and Weekly Times* [1978] VicRp 67, [1978] VR 727; *Raybos Australia Pty Ltd v Jones* (1985) 2 NSWLR 47, per Kirby P at 55 and 57; *John Fairfax and Sons Ltd v Police Tribunal (NSW)* (1986) 5 NSWLR 465, per McHugh JA at 477 and Glass JA agreeing at 467; *"Mr C"* (1993) 67 A Crim R 562, per Hunt CJ at CL at 563 and Smart and James JJ agreeing at 566; *Independent Publishing Co Ltd v Attorney-General of Trinidad and Tobago* [2005] 1 AC 190 at 216, [2005] 1 All ER 499, [2004] UKPC 26, [2004] 3 WLR 611; *Ex parte The Queensland Law Society Inc* [1984] 1 Qd R 166, per McPherson J at 170; *John Fairfax Publications Pty Ltd v District Court (NSW)* (2004) 61 NSWLR 344, per Spigelman CJ at 357 and Handley JA and M W Campbell A-JA agreeing at 368; *Re Applications by Chief Commissioner of Police (Vic)* (2004) 9 VR 275 at 288; *General Television Corporation Pty Ltd v DPP* (2008) 19 VR 68 at 77; *Herald and Weekly Times Pty Ltd v A* (2005) 160 A Crim R 299 at 305; *R v McArthur* (1984) 13 CCC (3d) 152; *R v Unnamed Person* (1985) 22 CCC (3d) 284 at 286; *R v Church of Scientology of Toronto* (1986) 27 CCC (3d) 193 at 207; *R v Barrow* (1989) 48 CCC (3d) 308 (NSSC) at 315 and *Dagenais v Canadian Broadcasting Corp* [1994] 3 SCR 835, [1994] SCC 39.

[580] As pointed out by Lord Donaldson MR pointed in *P v Liverpool Post and Echo Newspapers Plc* [1991] 2 AC 370 at 381.

[581] See *Mokbel* (2010) 30 VR 248 at 271.

## SUB-JUDICE RULE

The test applicable to the determination of an accused person's application for a non-publication order is whether or not there is a real and substantial risk of prejudice to a fair trial.[582]

That test involves a fact/value assessment[583] whilst balancing the interests of society in ensuring that the accused person receives a fair trial against the competing interests of society in the freedom of expression[584].

Freedom of speech and of the press has historically been viewed as indispensable to a free socity and its government.[585]

It is axiomatic that the question of prior restraint of publication of material proposed to be published in a public newspaper is a matter of the utmost seriousness.[586]

The role of contempt law in protecting the right to a fair trial is that it punishes publication of information that would not be admissible at the trial. In so doing it protects the integrity of the trial itself and the rules that govern the way the trial is run.[587]

While the most fundamental tenet of fairness extended to accused persons, the presumption of innocence, is easily justifiable from a rational, analytical point of view, it must constantly do battle against what appears to be an inherent tendency of people to jump to conclusions. Coupled with the strong desire many people feel to find 'closure' in distressing situations by identifying a culprit, the tendency to assume that a person charged with an offence is probably guilty of it poses a strong challenge to the presumption of innocence.[588]

---

582 See *Nationwide News Pty Ltd v Farquharson and another* (2010) 28 VR 473 at 474, [2010] VSCA 131.

583 See *Nationwide News Pty Ltd v Farquharson and another* (2010) 28 VR 473 at 477, [2010] VSCA 131.

584 See *Ex parte Bread Manufacturers Ltd; Re Truth and Sportsman Ltd* (1937) 37 SR (NSW) 242 at 249.

585 See *Smith v Daily Mail Publishing Co* (1979) 443 US 97, per Rehnquist J at 106 and *Hector v Attorney-General of Antigua* [1990] 2 AC 312, per Bridge LJ at 318.

586 See *Civil Aviation Authority v Australian Broadcasting Corporation* (1995) 39 NSWLR 540, per Kirby P at 549.

587 See Western Australia Law Reform Commission, 2003, 'Final Report on Report on the Law of Contempt', Report No. 93, Part II 'Contempt by Publication'.

588 See Western Australia Law Reform Commission, 2003, 'Final Report on Report on the Law of Contempt', Report No. 93, Part II 'Contempt by Publication'.

For a range of reasons, but mainly because of the desire to maximise audiences, media organisations are interested in playing to those psychological tendencies.[589]

With respect to publications that interfere with the due course of justice in particular legal proceedings this type of conduct is often referred to as 'trial by media'.[590]

The fear is that media trials could usurp the power of the Court, without giving litigants any of the safeguards found in the courts and thereby undermine confidence in the legal system generally.[591]

Justice Wheeler in *Re Coroners Court of Western Australia; ex Parte Porteous*[592] stated that that term refers to the capacity for published criticisms of court decisions to tend to suggest that the truth is easy to get at and that the Court has failed to do so.

To attract liability for sub-judice contempt, a person or organisation must be found to be 'responsible' for the publication in question. At present, the common law is flexible in its approach to assigning responsibility: a person or organisation is generally responsible for a publication if they are in a position to exercise control over its contents, production, distribution, or broadcast.[593]

Most often, it is the proprietor of the media organisation, and/or the program producer or editor, who is prosecuted for contempt.[594]

---

[589] See Western Australia Law Reform Commission, 2003, 'Final Report on Report on the Law of Contempt', Report No. 93, Part II 'Contempt by Publication'.

[590] See *Attorney-General (NSW) v John Fairfax and Sons Ltd* [1980] 1 NSWLR 362 at 370 and *Hinch and Macquarie Broadcasting Holdings Ltd v The Attorney-General for the State of Victoria* (1987) 164 CLR 15, [1987] HCA 56.

[591] See *Charles Maino v Moi Avei and Electoral Commission* [1998] PNGLR 165.

[592] [2002] WASCA 144.

[593] See *Attorney-General (NSW) v TCN Channel Nine Pty Ltd* (1990) 20 NSWLR 368 at 379.

See also:

- New South Wales Law Reform Commission, 2000, 'Contempt by Publication', Discussion Paper No. 43, Ch. 3 'Basic Concepts: Publication and Responsibility'; and
- S Walker, 1989, 'The Law of Journalism in Australia', Law Book Company, Sydney, para. 1.3.02.

[594] See New South Wales Law Reform Commission, 2000, 'Contempt by Publication', Discussion Paper No. 43, Ch. 3 'Basic Concepts: Publication and Responsibility'.

An editor can be held guilty of contempt even if he or she had no personal knowledge of the article.[595]

However, the common law notion of 'responsibility' is broad enough to encompass a wide class of people or bodies, including:

- journalists[596];
- newspaper publishers[597]; and
- radio[598] and television licensees[599].[600]

Such contemptuous behavior includes conducting public discussion that dissuades or is likely to have the effect of dissuading the institution of proceedings by a litigant, or his or her conduct of legal proceedings[601] including:

- injurious misrepresentations concerning a party to a proceedings[602];

---

[595] See *R v David Syme and Co Ltd* [1982] VicRp 16, [1982] VR 173 at 178.

[596] See *R v Thompson* [1989] WAR 219.

[597] See *R v West Australian Newspapers Ltd; ex parte The Minister for Justice* (1958) 60 WALR 108; *R v Regal Press Pty Ltd* [1972] VicRp 9, [1972] VR 67; *R v Scott and Downland Publications Ltd* [1972] VicRp 77, [1972] VR 663; *Attorney-General (NSW) v John Fairfax and Sons Ltd* [1980] 1 NSWLR 362; *Attorney-General (NSW) v Mirror Newspapers Ltd* [1980] 1 NSWLR 374; *R v David Syme and Co Ltd* [1982] VicRp 16, [1982] VR 173; *Director of Public Prosecutions (Cth) v Wran* (1987) 7 NSWLR 616 and *Director of Public Prosecutions (Cth) v John Fairfax and Sons Ltd* (1987) 8 NSWLR 732.

[598] See *R v Pacini* [1956] VicLawRp 84, [1956] VLR 544 and *Hinch v Attorney-General* [1987] VicRp 62, [1987] VR 721.

[599] See *Attorney-General (NSW) v Willesse* [1980] 2 NSWLR 143; *Director of Public Prosecution (Cth) v United Telecasters Sydney Ltd (in liquidation)* (1992) 7 BR 364; *R v Australian Broadcasting Corp* [1983] TasR 161 and *Director of Public Prosecutions (Cth) v Australian Broadcasting Corp* (1987) 7 NSWLR 588.

[600] See also: New South Wales Law Reform Commission, 2000, 'Contempt by Publication', Discussion Paper No. 43, Ch. 3 'Basic Concepts: Publication and Responsibility'.

[601] See also: Australian Law Reform Commission, 1987, 'Contempt', Report No. 35, p. 105.

[602] See *Re William Thomas Shipping Co Ltd* [1930] 2 Ch 368; *Fry v Bray* (1959) 1 FLR 366; *Commercial Bank of Australia Ltd v Preston* [1981] 2 NSWLR 554 and *Critchley v Australian Urban Investments Ltd* [1979] VicRp 39, [1979] VR 374.

- abuse of a party or holding a party up to public obloquy[603]; and
- public and prejudicial discussion of the merits or facts of a party's case[604].

The Courts must not only be free, but must also appear to be free, from any extraneous influence. The appearance of freedom from any such influence is just as important as the reality. Public confidence must necessarily be shaken if there is the least ground for any suspicion of outside interference in the administration of justice.[605]

Contempt law assumes that witnesses are susceptible to influence by media publicity (whether they be witnesses in civil or criminal proceedings). It is feared that media publicity may deter a witness from coming forward to give evidence, or may influence the evidence that witness gives, either consciously or subconsciously.[606]

A publication has been found to constitute contempt on the basis that it influences a witness in one of the following ways[607]:

- it criticises a potential witness[608];
- it criticises one of the parties to the proceedings[609]; or

---

[603] See *Attorney-General v Times Newspapers Ltd* [1973] 3 All ER 54, [1974] AC 273; *Fry v Bray* (1959) 1 FLR 366 and *Commercial Bank of Australia Ltd v Preston* [1981] 2 NSWLR 554.

[604] See *Re Truth and Sportsman Ltd; ex parte Attorney-General* (1961) 61 SR (NSW) 484.

[605] See *Attorney-General v Tanks* [1939] NZLR 533, per Myers CJ at 537.

[606] See *Vine Products Ltd v Green* [1966] Ch 484, per Buckley LJ at 495.

See also: *Victoria v Australian Building Construction Employees' and Builders Labourers' Federation* (1981-82) 152 CLR 25, [1982] HCA 31 and *Civil Aviation Authority v Australian Broadcasting Corp* (1995) 39 NSWLR 540.

[607] See Australian Law Reform Commission, 1987, 'Contempt', Report No. 35, para. 387; G Borrie and N Lowe, 1996, 'The Law of Contempt' 3rd ed., Butterworths, London, p. 197; United Kingdom Committee on Contempt of Court, 1974, 'Report of the Committee on Contempt of Court', HMSO, London, Cmnd 5794, paras. 53 and 55; CJ Miller, 1989, 'Contempt of Court' 2nd ed., Clarendon Press, Oxford, p. 245 and New South Wales Law Reform Commission, 2000, 'Contempt by Publication', Discussion Paper No. 43, Ch. 4 'Prejudice to Criminal Proceedings'.

[608] See *Re Doncaster and Retford Co-operative Societies Agreement* [1960] 1 WLR 1186.

[609] See *Victoria v Australian Building Construction Employees' and Builders Labourers' Federation* (1981-82) 152 CLR 25, [1982] HCA 31.

- it contains an interview with a witness on matters to which that witness, or another witness, will subsequently testify in court[610].

  The potential for a witness' testimony to be distorted because of a previous media interview may increase if the witness has been offered money for the interview.[611]

Historically it has been suggested that judicial officers may be susceptible to influence by media publicity in the same way as witnesses.[612] However, the general view of the Courts now is that any such influence on judicial officers will not be sufficient to amount to a 'real and definite tendency' so as to constitute contempt, because judicial officers have training and experience in disregarding information that is not obtained by way of evidence admitted in court.[613]

[610] See *Attorney-General (NSW) v Mirror Newspapers Ltd* [1980] 1 NSWLR 374 and *Civil Aviation Authority v Australian Broadcasting Corp* (1995) 39 NSWLR 540.

See also: United Kingdom Home Office and the Scottish Home and Health Department, Interdepartmental Committee on the Law of Contempt as it Affects Tribunals of Inquiry, 1969, 'Report of the Interdepartmental Committee on the Law of Contempt as it Affects Tribunals of Inquiry', HMSO, London, Cmnd 4078, para. 31 and United Kingdom Committee on Contempt of Court, 1974, 'Report of the Committee on Contempt of Court', HMSO, London, Cmnd 5794, para. 55.

[611] See United Kingdom, Committee on Contempt of Court, 1974, 'Report of the Committee on Contempt of Court', HMSO, London, Cmnd 5794, para. 56 and S Pugh, 'Checkbook Journalism, Free Speech and Fair Trials' (1995) 143 University of Pennsylvania Law Review 1739.

[612] See *Bell v Stewart* (1920) 28 CLR 419 at 433 and *Kerr v O'Sullivan* [1955] SASR 204.

[613] See *SCR No 3 of 1984; Ex parte Callick and Koroma* [1985] PNGLR 67, [1985] PGSC 20.

See also: *Victoria v Australian Building Construction Employees' and Builders Labourers' Federation* (1981-82) 152 CLR 25, per Gibbs CJ at 58, Mason J at 102 and Wilson J at 136, [1982] HCA 31; *Attorney-General (SA) v Nationwide News Pty Ltd* (1986) 43 SASR 374, per Jacobs J at 381; *Attorney-General (NSW) v Mirror Newspapers Ltd* [1980] 1 NSWLR 374 at 387; *Civil Aviation Authority v Australian Broadcasting Corporation* (1995) 39 NSWLR 540, per Kirby P at 548, Handley JA at 564 and Sheller JA at 574; *X v Amalgamated Television Services Pty Ltd (No. 2)* (1987) 9 NSWLR 575, per Kirby P at 590; *R v Regal Press Pty Ltd* [1972] VicRp 9, [1972] VR 67 at 79; *R v Duffy; ex parte Nash* [1960] 2 QB 188 at 198; *Ex parte McRae; Re John Fairfax and Sons Pty Ltd* (1954) 54 SR(NSW) 165 at 177, (1954) 71 WN 113 at 121; *Vine Products Ltd v Green* [1966] Ch 484 at 496 and *Attorney-General v Times Newspapers Ltd* [1973] 3 All ER 54, [1974] AC 273 at 301.

## SUB-JUDICE RULE

As Salmon LJ said in *Attorney-General v BBC*[614]

> I am and always have been satisfied that no Judge would be influenced in his judgment by what may be said by the media. If he were, he would not be fit to be a Judge.

However, all human beings are susceptible to the opinions put forward every day by the media or indeed by other institutions having a public voice. To deny this in the cases of judges would be suggesting that judges were in some sense superhuman, entirely aloof from the pressures to which other members or the public are susceptible.[615]

Whilst a Judge may be influenced by what they may read or hear[616], they are, however, by their training and experience capable of putting an extraneous matter out of their minds[617].

---

[614] [1981] AC 303 at 342.

McDermott J agreed with that statement in *SCR No 3 of 1984; Ex parte Callick and Koroma* [1985] PNGLR 67, [1985] PGSC 20 as did Gibbs CJ in *Victoria v Australian Building Construction Employees' and Builders Labourers' Federation* (1981-82) 152 CLR 25 at 58, [1982] HCA 31.

See also:

- *Bell v Stewart* (1920) 28 CLR 419 at 425; *Vine Products Ltd v Green* [1966] 1 Ch 484 at 496; *In re The William Thomas Shipping Co Ltd* [1930] 2 Ch 368 at 373; and *Attorney-General v Times Newspapers Ltd* [1973] 3 All ER 54, [1974] AC 273 at 297; and
- Report of the Salmon Committee on The Law of Contempt as it Affects Tribunals of Inquiry (1969) Cmnd. 4078, para. 26 and G Borrie and N Lowe, 1973, 'Law of Contempt', Butterworths, London, pp. 96 and 302.

[615] As commented by Kirby P in *Civil Aviation Authority v Australian Broadcasting Corporation* (1995) 39 NSWLR 540 at 550.

[616] As commented by Frankfurter J in *Pennekamp v Florida* (1946) 328 US 331 at 358, [1946] USSC 101 (90 Law Ed 1295 at p 1309) and *R v Davies; ex parte Delbert-Evans* (1945) 1 KB 435, per Humphreys LJ at 442.

See also: United Kingdom, Committee on Contempt of Court, 1974, 'Report of the Committee on Contempt of Court', HMSO, London, Cmnd 5794, para. 49.

[617] See United Kingdom, Committee on Contempt of Court, 1974, 'Report of the Committee on Contempt of Court', HMSO, London, Cmnd 5794, para. 49.

See also: *Charles Maino v Moi Avei and Electoral Commission* [1998] PNGLR 165.

See however: the comments of Viscount Dilhorne in *Attorney-General v BBC* [1981] AC 303 at 335.

## SUB-JUDICE RULE

Objectivity and independence are the qualities which judges are expected to bring to judicial determination.[618]

It is only natural that judges should prefer to decide cases in an atmosphere that is clinically free from prejudice. No one enjoys making a decision to which government or public is hostile or antagonistic.[619]

A publication that only embarrasses a judicial officer is not sufficient to find liability for sub-judice contempt.[620]

However, a publication would be contemptuous if it had a tendency, or was objectively likely, to undermine public confidence in the administration of justice by giving rise to a serious risk that the Court would appear not to have been free from any extraneous influence.[621]

At common law, a person or organisation will breach the 'sub-judice rule' and so be liable for contempt if the following conditions are met:

- material is 'published';
- the publication presents a real risk as opposed to a mere possibility, of interference with the due administration of justice;
- the publication has a real and definite tendency, as a matter of practical reality, to interfere with the due administration of justice in specific legal proceedings; or
- the publication prejudges the issues to be decided in those proceedings;
- the person or organisation charged with contempt is responsible for the publication;

---

[618] As stated by Mason J in *Victoria v Australian Building Construction Employees' and Builders Labourers' Federation* (1981-82) 152 CLR 25 at 102, [1982] HCA 31.

[619] As stated by Mason J in *Victoria v Australian Building Construction Employees' and Builders Labourers' Federation* (1981-82) 152 CLR 25 at 102, [1982] HCA 31.

[620] See *Victoria v Australian Building Construction Employees' and Builders Labourers' Federation* (1981-82) 152 CLR 25, [1982] HCA 31.

[621] See *Public Prosecutor v Nahau Rooney (No. 2)* [1979] PNGLR 448, [1979] PGSC 23.

See also: *R v The Herald and Weekly Times Ltd* [1999] VSC 432; *R v The Herald and Weekly Times Ltd (No. 2)* [2000] VSC 35 and *R v Duffy; ex parte Nash* [1960] 2 QB 188 at 18.

- at the time of publication, the relevant legal proceedings were imminent, pending or current;
- the severity of possible prejudice to the administration of justice is not outweighed by the public interest in freedom of discussion of matters of public importance which form the subject of the publication; and
- the publication is not a fair and accurate report of proceedings in open court.

However, the actual consequences which flow from a publication are irrelevant to the existence of a contempt.[622]

## [2.0] MATERIAL IS PUBLISHED

The common law of contempt treats as a 'publication' any material disseminated by recognized institutions of the media, such as newspapers, radio stations or television stations[623] and the internet[624].

The courts have not considered in any detail the meaning of 'publication' in the context of sub-judice contempt. Publications that have attracted prosecution for contempt have typically involved the dissemination of material whether written, visual, or audio, by media organisations, through newspapers, radio stations, or television channels. A film shown in a cinema may also amount to a publication for the purposes of sub-judice contempt[625].[626]

---

[622] See *R v West Australian Newspapers Ltd; Ex parte DPP (WA)* (1996) 16 WAR 518 at 533; *John Fairfax and Sons Pty Ltd v McRae* (1955) 93 CLR 351 at 371, [1955] HCA 12 and *Hinch and Macquarie Broadcasting Holdings Ltd v The Attorney-General for the State of Victoria* (1987) 164 CLR 15 at 46, 69 and 85, [1987] HCA 56.

[623] See Australian Law Reform Commission, 1987, 'Contempt', Report No. 35, p. 135.

[624] See *Dow Jones and Co Inc v Gutnick* (2002) 210 CLR 575 at 597.

[625] See *R v Hutchinson; ex parte McMahon* [1936] 2 All ER 1514.

[626] See New South Wales Law Reform Commission, 2000, 'Contempt by Publication', Discussion Paper No. 43, Ch. 3 'Basic Concepts: Publication and Responsibility'.

A private communication to a single individual would not usually be considered as a 'publication' under the 'sub-judice rule'.[627]

In order to have the requisite tendency, the material must be published to a sufficiently wide class of people.[628]

## [3.0] IMMINENT, PENDING OR CURRENT LEGAL PROCEEDINGS

In general, a publication will only constitute a contempt under the 'sub-judice rule' if it relates to legal proceedings which are:

- imminent[629].

  'Imminent' proceedings covers acts occurring before the legal process has formally been set in motion, such as, for example, police questioning of a suspect.[630]

---

[627] See *Attorney-General (NSW) v TCN Channel Nine Pty Ltd* (1990) 20 NSWLR 368 at 378.

See also: New South Wales Law Reform Commission, 2000, 'Contempt by Publication', Discussion Paper No. 43, Ch. 3 'Basic Concepts: Publication and Responsibility'.

[628] See *Registrar of the Court of Appeal v Collins* [1982] 1 NSWLR 682.

[629] See *Public Officers Superannuation Fund Board v Paul Paraka Trading as Paul Paraka Lawyers and Paul Paraka Trading as Paul Paraka Lawyers v Public Officers Superannuation Fund Board* (2005) N2791.

See also: *R v Savundrayanagan and Walker* [1968] 3 All ER 439 at 441; *R v Odham's Press Ltd; ex parte Attorney-General* [1957] 1 QB 73; *Attorney-General v Times Newspaper Ltd* [1973] 3 All ER 54, [1974] AC 273, per Reid LJ at 301; *Attorney-General v Leveller Magazine Ltd and others* [1979] AC 440, per Diplock LJ at 449; *R v Beaverbrook and Associated Newspapers Ltd* [1962] NI 15 and *The State (Director of Public Prosecutions) v Independent Newspapers Limited and others* [1985] ILRM 183.

[630] See New South Wales Law Reform Commission, 2000, 'Contempt by Publication', Discussion Paper No. 43, Ch. 7 'Time Limits on Liability for Sub-judice Contempt'.

The English courts have justified the inclusion of imminent proceedings within the sub-judice period on the basis that media publicity at that stage may cause just as serious a degree of prejudice to a case as publicity at the time when proceedings are pending or current[631];

- pending[632].

Criminal proceedings are generally regarded as 'pending' once a person has been arrested and charged or arrested with a view to being charged.[633]

---

[631] As Justice Wills commented in *R v Parke* [1903] 2 KB 432 at 437:

'It is possible very effectually to poison the fountain of justice before it begins to flow'.

See also: New South Wales Law Reform Commission, 2000, 'Contempt by Publication', Discussion Paper No. 43, Ch. 7 'Time Limits on Liability for Sub-judice Contempt'.

[632] See *Public Prosecutor v Nahau Rooney (No. 2)* [1979] PNGLR 448, [1979] PGSC 23 and *Public Officers Superannuation Fund Board v Paul Paraka Trading as Paul Paraka Lawyers and Paul Paraka Trading as Paul Paraka Lawyers v Public Officers Superannuation Fund Board* (2005) N2791.

See also: *R v O'Dogherty* (1848) 5 Cox CC 348; *Skipworth's Case* (1873) LR 9 QB 230, per Blackburn LJ at 232; *R v Payne and Cooper* [1896] 1 QB 577, per Russell LCJ at 580; *Attorney-General v Times Newspapers Ltd* [1973] 3 All ER 54, [1974] AC 273; *Porter v R; ex parte Yee* (1926) 37 CLR 432, per Isaacs J at 443 and Higgins J at 447, [1926] HCA 9; *Metzler v Gounod* (1874) 30 LT 264 at 603; *R v Daily Mirror; ex parte Smith* [1927] 1 KB 845 at 851 and *John Fairfax and Sons Pty Ltd v McRae* (1955) 93 CLR 35, [1955] HCA 12.

See however: *James v Robinson* (1963) 109 CLR 593 at 607, [1963] HCA 32; *R v Parke* [1903] 2 KB 432 at 437 and *R v Daily Mirror; ex parte Smith* [1927] 1 KB 845 at 851 as to whether court proceedings should have commenced for this rule of contempt to apply.

[633] See *James v Robinson* (1963) 109 CLR 593, [1963] HCA 32 and *Attorney-General (NSW) v TCN Channel Nine Pty Ltd* (1990) 20 NSWLR 368.

See also: New South Wales Law Reform Commission, 2000, 'Contempt by Publication', Discussion Paper No. 43, Ch. 7 'Time Limits on Liability for Sub-judice Contempt'.

Civil proceedings are pending once the initiating process to bring a civil action has been set in motion, for example, by the issue of a writ or statement of claim.[634] It is not necessary that the matter actually be set down for trial in order for the sub-judice period to begin[635]; or

- current[636]

This rule does apply to all other stages of legal proceedings, including after an accused person has been convicted and before sentence.[637]

However, this rule does not apply to appeal proceedings.[638]

---

[634] See *Dunn v Bevan* [1922] 1 Ch 276, per Sargant LJ at 284 and *Re Crown Bank* (1890) 44 Ch D 649, per North LJ at 651.

See also: *James v Robinson* (1963) 109 CLR 595, per Windeyer J at 615.

[635] See New South Wales Law Reform Commission, 2000, 'Contempt by Publication', Discussion Paper No. 43, Ch. 7 'Time Limits on Liability for Sub-judice Contempt'.

[636] See New South Wales Law Reform Commission, 2000, 'Contempt by Publication', Discussion Paper No. 43, Ch. 7 'Time Limits on Liability for Sub-judice Contempt'.

[637] See *Attorney-General v Tonks* [1939] NZLR 533.

Refer also to the text titled 'Injia on Sentencing in Papua New Guinea and the Pacific'.

[638] See *Charles Maino v Moi Avei and Electoral Commission* [1998] PNGLR 165 and *SCR No 3 of 1984; Ex parte Callick and Koroma* [1985] PNGLR 67, [1985] PGSC 20.

See also: *Attorney-General v Times Newspaper Ltd* [1973] 3 All ER 54, [1974] AC 273, per Reid LJ at 301.

See however: *R v Davies; ex parte Delbert-Davies* [1945] KB 435.

Refer also to:
- the chapter titled 'Appeals' in the text titled 'Injia on Criminal Practice and Procedure in Papua New Guinea and the Pacific'; and
- the chapter titled 'Appeals Against Sentence' in the text titled 'Injia on Sentencing in Papua New Guinea and the Pacific'.

## SUB-JUDICE RULE

### [4.0] ISSUES OF RISK AND TENDENCY

In order to be convicted of contempt in contrary to the 'sub-judice rule' it must proven beyond reasonable doubt that the conduct of the alleged contemnor posed a real risk[639], as opposed to a mere possibility, of interference with the due administration of justice.[640]

That test relates to the inherent tendency of the matter published.[641]

---

[639] See *Public Officers Superannuation Fund Board v Paul Paraka Trading as Paul Paraka Lawyers and Paul Paraka Trading as Paul Paraka Lawyers v Public Officers Superannuation Fund Board* (2005) N2791.

[640] See *Public Prosecutor v Nahau Rooney (No. 2)* [1979] PNGLR 448 at 467, [1979] PGSC 23; *SCR No. 3 of 1984; Ex parte Callick and Koroma* [1985] PNGLR 67 at 73 and 77, [1985] PGSC 20; *Charles Maino v Moi Avei and Electoral Commission* [1998] PNGLR 165 and *Andrew Kwimberi of Paulus M Dowa Lawyers v The State* (1998) SC545, [1998] PGSC 9.

See also: *Attorney-General v Times Newspapers Ltd* [1973] 3 All ER 54, [1974] AC 273, per Reid LJ at 298; *R v Duffy; ex parte Nash* [1960] 2 QB 188, per Parker LCJ at 200; *Hinch and Macquarie Broadcasting Holdings Ltd v The Attorney-General for the State of Victoria* (1987) 164 CLR 15, [1987] HCA 56; *Re Coroner's Court of Western Australia; ex parte Porteous* [2002] WASCA 144; *Victoria v Australian Building Construction Employees' and Builders' Labourers Federation* (1981-82) 152 CLR 25, [1982] HCA 31; *Solicitor-General v Radio Avon Ltd* [1978] 1 NZLR 225 at 234; *R v Kopyto* (1988) 47 DLR (4th) 213 at 290; *Wong Yeung Ng v Secretary for Justice* [1999] 2 HKLRD 293; *Secretary for Justice v The Oriental Press Group Ltd and others* (1998) 2 HKLRD 123, [1998] 2 HKC 627; *John Fairfax and Sons Pty Ltd v McRae* (1955) 95 CLR 351 at 370, [1955] HCA 12; *Attorney-General (NSW) v John Fairfax and Sons Ltd and Bacon* (1985) 6 NSWLR 695, per Samuels JA at 697; *Attorney-General (NSW) v John Fairfax and Sons Ltd* [1980] NSWLR 362 at 368 and *Hammond v The Commonwealth* (1982) 152 CLR 188, per Gibbs CJ at 198, [1982] HCA 42.

See however: *Ian Augerea, Registrar of the National Court v David Tigavu* (2010) N4185, [2010] PGNC 182.

[641] See *John Fairfax and Sons Pty Ltd v McRae* (1955) 93 CLR 351, at 371, [1955] HCA 12; *Lane v Registrar of the Supreme Court of New South Wales* (1981) 148 CLR 245 at 257, (1981) 55 ALJR 529, (1981) 35 ALR 322, [1981] HCA 35 and *The Prothonotary v Collins* (1985) 2 NSWLR 549, per Kirby P at 550 and McHugh JA at 570.

## SUB-JUDICE RULE

The critical question is whether the publication in question has, as a matter of practical reality, a real (or clear[642]) and definite tendency to interfere with the course of justice[643] by prejudicing or embarrassing imminent, pending[644] or current proceedings.[645]

The tendency to interfere with, or prejudice, pending proceedings is to be determined at the time of the publication.[646]

---

642 See *Hinch and Macquarie Broadcasting Holdings Ltd v The Attorney-General for the State of Victoria* (1987) 164 CLR 15, per Deane J at 46, [1987] HCA 56; *John Fairfax and Sons Pty Ltd v McRae* (1955) 93 CLR 351 at 372, [1955] HCA 12 and *R v West Australian Newspapers Ltd; ex parte Director of Public Prosecutions (WA)* (1996) 16 WAR 518 at 533.

643 See *Hinch and Macquarie Broadcasting Holdings Ltd v The Attorney-General for the State of Victoria* (1987) 164 CLR 15, per Wilson.

644 See *John Fairfax and Sons Pty Ltd v McRae* (1955) 93 CLR 351 at 370 and 372, [1955] HCA 12; *Victoria v Australian Building Construction Employees' and Builders Labourers' Federation* (1981-82) 152 CLR 25 at 56, 99, 133 and 166, [1982] HCA 31 and *Hinch and Macquarie Broadcasting Holdings Ltd v The Attorney-General for the State of Victoria* (1987) 164 CLR 15, per Wilson J at 34, Deane J at 46, Toohey J at 70 and Gaudron J at 88, [1987] HCA 56.

645 See also:

- *R v Parke* [1903] 2 KB 432 at 437; *R v Daily Mirror; ex parte Smith* [1927] 1 KB 845 at 851; *Registrar of the Court of Appeal v Willesee* (1985) 3 NSWLR 650, per Kirby P at 658; Hope JA at 673; *Resolute Ltd and another v Warnes* [2000] WASCA 359, per Ipp J; *Harkianakis v Skalkos* (1997) 42 NSWLR 22, per Mason P at 27; *R v Pearce* (1991) 2 WAR 395; *Nationwide News; ex parte Director of Public Prosecutions (Cth)* (1997) 94 A Crim R 57 at 62; *Attorney-General (NSW) v John Fairfax and Sons Ltd and Bacon* (1985) 6 NSWLR 695, per Samuels JA at 697 and McHugh JA at 708; *Attorney-General (NSW) v Mayas Pty Ltd* (1988) 14 NSWLR 352, per McHugh JA at 350; *Director of Public Prosecutions (Cth) v Australian Broadcasting Corp* (1987) 7 NSWLR 588; *Director of Public Prosecutions (Cth) v Wran* (1987) 7 NSWLR 616 and *Attorney-General (NSW) v Dean* (1990) 20 NSWLR 650; and
- United Kingdom, Committee on Contempt of Court, 1974, 'Report of the Committee on Contempt of Court', HMSO, London, Cmnd 5794, para. 1 and New South Wales Law Reform Commission, 2000, 'Contempt by Publication', Report 100, Ch. 4 'Prejudice to Criminal Proceedings'.

646 See *Ex parte Auld; Re Consolidated Press Ltd* (1936) 36 SR (NSW) 596, per Jordan CJ at 598; *Hinch and Macquarie Broadcasting Holdings Ltd v The Attorney-General for the State of Victoria* (1987) 164 CLR 15, per Toohey J at 70, [1987] HCA 56; *Director of Public Prosecutions (Cth) v John Fairfax and Sons Ltd* (1987) 8 NSWLR 732, per Kirby P at 736; *Attorney-General (NSW) v TCN Channel Nine Pty Ltd* (1990) 20 NSWLR 368 at 382; *R v Glennon* (1992) 173 CLR 592, per Mason CJ and Toohey J at at 605, [1992] HCA 16; *John Fairfax and Sons Pty Ltd v McRae* (1955) 93 CLR 351 at 372, [1955] HCA 12 and *R v Regal Press Pty Ltd* [1972] VicRp 9, [1972] VR 67, per McInerney J at 73.

The degree of likelihood required by the word 'tendency' in this context is not one of probability, but rather a 'real possibility' and not a 'remote possibility' of interference[647].[648]

The 'objective test' is judged by reference to its impact upon:

- the ordinary reader[649]; or
- a reasonable person[650].

If the publication is of a character which might have an effect on the proceedings, it will have the necessary tendency, unless the possibility of interference is so remote or theoretical that the *de minimis* principle should be applied.[651]

In determining whether the publication, as a matter of practical reality, had a real tendency to prejudice the fair trial of a pending proceeding, the Court should 'objectively[652]' take into consideration all the relevant factors, including:

- the nature of the publication[653];

---

647 See *Attorney-General (NSW) v John Fairfax and Sons Ltd and Bacon* (1985) 6 NSWLR 695, per Samuels JA at 697.

648 See *Victoria v Australian Building Construction Employees' and Builders Labourers' Federation* (1981-82) 152 CLR 25, per Gibbs CJ at 56, [1982] HCA 31.

649 See *R v Brett* [1950] VicLawRp 42, [1950] VLR 226, per O'Bryan J at 232.

650 See *Bell v Stewart* (1920) 28 CLR 419 at 425; *Fry v Bray* (1959) 1 FLR 366 at 376; *Resolute Ltd and another v Warnes* [2000] WASCA 359; *Attorney-General v Hislop* [1991] 1 QB 514 at 526 and *Vajda v Nine Network Australia Limited* [2000] NSWSC 873, per Bell J.

651 See *Attorney-General (NSW) v John Fairfax and Sons Ltd* (1980) 1 NSWLR 362 at 368; *R v Thompson* [1989] WAR 219 at 223 and *R v Saxon* [1984] WAR 283, per Kennedy J at 292.

652 See *Resolute Ltd and another v Warnes* [2000] WASCA 359; *Attorney-General v Hislop* [1991] 1 QB 514 at 526 and *Vajda v Nine Network Australia Ltd* [2000] NSWSC 873.

See however: *Bhagat v Global Custodians Ltd* [2002] NSWCA 160.

See also: R Baker, 'Determining contempts by improper pressure on a litigant: an objective or subjective test?', (2003), 8 Media and Arts Law Review 19, p. 20.

653 See *Secretary for Justice v The Oriental Press Group Ltd and others* (1998) 2 HKLRD 123, [1998] 2 HKC 627; *Attorney-General (NSW) v John Fairfax and Sons Ltd* [1980] 1 NSWLR 362 and *Director of Public Prosecutions v Wran* (1987) 7 NSWLR 616 at 626.

- the actual readership in the case of an internet publication[654];
- the circumstances in which it was made[655];
- the content of the publication[656];
- the nature of the proceedings liable to be affected and whether they are civil or criminal proceedings[657];
- whether at the time of publication the proceedings are pending at the committal, trial or appellate stage[658];
- the persons to whom the publication was addressed[659];
- the likely durability of the influence of the publication on its audience[660];
- as at the date of publication, the probable period of time which would pass between the publication and the trial of the pending proceeding[661]; and

---

[654] See *Attorney-General (NSW) v John Fairfax and Sons Ltd and Bacon* (1985) 6 NSWLR 695, per McHugh JA at 713 and *Attorney-General v Independent Television News Ltd* [1995] 2 All ER 370, per Leggett LJ at 383.

[655] See *Secretary for Justice v The Oriental Press Group Ltd and others* (1998) 2 HKLRD 123, [1998] 2 HKC 627; *Attorney-General (NSW) v John Fairfax and Sons Ltd* [1980] 1 NSWLR 362 and *Director of Public Prosecutions v Wran* (1987) 7 NSWLR 616 at 626.

[656] See *Hinch and Macquarie Broadcasting Holdings Ltd v The Attorney-General for the State of Victoria* (1987) 164 CLR 15, per Wilson J at 34, [1987] HCA 56.

[657] See *Hinch and Macquarie Broadcasting Holdings Ltd v The Attorney-General for the State of Victoria* (1987) 164 CLR 15, per Wilson J at 34, [1987] HCA 56.

[658] See *Hinch and Macquarie Broadcasting Holdings Ltd v The Attorney-General for the State of Victoria* (1987) 164 CLR 15, per Wilson J at 34, [1987] HCA 56.

[659] See *Hinch and Macquarie Broadcasting Holdings Ltd v The Attorney-General for the State of Victoria* (1987) 164 CLR 15, per Wilson J at 34, [1987] HCA 56.

[660] See *Hinch and Macquarie Broadcasting Holdings Ltd v The Attorney-General for the State of Victoria* (1987) 164 CLR 15, per Wilson J at 34, [1987] HCA 56.

[661] See *Attorney-General (NSW) v John Fairfax and Sons Ltd and Bacon* (1985) 6 NSWLR 695, per Samuels JA at 699 and McHugh JA at 711.

- the effect of other prejudicial matter which had already been published, before the date of the criminal charges, concerning the accused person[662].

In performing that assessment it is not permissible to take into account any prejudicial material published after the date of the laying of the charge against the accused person.[663]

However, it is permissible to take into account other material published after the laying of the charge against the accused person which did not constitute contempt.[664]

The publication of material in circumstances where the clear tendency of the publication is to preclude or prejudice the fair and effective administration of justice in particular pending legal proceedings constitutes contempt of court unless, as a matter of weighing competing public interests, the detriment of the possibility of prejudice to the administration of justice is outweighed by other identified factors such as the public interest served by freedom of discussion of matters of public importance and by the exposure of public dangers and abuses.[665]

While the act of publication must be intentional, an intention or purpose of prejudicing the due administration of justice is not an essential ingredient of this type of contempt of court.[666]

The critical question is whether the act is likely to have that effect, but the intention with which the act was done is relevant and sometimes important.[667]

It is not relevant to consider the actual effect of the publication upon the pending proceedings.[668]

---

662 See *Attorney-General (NSW) v John Fairfax and Sons Ltd and Bacon* (1985) 6 NSWLR 695, per Samuels JA at 700 and McHugh at 711.

663 See *Director of Public Prosecutions v Wran* (1987) NSWLR 616 at 629.

664 See *Director of Public Prosecutions v Wran* (1987) NSWLR 616 at 629.

665 See *Victoria v Australian Building Construction Employees' and Builders Labourers' Federation* (1981-82) 152 CLR 25, [1982] HCA 31 and *Ex parte Bread Manufacturers Ltd; Re Truth and Sportsman Ltd* [1937] NSWStRp 22, (1937) 37 SR (NSW) 242 at 249.

666 See *John Fairfax and Sons Pty Ltd v McRae* (1955) 93 CLR 351 at 371, [1955] HCA 12.

667 See *Lane v Registrar of Supreme Court of NSW* (1981) 148 CLR 245 at 258, [1981] HCA 35 and *Registrar of the Court of Appeal v Willesee* (1985) 3 NSWLR 650, per Kirby P at 658 and Hope JA at 673.

668 See *Director of Public Prosecutions v Wran* (1987) 7 NSWLR 616 at 626.

A Court should not have regard to later events, such as relevant proceedings that were not in fact affected by the publication.[669]

## [6.0] ISSUE OF PREJUDGEMENT

It is 'Contempt of Court' to publish material which prejudges the issue or is likely to cause public prejudgment of the issue the subject of pending litigation[670], however accurately or temperately that material may be expressed.[671]

Whether published material purports to prejudge an issue before the Court depends on whether or not, in the circumstances of the particular case:

- what has happened is something which is likely to prejudice the fair trial; and
- the risk that it will prejudice the fair trial must be a real risk.[672]

---

[669] See *Ex parte Auld; Re Consolidated Press Ltd* (1936) 36 SR (NSW) 596, per Jordan CJ at 598; *Hinch and Macquarie Broadcasting Holdings Ltd v The Attorney-General for the State of Victoria* (1987) 164 CLR 15, per Toohey J at 70, [1987] HCA 56; *Director of Public Prosecutions (Cth) v John Fairfax and Sons Ltd* (1987) 8 NSWLR 732, per Kirby P at 736; *Attorney-General (NSW) v TCN Channel Nine Pty Ltd* (1990) 20 NSWLR 368 at 382 and *R v Glennon* (1992) 173 CLR 592, per Mason CJ and Toohey J at 605, [1992] HCA 16.

[670] See *SCR No 3 of 1984; Ex parte Callick and Koroma* [1985] PNGLR 67, [1985] PGSC 20.

See also: *Attorney-General v Times Newspaper Ltd* [1973] 3 All ER 54, [1974] AC 273.

[671] See *Commercial Bank of Australia Ltd v Preston* [1981] 2 NSWLR 554 at 561 and *Victoria v Australian Building Construction Employees and Builders Labourers Federation* (1981-82) 152 CLR 25 at 167, [1982] HCA 31.

[672] See *Public Prosecutor v Nahau Rooney (No. 2)* [1979] PNGLR 448, [1979] PGSC 23 and *SCR No. 3 of 1984; Ex parte Callick and Koroma* [1985] PNGLR 67, [1985] PGSC 20.

See also: *Vine Products Ltd v Green* [1966] 1 Ch 484 at 498 and *Meriden Britannia Co Ltd v Walters* (1915) 25 DLR 167 at 168.

As regards the disclosure of a prior conviction, see *Davis v Baillie* [1946] VicLawRp 76, (1946) VLR 486, per Fullagar J at 496 and *R v Regal Press Pty Ltd* [1972] VicRp 9, (1972) VR 67, per McInerney J at 73.

## [7.0] DEFENCES

## [7.1] INTRODUCTION

There are limited defences to sub-judice contempt by publication, including:

- publication in the public interest; and
- fair and accurate reporting.

## [7.2] ISSUE OF PUBLIC INTEREST

Freedom of speech and of the press has historically been viewed as indispensable to a free society and its government.[673]

Freedom of speech is one of the hallmarks of a democratic society.[674]

As the legal philosopher Jeremy Bentham said in the 19th century[675]:

> Publicity is the very soul of justice .... It keeps the judge himself, while trying, under trial.

The law of contempt is not to protect the private interests of publishers or any other person[676], but to protect the public interest in the unconstrained expression of ideas and the provision of information.

However, the law of contempt does not punish people for ideas or views; it is the communication of those ideas in circumstances which lead, or may lead, to an interference with the administration of justice that creates the offence.[677]

---

673 See *Smith v Daily Mail Publishing Co* (1979) 443 US 97, per Rehnquist J at 106 and *Hector v Attorney-General of Antigua* (1990) 2 AC 312, per Bridge LJ at 318.

674 See section 46 of the *Constitution of the Independent State of Papua New Guinea* ['Freedom of Expression'].

675 See J Bentham, 1843, 'Works of Jeremy Bentham', p. 305.

676 See *Attorney-General v Times Newspapers Ltd* [1973] 3 All ER 54, [1974] AC 273.

See also: *R v West Australian Newspapers Ltd; ex parte Director of Public Prosecutions (WA)* (1996) 16 WAR 518 at 533.

677 See *Attorney-General for New South Wales* v *Mundey* [1972] 2 NSWLR 887, per Hope JA at 916.

## SUB-JUDICE RULE

As Mahoney J observed in *Ballina Shire Council v Ringland*[678] the objectives which might be achieved by giving full weight to the protection of freedom of expression include that:

> ideas may be developed freely, culture may be refined, and the arrogance or abuse of power may be controlled.

The importance of minimal interference with freedom of speech[679] is one of the reasons why the jurisdiction to punish for contempt is a jurisdiction which is to be exercised 'with great caution'.[680]

In order to safeguard the proper administration of justice, the Courts will, however, curb conduct, including freedom of speech, to the extent necessary to prevent prejudice to proceedings.[681]

The sub-judice rule involves a balancing exercise between:

- the public interest in freedom of speech and therefore, discussion[682]; and

---

678 (1994) 33 NSWLR 680 at 720.

679 See *Lange v Australian Broadcasting Corporation* (1997) 189 CLR 520, [1997] HCA 25 and *Theophanous v Herald and Weekly Times Ltd* (1994) 182 CLR 104, [1994] HCA 46.

680 See *John Fairfax and Sons Pty Ltd v McRae* (1955) 93 CLR 351 at 370, [1955] HCA 12.

681 See *Victoria v Australian Building Construction Employees' and Builders Labourers' Federation* (1981-82) 152 CLR 25, per Gibbs CJ at 56, [1982] HCA 31 and *Attorney-General v Times Newspapers Ltd* [1973] 3 All ER 54, [1974] AC 273 at 294.

682 See *Ex parte Bread Manufacturers Ltd; Re Truth and Sportsman Ltd* (1937) 37 SR (NSW) 242, per Jordan CJ at 249; *Hinch and Macquarie Broadcasting Holdings Ltd v The Attorney-General for the State of Victoria* (1987) 164 CLR 15 at 19, 35, 64 and 82, [1987] HCA 56; *Victoria v Australian Building Construction Employees' and Builders Labourers' Federation* (1981-82) 152 CLR 25 at 59, 95, 98, 133 and 175, [1982] HCA 31; *Registrar of the Court of Appeal v Willesee* (1985) 3 NSWLR 650, per Priestley JA at 682; *Attorney-General for New South Wales v John Fairfax and Sons Ltd and Bacon* (1985) 6 NSWLR 695, per McHugh JA at 714; *Attorney-General (NSW) v X* (2000) 49 NSWLR 653, [2000] NSWCA 199; *R v West Australian Newspapers Ltd; ex parte Director of Public Prosecutions (WA)* (1996) 16 WAR 518 at 531; *Director of Public Prosecutions (Cth) v United Telecasters Sydney Ltd (in liquidation)* (1992) 7 BR 364, per Kirby J at 371 and Sheller JA at 378; *R v Sun Newspapers Pty Ltd* (1992) 58 A Crim R 281, per Byrne J at 288; *John Fairfax Publications Pty Ltd v Doe* (1995) 37 NSWLR 81, per Gleeson CJ at 84; *R v Thompson* [1989] WAR 219 at 223; *Nationwide News Pty Ltd; ex parte Director of Public Prosecutions (Cth)* (1997) 94 A Crim R 57, per Ipp J at 62 and *R v Thompson* [1989] WAR 219 at 223.

See also: New South Wales Law Reform Commission, 2000, 'Contempt by Publication', Discussion Paper No. 43, Ch. 8 'Publications in the Public Interest'.

The public interest principle is formulated in section 5 of the *Contempt of Court Act 1981* (UK).

- the public interest in the administration of justice.

The publication of material in circumstances where the clear tendency of the publication is to preclude or prejudice the fair and effective administration of justice in particular pending legal proceedings constitutes 'Contempt of Court' unless, as a matter of weighing competing public interests, the detriment of the possibility of prejudice to the administration of justice is outweighed by other identified factors such as:

- the public interest served by freedom of discussion of matters of public importance; and
- the exposure of public dangers and abuses.[683]

The detriment arising from the possible prejudice is outweighed by the public interest served by freedom of discussion of, and dissemination of information about, a matter of public importance.[684]

---

[683] See *Hinch and Macquarie Broadcasting Holdings Ltd v The Attorney-General for the State of Victoria* (1987) 164 CLR 15, per Deane J at 46, Mason CJ at 27, Wilson J at 41, Toohey J at 68 and Gaudron J at 85, [1987] HCA 56; *Victoria v Australian Building Construction Employees' and Builders Labourers' Federation* (1981-82) 152 CLR 25, [1982] HCA 31 and *Ex parte Bread Manufacturers Ltd; Re Truth and Sportsman Ltd* (1937) 37 SR (NSW) 242 at 249.

[684] See *Hinch and Macquarie Broadcasting Holdings Ltd v The Attorney-General for the State of Victoria* (1987) 164 CLR 15, [1987] HCA 56; *Attorney-General (NSW) v John Fairfax Publications Pty Ltd* [1999] NSWSC 318, per Barr J and *Ex parte Bread Manufacturers Ltd; Re Truth and Sportsman Ltd* (1937) 37 SR (NSW) 242.

See also: G Borrie and N Lowe, 1996, 'The Law of Contempt' 3rd ed., Butterworths, London, at 169; CJ Miller, 1989, 'Contempt of Court' 2nd ed., Clarendon Press, Oxford, at 228 and J Mo, 'Freedom of Speech Versus Administration of Justice: Balancing of Public Interests in Contempt of Court Cases in New South Wales', (1992), 9 Australian Bar Review 215 at 217.

## [7.3] FAIR AND ACCURATE REPORTING

A publication may have a tendency to cause prejudice to proceedings, but may be found not to amount to a contempt, on the basis that it is a fair and accurate report of proceedings held in open court[685].[686]

The courts justify fair and accurate reporting as a ground of exoneration by emphasising the public interest in the administration of justice as an open process.[687]

However, the following conditions apply:

- The report must be of proceedings which are held in open court.[688]

  Where there is no publicity there is no justice. Publicity is the very soul of justice. It is the keenest spur to exertion and the surest of all guards against improbity.[689]

---

[685] See:

- Order 4, Division 4 of the *Criminal Practice Rules 1987* ['Prohibition of Publication'];
- section 19 of the *HIV/AIDS Management and Prevention Act 2003* ['Privacy of Proceedings'];
- section 28 of the *Juvenile Courts Act 1991* ['Restriction of Publication of Proceedings']; and
- section 30 of the *Coroners Court Act* (Ch. 32) ['Power of Exclusion'].

Refer also to the section titled 'Right To Be Heard In Open Court' in the chapter titled 'Rights Of An Accused Person' in the text titled 'Injia on Criminal Practice and Procedure in Papua New Guinea and the Pacific'.

[686] See *Attorney-General (NSW) v John Fairfax and Sons Ltd and Bacon* (1985) 6 NSWLR 695, per McHugh J at 714 and *Hinch and Macquarie Broadcasting Holdings Ltd v The Attorney-General for the State of Victoria* (1987) 164 CLR 15, per Mason CJ at 26 and Gaudron J at 83, [1987] HCA 56.

[687] See *Ex parte Terrill; Re Consolidated Press Ltd* (1937) 37 SR (NSW) 255 at 257 and *R v Sun Newspapers Pty Ltd* (1992) 58 A Crim R 281, per Bryne J at at 286.

[688] See New South Wales Law Reform Commission, 2000, 'Contempt by Publication', Discussion Paper No. 43, Ch. 9 'The Fair and Accurate Reporting Principle'.

[689] See Bowring, 1843, '*Works of Jeremy Bentham*', Vol. 4, p. 305.

The principle of open justice is considered to be of vital importance, not only as a means of informing the public of the processes of the courts, but also to ensure that those processes are carried out fairly, without abuse, and are seen to be carried out fairly. This public interest is considered to be of such significance that it takes precedence over the public interest in protecting legal proceedings from possible prejudice and influence by media publicity[690];

- The report must not be of material which is:
  - the subject of a 'suppression' or 'non-publication' order.

    Conduct outside the courtroom which deliberately frustrates the effect of an order made to enable a Court to act effectively within its jurisdiction may constitute a 'Contempt of Court'[691]; or
  - for some other reason not permitted to be reported[692];
- The report must be of 'proceedings'.[693]

  This includes events occurring in the vicinity of the relevant hearing, arising out of it and directly connected with it, such as a shouted interjection by a spectator in the courtroom or a demonstration outside the court asserting strong views as to what the outcome should be[694];
- The report must be presented as a report.[695]

---

[690] See New South Wales Law Reform Commission, 2000, 'Contempt by Publication', Discussion Paper No. 43, Ch. 9 'The Fair and Accurate Reporting Principle'.

[691] As explained by McHugh JA in *John Fairfax and Sons v Police Tribunal* (1986) 5 NSWLR 465 at 477.

[692] See New South Wales Law Reform Commission, 2000, 'Contempt by Publication', Discussion Paper No. 43, Ch. 9 'The Fair and Accurate Reporting Principle'.

[693] See New South Wales Law Reform Commission, 2000, 'Contempt by Publication', Discussion Paper No. 43, Ch. 9 'The Fair and Accurate Reporting Principle'.

[694] See *Ex parte Fisher; Re Associated Newspapers Ltd* (1941) 41 SR (NSW) 272, per Jordan CJ at 278.

[695] See New South Wales Law Reform Commission, 2000, 'Contempt by Publication', Discussion Paper No. 43, Ch. 9 'The Fair and Accurate Reporting Principle'.

The immunity will not apply where the fact that the relevant prejudicial statements were made during court proceedings is not mentioned[696];

- The report must be fair and accurate.[697]

  A report is fair and accurate if it is one which a person of ordinary intelligence using reasonable care might regard as giving a fair summary of the proceedings.[698]

  A report may be unfair by virtue of its mode of presentation or its content, including:

  - the inclusion or exclusion of testimony[699];
  - the inclusion of extraneous matters or comment[700]; and
  - an absence of a proper balance[701].

  An inaccurate report is capable of constituting a contempt[702]; and

- The report must be published in good faith.[703]

---

[696] See *R v Scott and Download Publications Ltd* [1972] VicRp 77, [1972] VR 663, per Menhennitt J at 673.

[697] See New South Wales Law Reform Commission, 2000, 'Contempt by Publication', Discussion Paper No. 43, Ch. 9 'The Fair and Accurate Reporting Principle'.

[698] See *Ex parte Terrill; Re Consolidated Press Ltd* (1937) 37 SR (NSW) 255, per Jordan CJ at 259.

[699] See *Minister for Justice v Western Australian Newspapers Ltd* [1970] WAR 202, per Jackson CJ at 207.

[700] See *Attorney-General v Davidson* [1925] NZLR 849.

[701] See *Minister for Justice v Western Australian Newspapers Ltd* [1970] WAR 202, per Jackson CJ at 207.

[702] See *Ex parte Norton; Re John Fairfax and Sons Pty Ltd* (1952) 69 WN (NSW) 312; *R v Evening Standard Co Ltd* [1954] 1 QB 578; *R v West Australian Newspapers Ltd; ex parte The Minister for Justice* (1958) 60 WALR 108 and *Davis v Baillie* [1946] VicLawRp 76, [1946] VLR 486 at 496.

[703] See New South Wales Law Reform Commission, 2000, 'Contempt by Publication', Discussion Paper No. 43, Ch. 9 'The Fair and Accurate Reporting Principle'.

When good faith is to be considered, factors include:

- whether the report is fair[704];
- whether there has been a delay in reporting the proceedings[705];
- if it is published for its news value and in complete and serious disregard of its consequences on the trial of an accused person[706]. An intention to prejudice a trial is unnecessary[707];
- the application of force, intimidation and financial inducement motivated by the private concerns of the payer[708]; and
- whether there has been numerous repetitions in the media of the nature of the evidence available against a party to pending proceedings[709].

Where criticism of a person's conduct is in issue, the fairness and temperate nature of the criticism may be determinative.[710]

Improper pressure will be held to constitute contempt.[711]

As Reid LJ stated in *Attorney General v Times Newspapers Ltd*[712]:

> [W]here the only matter to be considered is pressure put on a litigant, fair and temperate criticism is legitimate, but anything which goes beyond that may well involve contempt of court.

[704] See *Ex parte Terrill; Re Consolidated Press Ltd* (1937) 37 SR (NSW) 255, per Jordan CJ at 259.

[705] See *R v Scott and Download Publications Ltd* [1972] VicRp 77, [1972] VR 663, per Menhennitt J at 675.

[706] See *R v Scott and Download Publications Ltd* [1972] VicRp 77, [1972] VR 663, per Menhennitt J at 675.

[707] See *R v David Syme and Co Ltd* [1982] VicRp 16, [1982] VR 173.

[708] See *Harkianakis v Skalkos* (1997) 42 NSWLR 22.

[709] See *Attorney-General v TCN Channel Nine Pty Ltd* (1990) 5 BR 10, per Hunt J at 29.

[710] See *Attorney-General v Times Newspapers Ltd* [1973] 3 All ER 54, [1974] AC 273

[711] See *Attorney-General v Hislop* [1991] 1 QB 514, per Nicholls LJ at 531.

[712] [1973] 3 All ER 54, [1974] AC 273 at 297.

## [8.0] ISSUE OF INTENTION OR PURPOSE

While the act of publication must be intentional, an actual intention or purpose to prejudice the due administration of justice is not an essential ingredient of this type of contempt of court.[713]

However, the intention with which the act was done is relevant and sometimes important.[714]

---

[713] See *R v Odhams Press Ltd* [1957] QBD 73, per Goddard LCJ at 80; *R v Editor of New Statesman; ex parte Director of Public Prosecutions* (1928) 44 Times LR 301, per Hewart LCJ; *Attorney-General v Butterworth and others* [1963] 1 QB 696, per Donovan LJ at 726; *R v Parke* [1903] 2 KB 432 at 437 and *R v Daily Mirror; ex parte Smith* (1927) 1 KB 845 at 851.

See also: *Rex v Dolan* [1907] 2 IR 260, per Palles CB; *Secretary for Justice v The Oriental Press Group Ltd and others* (1998) 2 HKLRD 123, [1998] 2 HKC 627; *Attorney-General (NSW) v Mundey* [1972] 2 NSWLR 887, per Hope JA at 911; *Solicitor-General v Radio Avon Ltd* [1978] 1 NZLR 225; *Solicitor-General v Radio New Zealand Ltd* [1994] 1 NZLR 48; *Chokolingo v Law Society of Trinidad and Tobago* (1978) 30 WIR 372, per Corbin JA at 396; *John Fairfax and Sons Pty Ltd v McRae* (1955) 93 CLR 351 at 371, [1955] HCA 12; *Hinch and Macquarie Broadcasting Holdings Ltd v The Attorney-General for the State of Victoria* (1987) 164 CLR 15, per Deane J at 46, Toohey J at 69 and Gaudron J at 85, [1987] HCA 56; *Registrar, Court of Appeal v Collins* [1982] 1 NSWLR 682; *Registrar of the Court of Appeal v Willesee* (1985) 3 NSWLR 650, per Kirby P at 652; *Attorney-General (NSW) v John Fairfax and Sons Pty Ltd and Bacon* (1985) 6 NSWLR 695, per McHugh JA at 708; *Attorney-General (SA) v Nationwide News Pty Ltd* (1986) 43 SASR 374 at 386; *Lane v Registrar, Supreme Court of New South Wales* (1981) 148 CLR 245, (1981) 55 ALJR 529, (1981) 35 ALR 322, [1981] HCA 35; *Victoria v Australian Building Construction Employees' and Builders Labourers' Federation* (1981-82) 152 CLR 25, per Gibbs CJ at 56, [1982] HCA 31; *R v Pearce* (1992) 7 WAR 395; *R v WA Newspapers Ltd; ex parte Director of Public Prosecutions (WA)* (1996) 16 WAR 518 and *The Swan Brewery Co Pty Ltd v Newman* [1998] WASC 271.

See however: *The State v Van Niekerk* (1970) (3) SA 655 (T), per Claasen J at 657.

[714] See *Attorney-General v Butterworth* [1963] 1 QB 696 at 725.

See also: *Lane v Registrar of Supreme Court of New South Wales* (1981) 148 CLR 245 at 258, (1981) 55 ALJR 529, (1981) 35 ALR 322, [1981] HCA 35; *Registrar of the Court of Appeal v Willesee* (1985) 3 NSWLR 650, per Kirby P at 658 and Hope JA at 673; *Hinch and Macquarie Broadcasting Holdings Ltd v The Attorney-General for the State of Victoria* (1987) 186 CLR 15, [1987] HCA 56 and *John Fairfax and Sons Pty Ltd v McRae* (1955) 93 CLR 351 at 371, [1955] HCA 12.

## SUB-JUDICE RULE

The proof of an intention to interfere with the due administration of justice may assist the conclusion that the publication had the required tendency, and its presence or absence would also be relevant to penalty[715]; but the absence of such an intention will not necessarily lead to the conclusion that no contempt has been committed.[716]

---

[715] See *Hinch and Macquarie Broadcasting Holdings Ltd v The Attorney-General for the State of Victoria* (1987) 186 CLR 15, per Wilson J at 42, [1987] HCA 56; *Director of Public Prosecutions (Cth) v Wran* (1987) 7 NSWLR 616 and *Attorney-General (NSW) v Dean* (1990) 20 NSWLR 650.

[716] See *Solicitor General v Radio New Zealand Limited* [1994] 1 NZLR 48.

## RULES OF NATURAL JUSTICE

### [1.0] CONSTITUTIONAL PROVISION

Section 59 of the *Constitution of the Independent State of Papua New Guinea* ['Principles of Natural Justice'] states:

> '(1) Subject to this Constitution and to any statute, the principles of natural justice are the rules of the underlying law known by that name developed for control of judicial and administrative proceedings.
>
> (2) The minimum requirement of natural justice is the duty to act fairly and, in principle, to be seen to act fairly'.

### [2.0] GENERAL PRINCIPLES

Whether it is a trial or some other form of proceedings involving the life or liberty of an individual – the Court must control the proceedings in accordance with the principles of natural justice.[717]

The overriding principle, in the conduct of contempt proceedings is the principle of fairness as provided for in section 59 of the *Constitution of the Independent State of Papua New Guinea* ['Principles of Natural Justice']. It is the duty to act fairly and be seen to be acting fairly[718].[719]

The principles of 'natural justice' are part of the underlying law.[720]

However, those principles do not have a constitutional status.[721]

---

[717] See *Sela Gipe v The State* (2001) SC661 and *Tom Longman Yaul v The State* (2005) SC803, [2005] PGSC 29.

[718] See section 59(2) of the *Constitution of the Independent State of Papua New Guinea* ['Principles of Natural Justice'].

[719] See also: *Tom Longman Yaul v The State* (2005) SC803, [2005] PGSC 29 and *Gipe v The State* (2001) SC661.

[720] See *Tindiwi, for and on behalf of Members of the Suspended Enga Provincial Government v Nilkare, Minister for Provincial Affairs, and The State* [1984] PNGLR 191, [1984] PGSC 18; *Premdas v The State* [1979] PNGLR 329 and *Lambakey Okuk v Fallscheer* [1980] PNGLR 274.

[721] See *Parakas v The State* [1985] PNGLR 224, [1985] PGSC 16.

## RULES OF NATURAL JUSTICE

An alleged contemnor:

- should not be convicted for the offence of 'Contempt of Court', unless there has been a fair hearing because no person shall be liable to penalty or punishment without a fair hearing[722];

- should suffer no conviction at the hands of another who is his or her prosecutor and his and her judge[723];

- should not be judged by one in whom there is a reasonable apprehension of bias.[724]

  The principles relating to bias apply in contempt proceedings and therefore, there should not be a reasonable apprehension of bias that a fair hearing was not possible.[725]

---

722 See *SCR No 3 of 1984; Ex parte Callick and Koroma* [1985] PNGLR 67 at 70, [1985] PGSC 20 and *Andrew Kwimberi of Paulus M Dowa Lawyers v The State* (1998) SC545, [1998] PGSC 9.

See also: *McKeown v R* (1971) 16 DLR (3d) 390, per Laskin J at 398 and *Fraser v R* (1984) 3 NSWLR 212 at 224.

723 See *SCR No 3 of 1984; Ex parte Callick and Koroma* [1985] PNGLR 67 at 70, [1985] PGSC 20 and *Andrew Kwimberi of Paulus M Dowa Lawyers v The State* (1998) SC545, [1998] PGSC 9.

See also: *McKeown v R* (1971) 16 DLR (3d) 390, per Laskin J at 398.

724 See *SCR No 3 of 1984; Ex parte Callick and Koroma* [1985] PNGLR 67 at 70, [1985] PGSC 20 and *Andrew Kwimberi of Paulus M Dowa Lawyers v The State* (1998) SC545, [1998] PGSC 9.

See also: *McKeown v R* (1971) 16 DLR (3d) 390, per Laskin J at 398.

725 See *SCR No. 3 of 1984; Ex parte Callick and Koroma* [1985] PNGLR 67 at 70, [1985] PGSC 20; *Andrew Kwimberi of Paulus M Dowa Lawyers v The State* (1998) SC545, [1998] PGSC 9; *Tzen Pacific Ltd v Innovest Ltd* [2012] PGNC 60, (2012) N4713 and *In the Matter of The Organic Law on National and Local Government Elections, Pato v Kaiulo, Electoral Commissioner of Papua New Guinea* [2003] PGNC 67, (2003) N2455.

See also: *Mc Keown v R* (1971) 16 DLR (3d) 390, per Laskin J at 398.

Refer also to the section titled 'Right To An Independent And Impartial Court' in the chapter titled 'Rights Of An Accused Person' in the text titled 'Injia on Criminal Practice and Procedure in Papua New Guinea and the Pacific'.

If a contemnor allegedly uses words that were scandalous of the presiding Judge in person then it is necessary to bring the Contempt charge before another judge by way of Notice of Motion or Originating Summons supported by affidavits[726];

- should not be convicted unless the specific offence charged against him or her has been distinctly stated in a 'Statement of Charge'[727], thereby enabling the contemnor to understand the alleged charge[728].

  Compliance with this rule will be strictly insisted upon since the liberty of the contemnor is at stake[729]; and

---

[726] See *Andrew Kwimberi of Paulus M Dowa Lawyers v The State* (1998) SC545, [1998] PGSC 9.

[727] See *In re Pollard* [1868] LR 2 PC 106 at 120.

See also: *Ditford v Brown* (1990) 19 NSWLR 49; *Coward v Stapleton* (1953) 90 CLR 573 at 579, [1953] HCA 48; *Anthony Radcliffe Lewis v His Honour Judge Ogden* (1984) 153 CLR 682 at 693, [1984] HCA 26; *MacGroarty v Clauson* (1989) 167 CLR 251 at 255, (1989) 86 ALR 513, [1989] HCA 34; *Gliosca v Ninyett* (1992) 10 WAR 562, per Murray J at 567; *Attorney-General for Tuvalu v Philatelic Distribution* [1990] 1 WLR 926, per Woolf LJ at 934; *Chiltern District Council v Keane* [1985] 1 WLR 1401; *Harmsworth v Harmsworth* [1987] 1 WLR 1676, per Nicholls LJ at 1683 and Woolf LJ at 1685; *R v Foster; ex parte Isaacs* [1941] VLR 77 at 81; *Re B (JA) (an Infant)* [1965] Ch 1112, per Cross LJ at 1117; *Doyle v The Commonwealth* (1985) 156 CLR 510 at 516, [1985] HCA 46; *Chiltern District Council v Keane* [1985] 1 WLR 619, per Lord Donaldson MR at 622; *McDonnell v Novello* [2006] NSWSC 1186; *Concrete Constructions Pty Ltd v Plumbers and Gasfitters Employees' Union (No. 2)* (1987) 15 FCR 64, per Wilcox J at 73, [1987] FCA 117 and *Inghams Enterprises Pty Ltd v Timania Pty Ltd* [2005] FCAFC 155.

[728] See *Balogh v Crown Court at Saint Albans* [1974] 3 All ER 283, [1975] QB 73 and *Re K* [1983] 78 Cr App R 82.

[729] See *Re B (JA) (an Infant)* [1965] Ch 1112, per Cross LJ at 1117.

See also: *Attorney-General for Tuvalu v Philatelic Distribution* [1990] 1 WLR 926, per Woolf LJ at 934.

Refer also to the chapter titled 'Statement Of Charge' in the section titled 'Motion or Proceedings for Punishment' in this chapter.

- should not be convicted, unless he or she has been given a reasonable opportunity to answer the charge[730], that is to say a reasonable opportunity to defend himself or herself[731] by:
    - the giving[732] and calling of evidence; and
    - the making of a submission as to fact and/or law which he or she may wish the Court to consider in relation to:
        - the charge itself; and
        - the question of punishment[733].[734]

Where a contemnor is brought before the Court, the Court shall require him or her to make his or her defence to the charge.[735]

---

730 See *SCR No 3 of 1984; Ex parte Callick and Koroma* [1985] PNGLR 67, [1985] PGSC 20; *Tom Longman Yaul v The State* (2005) SC803, [2005] PGSC 29 and *Re: Contempt of Court; Re: Assistant Registrar, Philip Kaumba* (2004) N2763.

See also: *In re Pollard* (1868) LR 2 PC 106 at 120; *Re B (JA) (an Infant)* [1965] Ch 1112, per Cross LJ at 1117; *R v Foster; ex parte Isaacs* [1941] VLR 77 at 81; *Fraser v R* [1984] 3 NSWLR 212 at 224; *Coward v Stapleton* (1953) 90 CLR 573 at 579, [1953] HCA 48; *Varnavides v VCAT* (2005) 12 VR 1, [2005] VSCA 231 and *Doyle v The Commonwealth* (1985) 156 CLR 510 at 516, [1985] HCA 46.

731 See *Bradshaw v Beanland* [1998] QCA 224.

732 See *Zakanovich v Magistrates Court of Victoria at Moorabbin* (2011) 32 VR 216, [2011] VSC 141 and *Gliosca v Ninyett* (1992) 10 WAR 562.

733 See *Zakanovich v Magistrates Court of Victoria at Moorabbin* (2011) 32 VR 216, [2011] VSC 141; *Gliosca v Ninyett* (1992) 10 WAR 562 and *Castle City Pty Ltd v New Vintage Nominees Pty Ltd* [2003] WASCA 30.

734 See *In re Pollard* [1868] LR 2 PC 106 at 120.

See also: *Coward v Stapleton* (1953) 90 CLR 573 at 579, [1953] HCA 48; *Anthony Radcliffe Lewis v His Honour Judge Ogden* (1984) 153 CLR 682 at 693, [1984] HCA 26; *MacGroarty v Clauson* (1989) 167 CLR 251 at 255, (1989) 86 ALR 513, [1989] HCA 34; *Gliosca v Ninyett* (1992) 10 WAR 562, per Murray J at 56; *Balogh v Crown Court at Saint Albans* [1974] 3 All ER 283, [1975] QB 73 and *Re K* [1983] 78 Cr App R 82.

735 See Order 14, rule 39(b) ['Charge, Defence and Determination'] in relation to 'Contempt in the Face or Hearing of the Court'.

In order to defend himself or herself a contemnor should be given the opportunity to seek legal advice[736], whether or not the Court is applying the provisions of Subdivision B of Division 6 of Order 14 of the *National Court Rules 1983*[737].

Salmon LJ speaking for the Privy Council, in *Maharaj v Attorney-General for Trinidad and Tobago*[738] said:

> Their Lordships recognize how important it is not to waste judicial time. But if this can be avoided only by finding against a party without giving him a fair chance of being heard, then such a price for saving judicial time is far too high.

---

[736] See:

- section 37(4)(e) of the *Constitution of the Independent State of Papua New Guinea* ['Protecton of the Law']; and
- *Balogh v Crown Court at Saint Albans* [1974] 3 All ER 283, [1975] QB 73 and *Re K* [1983] 78 Cr App R 82.

See however: *Moran* (1985) 81 Cr App R 51 at 53 and *Murphy v Magistrates Court at Prahran* [1995] A Crim R 92.

[737] See:

- *The State v Re Awaita; Contempt Proceedings* [1985] PNGLR 179, [1985] PGNC 29, (1985) N508 and *The State v Foxy Kia Tala; Re Corney Winjan* [1995] PNGLR 303, (1995) N1192; and
- section 37(4)(e) of the *Constitution of the Independent State of Papua New Guinea* ['Protection of the Law'].

[738] [1977] 1 All ER 411.

## NATIONAL COURT RULES

### [1.0] INTRODUCTION

The offence of 'Contempt of Court' is an exception to the requirements under section 37(2) of the *Constitution of the Independent State of Papua New Guinea* ['Protection of the Law'] that:

- a criminal offence must be defined; and
- the penalty must prescribed by a written law.[739]

It is now established that 'Contempt of Court' is a matter of the underlying law.[740]

When dealing with a charge of 'Contempt of Court':

- the elementary requirements of justice in the circumstances need to be observed[741]; and
- the correct procedures must be followed[742].

Notwithstanding that contempt proceedings are criminal in nature, a contemnor can be charged, convicted and punished without following the usual criminal procedure prescribed by written law.[743]

The *National Court Rules 1983*[744] provides the procedure to be followed in dealing with contempt committed in connection with proceedings in Court. The rules have been promulgated by the National Court judges pursuant to:

- section 8 of the *National Court Act* (Ch. 38) ['Rules of Court of the National Court']; and
- section 184 of the *Constitution of the Independent State of Papua New Guinea* ['Rules of Court']

[739] See *Public Prosecutor v Nahau Rooney (No. 2)* [1979] PNGLR 448, [1979] PGSC 23.

[740] See *Public Prosecutor v Nahau Rooney (No. 2)* [1979] PNGLR 448, [1979] PGSC 23 and *Agnes Okona Meten v William Seneka and Magisterial Services* (2011) N4462, [2011] PGNC 169.

[741] See *State (Director of Public Prosecutions) v Walsh* [1981] IR 412.

[742] See *Alan Robinson v The State* [1986] PNGLR 307; *The State v Mark Taua, Re Awaita - Contempt Proceedings* [1985] PNGLR 179 and *David Toll v The State* (1989) SC378, [1989] PGSC 1.

[743] See *Andrew Kwimberi of Paulus M Dowa Lawyers v The State* (1998) SC545, [1998] PGSC 9.

[744] See Order 14, Division 6 ['Contempt of Court'].

Such rules are legislative in nature and not a product generated within the common law, as explained by Estey J in *R v Clement* [1981] 2 SCR 468 at 477, [1981] SCC 212.

provide a comprehensive statement of the formal procedure to be followed in cases involving 'Contempt of Court'.[745]

Order 14, Division 6, rules 37-50 of the *National Court Rules 1983* provides 'a comprehensive statement of the procedure to be followed in cases involving contempt of Court (O. 14 r. 38) and in other situations where the contempt complained of is in connection with proceedings in the Court (O. 14 r. 42)[746, 747]

However, those rules are only a guide for use in the Supreme Court.[748]

The Rules are intended to ensure fairness in the summary procedure.[749]

It should also be borne in mind that the Rules were designed to guide and assist:

- the Court; and
- the parties

to reach a fair, orderly and expeditious disposition of matters before the Court.[750]

It is now settled law that those Rules are not an end in themselves, but are a means to an end in all matters going before the Courts.[751]

---

[745] See *Andrew Kwimberi of Paulus M Dowa Lawyers v The State* (1998) SC545, [1998] PGSC 9; *Alan Robinson v The State* [1986] PNGLR 307 at 309; *Paul Metta v The State* [1992] PNGLR 176 at 183; *The State v Foxy Kia Tala; Re Corney Winjan* [1995] PNGLR 303, (1995) N1192; *David Toll v The State* (1989) SC378, [1989] PGSC 1 and *The State v Mark Taua, Re Awaita - Contempt Proceedings* [1985] PNGLR 179.

[746] See *Alan Robinson v The State* [1986] PNGLR 307 at 309.

[747] See *Andrew Kwimberi of Paulus M Dowa Lawyers v The State* (1998) SC545, [1998] PGSC 9.

[748] See *In the Matter of Jeffrey Balakau v Panuel Mogish and others* (1996) SC497.

A summons to show cause for contempt of the Supreme Court may be issued for attendance of the alleged contemnor in the Supreme Court, see *SCR No 3 of 1984; Ex parte Callick and Koroma* [1985] PNGLR 67, [1985] PGSC 20.

[749] See *Andrew Kwimberi of Paulus M Dowa Lawyers v The State* (1998) SC545, [1998] PGSC 9.

[750] See *Andrew Kwimberi of Paulus M Dowa Lawyers v The State* (1998) SC545, [1998] PGSC 9 and *Kurt Reimann, Dominic Anis, Francis Alou, Peia Waea, Collectively known as the Executives of South Coast Soccer Club v George Skell and another* (2001) N2093, [2001] PGNC 84.

[751] See *Kurt Reimann, Dominic Anis, Francis Alou, Peia Waea, Collectively known as the Executives of South Coast Soccer Club v George Skell and another* (2001) N2093, [2001] PGNC 84.

They are to be considered as a code of practice.[752]

Their application is flexible.[753]

There is no doubt that, where justice so requires, strict adherence to the Rules can be dispensed with in the circumstances of a particular case.[754]

Non-compliance with any of the Rules do not render any proceedings void[755], unless the Court otherwise orders.[756]

---

[752] See *Kurt Reimann, Dominic Anis, Francis Alou, Peia Waea, Collectively known as the Executives of South Coast Soccer Club v George Skell and another* (2001) N2093, [2001] PGNC 84.

[753] See *Andrew Kwimberi of Paulus M Dowa Lawyers v The State* (1998) SC545, [1998] PGSC 9; *Reimann v Skell* [2001] PGNC 84, (2001) N2093; *Kurt Reimann, Dominic Anis, Francis Alou, Peia Waea, Collectively known as the Executives of South Coast Soccer Club v George Skell and another* (2001) N2093, [2001] PGNC 84; *Anthony John Polling v Motor Vehicles Insurance (PNG) Trust* [1996] PNGLR 228 at 230 and *South Pacific Post Pty Ltd v Ephraim Ikenna Maduabuchi Nwokolo* [1984] PNGLR 38 at 46.

[754] See *Kurt Reimann, Dominic Anis, Francis Alou, Peia Waea, Collectively known as the Executives of South Coast Soccer Club v George Skell and another* (2001) N2093; *Anthony John Polling v Motor Vehicles Insurance (PNG) Trust* [1996] PNGLR 228 at 230; *South Pacific Post Pty Ltd v Ephraim Ikenna Maduabuchi Nwokolo* [1984] PNGLR 38 at 46; *Kurt Reimann, Dominic Anis, Francis Alou, Peia Waea, Collectively known as the Executives of South Coast Soccer Club v George Skell and another* (2001) N2093, [2001] PGNC 84; *Wau Ecology Institute Ltd v Neale* [2007] PGNC 28, (2007) N3130; *Dennis Charles Young v Niugini Nius Pty Ltd* [1988-89] PNGLR 45; *Anthony John Polling v MVIT* [1986] PNGLR 228; *Sai-Sail Beseoh v Yuntivi Bao* (2003) N2348 and *Graham B Price and Swanita Ltd v Pacific Legal Group Lawyers* (2004) N2509.

[755] See *Park Sung Soo and another v Hankin Emboge and others* (2002) N2248.

[756] See *Andrew Kwimberi of Paulus M Dowa Lawyers v The State* (1998) SC545, [1998] PGSC 9; *Anthony John Polling v Motor Vehicles Insurance (PNG) Trust* [1996] PNGLR 228 at 230; *Bowmans Bougainville Pty Ltd and Bougainville Development Corporation Ltd* [1986] PNGLR 228 at 230; *Kurt Reimann, Dominic Anis, Francis Alou, Peia Waea, Collectively known as the Executives of South Coast Soccer Club v George Skell and another* (2001) N2093, [2001] PGNC 84; *Anthony John Polling v Motor Vehicles Insurance (PNG) Trust* [1996] PNGLR 228; *Soo v Emboge* [2002] PGNC 84, (2002) N2248 and *Wau Ecology Institute Ltd v Neale* [2007] PGNC 28, (2007) N3130.

There is also ample authority for the proposition that, the Court does have the power under Order 1, rule 7 of the *National Court Rules 1983* ['Relief from Rules'][757] to dispense with the requirements of the rules either before or after the need to comply has arisen.[758]

When an application under this rule is made the Court will have regard to:

- the urgency of the matter[759];
- the interests of justice;
- the impact of the non-compliance on the parties with reference to:
  - whether in reality the other party is in as good a position as if the rules had been complied with; or
  - whether the party has been disadvantaged in regard to its rights in the matter;
- whether the application for dispensation is made within a reasonable time[760]; and
- whether or not the intent and/or purpose of the rule in question has been met[761].[762]

---

[757] Order 1, rule 7 of the *National Court Rules 1983* ['Relief from Rules'] states:

> The Court may dispense with compliance with any of the requirements of these Rules, either before or after the occasion for compliance arises.

Order 1, rule 8 ['Non-compliance with Rules Not to Render Proceedings Void'] states:

> 'Non-compliance with any of these Rules, or with any rule of practice for the time being in force, shall not render any proceedings void, unless the Court so directs, but the proceedings may be set aside, either wholly or in part, as irregular, or may be amended or otherwise dealt with, in such a manner, and on such terms, as the Court thinks fit'.

[758] See *Kurt Reimann, Dominic Anis, Francis Alou, Peia Waea, Collectively known as the Executives of South Coast Soccer Club v George Skell and another* (2001) N2093, [2001] PGNC 84.

[759] See *The Public Prosecutor v The Chief Justice* [1992] PNGLR 316 at 321.

[760] See *Anthony John Polling v Motor Vehicles Insurance (PNG) Trust* [1996] PNGLR 228 and *Bowmans Bougainville Pty Ltd and Bougainville Development Corporation Ltd* [1986] PNGLR 228 at 231.

[761] See *Kuijk v Kuijk* [1977] PNGLR 253.

[762] See *Kurt Reimann, Dominic Anis, Francis Alou, Peia Waea, Collectively known as the Executives of South Coast Soccer Club v George Skell and another* (2001) N2093, [2001] PGNC 84.

If the Court is satisfied that the purpose of a Rule has been substantially fulfilled, the Court has an inherent jurisdiction under section 155(4) of the *Constitution of the Independent State of Papua New Guinea* ['The National Judicial System'], in the interests of justice to waive strict compliance with the Rule.[763]

## [2.0] CONTEMPT IN THE FACE OR HEARING OF THE COURT

## [2.1] STATUTORY PROVISION

Subdivision B of Division 6 of Order 14 of the *National Court Rules 1983* states:

### Rule 38 Arrest

'Where it is alleged, or appears to the Court on its own view, that a person is guilty of contempt of Court, committed in the face of the Court or in the hearing of the Court, the Court may –

(a) by oral order direct that the contemnor[764] be brought before the Court; or

(b) issue a warrant[765] for the arrest of the contemnor.'

### Rule 39 Charge, Defence And Determination

'Where a contemnor is brought before the Court, the Court shall --

(a) cause him to be informed orally of the contempt with which he is charged; and

(b) require him to make his defence to the charge; and

(c) after hearing him, determine the matter of the charge; and

(d) make an order for the punishment or discharge of the contemnor.'

---

[763] See *Kuijk v Kuijk* [1977] PNGLR 253 and *Lindsay Kivia, Peter N' Draku and Peter Seski v The State* [1988-89] PNGLR 107.

[764] The term 'contemnor' is defined in Order 14, rule 37 of the *National Court Rules 1983* for the purpose of Division 6 as meaning:
'a person guilty or alleged to be guilty of contempt of the Court'.

[765] Order 14, rule 48 of the *National Court Rules 1983* ['Warrant'] states:
'A warrant in Form 65 for the arrest and detention under this Division of a contemnor shall be addressed to the Sheriff and may be issued under the hand of the Judge presiding in the Court directing the arrest or detention'.

See also: Form 65 ['Warrant for Committal'] in Schedule 1 of the *National Court Rules 1983*.

**Rule 40 Interim Custody**

'(1) The Court may, pending disposal of the charge --

(a) direct that the contemnor be kept in such custody as the Court may determine; or

(b) direct that the contemnor be released.

(2) The Court may make a direction under Sub-rule (1)(b) on terms, which may include a requirement that the contemnor give security, in such sum as the Court directs, for his appearance in person to answer the charge.'

## [2.2] GENERAL PRINCIPLES

The offence of 'Contempt of Court' is an offence of a criminal nature for which a contemnor may be charged, convicted and punished by the Court, without following the usual criminal procedure prescribed by written law.[766]

[766] See *Andrew Kwimberi of Paulus M Dowa Lawyers v The State* (1998) SC545, [1998] PGSC 9.

The procedure under Order 14, rules 37-50 of the *National Court Rules 1983* ['Contempt of Court'] reflects practice developed in the common law over centuries.

The ability of a judge to forego the formal trappings of a criminal trial and summarily, and in some cases instantly, punish for contempt is a power that is recognized in a number of common law countries including:

- Australia [see the cases referred to];
- England [see *Morris v The Crown Office* [1970] 1 All ER 1079, [1970] 2 QB 114; *Balogh v Crown Court at Saint Albans* [1974] 3 All ER 283 at 287; CJ Miller, 1989, 'Contempt of Court' 2nd ed., Clarendon Press, Oxford, p. 45 and the other cases referred to];
- United States for 'petty' contempt offences [see *Sacher v United States* (1952) 343 US 1; *Bloom v Illinois* (1968) 391 US 194. According to *Baldwin v New York* (1970) 399 US 66 at 69, a 'petty' offence is one with a maximum punishment of six months' imprisonment];
- Hong Kong [see the cases referred to];
- Scotland [see the cases referred to]; and
- Canada [see *R v Vermette* [1987] 1 SCR 577 at 582, [1987] SCC 51; *Paul v R* [1980] 2 SCR 169, [1980] SCC 37; *United Nurses of Alberta v Alberta (Attorney-General)* [1992] 1 SCR 901 at 924, [1992] SCC 99; *British Columbia Government Employees Union v British Columbia (Attorney-General)* [1988] 2 SCR 214 at 238, [1988] SCC 3 and *R v K (B)* [1995] 4 SCR 186, [1995] SCC 45 and the other cases referred to].

The summary procedure allows the presiding Judge to avoid the formalities of a criminal trial to convict a person for contempt of court, even *instanter*, in some cases.[767]

The *National Court Rules 1983* contain a comprehensive statement of the procedure to be followed in cases involving contempt of court [Order 14, rule 38].[768]

Under Sub-division 'B' of Order 14, rules 38-40 ['Contempt in the Face or Hearing of the Court'] there is a summary procedure for dealing with contemnors.[769]

The procedure to be applied where the Court is exercising its summary jurisdiction and dealing with contempt, of its own motion, for contempt committed in the face of the Court (within the view or hearing of the Judge or Court), is flexible and allows for:

- the charge to be put to the alleged contemnor;
- opportunity to be given to the alleged contemnor to reply to the charge;
- separate findings on the question of guilt or innocence; and
- opportunity to be given to the alleged contemnor to be heard on penalty before a decision on penalty is made.[770]

Ordinarily, an evidentiary hearing may not be required because the contempt is committed in the face of the Court and the contemptous act will be taken judicial notice[771] of and put before the alleged contemnor. If the alleged contempt is committed away from the Court's view or hearing and the Judge or Court concerned were to deal with the matter, an evidentiary hearing following the procedures set out in Subdivision C of Division 6 of Order 14 of the *National Court Rules 1983* may be necessary.[772]

---

767 See *R v Almon* (1765) 97 ER 94 at 100, (1765) Wilm 243 at 254, [1765] EngR 25.

See also: *British Columbia Government Employees Union v British Columbia (Attorney-General)* [1988] 2 SCR 214, per Dickson CJ at 238, [1988] SCC 3; *R v K (B)* [1995] 4 SCR 186, [1995] SCC 45 and *Hébert v Procureur général du Québec* [1966] Que QB 197 at 227.

768 See *Alan Robinson v The State* [1986] PNGLR 307 at 309.

769 See *Andrew Kwimberi of Paulus M Dowa Lawyers v The State* (1998) SC545, [1998] PGSC 9.

770 See *Andrew Kwimberi of Paulus M Dowa Lawyers v The State* (1998) SC545, [1998] PGSC 9.

771 Refer also to the section titled 'Judicial Notice' in the chapter titled 'Court Procedure' in the text titled 'Injia on Criminal Practice and Procedure in Papua New Guinea and the Pacific'.

772 See *Andrew Kwimberi of Paulus M Dowa Lawyers v The State* (1998) SC545, [1998] PGSC 9.

However, the summary procedure should not be used if the contempt was not committed:

- in the face of the presiding Judge (Court); or
- within the hearing of the presiding Judge (Court); and
- the presiding Judge is relying on information put to him or her.[773]

Where it appears to the Court 'on its own view, that a person is guilty of contempt of court, committed in the face of the Court or in the hearing of the Court, the Court may' issue oral orders directing the contemnor to be brought before the Court or issue a warrant for his or her arrest [Rule 38].[774]

When the contemnor is brought before the Court, the Court informs the contemnor of the charge orally, requires him or her to make his or her statement in defence, hears him or her and determines the matter of the charge and makes such order as to punishment [Rule 39].[775]

The Court may direct the contemnor to be kept in custody pending the Court's determination of the charge [Rule 40].[776]

The rules do not prevent the Court, which is the subject of the alleged contempt, from dealing with the charge, whether the contempt is committed on the face of the court or outside the court. However, the Court must adhere to the principles of natural justice, more particularly the need to:

- conduct a fair hearing; and
- avoid appearances of bias.[777]

[773] See *Andrew Kwimberi of Paulus M Dowa Lawyers v The State* (1998) SC545, [1998] PGSC 9.

[774] See *Andrew Kwimberi of Paulus M Dowa Lawyers v The State* (1998) SC545, [1998] PGSC 9.

[775] See *Andrew Kwimberi of Paulus M Dowa Lawyers v The State* (1998) SC545, [1998] PGSC 9.

[776] See *Andrew Kwimberi of Paulus M Dowa Lawyers v The State* (1998) SC545, [1998] PGSC 9.

[777] See *SCR No. 3 of 1984; Ex parte Callick and Koroma* [1985] PNGLR 67 at 69, [1985] PGSC 20; *Andrew Kwimberi of Paulus M Dowa Lawyers v The State* (1998) SC545, [1998] PGSC 9 and *Kurt Reimann, Dominic Anis, Francis Alou, Peia Waea, Collectively known as the Executives of South Coast Soccer Club v George Skell and another* (2001) N2093.

## NATIONAL COURT RULES

The general rule is that a contempt of court is punishable by the Court before or against whom it is committed.[778]

There are advantages in a contempt matter being dealt by the same judge:

- the presiding Judge would be in the best position to deal with it because he or she had witnessed what had taken place;
- the presiding Judge might well be more inclined to take a lenient view after a period of reflection than another Judge who simply reads the transcript and would be naturally anxious to protect another Judge;
- the threat of immediate punishment is an effective deterrent;
- there will not be a lapse of time between the events the subject of the charge and the trial[779]; and
- the necessity for prompt action in cases where the trial is still going on and the impracticability of arranging for another Judge to deal with it if there is still a risk that the contempt hearing will itself be disrupted.[780]

A significant consequence of prosecution by summary process is that it results in the bypassing of the traditional safeguards of criminal proceedings.[781]

---

[778] See *SCR No. 3 of 1984; Ex parte Callick and Koroma* [1985] PNGLR 67 at 69-70, [1985] PGSC 20; *The State v Mark Tava: Re Awaita* [1985] PNGLR 179 at 180-181; *Andrew Kwimberi of Paulus M Dowa Lawyers v The State* (1998) SC545, [1998] PGSC 9 and *Ian Augerea, Registrar of the National Court v David Tigavu* (2010) N4185, [2010] PGNC 182.

[779] See *Kift v R* [1993] VicRp 51, [1993] 1 VR 703 at 707.

[780] *See Robertson and another v Her Majesty's Advocate* [2008] SCCR 20, [2007] GWD 37-643, [2008] JC 146, [2007] SLT 1153, [2007] ScotHC HCJAC_63, [2007] HCJAC 63.

See also: United Kingdom, Committee on Contempt of Court, 1974, 'Report of the Committee on Contempt of Court', HMSO, London, Cmnd 5794, para. 30.

[781] See *Re Colina; ex parte Torney* (1999) 200 CLR 386, (1999) 166 ALR 545 at 548, (1999) 73 ALJR 1576, [1999] HCA 57.

See also: D Eady and ATH Smith, 1999, 'Arlidge, Eady and Smith on Contempt' 2nd ed., Sweet and Maxwell, London, para. 2-26.

However, there is no room to invoke the ordinary criminal procedure.[782]

The summary procedure to be adopted is comprehensive.[783]

The rules of practice and procedure in ordinary criminal cases, as technical and rigid as they are, are never intended to apply to contempt proceedings.[784]

In such a case, which usually arises from events of which the Court itself is a witness, special procedures are permitted, including the receiving of hearsay evidence[785].[786]

Moreover, the alleged contemnor does not have an unrestricted right to cross-examine witnesses against him or her.[787]

The overriding principle however, is the principle of fairness as provided for by section 59 of the *Constitution of the Independent State of Papua New Guinea* ['Principles of Natural Justice'].[788] It is the duty to act fairly and be seen to be acting fairly. The procedure set out in Order 14, rule 39 is intended to ensure fairness in the summary procedure.[789]

---

[782] See *Andrew Kwimberi of Paulus M Dowa Lawyers v The State* (1998) SC545, [1998] PGSC 9.

See however: *Stephen John Rose and John Charles Harrison v Neville Devete, Acting Solicitor-General and The State* (2007) N3327.

[783] See *Andrew Kwimberi of Paulus M Dowa Lawyers v The State* (1998) SC545, [1998] PGSC 9 and *Alan Robinson v The State* [1986] PNGLR 307 at 309.

[784] See *Andrew Kwimberi of Paulus M Dowa Lawyers v The State* (1998) SC545, [1998] PGSC 9.

See however: *Stephen John Rose and John Charles Harrison v Neville Devete, Acting Solicitor-General and The State* (2007) N3327.

[785] Refer also to the chapter titled 'Hearsay Evidence' in the text titled 'Injia on Evidence in Papua New Guinea and the Pacific'.

[786] See *Kift v R* [1993] VicRp 51, [1993] 1 VR 703 at 707.

[787] See *Keeley v The Honourable Mr Justice Brooking* (1979) 143 CLR 162 at 173, (1979) 25 ALR 45 at 52, [1979] HCA 28; *Fraser v R* [1984] 3 NSWLR 212 at 227 and *Kift v R* [1993] VicRp 51, [1993] 1 VR 703 at 707.

[788] Refer also to the chapter titled 'Rules Of Natural Justice'.

[789] See *Andrew Kwimberi of Paulus M Dowa Lawyers v The State* (1998) SC545, [1998] PGSC 9.

The summary procedure does not offend against the rule of natural justice, *nemo iudex in sua causa* [no-one shall be judge in his own case], since the prosecution of the offence is not aimed at protecting the Judge personally, but protecting the administration of justice.[790]

This summary procedure, however, gives the Court the immediate and ultimate power to decide the fate of the contemnor.[791]

To some extent, it works to the detriment of the contemnor in that he or she may be deprived of his or her personal liberty without first being heard., e.g. arrest upon oral order. The summary procedure has some associated risks such as:

- the presiding Judge's perception of contempt committed before hearing the contemnor.[792]

  The presiding Judge may have witnessed the contemptuous behavior and therefore be the repository of the knowledge of the relevant events as the personification of the Court in whose face the contempt has occurred[793];

- the arrest of the contemnor on an oral order before hearing the contemnor[794];

- the absence of any formal documentation of the contempt charge, etc[795];

- the presiding Judge being be placed in an unusual concatenation of roles[796] of:

  - initiating the formal curial proceedings to bring the contemnor before the Court;

  - deciding the issues of fact;

  - determining the charge; and

---

790 See *Robertson and another v Her Majesty's Advocate* [2008] SCCR 20, [2007] GWD 37-643, [2008] JC 146, [2007] SLT 1153, [2007] ScotHC HCJAC_63, [2007] HCJAC 63.

See also: G Borrie and N Lowe, 1996, 'The Law of Contempt' 3rd ed., Butterworths, London, p. 522.

791 See *Andrew Kwimberi of Paulus M Dowa Lawyers v The State* (1998) SC545, [1998] PGSC 9.

792 See *Andrew Kwimberi of Paulus M Dowa Lawyers v The State* (1998) SC545, [1998] PGSC 9.

793 See *Clampett v Attorney-General (Cth)* (2009) 181 FCR 473 at 507, [2009] FCAFC 151.

794 See *Andrew Kwimberi of Paulus M Dowa Lawyers v The State* (1998) SC545, [1998] PGSC 9.

795 See *Andrew Kwimberi of Paulus M Dowa Lawyers v The State* (1998) SC545, [1998] PGSC 9.

796 See *Fraser v R* [1984] 3 NSWLR 212 at 224.

- making orders for punishment or dismissal.[797]

Those roles impose on the presiding Judge a special obligation to ensure that he or she has not made up his or her mind until everything that can reasonably be put on the scale is allowed to be put there[798]; and

- perceived bias of the presiding Judge.[799]

The presiding Judge may be the 'victim'.[800]

In certain situations, it may become desirable for the presiding Judge to disqualify himself or herself and refer the matter to:

- another judge to deal with it; or
- the Public Prosecutor for prosecution under Order 14, rule 42 ['Procedure Generally'].[801]

The test is one of whether:

- the contemptuous behavior is one of personal affront to, scandalous of or criticism of to the judge concerned[802]; or
- the contemptuous behavior goes against the system of administration of justice.[803]

---

797 See *Fraser v R* [1984] 3 NSWLR 212 at 225.

798 See *Fraser v R* [1984] 3 NSWLR 212 at 225.

799 See *Robertson and another v Her Majesty's Advocate* [2008] SCCR 20, [2007] GWD 37-643, [2008] JC 146, [2007] SLT 1153, [2007] ScotHC HCJAC_63, [2007] HCJAC 63.

800 See *Fraser v R* [1984] 3 NSWLR 212 at 224.

801 See *Andrew Kwimberi of Paulus M Dowa Lawyers v The State* (1998) SC545, [1998] PGSC 9.

802 See *Alan Robinson v The State* [1986] PNGLR 307.

803 See *The State v Mark Tava: Re Awaita* [1985] PNGLR 179, per Woods J at 181 and *SCR No 3 of 1984; Ex parte Callick and Koroma* [1985] PNGLR 67, [1985] PGSC 20.

If the contempt:

- is a personal affront to the presiding Judge, he or she should disqualify himself or herself[804]; and

- goes to public confidence in the judicial system, then the judge before whom the contempt is committed is entitled to deal to with it.[805]

  However, time for reflection presents an opportunity to consider whether a less stringent course may be taken[806], rather than in the heat of the moment[807].

There is the need for the presiding Judge to have the available machinery by which, speedily and effectively, they can protect the proceedings over which they have control.[808]

But this procedure is of necessity that the Court must possess[809] although its usefulness depends on the wisdom and restraint with which it is exercised[810].

It is given so as to maintain the dignity and authority of the presiding Judge to ensure a fair trial.[811]

---

804 See *Wilkinson v S and another* [2003] EWCA Civ 95, [2003] 1 WLR 1254 and *Robertson and another v Her Majesty's Advocate* [2008] SCCR 20, [2007] GWD 37-643, [2008] JC 146, [2007] SLT 1153, [2007] ScotHC HCJAC_63, [2007] HCJAC 63.

805 See *SCR No 3 of 1984; Ex parte Callick and Koroma* [1985] PNGLR 67, per McDermott J at 69, [1985] PGSC 20; *Re: Contempt of Court; Re: Assistant Registrar, Philip Kaumba* (2004) N2763; *Andrew Kwimberi of Paulus M Dowa Lawyers v The State* (1998) SC545, [1998] PGSC 9 and *The State v Re Awaita; Contempt Proceedings* [1985] PNGLR 179, [1985] PGNC 29, (1985) N508.

806 See *R v Huggins* [1995] EWCA Crim 6, [2007] 2 Cr App R 108, per Moses LJ at 110; *Kift v R* [1993] VicRp 51, [1993] 1 VR 703 at 709 and *R v Phillips* (1984) 78 Cr App R 88 at 94.

807 See *The State v Foxy Kia Tala; Re Corney Winjan* [1995] PNGLR 303, (1995) N1192.

808 See *Attorney-General v Sport Newspapers Ltd* [1991] 1 WLR 1194, per Hodgson LJ at 1225.

809 See *Andrew Kwimberi of Paulus M Dowa Lawyers v The State* (1998) SC545, [1998] PGSC 9.

See also: *Shamdasani v King-Emperor* [1945] AC 264, per Goddard LJ at 270.

810 See *Shamdasani v King-Emperor* [1945] AC 264, per Goddard LJ at 270.

811 See *Andrew Kwimberi of Paulus M Dowa Lawyers v The State* (1998) SC545, [1998] PGSC 9.

But then again, the overriding principle is one of fairness.[812]

Notwithstanding that 'Contempt of Court' is a criminal offence, the summary nature of the proceedings cannot be permitted to:

- subvert principles of fairness; or
- become an instrument of oppression to an alleged contemnor.[813]

In order to ensure fairness, if a judge opts to employ facets of the procedure under Order 14, rules 41-47 of the *National Court Rules 1983* such as by motion or originating summons through the Registrar to afford the contemnor adequate time and opportunity to respond to the charge of contempt, then there can be no argument of irregularity in the contempt procedure working to the detriment of the contemnor. In any case, the use of such combined procedure would not void the summary proceeding[814].[815]

It is of particular importance in contempt applications, where the Court is often in a sense an interested party, that the presiding Judge do whatever is possible to ensure that there be observed not only the requirements of a just and open-minded hearing, but also that this be apparent to the accused person and to the world.[816]

---

[812] See *Andrew Kwimberi of Paulus M Dowa Lawyers v The State* (1998) SC545, [1998] PGSC 9.

See also: *Zukanovic v Magistrates' Court at Moorabbin* (2012) 32 VR 216, per Forrest J at 224, [2011] VSC 141.

[813] See *Rich v Attorney-General for the State of Victoria* [1999] VSCA 14 and *Murphy v R* [1997] 2 VR 186.

[814] Order 1, rule 8 of the *National Court Rules 1983* ['Non-compliance with Rules Not to Render Proceedings Void'] states:

> 'Non-compliance with any of these Rules, or with any rule of practice for the time being in force, shall not render any proceedings void, unless the Court so directs, but the proceedings may be set aside, either wholly or in part, as irregular, or may be amended or otherwise dealt with, in such a manner, and on such terms, as the Court thinks fit'.

[815] See *Andrew Kwimberi of Paulus M Dowa Lawyers v The State* (1998) SC545, [1998] PGSC 9.

[816] See *Kift v R* [1993] VicRp 51, [1993] 1 VR 703 at 709.

## NATIONAL COURT RULES

The power to summarily punish a contemnor in accordance with Order 14, rules 38-40 of the *National Court Rules 1983* ['Contempt in the Face or Hearing of the Court'] is an extraordinary[817] and very significant[818] power, not to be embarked upon lightly[819], and to be exercised:

- sparingly[820];
- extremely rarely[821];
- with scrupulous care[822];
- with great caution.[823]

---

[817] See *Fraser v R* (1984) 3 NSWLR 212 at 224.

[818] See *Kift v R* [1993] VicRp 51, [1993] 1 VR 703 at 707 and *Balogh v Crown Court at St Albans* [1975] QB 73, per Lord Denning MR at 85 and Stephenson LJ at 89, [1974] 3 All ER 283.

[819] See *Wilkinson v S and another* [2003] EWCA Civ 95, [2003] 1 WLR 1254.

[820] See *Shamdasani v King-Emperor* [1945] AC 264, per Goddard LJ at 270.

See also: *Kift v R* [1993] VicRp 51, [1993] 1 VR 703 at 707; *Balogh v Crown Court at St Albans* [1975] QB 73, per Lord Denning MR at 85 and Stephenson LJ at 89, [1974] 3 All ER 283; *HKSAR v Yau* [1999] 2 HKLRD 633, per Keith J; *Keeley v The Honourable Mr Justice Brooking* (1979) 143 CLR 162, per Stephen J at 174, [1979] HCA 28 and *Anthony Radcliffe Lewis v His Honour Judge Ogden* (1984) 153 CLR 682 at 693, [1984] HCA 26.

[821] See *Keeley v The Honourable Mr Justice Brooking* (1979) 143 CLR 162, per Stephen J at 174, [1979] HCA 28.

[822] See *Andrew Kwimberi of Paulus M Dowa Lawyers v The State* (1998) SC545, [1998] PGSC 9.

See also: *R v Gray* [1900] 2 QB 36, per Russell LCJ; *Balogh v Crown Court at Saint Albans* [1975] QB 73, [1974] 3 All ER 283, per Lord Denning MR at 288; *BK v R* (1995) 129 DLR (4th) 500; *Re Colina; ex parte Torney* (1999) 200 CLR 386, (1999) 166 ALR 545 at 548, (1999) ALJR 1576, [1999] HCA 57; *Keeley v The Honourable Mr Justice Brooking* (1979) 143 CLR 162, per Stephen J at 174, [1979] HCA 28 and *R v K (B)* [1995] 4 SCR 186, [1995] SCC 45, per Lamer CJ.

[823] As commented by Lindley LJ in *Seaward v Paterson* [1897] 1 Ch 545 at 553.

See also: *HKSAR v Yau* [1999] 2 HKLRD 633, per Keith J; *Bradshaw v Attorney-General for the State of Queensland* [1998] QCA 224 and *John Fairfax and Sons Pty Ltd v McRae* (1955) 93 CLR 351, [1955] HCA 12.

The need for great caution is obvious, since the presiding Judge places himself or herself in the position of prosecutor, witness, jury and judge.[824]

The presiding Judge should not appear to be a prosecutor acting in his or her own cause.[825]

However, the *National Court Rules 1983* do not prevent the Court itself from dealing with the contempt[826];

- only in serious cases[827];
- when necessity demands in order to meet the ends of justice[828].

[824] See *Fraser v R* [1984] 3 NSWLR 212, per Kirby P and McHugh JA at 224; *Zukanovic v Magistrates' Court at Moorabbin* (2012) 32 VR 216, per Forrest J at 224, [2011] VSC 141 and *Robertson and another v Her Majesty's Advocate* [2008] SCCR 20, [2007] GWD 37-643, [2008] JC 146, [2007] SLT 1153, [2007] ScotHC HCJAC_63, [2007] HCJAC 63.

[825] See *Schot and Barclay* [1997] 2 Cr App R 383 and *Robertson and another v Her Majesty's Advocate* [2008] SCCR 20, [2007] GWD 37-643, [2008] JC 146, [2007] SLT 1153, [2007] ScotHC HCJAC_63, [2007] HCJAC 63.

[826] See *Andrew Kwimberi of Paulus M Dowa Lawyers v The State* (1998) SC545, [1998] PGSC 9; *SCR No 3 of 1984; Ex parte Callick and Koroma* [1985] PNGLR 67 at 69, [1985] PGSC 20 and *The State v Mark Tava: Re Awaita* [1985] PNGLR 179 at 180.

[827] See *Andrew Kwimberi of Paulus M Dowa Lawyers v The State* (1998) SC545, [1998] PGSC 9 and *David Gwaya Poka v The State* [1988-89] PNGLR 218 at 221, [1988] PGSC 27.

See also: *Anthony Radcliffe Lewis v His Honour Judge Ogden* (1984) 153 CLR 682 at 693, [1984] HCA 26 and *Shamdasani v King-Emperor* [1945] AC 264, per Goddard LJ at 270.

[828] See *In re Clements, Republic of Costa Rica v Erlanger* (1877) 46 L J Ch 375, per Sir George Jessel MR at 383 and *R v Gray* [1900] 2 QB 36, per Russell LCJ at 41.

See also: *Re Colina; ex parte Torney* (1999) 200 CLR 386, (1999) 166 ALR 545 at 548, (1999) ALJR 1576, [1999] HCA 57 and *Keeley v The Honourable Mr Justice Brooking* (1979) 143 CLR 162, per Stephen J at 174, [1979] HCA 28.

Such circumstances include where the conduct is such that 'it cannot wait to be punished'[829] because it is urgent[830] and imperative to act immediately[831] so as to maintain the authority of the Court[832] by removing at once the immediate obstruction to the demonstration of justice[833] including:

- to prevent disorder[834]; and
- to enable witnesses to be free from fear[835].

In the case of contempt by a witness there is much to be said for the view that, in the administration of justice, prompt and effective steps should be taken to deal with the situation[836]; and

---

829 See *Keeley v The Honourable Mr Justice Brooking* (1979) 143 CLR 162, per Stephen J at 174, [1979] HCA 28.

830 See *Griffin* (1989) 88 Cr App R 63, per Mustill LJ at 69.

831 See *Balogh v Crown Court at Saint Albans* [1975] QB 73, [1974] 3 All ER 283, per Lord Denning MR at 287; *BK v R* (1995) 129 DLR (4th) 500; *Kift v R* [1993] VicRp 51, [1993] 1 VR 703 at 707 and *Keeley v The Honourable Mr Justice Brooking* (1979) 143 CLR 162, per Stephen J at 174, [1979] HCA 28.

832 See *Andrew Kwimberi of Paulus M Dowa Lawyers v The State* (1998) SC545, [1998] PGSC 9.

See also: *Balogh v Crown Court at St Albans* [1975] QB 73, [1974] 3 All ER 283 at 287 and *R v K (B)* [1995] 4 SCR 186, [1995] SCC 45, per Lamer CJ.

833 See *Attorney-General (NSW) v Mundey* [1972] 2 NSWLR 887 at 912 and *R v Wright (No. 1)* [1968] VicRp 15, [1968] VR 164 at 165.

834 See *Andrew Kwimberi of Paulus M Dowa Lawyers v The State* (1998) SC545, [1998] PGSC 9 and *Re: Contempt of Court; Re: Assistant Registrar, Philip Kaumba* (2004) N2763.

See also: *Balogh v St Albans Crown Court* [1975] QB 73, [1974] 3 All ER 283, per Lord Denning MR at 287 and *R v K (B)* [1995] 4 SCR 186, [1995] SCC 45, per Lamer CJ.

835 See *Andrew Kwimberi of Paulus M Dowa Lawyers v The State* (1998) SC545, [1998] PGSC 9 and *Re: Contempt of Court; Re: Assistant Registrar, Philip Kaumba* (2004) N2763.

See also: *Balogh v St Albans Crown Court* [1975] QB 73, [1974] 3 All ER 283, per Lord Denning MR at 287 and *R v K (B)* [1995] 4 SCR 186, [1995] SCC 45, per Lamer CJ.

836 See *Mayer v HM Advocate* [2005] JC 121.

- only when the case is clearly proven 'beyond reasonable doubt[837]'.[838]

Such a power properly exercised is a power of the utmost value and importance that should not be curtailed.[839]

However, it is not limited to cases where it is necessary to preserve the integrity of a trial that is:

- in progress; or
- about to begin.[840]

In a case where there are ongoing proceedings between the same parties, it may be entirely proper to invoke the summary procedure even though the immediate hearing is over.[841]

## [2.3] SUMMARY OF PROCEDURE

### [2.3.1] INTRODUCTION

The procedure to be followed in the taking of a plea or conducting a trial in accordance with Order 14, rules 38-40 of the *National Court Rules 1983* ['Contempt in the Face or Hearing of the Court'] is not provided for in the relevant statutes or the rules of Court. Often Courts resort to section 185 of the *Constitution of the Independent State of Papua New Guinea* ['Lack of Procedural Provision'] to develop ad hoc procedures in each case. It is helpful for the guidance of lawyers, parties and Judges or Courts to set out the main steps to be followed which will ensure that principles of natural justice and fairness are observed.

---

837 Refer also to the chapter titled 'Determination Of Guilt'.

838 See *HKSAR v Yau* [1999] 2 HKLRD 633, per Keith J and *R v K (B)* [1995] 4 SCR 186, [1995] SCC 45, per Lamer CJ and *Balogh v Crown Court at Saint Albans* [1975] QB 73 at 85, [1974] 3 All ER 283.

839 See *Andrew Kwimberi of Paulus M Dowa Lawyers v The State* (1998) SC545, [1998] PGSC 9.

See also: *Balogh v Crown Court at Saint Albans* [1975] QB 73, [1974] 3 All ER 283, per Lord Denning MR at 288.

840 See *Director of Public Prosecutions v Channel Four Television Co Ltd* [1993] 2 All ER 517 and *Wilkinson v S and another* [2003] EWCA Civ 95, [2003] 1 WLR 1254.

841 See *Wilkinson v S and another* [2003] EWCA Civ 95, [2003] 1 WLR 1254.

## [2.3.2] PLEA OF GUILTY

The following steps are recommended to be followed:

**Step 1: Arraignment**

The Court states the essence of or reads the charge to the alleged contemnor ('the defendant'), as per the 'Statement of Charge'.

**Step 2: Bail**

The Court considers the question of bail or remand.

**Step 3: Plea**

The Court invites the defendant to plead to the charge (whether the charge is true or untrue or whether the charge is admitted or denied).

**Step 4: Answer on Plea**

The defendant pleads Guilty to the charge.[842]

**Step 5: Formal Conviction**

The Court formally enters a conviction.

**Step 6: Allocatus**

The Court asks the defendant if he or she wishes to say anything on penalty.

**Step 7: Statement on Allocatus**

The defendant makes a statement on penalty.

**Step 8: Submissions on Penalty**

The defendant and complainant or their counsel make submissions on penalty. This process may include the defendant calling character evidence and reports. If evidence is called, the witness may be cross-examined and findings of fact made.

---

[842] However, the plea may be vacated, see *Park Sung Soo and another v Hankin Emboge and others* (2002) N2248.

**Step 9:** **Punishment**

The Court pronounces punishment with reasons for decision.

**Step 10:** **Costs**

The Court makes a decision as to costs.

## [2.3.3] PLEA OF NOT GUILTY

The following steps are recommended to be followed:

**Step 1:** **Arraignment**

The Court states the essence of or reads the charge to the alleged contemnor ('the defendant'), as per the 'Motion for Contempt'.

**Step 2:** **Bail**

The Court considers the question of bail or remand.

**Step 3:** **Plea**

The Court invites the defendant to plead to the charge (whether the charge is true or untrue or whether the charge is admitted or denied). The defendant pleads Not Guilty.

**Step 4:** **Answer on Plea**

The Court enters a plea of Not Guilty.

**Step 5:** A trial is conducted in the following order:

**Complainant's Case**

Complainant's case opens

Complainant produces evidence-in-chief (and is examined by counsel, if represented by a lawyer)

Cross-examination by defendant or counsel

Re-examination by complainant or counsel

Close of complainant's case

**Ruling on No Case to Answer Submission**[843]

If the Court upholds the No Case to Answer Submission, the charge is dismissed.

If the matter survives the No Case to Answer Submission, the matter proceeds.

**Defendant's Case**

Defendant's case opens

Defendant elects whether to call evidence

Defendant produces evidence-in-chief (and is examined by counsel, if represented by a lawyer)

Cross-examination by complainant or counsel

Re-examination by defendant or counsel

Close of the defendant's case

**Submissions of complainant and defendant or their counsel on the issue of guilt or innocence**

**Judgement of the Court on the issue of guilt or innocence**

**Verdict:** If the defendant is found not guilty, he or she is acquitted and discharged.

If the defendant is found guilty, he or she is convicted and the steps for a plea of guilty are then followed.

**Step 6: Allocatus**

The Court asks the defendant if he or she wishes to say anything on penalty.

**Step 7: Statement on Allocatus**

The defendant makes a statement on penalty.

[843] See *C Com Pty Ltd v Jiejing Pty Ltd* (1992) 36 FCR 524 at 527, [1992] FCA 325.

**Step 8:** **Submissions on Penalty**

The defendant and complainant or their counsel make submissions on penalty. This process may include the defendant calling character evidence and reports. If evidence is called, the witness may be cross examined and findings of fact made.

**Step 9:** **Punishment**

The Court pronounces punishment with reasons for decision.

**Step 10:** **Costs**

The Court makes a decision as to costs.

The above recommended procedure is similar to the ordinary criminal trial process, but is applied flexibly.

## [3.0] MOTION OR PROCEEDINGS FOR PUNISHMENT

### [3.1] STATUTORY PROVISION

Subdivision C of Division 6 of Order 14 of the *National Court Rules 1983* states:

**Rule 41** **Application**

'This Subdivision does not apply to a case in which the Court proceeds under Rules 38 to 40.'

**Rule 42** **Procedure Generally**

'(1) Where contempt is committed in connection with proceedings in the Court, an application for punishment for the contempt must be made by motion on notice in the proceedings, but, if separate proceedings for punishment of the contempt are commenced, the proceedings so commenced may be continued unless the Court otherwise orders.

(2) Where contempt is committed, but not in connection with proceedings in the Court, proceedings for punishment of the contempt must be commenced by originating summons, but, if an application for punishment of the contempt is made by motion on notice in any proceedings, the application may be heard and disposed of in the latter proceedings, unless the Court otherwise orders.'

**Rule 43 Statement of Charge**

'A statement of charge, that is, a statement specifying the contempt of which the contemnor[844] is alleged to be guilty, shall be subscribed to, or filed with, the notice of motion or originating summons.'

**Rule 44 Evidence**

'(1) Subject to Sub-rule (2), the evidence in support of the charge shall be by affidavit.

(2) The Court may, on terms, permit evidence in support of the charge to be given otherwise than by affidavit.'

**Rule 45 Service**

'The notice of motion or summons, the statement of charge, and the affidavits shall be served personally on the contemnor.'

**Rule 46 Arrest**

'Where --

(a) notice of a motion for punishment of a contempt has been filed or proceedings have been commenced for punishment of a contempt; and

(b) it appears to the Court that the contemnor is likely[845] to abscond or otherwise withdraw himself from the jurisdiction of the Court,

the Court may issue a warrant in Form 64[846] for the arrest of the contemnor and his detention in custody until he is brought before the Court to answer the charge, unless he, in the meantime, gives security in such manner and in such sum as the Court directs, for his appearance in person to answer the charge and to submit to the judgement or order of the Court.'

---

[844] The term 'contemnor' is defined in Order 14, rule 37 of the *National Court Rules 1983* for the purpose of Division 6 as meaning:

'a person guilty or alleged to be guilty of contempt of the Court'.

[845] This term means 'a tendency with real possibility and not "more likely than not", "probably", or "very likely"', see *Kurt Reimann, Dominic Anis, Francis Alou, Peia Waea, Collectively known as the Executives of South Coast Soccer Club v George Skell and another* (2001) N2093.

[846] See also: Form 64 ['Warrant for Arrest'] in Schedule 1 of the *National Court Rules 1983.*

**Rule 47 Motion Or Proceedings By Registrar**

'(1) Where it is alleged, or appears to the Court on its own view, that a person is guilty of contempt of the court or of any other court, the Court may, by order, direct the Registrar to apply by motion for, or to commence proceedings for, punishment of the contempt.

(2) Sub-rule (1) does not affect the right that any person other than the Registrar may have to apply by motion for, or to commence proceedings for, punishment of contempt.'

## [3.2] GENERAL PRINCIPLES

The *National Court Rules 1983* contain a comprehensive statement of the procedure to be followed in situations where the contempt complained of is in connection with proceedings in the Court [Order 14, rule 42].[847]

Proceedings under subdivision C of Division 6 of Order 14 of the *National Court Rules 1983* are commenced either by:

- motion if in relation to contempt in connexion with proceedings in Court; or
- originating summons if the contempt is not 'in connection with proceedings in Court' [Rules 42 and 47].

A 'Statement of Charge' is prepared together with a 'Notice of Motion' [Rule 43].

Evidence may be given by affidavit or otherwise as ordered by the Court [Rule 44].

The documents are served on the alleged contemnor personally [Rule 45].

However, Order 1, rule 7 of the *National Court Rules 1983* ['Relief from Rules'] empowers the Court to dispense with the mandatory requirement of personal service under Order 14, rule 45.[848]

[847] See *Alan Robinson v The State* [1986] PNGLR 307 at 309.

[848] See *Wau Ecology Institute Ltd v Trevor Neale and others* (2007) N3130.

Order 1, rule 1 of the *National Court Rules 1983* ['Relief from Rules'] states:
'The Court may dispense with compliance with any of the requirements of these Rules, either before or after the occasion for compliance arises'.

As to whether there should be strict compliance, see *In re Pollard* (1868) LR 2 PC 106 at 120; *Rich v Attorney-General for the State of Victoria* [1999] VSCA 14 and *Murphy v R* [1997] 2 VR 186.

If it appears to the Court that the alleged contemnor is likely to abscond or otherwise withdraw himself or herself from the jurisdiction of the Court, the Court may issue a warrant of arrest [Rule 46].

The Court may refer the matter to the Public Prosecutor for prosecution.[849]

This procedure provides the alleged contemnor with the usual procedural guarantees of a criminal trial.[850]

When considering the seriousness of the offence the procedures of a criminal prosecution must be strictly observed as far as possible.[851]

The right to a fair and unprejudiced trial is an essential safeguard of the liberty of the individual under the law. The ability of a society to provide a fair and unprejudiced trial is an indispensable basis of any acceptable justification of the restraints and penalties of the criminal law. Indeed, it is a touchstone of the existence of the 'Rule of Law'.[852]

The power to be exercised in such cases is not merely to determine private rights between litigants, but is a power to ensure the right of the accused and the prosecution to a fair trial.[853]

---

[849] See *Andrew Kwimberi of Paulus M Dowa Lawyers v The State* (1998) SC545, [1998] PGSC 9 and *Alan Robinson v The State* [1986] PNGLR 307.

[850] See *British Columbia Government Employees Union v British Columbia (Attorney-General)* [1988] 2 SCR 214, per Dickson CJ at 238, [1988] SCC 3; *R v K (B)* [1995] 4 SCR 186, [1995] SCC 45; *Hébert v Procureur général du Québec* [1966] Que QB 197 at 227 and *Doyle v The Commonwealth* (1985) 156 CLR 510 at 516, [1985] HCA 46.

[851] See *Spindler v Balog* (1959) 76 WN (NSW) 391 at 393; *Registrar of the Court of Appeal v Maniam (No. 2)* (1992) 26 NSWLR 309, per Kirby P at 315; *Kennedy v Lovell* [2002] WASCA 226 and *Varnavides v Victorian Civil and Administrative Tribunal* [2005] 12 VR 1, [2005] VSCA 231.

[852] As stated by Deane J in *Hinch and Macquarie Broadcasting Holdings Ltd v The Attorney-General for the State of Victoria* (1987) 164 CLR 15 at 58, [1987] HCA 56.

[853] See *General Television Corporation Pty Ltd v Director of Public Prosecutions and others* [2008] VSCA 49.

Therefore, the correspondingly appropriate safeguards ought apply[854], including:

- the right of cross-examination[855], as provided for by section 37(4)(f) of the *Constitution of the Independent State of Papua New Guinea* ['Protection of the Law'].

  However, the right of cross-examination is not unlimited.[856]

  All cross-examination is subject to the discretion of the presiding Judge to refuse irrelevant cross-examination.[857]

  Furthermore, the rule in *Browne v Dunn*[858] applies[859];

- the right to call witnesses[860], as provided for by section 37(4)(f) of the *Constitution of the Independent State of Papua New Guinea*; and

- the right to decide whether to give evidence[861], as provided for by section 37(4)(10) of the *Constitution of the Independent State of Papua New Guinea*.

---

[854] See *Doyle v The Commonwealth* (1985) 156 CLR 510 at 516, [1985] HCA 46 and *In re B (Contempt of Court)* (1996) 1 WLR 627, per Wall LJ at 639.

[855] See *United Nurses of Alberta v Alberta (Attorney-General)* [1992] 1 SCR 901, [1992] SCC 99, per McLachlin J and *Tilco Plastics Ltd v Skurat* (1966) 57 DLR (2d) 596, per Gale CJ at 610.

Refer also to the section titled 'Cross-Examination' in the chapter titled 'Examination Of Witnesses' in the text titled 'Injia on Criminal Practice and Procedure in Papua New Guinea and the Pacific'.

[856] See *United Nurses of Alberta v Alberta (Attorney-General)* [1992] 1 SCR 901, [1992] SCC 99, per McLachlin J.

[857] See *United Nurses of Alberta v Alberta (Attorney-General)* [1992] 1 SCR 901, [1992] SCC 99, per McLachlin J.

[858] (1893) 6 R 7 (HL).

[859] See *TPC v Feather Mills Pty Ltd* (1990) 26 FCR 555 at 559, [1990] FCA 415.

Refer also to the subsection titled 'Rule In Browne v Dunn' in the section titled 'Cross-examination' in the chapter titled 'Examination Of Witnesses' in the text titled 'Injia on Criminal Practice and Procedure in Papua New Guinea and the Pacific'.

[860] See *Tilco Plastics Ltd v Skurat* (1966) 57 DLR (2d) 596, per Gale CJ at 610.

[861] See *Conmet Products UK Ltd v Hawkex Plastics Ltd* [1971] 2 QB 67 at 73.

See also: *Tilco Plastics Ltd v Skurat* (1966) 57 DLR (2d) 596, per Gale CJ at 610 and *Kift v R* [1993] VicRp 51, [1993] 1 VR 703 at 708.

## [3.3] SUMMARY OF PROCEDURE

### [3.3.1] INTRODUCTION

The procedure to be followed in conducting a trial or the taking of a plea on a motion for contempt is not provided for in either the relevant statutes or the *National Court Rules 1983*. Often Courts resort to section 185 of the *Constitution of the Independent State of Papua New Guinea* ['Lack of Procedural Provision'] to develop ad hoc procedures in each case. It is helpful for the guidance of lawyers, parties and Judges or Courts to set out the main steps to be followed which will ensure that principles of natural justice and fairness are observed.

### [2.3.2] PLEA OF GUILTY

The following steps are recommended to be followed:

**Step 1:** **Presentation of Motion for Contempt**

Motion for Contempt, Statement of Charge and affidavits (if any) is presented by Complainant and scrutinized by the Court to ensure it complies with the Rules of Court.

**Step 2:** **Bail**

The Court considers the question of bail or remand.

**Step 3:** **Arraignment**

The Court states the essence of or reads the charge to the alleged contemnor ('the defendant'), as per the 'Statement of Charge'.

**Step 4:** **Plea**

The Court invites the defendant to plead to the charge (whether the charge is true or untrue or whether the charge is admitted or denied).

**Step 5:** **Answer on Plea**

The defendant pleads Guilty to the charge.[862]

[862] However, the plea may be vacated, see *Park Sung Soo and another v Hankin Emboge and others* (2002) N2248.

**Step 4:** **Formal Conviction**

The Court formally enters a conviction.

**Step 5:** **Allocatus**

The Court asks the defendant if he or she wishes to say anything on penalty.

**Step 6:** **Statement on Allocatus**

The defendant makes a statement on penalty.

**Step 7:** **Submissions on Penalty**

The defendant and complainant or their counsel make submissions on penalty. This process may include the defendant calling character evidence and reports. If evidence is called, the witness may be cross examined and findings of fact made.

**Step 9:** **Punishment**

The Court pronounces punishment with reasons for decision.

**Step 10:** **Costs**

The Court makes a decision as to costs.

### [2.3.3] PLEA OF NOT GUILTY

The following steps are recommended to be followed:

**Step 1:** **Presentation of Motion for Contempt**

Motion for Contempt, Statement of Charge and affidavits (if any) is presented by Complainant and scrutinized by the Court to ensure it complies with the Rules of Court.

**Step 2:** **Bail**

The Court considers the question of bail or remand.

**Step 3:** **Arraignment**

The Court states the essence of or reads the charge to the alleged contemnor ('the defendant'), as per the 'Motion for Contempt'.

**Step 4:** **Plea**

The Court invites the defendant to plead to the charge (whether the charge is true or untrue or whether the charge is admitted or denied). The defendant pleads Not Guilty.

**Step 5:** **Answer on Plea**

The Court enters a plea of Not Guilty.

**Step 6:** A trial is conducted in the following order:

**Complainant's Case**

Complainant's case opens

Complainant produces evidence-in-chief (and is examined by counsel, if represented by a lawyer).

Cross-examination by defendant or counsel.

Re-examination by complainant or counsel.

Close of complainant's case

**Ruling on No Case to Answer Submission**[863]

If the Court upholds the No Case to Answer Submission, the charge is dismissed.

If the matter survives the No Case to Answer Submission, the matter proceeds.

**Defendant's Case**

Defendant's case opens

Defendant elects whether to call evidence.

Defendant produces evidence-in-chief (and is examined by counsel, if represented by a lawyer).

Cross-examination by complainant or counsel.

Re-examination by defendant or counsel.

Close of the defendant's case

---

[863] See *C Com Pty Ltd v Jiejing Pty Ltd* (1992) 36 FCR 524 at 527, [1992] FCA 325.

**Submissions of complainant and defendant or their counsel on the issue of guilt or innocence**

**Judgement of the Court on the issue of guilt or innocence**

**Verdict:** If the defendant is found not guilty, he or she is acquitted and discharged.

If the defendant is found guilty, he or she is convicted and the steps for a plea of guilty are then followed.

**Step 7: Allocatus**

The Court asks the defendant if he or she wishes to say anything on penalty.

**Step 8: Statement on Allocatus**

The defendant makes a statement on penalty.

**Step 9: Submissions on Penalty**

The defendant and complainant or their counsel make submissions on penalty. This process may include the defendant calling character evidence and reports. If evidence is called, the witness may be cross examined and findings of fact made.

**Step 10: Punishment**

The Court pronounces punishment with reasons for decision.

**Step 11: Costs**

The Court makes a decision as to costs.

The above recommended procedure is similar to the ordinary criminal trial process, but is applied flexibly.

# STATEMENT OF CHARGE

## [1.0] NATIONAL COURT RULES

Order 14, rule 43 of the *National Court Rules 1983* ['Statement of Charge'] states:

> 'A statement of charge, that is, a statement specifying the contempt of which the contemnor[864] is alleged to be guilty, shall be subscribed to, or filed with, the notice of motion or originating summons'.[865]

Rule 45 ['Service'] states:

> 'The notice of motion or summons, the statement of charge, and the affidavits shall be served personally on the contemnor'.[866]

## [2.0] GENERAL PRINCIPLES

It is clear from Order 14, rules 42(1) to 45 of the *National Court Rules 1983* inclusive that a 'Statement of Charge' is different from a Notice of Motion and affidavits.[867]

The 'Statement of Charge' must either be:

- filed as a separate document; or
- 'subscribed' to the Notice of Motion or originating summons[868]

and served personally on the alleged contemnor.[869]

---

[864] The term 'contemnor' is defined in Order 14, rule 37 of the *National Court Rules 1983* for the purpose of Division 6 as meaning:

'a person guilty or alleged to be guilty of contempt of the Court'.

[865] This Rule does not apply to a case in which the Court proceeds under Rules 38 to 40 ['Contempt in the Face or Hearing of the Court'], see Rule 41 ['Application'].

[866] This Rule does not apply to a case in which the Court proceeds under Rules 38 to 40 ['Contempt in the Face or Hearing of the Court'], see Rule 41 ['Application'].

[867] See *Gaman Holdings Pty Ltd v Labu Holdings Pty Ltd* [2000] PGNC 47, (2000) N2016.

[868] See Order 14, rule 43 ['Statement of Charge'].

[869] See *Nonga Hospital Board v Sr Theonila Watt and others* (2016) N3055.

## STATEMENT OF CHARGE

The word 'subscribe' means 'to write under[870]' the 'Notice of Motion' or originating summons.

The phrase 'a statement specifying the contempt of which the contemnor is alleged to be guilty' in rule 43[871] of the *National Court Rules 1983* should be given its broad meaning. It is to mean, a clear statement of relevant facts alleged against the contemnor by the applicant and the grounds constituting the alleged contempt.[872]

The statement should clearly be entitled 'Statement of Charge'.[873]

It is the 'Statement of Charge' and no other documentation that sets out the charge.[874]

The purpose of the 'Statement of Charge' is to clearly and sufficiently inform the alleged contemnor and the Court, at first glance, as to what is alleged against him or her as constituting the contempt. Any 'Statement of Charge' which falls short of these requirements should be struck down as incompetent.[875]

The 'Statement of Charge' is no ordinary statement; it is a 'charge' document, because the contempt procedure has penal outcomes and could well result in deprivation of personal liberty of the alleged contemnor if found guilty. It is for this reason that procedural rules for instituting contempt proceedings are in explicit and mandatory terms.[876]

Compliance should be strictly insisted upon since the liberty of the alleged contemnor is at stake.[877]

---

[870] See *Gaman Holdings Pty Ltd v Labu Holdings Pty Ltd* [2000] PGNC 47, (2000) N2016.

[871] See Order 14, rule 43 ['Statement of Charge'].

[872] See *Gaman Holdings Pty Ltd v Labu Holdings Pty Ltd* [2000] PGNC 47, (2000) N2016.

[873] See *Gaman Holdings Pty Ltd v Labu Holdings Pty Ltd* [2000] PGNC 47, (2000) N2016.

[874] See *Harmsworth v Harmsworth* [1987] 1 WLR 1676, per Nicholls LJ at 1683 and *Chiltern District Council v Keane* [1985] 1 WLR 1401, per Lord Donaldson MR.

[875] See *Gaman Holdings Pty Ltd v Labu Holdings Pty Ltd* [2000] PGNC 47, (2000) N2016.

[876] See *Gaman Holdings Pty Ltd v Labu Holdings Pty Ltd* [2000] PGNC 47, (2000) N2016.

[877] See *Re B (JA) (an Infant)* [1965] Ch 1112, per Cross LJ at 1117.

See also: *Attorney-General for Tuvalu v Philatelic Distribution* [1990] 1 WLR 926, per Woolf LJ at 934.

## STATEMENT OF CHARGE

A 'Statement of Charge' is a statement:

- of alleged facts in clear and precise terms; and
- with sufficient particularity

which should sufficiently inform the alleged contemnor of the precise nature of the contempt alleged against him or her.[878]

It should state:

- the full name, description and address of the applicant;
- the full name, description and address of the alleged contemnors; and
- precisely the grounds upon which the alleged contemnor is alleged to be guilty[879],[880]

notwithstanding the allegations are contained in the supporting affidavits.

If the 'Statement of Charge' itself does not sufficiently specify the contempt, the affidavit evidence served with the statement cannot be relied upon to remedy the deficiency.[881]

The charge must be sufficiently explicit in the 'Statement of Charge', read fairly and as a whole.[882]

It is not enough to state the grounds of the application in general terms.[883]

---

878 See *Gaman Holdings Pty Ltd v Labu Holdings Pty Ltd* [2000] PGNC 47, (2000) N2016.

See also: *Ditford v Brown* (1990) 19 NSWLR 49.

879 See *Re B (JA) (An Infant)* [1965] Ch 1112 at 1117.

880 See *Gaman Holdings Pty Ltd v Labu Holdings Pty Ltd* [2000] PGNC 47, (2000) N2016.

881 See *Harmsworth v Harmsworth* [1987] 1 WLR 1676, per Nicholls LJ at 1683; *Construction, Forestry, Mining and Energy Union v BHP Steel (AIS) Pty Ltd* [2001] FCA 1758 and *Chanel Ltd v FGM Cosmetics* (1981) FSR 471 at 478.

882 See *Coward v Stapleton* (1953) 90 CLR 573 at 579, [1953] HCA 48 and *Australian Building Construction Employees' and Builders' Labourers' Federation v Minister of State for Industrial Relations* (1982) 43 ALR 189 at 211.

883 See *Chiltern District Council v Keane* [1985] 1 WLR 619.

## STATEMENT OF CHARGE

It is essential that the alleged contemnor understands the nature of the conduct that is said to constitute the offence.[884]

An alleged contemnor is entitled to know with sufficient particularity in the charge exactly or precisely what he or she is said to:

- have done; or
- omitted to do.[885]

The requirement for particularity must be strictly complied with.[886]

What matters is that the alleged contemnor is given particulars sufficient to let him or her know the subject matter of the breach which is alleged.[887]

Precision is necessary if the alleged contemnor is to be able to defend himself or herself effectively.[888]

The gist of the accusation must be made clear to the person charged, though it is not always necessary to formulate the charge in a series of specific allegations.[889]

---

[884] See *Anthony Radcliffe Lewis v His Honour Judge Ogden* (1984) 153 CLR 682 at 688, [1984] HCA 26; *Balogh v Crown Court at Saint Albans* [1974] 3 All ER 283, [1975] QB 73 and *Re K* [1983] 78 Cr App R 82.

[885] See *Attorney-General for Tuvalu v Philatelic Distribution* [1990] 1 WLR 926, per Woolf LJ at 934; *Harmsworth v Harmsworth* [1987] 1 WLR 1676, per Woolf LJ; *Attorney-General for Tuvalu v Philatelic Distribution Corporation Ltd* [1990] 1 WLR 926 at 934; *Chiltern District Council v Keane* [1985] 1 WLR 619, per Lord Donaldson MR at 622; *McDonnell v Novello* [2006] NSWSC 1186; *Dublin City Council v Thomas McFeely* [2012] IESC 45; *Johnson v Miller* (1937) 59 CLR 467, per Evatt J at 498, [1937] HCA 77; *Walsh v Tattersall* (1996) 188 CLR 77 at 105; *Macgroarty v Clauson* (1989) 167 CLR 251 at 255, (1989) 86 ALR 513, [1989] HCA 34; *Anthony Radcliffe Lewis v His Honour Judge Ogden* (1984) 153 CLR 682, [1984] HCA 26; *Gliosca v Ninyett* (1992) 10 WAR 562; *Coward v Stapleton* (1953) 90 CLR 573 at 580, [1953] HCA 48 and *Morriss v Withers* [1954] VicLawRp 15, [1954] VLR 100 at 103.

[886] See *Chiltern District Council v Keane* [1985] 1 WLR 619.

[887] See *Harmsworth v Harmsworth* [1987] 1 WLR 1676, per Woolf LJ at 1685.

[888] See *Cotroni v Quebec Police Commission* (1977) 80 DLR (3d) 490 at 497.

[889] See *Chang Hang Kiu v Piggott* [1990] AC 312 at 315; *Doyle v The Commonwealth* (1985) 156 CLR 510 at 516, [1985] HCA 46; *Macgroarty v Clauson* (1989) 167 CLR 251 at 255, (1989) 86 ALR 513, [1989] HCA 34; *Coward v Stapleton* (1953) 90 CLR 573 at 579, [1953] HCA 48; *Harmsworth v Harmsworth* [1987] 1 WLR 1676, per Woolf LJ at 1686; *Coward v Stapleton* (1953) 90 CLR 573 at 579, [1953] HCA 48 and the observations of Winneke P in *Hugo Rich v The Attorney-General for the State of Victoria* [1999] VSCA 14.

## STATEMENT OF CHARGE

If a breach of an earlier Court order is relied upon as constituting the alleged contempt the alleged contemnor is entitled to be given particulars sufficient to let him or her know the subject matter of the breach which is alleged.[890]

Therefore, the 'Statement of Charge' should set out clearly and precisely:

- the order that is alleged to have been broken[891]; and
- the relevant facts alleged as constituting a breach of that order.[892]

The law relating to 'duplicity' applies to contempt proceedings and therefore 'latent duplicity' that may give rise to uncertainty as to the charge to be met should be corrected if the alleged contemnor is to have a fair trial.[893]

Where an alleged contemnor is brought before the Court, the Court shall cause him or her to be informed orally of the contempt with which he or she is charged.[894]

---

[890] See *Harmsworth v Harmsworth* [1987] 1 WLR 1676, per Woolf LJ at 1685.

[891] See *Dublin City Council v Thomas McFeely* [2012] IESC 45.

[892] See *Gaman Holdings Pty Ltd v Labu Holdings Pty Ltd* [2000] PGNC 47, (2000) N2016.

See also: *Dublin City Council v Thomas McFeely* [2012] IESC 45; *Attorney-General for Tuvalu v Philatelic Distribution* [1990] 1 WLR 926, per Woolf LJ at 934; *Harmsworth v Harmsworth* [1987] 1 WLR 1676, per Woolf LJ; *Chiltern District Council v Keane* [1985] 1 WLR 619, per Lord Donaldson MR at 622 and *McDonnell v Novello* [2006] NSWSC 1186.

[893] See *S v R* (1989) 168 CLR 266, per Dawson J at 274 and Toohey J at 280, [1989] HCA 66; *Hannes v Director of Public Prosecutions (Cth) (No. 2)* (2006) 60 ACSR 1, (2006) 165 A Crim R 151, [2006] NSWCCA 373 and *Australian Securities and Investments Commission v Jorgensen and others* [2008] QSC 91.

See however: *Concrete Constructions Pty Ltd v Plumbers and Gasfitters Employees' Union (No. 2)* (1987) 15 FCR 64, per Wilcox J at 74, [1987] FCA 117; *Harmsworth v Harmsworth* [1987] 1 WLR 1676, per Woolf LJ at 1686 and the observations of Winneke P in *Hugo Rich v The Attorney-General for the State of Victoria* [1999] VSCA 14.

Refer also to the section titled 'Duplicity' in the chapter titled 'Charges' in the text titled 'Injia on Criminal Procedure and Practice in Papua New Guinea and the Pacific'.

[894] See Order 14, rule 39(a) ['Charge, Defence and Determination'] in relation to 'Contempt in the Face or Hearing of the Court'.

## STATEMENT OF CHARGE

Unless and until an application is allowed to alter a particularised 'Statement of Charge', the alleged contemnor is entitled to insist that he or she is only required to meet the charge as made.[895]

Where a charge is defective because of lack of precision the error may go to the root of the proceedings.[896]

---

[895] As was observed by Evatt and Deane JJ *Australian Building Construction Employees' and Builders Labourers' Federation v Minister of State for Industrial Relations* (1982) 43 ALR 189 at 206.

[896] See *Wilde v R* (1988) 164 CLR 365 at 373, [1988] HCA 6.

## EVIDENCE

### [1.0] STATUTORY PROVISION

Order 14, rule 44 of the *National Court Rules 1983* ['Evidence'] states:

> '(1) Subject to Sub-rule (2), the evidence in support of the charge shall be by affidavit.
>
> (2) The Court may, on terms, permit evidence in support of the charge to be given otherwise than by affidavit'.[897]

### [2.0] GENERAL PRINCIPLES

Depending on the circumstances there may be no need for evidence to be called, such as contempt in the view of the Court.[898]

The judge can act on any information which is:

- before him or her; or
- within his or her personal knowledge.[899]

When considering that punishment for being found guilty may include a term of imprisonment, the evidence required to establish it must be appropriately cogent.[900]

Evidence in support of a charge of 'Contempt of Court' may be by:

- affidavit; or
- oral evidence.[901]

---

897 This Rule does not apply to a case in which the Court proceeds under Rules 38 to 40 ['Contempt in the Face or Hearing of the Court'], see Rule 41 ['Application'].

898 See *David Gwaya Poka v The State* [1988-89] PNGLR 218, per Woods J at 223, [1988] PGSC 27 and *Andrew Kwimberi of Paulus M Dowa Lawyers v The State* (1998) SC545, [1998] PGSC 9.

899 See *David Gwaya Poka v The State* [1988-89] PNGLR 218, per Woods J at 223, [1988] PGSC 27 and *Andrew Kwimberi of Paulus M Dowa Lawyers v The State* (1998) SC545, [1998] PGSC 9.

900 See *Knight v Clifton* [1971] Ch 700, [1971] 2 All ER 378, per Russell LJ at 707 and 381.

901 See Order 14, rules 44 ['Evidence'] and 45 ['Service'].

Irrespective, the evidence must be admissible form.[902]

However, as to the nature of the facts or evidence before a judge under a summary procedure involving a lawyer failing to appear in Court on a fixed date, time and place; it is not necessary that evidence be placed before the Court in accordance with technical rules of evidence. The presiding Judge can act on any information which is:

- before him or her; or
- within his or her personal knowledge.[903]

[902] See *Ian Thomas Langford v The State* (1990) SC383, [1990] PGSC 3.

Refer also to the text titled 'Injia on Evidence in Papua New Guinea and the Pacific'.

[903] See *Andrew Kwimberi of Paulus M Dowa Lawyers v The State* (1998) SC545, [1998] PGSC 9 and *David Gwaya Poka v The State* [1988-89] PNGLR 218 at 223, [1988] PGSC 27.

## DETERMINATION OF GUILT

Upon hearing the evidence the Court must then determine the matter of the charge.[904]

It is the duty of the Court to:

- ensure that the contempt which is sought to be punished is properly established; and
- not proceed on something less than proper proof of the contempt.[905]

The onus of proof of contempt consisting of a breach of an order lies with the applicant.[906]

When the Court is concerned with the circumstances in which a contempt has been committed and thus with the gravity of the contemnor's conduct, it must be satisfied to the point of being sure of any matters which:

- it would regard as adverse to the alleged contemnor; or
- would tend to lead to it to view his or her action in a more serious light

and so affect its view of the appropriate penalty.[907]

---

[904] See Order 14, Rule 39(c) ['Charge, Defence and Determination'] in relation to 'Contempt in the Face or Hearing of the Court'.

[905] See *Augerea v Pambel* [2008] PGNC 81, (2008) N3332.

See also: *Spindler v Balog* (1959) 76 WN (NSW) 391 at 393.

[906] See *Yap v Tin Siew Tan, B and T Engineering Pty Ltd, Robert L Wong, William Baptiste and David F Tau* [1987] PNGLR 227, [1987] PGSC 21 and *Stephen John Rose and another v Neville Devete, Acting Solicitor-General and The State* (2007) N3327.

See also:

- *Witham v Holloway* (1995) 183 CLR 525 at 530, (1995) 131 ALR 401, (1995) 69 ALJR 847, [1995] HCA 3; *Australasian Meat Industry Employees' Union v Mudginberri Station Pty Ltd* (1986) 161 CLR 98 at 113, (1986) 66 ALR 577, [1986] HCA 46 and *Advan Investments Pty Ltd v Dean Gleeson Motor Sales Pty Ltd* (2003) VSC 2001, per Gillard J; and
- Australian Law Reform Commission, 1987, 'Contempt', Report No. 35, p. 335.

[907] See *Z Bank v D1* [1994] 1 Lloyd's Rep 656 at 667 and *Gulf Azov Shipping Co Ltd v Idis* [2001] EWCA Civ 21, per Lord Phillips MR.

## DETERMINATION OF GUILT

A charge of 'Contempt of Court' must be proven 'beyond reasonable doubt'.[908]

Uncertain inferences from inexact proof will not support such a charge.[909]

Such proof must be based on admissible evidence.[910]

It is the duty of the Court to see that the contempt which is sought to be punished is properly established and that the Court must not proceed on something less than proper proof of the contempt.[911]

Therefore, if at the end of the evidence the Court is left with any lingering doubt as to the liability or guilt of the contemnor, the law requires that the Court extend to that person the benefit of that doubt.[912]

Upon the determination of guilt of the charge the Court must then make the following orders:

- an order of punishment[913];

---

[908] This standard of proof applies in:

- Papua New Guinea, see for example, *Ross Bishop v Bishop Bros Engineering Pty Ltd* [1988-89] PNGLR 533, [1988] PGSC 8 and *Andrew Kwimberi of Paulus M Dowa Lawyers v The State* (1998) SC545, [1998] PGSC 9;
- England, see for example, *R v Gray* [1900] 2 QB 36, per Russell LCJ at 40;
- Solomon Islands, see for example, *Tubara v James* [1998] SBHC 94;
- Australia, see for example, *Witham v Holloway* (1995) 183 CLR 525 at 530, (1995) 131 ALR 401, (1995) 69 ALJR 847, [1995] HCA 3; and
- Hong Kong, see for example, *Kao Lee and Yip (a firm) v Donald Koo Hoi Yan* (2009) 12 HKCFAR 830.

[909] See *Consolidated Press Ltd v McRae* (1955) 93 CLR 325 at 333, [1955] HCA 11.

[910] See *Consolidated Press Ltd v McRae* (1955) 93 CLR 325 at 333, [1955] HCA 11.

[911] See *Ian Augerea in his Capacity as Registrar of The National and Supreme Courts v Jack Pambel as the Acting Public Prosecutor and others* (2008) N3332.

See also: *Spindler v Balog* (1959) 76 WN (NSW) 391 at 393.

[912] See *Stephen John Rose and John Charles Harrison v Neville Devete, Acting Solicitor-General and The State* (2007) N3327.

[913] See Order 14, rule 39(d) ['Charge, Defence and Determination'] in relation to 'Contempt in the Face or Hearing of the Court'.

- in the case of the National and Supreme Courts discharge of the contemnor[914]; or

- in the case of the District Court proceed to deal with the contemnor under the provisions of section 277(4) of the *District Courts Act* (Ch. 40) ['Contempt of Court'] which states:

  'If a person convicted of an offence against Subsection (1) makes to the Court, before its rising, such apology as it considers satisfactory, the Court may remit the fine wholly or in part'.

[914] See Order 14, rule 39(d) ['Charge, Defence and Determination'] in relation to 'Contempt in the Face or Hearing of the Court'.

# PUNISHMENT

## [1.0] CONSTITUTIONAL PROVISION[915]

Section 23 of the *Constitution of the Independent State of Papua New Guinea* ['Sanctions'] states

> '(1) Where any provision of a Constitutional Law prohibits or restricts an act, or imposes a duty, then unless a Constitutional Law or an Act of the Parliament provides for the enforcement of that provision the National Court may –
>
> (a) impose a sentence of imprisonment for a period not exceeding 10 years or a fine not exceeding K10 000.00; or
>
> (b) in the absence of any other equally effective remedy under the laws of Papua New Guinea, order the making of compensation by a person (including a governmental body) who is in default,
>
> or both, for a breach of the prohibition, restriction or duty, and may make such further order in the circumstances as it thinks proper.
>
> (2) Where a provision of a Constitutional Law prohibits or restricts an act or imposes a duty, the National Court may, if it thinks it proper to do so, make any order that it thinks proper for preventing or remedying a breach of the prohibition, restriction or duty, and Subsection (1) applies to a failure to comply with the order as if it were a breach of a provision of this Constitution.
>
> (3) Where the National Court considers it proper to do so, it may include in an order under Subsection (2) an anticipatory order under Subsection (1)'.

[915] See also: section 178 of the *Constitution of the Autonomous Region of Bougainville* ['Basic Rights'].

## [2.0] STATUTORY PROVISIONS

## [2.1] NATIONAL COURT RULES

Order 14, Division 6 of the *National Court Rules 1983* ['Contempt of Court'] states (in part):

**Punishment**

> '(1) Where the contemnor[916] is not a corporation, the Court may punish contempt by committal to prison or fine or both.
>
> (2) Where the contemnor is a corporation the Court may punish contempt by sequestration or fine or both.
>
> (3) The Court may make an order for punishment on terms, including a suspension of punishment or a suspension of punishment where the contemnor gives security in such manner and in such sum as the Court may approve for good behaviour and performs the terms of the security'.

**Discharge**

Rule 50 states:

> 'Where a contemnor is committed to prison for a term, the Court may order his discharge before the expiry of the term'.

## [2.2] CRIMINAL CODE ACT

Section 5 of the *Criminal Code Act* (Ch. 262) ['Contempt of Court'] states:

> '(1) Subject to Subsection (2), this Act or the Code does not affect the authority of any court of record to punish a person summarily for the offence commonly known as "Contempt of Court".
>
> (2) A person shall not be punished under Subsection (1) and under the Code for the same act or omission'.

---

[916] The term 'contemnor' is defined in Order 14, rule 37 of the *National Court Rules 1983* for the purpose of Division 6 as meaning:

> 'a person guilty or alleged to be guilty of contempt of the Court'.

## PUNISHMENT

### [3.0] GENERAL PRINCIPLES

The task of sentencing, though coming at the end of the trial process in the criminal justice system, is no less important than the other earlier stages of the process. This stage is the sanctioning stage, the enforcement stage and the vindication of the law stage.[917]

The penalty for the offence of 'Contempt of Court, even when it is used to enforce a purely private order, still involves an element of 'public law[918]', in a sense, because respect for the role and authority of the Court, one of the foundations of the 'Rule of Law', is always at issue.[919]

The Supreme Court[920] and the National Court[921] have the power to punish for contempt by virtue of the *Constitution of the Independent State of Papua New Guinea*.

The *National Court Rules 1983* does not fix a maximum punishment for contempt[922] and there is no other law that fixes a minimum or maximum punishment[923].

---

917 See *Peter Luga v Richard Sikani Commissioner, Correctional Services and The State* (2002) N2285.

918 'Public Law' prima facie is the law that governs the actions of bodies designated by statute or by the prerogative where those actions are concerned generally to protect the interests of or to control the activities of the public at large, see *Ereman Ragi and State Services and Statutory Authorities Superannuation Fund Board (Public Officers Superannuation Fund Board) v Joseph Maingu* (1994) SC459, [1994] PGSC 3.

919 See *Vidéotron Ltée v Industries Microlec Produits Électroniques Inc* [1992] 2 SCR 1065 at 1075, [1992] SCC 29.

920 See section 160(2) ['Establishment of the Supreme Court'].

921 See section 163(2) ['Establishment of the National Court'].

922 See *Elias Padura v Stephanie Valakvi* (2012) N4894, [2012] PGNC 254; *Madang Development Corporation Ltd v Rabtrad Niugini Ltd* [2003] PGNC 113, (2003) N5259 and *Bank of South Pacific Ltd v Sekum* [2011] PGNC 176, (2011) N4588.

923 See *Raikos Holdings Ltd v Porche Enterprise Ltd* [2011] PGNC 130, (2011) N4301.

See however: section 23 of the *Constitution of the Independent State of Papua New Guinea* ['Sanctions'].

## PUNISHMENT

When considering that the penalty for the offence of 'Contempt of Court' has no limit in the National and Supreme Courts, the punishment to be ordered is at the sole discretion of the Court[924], but subject to the general sentencing principles[925].[926]

However, the punishment should be commensurate with the offence.[927]

All punishment for offences is fundamentally for the protection of the community, but a Court in discharging its sentencing function should not impose a longer sentence than is otherwise fairly proportionate to the gravity of the offence assessed against its proper background.[928]

Sentences should be such as, having regard to all the proved circumstances, seem at the same time to accord with general community attitudes and to be likely to be a sufficient deterrent both to the offender and others. The circumstances of the offence, i.e. the objective factors, are of paramount importance in determining the gravity of the crime. The circumstances of the contemnor, i.e., the subjective factors, are also vital.[929]

---

[924] See *Public Prosecutor v Nahau Rooney (No. 2)* [1979] PNGLR 448, [1979] PGSC 23; *Luga v Sikani, Commissioner of Correctional Services (No. 2)* [2002] PGNC 60, (2002) N2286 and *Kalip Salo and others on behalf of Lawful Landowners and another v Peter Terry Gerari and others* (2005) N2923.

See also: section 42(1)(b) of the *Constitution of the Independent State of Papua New Guinea* ['Liberty of the Person'].

[925] Refer also to the text titled 'Injia on Sentencing in Papua New Guinea and the Pacific'.

[926] See *The State v Enni Mathew and others (No. 2)* (2003) N2563; *Elias Padura v Stephanie Valakvi* (2012) N4894, [2012] PGNC 254 and *Raikos Holdings Ltd v Porche Enterprise Ltd* [2011] PGNC 130, (2011) N4301.

See also:

- section 42(1)(b) of the *Constitution of the Independent State of Papua New Guinea* ['Liberty of the Person']; and
- *R v Pearce* (1992) 7 WAR 395, per Malcolm CJ at 431 and *Kennedy v Lovell* [2002] WASCA 226.

[927] See *Re Davies* (1888) 21 QBD 236 per Matthew J at 238.

[928] See See *Public Prosecutor v Nahau Rooney (No. 2)* [1979] PNGLR 448, [1979] PGSC 23, per Wilson J.

[929] See See *Public Prosecutor v Nahau Rooney (No. 2)* [1979] PNGLR 448, [1979] PGSC 23, per Wilson J.

## PUNISHMENT

The power to punish for contempt imposes a heavy responsibility upon a Court confronted with a determined challenge to its authority.[930]

Punishment is inflicted for contempt of court involving the depreciation of the Court not for the purpose of protecting either:

- the Court as a whole; or
- the individual judges of the Court

from a repetition of the attack, but for the purpose of protecting the public, and especially those who either voluntarily or by compulsion are subject to the jurisdiction of the Court, from the mischief that will occur if the authority of the Court is undermined or impaired.[931]

Punishment is inflicted for contempt of court involving an attempt to interfere with the due course of justice, not only for the purpose of protecting the Court as a whole and the individual judges, both present and future, from pressures of this kind, but also for the purpose of preserving the right of every litigant to have his or her case determined free from outside interference by an independent and impartial court.[932]

There is no 'victim' in the normal sense.[933]

---

[930] See *Australasian Meat Industry Employees' Union v Mudginberri Station Pty Ltd* (1986) 161 CLR 98, (1986) 66 ALR 577, [1986] HCA 46.

[931] See See *Public Prosecutor v Nahau Rooney (No. 2)* [1979] PNGLR 448, [1979] PGSC 23, per Wilson J.

[932] See See *Public Prosecutor v Nahau Rooney (No. 2)* [1979] PNGLR 448, [1979] PGSC 23, per Wilson J.

[933] See *Kennedy v Lovell* [2002] WASCA 226.

## PUNISHMENT

It is obviously desirable that punishment for contempt, as for other acts and omissions which are criminal or criminal in character should, so far as possible, be imposed by the Courts in a principled and even-handed way. An attempt should be made to ensure consistency between the approach to like cases[934], so that the imposition of penalties, if any, is seen to be coherent and not simply the idiosyncratic opinion of particular judges.[935] However, a minute comparison between the penalties imposed in other cases is not required. This is because the circumstances are infinitely variable as is the impact of different contempts upon the court process.[936]

The chosen sentence must be effective, no more but no less. For, if it is not effective, serious and lasting damage to the fabric of the law may result.[937]

A sentence for contempt is punitive, to vindicate the authority of the Court[938] and may depending on the circumstances be coercive[939].

---

934 See *R v Age Company Ltd* [2000] TASSC 62.

935 See *The State v Foxy Kia Tala; Re Corney Winjan* [1995] PNGLR 303, (1995) N1192; *Re: Contempt of Court; Re: Assistant Registrar, Philip Kaumba* (2004) N2763; *Bewa Tou on his own behalf and on behalf of Isou Clan of Krissa Village, Vanimo, Sandaun Province v Papua New Guinea Forest Authority and others* (2003) N2490 and *The State v Lucas Sasoruo* [1997] PNGLR 676.

See also: *The Age Company Ltd* (2000) 113 A Crim R 181, [2000] TASSC 62; *R v Holman* [2012] TASSC 75 and as commented by Kirby P in *Director of Public Prosecutions v John Fairfax and Sons Ltd* (1987) 8 NSWLR 732 at 742.

Refer also to the section titled 'Comparative Sentences' in this chapter.

936 As explained by Hunt CJ in *Wood v Galea* (1996) 84 A Crim R 274 at 277.

937 See *Australasian Meat Industry Employees' Union v Mudginberri Station Pty Ltd* (1986) 161 CLR 98, (1986) 66 ALR 577, [1986] HCA 46.

938 See *Australasian Meat Industry Employees' Union v Mudginberri Station Pty Ltd* (1986) 161 CLR 98 at 107, (1986) 66 ALR 577, [1986] HCA 46; *Australian Competition and Consumer Commission v INFO4PC.com Pty Ltd* [2002] FCA 949 and *Australian Competition and Consumer Commission v Purple Harmony Plates Pty Ltd (No. 3)* [2002] FCA 1487.

939 See *Lightfoot v Lightfoot* [1989] FCR 305 and *Burton v Winters* [1993] 3 All ER 847, per Lloyd LJ at 850.

## PUNISHMENT

The contempt power's exercise is a delicate one, and care is needed to avoid arbitrary and oppressive conclusions. This rule of caution is more mandatory where the contempt charged has in it the element of personal criticism or attack upon the presiding Judge. The judge must banish the slightest personal impulse to reprisal, but he or she should not bend backwards, and injure the authority of the Court by too greater leniency.[940]

The power to punish for contempt is not for the personal vindication of the judges; the real offence is the wrong done to the public by weakening the authority and influence of the Court which exists for the public good alone.[941]

The stand taken by the judges against the contemptuous remarks and statements is not out of a tender regard for their own feelings and not because they have false idea of their own dignity.[942]

A penalty should not be imposed unless the thing done is of such a nature as to require the arbitrary and summary interference of the Court in order to enable justice to be duly and properly administered without any interruption or interference.[943]

However, the power to punish for contempt should be used sparingly, and only in serious cases.[944]

A legal representative may be banned from appearing for a day or so in order to keep decorum and decency in the Court.[945]

---

[940] See *Peter Luga v Richard Sikani Commissioner, Correctional Services and The State* (2002) N2285 and *Luga v Sikani, Commissioner of Correctional Services (No. 2)* [2002] PGNC 60, (2002) N2286.

See also: *Cooke v United States* 267 US 517 (1925).

[941] See *R v Dunbabin; ex parte Williams* (1935) 52 CLR 248, [1935] HCA 1.

[942] As stated by Saldanha J in *Public Prosecutor v Nahau Rooney (No. 2)* [1979] PNGLR 448 at 482, [1979] PGSC 23.

[943] See *Hunt v Clarke* (1889) 58 LJ (QB) 490, per Cotton LJ at 493 and *R v Payne* [1896] 1 QB 577, per Russell CJ at 581.

[944] See *Parashuram Detaram Shamsdani v King-Emperor* [1945] AC 264 at 270.

[945] See *David Toll v The State* (1989) SC378, [1989] PGSC 1.

See also: *R v O'Neill* (1885) 6 NSWLR 43, per Marton CJ at 45 and *R v Matthews* (1887) 8 NSWLR 45, per Darley CJ at 50.

Upon a term of imprisonment being imposed a contemnor must show 'exceptional circumstances' in order to be granted bail whilst awaiting appeal.[946]

## [4.0] OBJECTIVES AND PURPOSES

In determining the punishment a Court should consider the following objectives and purposes of punishing a contemnor:

- to uphold and protect the effective administration of justice[947];
- to prevent interference with the due administration of justice[948];
- to maintain the supremacy of the law and the due and unobstructed administration of justice[949];
- to protect the public interest in the integrity of the Court and its administration of justice[950];
- to protect the dignity, quietness, and regularity of its proceedings[951];

---

946 See *Dr Jethro Usurup v Sr Dianne Liriope* (2009) SC1040, [2009] PGSC 44.

947 See *Attorney-General v Times Newspapers Ltd* [1973] 3 All ER 54, [1974] AC 273.

See also: *Australasian Meat Industry Employees Union v Mudginberri Station Pty Ltd* (1986) 161 CLR 98 at 107, (1986) 66 ALR 577 at 584, (1986) 66 ALR 577, [1986] HCA 46; *R v West Australian Newspapers Ltd; ex parte Director of Public Prosecutions (WA)* (1996) 16 WAR 518; *Miller v Eurovox Pty Ltd* [2004] VSCA 211 and *Registrar of the Court of Appeal v Maniam (No. 2)* (1992) 26 NSWLR 309 at 313.

948 See *Helmore v Smith (No. 2)* (1886) 35 Ch D 449, per Bowen LJ.

See also:
- *Commissioner of Taxation v De Vonk* (1995) 61 FCR 564, per Foster J at 569 and *Attorney-General v Times Newspapers Ltd and another* [1991] 2 All ER 398, [1991] 2 WLR 994, [1992] 1 AC 191, per Ackner LJ at 209; and
- Australian Law Reform Commission, 1987, 'Contempt', Report No. 35, p. 16.

949 See *Ruby Moy and others v Chan Luen Ying and another* [1964] HKLR 579 at 587.

950 See *Bewa Tou on his own behalf and on behalf of Isou Clan of Krissa Village, Vanimo, Sandaun Province v Papua New Guinea Forest Authority and others* (2003) N2490.

951 See *Petrie v Angus* (1889) 2 White 358, per Lord Justice Clerk Macdonald.

- to prevent defiance of its orders[952];
- to vindicate the integrity of the Court and of its proceedings[953];
- to protect the integrity of its operations[954];
- to keep the course of Justice free for by the exercise of them law and order prevails[955];
- to punish acts of contempt so as to maintain the dignity and authority of the Court and to ensure a fair trial[956];
- to ensure that justice will be done and solely to this end, it prohibits acts and words tending to obstruct the administration of justice[957];
- to ensure that justice shall be done by prohibiting acts and words tending to obstruct the administration of justice[958], either in a particular case or more generally as a continuing process in the case of criminal contempts[959];

---

952 See *Petrie v Angus* (1889) 2 White 358, per Lord Justice Clerk Macdonald.

953 See *Ex parte Ferandez* [1861] EngR 556, [1861] 30 LJCP 321 at 332 and *Skipworth's case* (1873) LR 9 QB 219 at 232.

See also: *Balanto* [1963] SRNSW 200 at 202 and *Anthony Radcliffe Lewis v His Honour Judge Ogden* (1984) 153 CLR 682 at 688, [1984] HCA 26.

954 See *Commissioner of Taxation v De Vonk* (1995) 61 FCR 564, per Foster J at 569.

See also: Australian Law Reform Commission, 1987, 'Contempt', Report No. 35, p. 16.

955 As stated by Dodds CJ in *R v Fowler* (1905) 1 Tas LR 53 at 56.

956 See *Balogh v Crown Court at Saint Albans* [1974] 3 All ER 283, per Denning LJ at 288, [1975] QB 73.

See also: *British Columbia Government Employees Union v British Columbia (Attorney-General)* [1988] 2 SCR 214, per Dickson CJ at 238, [1988] SCC 3.

957 See *The State v Foxy Kia Tala, Re Detective Constable Corney Winjan* [1995] PNGLR 303.

See also: *Jennison v Baker* [1972] 2 QB 52, per Salmon LJ at 61.

958 As stated by Salmon LJ in *Jennison v Baker* [1972] 2 QB 52 at 61.

959 As stated by Diplock LJ in *Attorney-General v Leveller Magazine Ltd and others* [1979] AC 440 at 449.

- to preserve and protect the general community interest, not the Court's own dignity[960], in suppressing unjustifiable interference in the authority of the Courts of the land[961];

- to ensure that justice shall be done and solely to this end, it prohibits acts and words tending to obstruct the administration of justice[962];

- to secure a better and more secure administration of justice. Every writing, letter or publication which has for its object to divert the course of justice is a contempt of the Court[963];

- to protect the authority of the Courts and preserve the impartial administration of justice[964];

- to uphold the undisturbed and orderly administration of justice in the Courts according to law[965];

---

960 See *Helmore v Smith (No. 2)* (1886) 35 Ch D 449, per Bowen LJ.

961 See *Paul Metta v The State* [1992] PNGLR 176 at 184 and *Andrew Kwimberi of Paulus M Dowa Lawyers v The State* (1998) SC545, [1998] PGSC 9.

See also: *Attorney-General v Times Newspapers Ltd* [1973] 3 All ER 54, [1974] AC 273 at 302.

962 See *Pioneers Health Services Limited v Gabriel Yer, Secretary of Department of Finance and The State* (2008) N3326.

See also: *Jennison v Baker* [1972] QB 52 at 61; *Gisborne Herald Co Ltd v Solicitor-General* [1995] 3 NZLR 563 and *Solicitor-General v Radio Avon Ltd* [1978] 1 NZLR 225 at 229.

963 As stated by Cottenham LC in *Re Ludlow Charities; Mr Lechmere Charlton's Case* (1837) 2 My and Cr 316 at 339, [1837] EngR 524, (1837) 40 ER 661 at 670.

964 See *R v David Syme and Co* [1982] VicRp 16, [1982] VR 173.

965 See *C v Registrar, Court of Appeal No. Ca 40130/94 Contempt* [1996] NSWSC 103; *Director of Public Prosecutions v John Fairfax and Sons Ltd* (1987) 8 NSWLR 732 at 741; *Kennedy v Lovell* [2002] WASCA 226; *Phelan* (1993) 66 A Crim R 446 at 449; *GDR* (1994) 35 NSWLR 376 at 378, (1994) 75 A Crim R 319 at 321; *Wood v Staunton (No. 5)* (1995) 86 A Crim R 183; *Registrar of the Court of Appeal v Maniam (No. 2)* (1992) 26 NSWLR 309, per Kirby P at 314 and *Pelechowski v The Registrar of the Court of Appeal of New South Wales* (1999) 198 CLR 435, per McHugh J at 462 and Kirby J at 484, [1999] HCA 19.

- to punish other acts which impede the administration of justice, such as obstructing proceedings in court while it is sitting or publishing comments on a pending case, which have both been described as 'criminal contempt'[966];

- to enforce the process and orders of the Court, disobedience to which has been described as 'civil contempt'[967];

- to deter the contemnor (specific deterrence[968]) from committing contemptuous behavior again;

---

[966] See *Australasian Meat Industry Employees' Union and others v Mudginberri Station Pty Ltd* (1986) 161 CLR 98 at 106, (1986) 66 ALR 577, [1986] HCA 46.

See also: J Fox, 1927, 'History of Contempt of Court', p. 1.

[967] See *Australasian Meat Industry Employees' Union and others v Mudginberri Station Pty Ltd* (1986) 161 CLR 98 at 106, (1986) 66 ALR 577, [1986] HCA 46 and *Witham v Holloway* (1995) 183 CLR 525 at 533, (1995) 131 ALR 401, (1995) 69 ALJR 847, [1995] HCA 3.

See also: J Fox, 1927, 'History of Contempt of Court', p. 1.

[968] See *Public Prosecutor v Nahau Rooney (No. 2)* [1979] PNGLR 448, [1979] PGSC 23, per Wilson J; *The State v Foxy Kia Tala; Re Corney Winjan* [1995] PNGLR 303, (1995) N1192; *Bewa Tou on his own behalf and on behalf of Isou Clan of Krissa Village, Vanimo, Sandaun Province v Papua New Guinea Forest Authority and others* (2003) N2490; *Kapil Salo and others v Peter Terry Gerari and others* (2005) N2923 and *The State v Lucas Sasoruo* [1997] PNGLR 676.

See also: *C v Registrar, Court of Appeal No. Ca 40130/94 Contempt* [1996] NSWSC 103; *Registrar of the Court of Appeal v Maniam (No. 2)* (1992) 26 NSWLR 309 at 314; *Director of Public Prosecutions v John Fairfax and Sons Ltd* (1987) 8 NSWLR 732 at 741; *Phelan* (1993) 66 A Crim R 446 at 449; *GDR* (1994) 35 NSWLR 376 at 378, (1994) 75 A Crim R 319 at 321; *Wood v Staunton (No. 5)* (1995) 86 A Crim R 183; *Kennedy v Lovell* [2002] WASCA 226; *Principal Registrar of the Supreme Court v Jando* (2001) 53 NSWLR 527, (2001) 125 A Crim R 473, [2001] NSWSC 969; *Haritopoulos Pty Ltd and another v Scott and others* [2007] VSCA 174; *R v Duncan* [2000] NSWSC 440; *Registrar of the Supreme Court v Nationwide News Ltd* (2004) 89 SASR 113 at 123, [2004] SASC 223; *Chief Executive Officer, Department of Environment and Conversation v Szulc* [2010] WASC 195; *Corruption and Crime Commission v Allbeury, Silvestro, Chikonga, Smith (No. 2)* [2011] WASC 26; *Australian Securities and Investments Commission v Michalik* (2004) 52 ACSR 115, [2004] NSWSC 1259; *Commissioner for the Police Integrity Commission v Walker* [2006] NSWSC 964; *Trad v Pickles Auction Pty Ltd; In the Matter of Carl Trad* [2006] NSWSC 1177; *Principal Registrar of Supreme Court v Tran* [2006] NSWSC 1183; *Dental Board of Australia v Traianou* [2011] WASC 293; *Legal Practice Board v Tee* [2009] WASC 5; *Registrar of the Court of Appeal v Gilby* [1991] NSWCA 235; *Legal Services Board v Forster (No. 3)* [2012] VSC 640; *Director of Public Prosecutions v Johnson* [2002] VSC 583; *R v General Television Corporation Pty Ltd* [2009] VSC 84; *R v The Herald and Weekly Times Pty Ltd and another* [2008] VSC 251; *R v The Herald and Weekly Times Ltd* [2009] VSC 85; *R v Vasiliou (No. 2)* [2012] VSC 242 and *Bydand Holdings Pty Ltd v Pineland Property Holdings Pty Ltd and others* [2009] NSWSC 584.

- to deter other possible contemnors (general deterrence[969]) in the future from committing like contempts; and

- to publicly denounce the contemptuous conduct[970].

[969] See *Public Prosecutor v Nahau Rooney (No. 2)* [1979] PNGLR 448, [1979] PGSC 23, per Wilson J; *The State v Foxy Kia Tala; Re Corney Winjan* [1995] PNGLR 303, (1995) N1192; *Re: Contempt of Court; Re: Assistant Registrar, Philip Kaumba* (2004) N2763; *Kapil Salo and others v Peter Terry Gerari and others* (2005) N2923; *Bewa Tou on his own behalf and on behalf of Isou Clan of Krissa Village, Vanimo, Sandaun Province v Papua New Guinea Forest Authority and others* (2003) N2490 and *The State v Lucas Sasoruo* [1997] PNGLR 676.

See also: *C v Registrar, Court of Appeal No. Ca 40130/94 Contempt* [1996] NSWSC 103; *Registrar of the Court of Appeal v Maniam (No. 2)* (1992) 26 NSWLR 309 at 314; *Director of Public Prosecutions v John Fairfax and Sons Ltd* (1987) 8 NSWLR 732 at 741; *Phelan* (1993) 66 A Crim R 446 at 449; *GDR* (1994) 35 NSWLR 376 at 378, (1994) 75 A Crim R 319 at 321; *Wood v Staunton (No. 5)* (1995) 86 A Crim R 183; *Kennedy v Lovell* [2002] WASCA 226, *Principal Registrar of the Supreme Court v Jando* (2001) 53 NSWLR 527, (2001) 125 A Crim R 473, [2001] NSWSC 969; *Haritopoulos Pty Ltd and another v Scott and others* [2007] VSCA 174; *R v Duncan* [2000] NSWSC 440; *Director of Public Prosecutions (Commonwealth) v United Telecasters Sydney Ltd* (1992) 7 BR 364, per Kirby P at 376; *Director of Public Prosecutions v Wran* (1986) 7 NSWLR 616 at 629 and 636; *Hinch v Attorney-General* [1987] VicRp 62, [1987] VR 721 at 733 and 750; *Registrar of the Supreme Court v Nationwide News Ltd* (2004) 89 SASR 113 at 123, [2004] SASC 223; *Commissioner for the Police Integrity Commission v Walker* [2006] NSWSC 964; *Trad v Pickles Auction Pty Ltd; In the Matter of Carl Trad* [2006] NSWSC 1177; *Principal Registrar of Supreme Court v Tran* [2006] NSWSC 1177; *Australian Securities and Investments Commission v Michalik* (2004) 52 ACSR 115, [2004] NSWSC 1259; *Chief Executive Officer, Department of Environment and Conversation v Szulc* [2010] WASC 195; *Corruption and Crime Commission v Allbeury, Silvestro, Chikonga, Smith (No. 2)* [2011] WASC 26; *Dental Board of Australia v Traianou* [2011] WASC 293; *Legal Practice Board v Tee* [2009] WASC 5; *Registrar of the Court of Appeal v Gilby* [1991] NSWCA 235; *Legal Services Board v Forster (No. 3)* [2012] VSC 640; *Director of Public Prosecutions v Johnson* [2002] VSC 583; *R v General Television Corporation Pty Ltd* [2009] VSC 84; *R v The Herald and Weekly Times Pty Ltd and another* [2008] VSC 251; *R v The Herald and Weekly Times Ltd* [2009] VSC 85; *R v Vasiliou (No. 2)* [2012] VSC 242 and *Bydand Holdings Pty Ltd v Pineland Property Holdings Pty Ltd and others* [2009] NSWSC 584.

[970] See *Director of Public Prosecutions v John Fairfax and Sons Ltd* (1987) 8 NSWLR 732 at 741; *C v Registrar, Court of Appeal No. Ca 40130/94 Contempt* [1996] NSWSC 103; *Principal Registrar of the Supreme Court v Jando* (2001) 53 NSWLR 527, (2001) 125 A Crim R 473, [2001] NSWSC 969; *Kennedy v Lovell* [2002] WASCA 226; *R v Duncan* [2000] NSWSC 440; *Chief Executive Officer, Department of Environment and Conversation v Szulc* [2010] WASC 195; *Corruption and Crime Commission v Allbeury, Silvestro, Chikonga, Smith (No. 2)* [2011] WASC 26; *Australian Securities and Investments Commission v Michalik* (2004) 52 ACSR 115, [2004] NSWSC 1259; *Dental Board of Australia v Traianou* [2011] WASC 293; *Legal Practice Board v Tee* [2009] WASC 5; *Registrar of the Court of Appeal v Gilby* [1991] NSWCA 235; *Legal Services Board v Forster (No. 3)* [2012] VSC 640; *Director of Public Prosecutions* v *Johnson* [2002] VSC 583; *R v Vasiliou (No. 2)* [2012] VSC 242; *Bydand Holdings Pty Ltd v Pineland Property Holdings Pty Ltd and others* [2009] NSWSC 584; *Registrar of the Court of Appeal v Maniam (No. 2)* (1992) 26 NSWLR 309 and *Director of Public Prosecutions (Cth) v United Telecasters Sydney Ltd* (1992) 7 BR 364 at 376.

## [5.0] PRACTICE AND PROCEDURE

'Contempt of Court' is a serious offence that should be approached, as far as possible, in a way which is consistent with that adopted when dealing with criminal conduct generally.[971]

The standard of proof used in deciding factual matters for the purpose of imposing a sentence for contempt of court should be the same as is used in imposing a sentence in criminal matters[972], including aggravating features relevant to penalty such as the question whether the conduct constituted a 'contumacious' breach of an order or undertaking[973].

## [6.0] NATURAL JUSTICE

The allocutus is a part of the Court's duty to act fairly and, in principle, to be seen to act fairly. Failure to administer an allocutus can nullify the sentence.[974]

---

[971] See *Varnavides v Victorian Civil and Administrative Tribunal and another* [2005] VSCA 231; *Registrar of the Court of Appeal v Maniam (No. 2)* (1992) 26 NSWLR 309 at 314; *Attorney-General (NSW) v Whiley* (1993) 31 NSWLR 314 at 320 and *Bydand Holdings Pty Ltd v Pineland Property Holdings Pty Ltd and others* [2009] NSWSC 584.

Refer also to the text titled 'Injia on Sentencing in Papua New Guinea and the Pacific'.

[972] See *NCR Australia Pty Ltd v Credit Connection Pty Ltd* [2005] NSWSC 1118.

[973] See *Primelife Corp Ltd v Newpark Pty Ltd* [2003] VSC 106 and *Pico Holdings Inc v Voss* [2002] VSC 319.

[974] See *Tom Longman Yaul v The State* (2005) SC803, [2005] PGSC 29; *Moses Aikaba v Tami* [1971-72] PNGLR 155; *Agiru Aieni and Others v Paul T Tahain* [1978] PNGLR 37 and *Michael Gende v The State* (1999) SC626.

## PUNISHMENT

Applying a rule of 'natural justice' a contemnor is entitled to be heard on penalty or punishment before it is imposed.[975]

## [7.0] SENTENCES

### [7.1] INTRODUCTION

At common law, the Court has the power in respect of a criminal contempt to both fine and impose a term of imprisonment and in an appropriate case, to order the giving of security for good behaviour.[976]

Traditionally, the sentencing options available to a Court at common law depended upon whether or not the disobedience was contumacious. 'Mere' disobedience attracted the sentence of open-handed imprisonment or sequestration of assets, whereas contumacious disobedience was punishable by fixed term imprisonment. A fine was not considered to be an appropriate sanction for any form of civil contempt.[977]

Such a power has long been part of the coercive power of the Courts.[978]

---

[975] See *SCR No. 3 of 1984; Ex parte Callick and Koroma* [1985] PNGLR 67 at 70, [1985] PGSC 20 and *Andrew Kwimberi of Paulus M Dowa Lawyers v The State* (1998) SC545, [1998] PGSC 9.

See also:
- *Mc Keown v R* (1971) 16 DLR (3rd) 390, per Laskin J at 398; *Zakanovich v Magistrates Court of Victoria at Moorabbin* (2011) 32 VR 216, [2011] VSC 141; *Castle City Pty Ltd v New Vintage Nominees Pty Ltd* [2003] WASCA 30; *In re Pollard* [1868] LR 2 PC 106 at 120; *Coward v Stapleton* (1953) 90 CLR 573 at 579, [1953] HCA 48; *Anthony Radcliffe Lewis v His Honour Judge Ogden* (1984) 153 CLR 682 at 693, [1984] HCA 26; *MacGroarty v Clauson* (1989) 167 CLR 251 at 255, (1989) 86 ALR 513, [1989] HCA 34; *Gliosca v Ninyett* (1992) 10 WAR 562, per Murray J at 56; *Balogh v Crown Court at Saint Albans* [1974] 3 All ER 283, [1975] QB 73 and *Re K* [1983] 78 Cr App R 82; and
- section 59(2) of the *Constitution of the Independent State of Papua New Guinea* ['Principles of Natural Justice'].

[976] See *Skipworth's Case* [1873] LR 9 QB 230 and *Morris v The Crown Office* [1970] 1 All ER 1079, [1970] 2 QB 114, per Lord Denning MR at 125.

[977] See *Peter Luga v Richard Sikani Commissioner, Correctional Services and The State* (2002) N2285.

[978] See *Bakir v Doueihi and others* [2001] QSC 414.

## PUNISHMENT

### [7.2] INDIVIDUAL

The National and Supreme Court may punish contempt committed by an individual by the imposition of:

- a term of imprisonment[979];
- the payment of a fine[980]; or
- both[981].

### [7.3] CORPORATION

The National and Supreme Court may punish contempt committed by a corporation by:

- sequestration;
- the imposition of a fine[982]; or
- both.

---

[979] See however: Order 14, rule 50 ['Discharge'].

[980] See *Milupol Development Corporation Ltd v Garai* [2012] PGNC 29, (2012) N4635 and *Bank of South Pacific Ltd v Anton Sekum and others* (2011) N4588.

[981] See Order 14, rule 49(1) ['Punishment'].

See also: section 42(1)(b) of the *Constitution of the Independent State of Papua New Guinea* ['Liberty of the Person'].

[982] See *Newsat Ltd v Telikom PNG Ltd* [2008] PGNC 227, (2008) N3673 and *Raikos Holdings Ltd v Porche Enterprise Ltd* [2011] PGNC 130, (2011) N4301.

## [8.0] IMPRISONMENT

### [8.1] NATIONAL COURT RULES

Order 14, Rule 50 of the *National Court Rules 1983* ['Discharge'] states:

> 'Where a contemnor is committed to prison for a term, the Court may order his discharge before the expiry of the term'.

### [8.2] GENERAL PRINCIPLES

There is theoretically, at common law, no limit as to the length of the term of imprisonment that may be imposed.[983]

The *National Court Rules 1983* does not fix a maximum punishment for contempt[984] and there is no other law that fixes a minimum or maximum punishment[985].

When considering that the penalty for the offence of 'Contempt of Court' has no limit in the National and Supreme Courts, the punishment to be ordered is at the sole discretion of the Court, but subject to the general sentencing principles[986].[987]

---

[983] See *Registrar v Maniam (No. 2)* (1992) 26 NSWLR 309, per Kirby J at 314; *Attorney General (NSW) v Whiley* (1993) 31 NSWLR 314 at 320; *Gallagher v Durack* (1983) 152 CLR 238, per Murphy J at 249, (1982) 44 ALR 272, [1983] HCA 2 and *Re Colina; ex parte Torney* (1999) 200 CLR 386 at 429, (1999) 73 ALJR 1576, (1999) 166 ALR 545, [1999] HCA 57.

See also: Australian Law Reform Commission, 1987, 'Contempt', Report No. 35, p. 299.

[984] See *Elias Padura v Stephanie Valakvi* (2012) N4894, [2012] PGNC 254; *Madang Development Corporation Ltd v Rabtrad Niugini Ltd* [2003] PGNC 113, (2003) N5259 and *Bank of South Pacific Ltd v Sekum* [2011] PGNC 176, (2011) N4588.

[985] See *Raikos Holdings Ltd v Porche Enterprise Ltd* [2011] PGNC 130, (2011) N4301.

See however: section 23 of the *Constitution of the Independent State of Papua New Guinea* ['Sanctions'].

[986] Refer also to the text titled 'Injia on Sentencing in Papua New Guinea and the Pacific'.

[987] See *The State v Enni Mathew and others (No. 2)* (2003) N2563.

See also: section 42(1)(b) of the *Constitution of the Independent State of Papua New Guinea* ['Liberty of the Person'].

However, it is arguable that the unexpressed limits derived from constitutional principles prevent the imposition of an excessive term of imprisonment if this amounts to a cruel and unusual punishment.[988]

Furthermore, it is also established that such a contemnor should not be kept in custody for any period longer than would be appropriate as punishment for the contempt without regard to coercion.[989]

Imprisonment for 'Contempt of Court' should only be imposed where a serious contempt has been committed.[990]

In deciding whether an act of contempt is serious enough to warrant imprisonment, the following factors are determinative:

- the likely interference with the due administration of justice; and
- the culpability of the contemnor.[991]

---

[988] See *Registrar v Maniam (No. 2)* (1992) 26 NSWLR 309, per Kirby J at 314; *Smith v R* (1991) 25 NSWLR 1 and *Gallagher v Durack* (1983) 152 CLR 238, per Murphy J at 249, (1982) 44 ALR 272, [1983] HCA 2.

See also: section 36(1) of the *Constitution of the Independent State of Papua New Guinea* ['Freedom From Inhuman Treatment'].

[989] See *Re Barrell Enterprises* [1973] 1 WLR 19 at 27.

See also: *Wood v Galea* (1997) 92 A Crim R 287 at 288 and *Enfield London Borough Council v Mahoney* [1983] 1 WLR 749 at 755.

[990] See *Public Prosecutor v Nahau Rooney (No. 2)* [1979] PNGLR 448, [1979] PGSC 23, per Wilson J.

See for example, *Peter Terry Gerari and others v Kalip Salo and others* (2009) SC1009.

See also: *Varnavides v VCAT* (2005) 12 VR 1 at 12, [2005] VSCA 231; *Haritopoulos Pty Ltd and another v Scott and others* [2007] VSCA 174 and *Registrar, Court of Appeal v Maniam (No. 2)* (1992) 26 NSWLR 309 at 313.

[991] See *Public Prosecutor v Nahau Rooney (No. 2)* [1979] PNGLR 448, [1979] PGSC 23.

See also: *R v Thomson Newspapers Ltd* [1968] 1 All ER 268 at 269 and *Re Application by the Attorney General of Fiji* [2009] FJHC 8.

## PUNISHMENT

In the case of attacks upon the Court or its members, the summary remedy of a fine or imprisonment is applied only where the Court is satisfied that it is necessary in the interests of the ordered and fearless administration of justice and where the attacks are unwarrantable.[992]

In criminal contempt, which involves interference with the administration of justice, a term of imprisonment is generally called for.[993]

In the case of persons found guilty of wilfully disobeying a subpoena to attend court as a witness, and especially in criminal proceedings, it is by no means unusual for a custodial sentence to be imposed.[994]

### [9.0] FINE

There is theoretically, at common law, no limit as to the amount of the fine that may be imposed.[995]

The *National Court Rules 1983* does not fix a maximum punishment for contempt[996] and there is no other law that fixes a minimum or maximum punishment[997].

---

[992] See *Bell v Stewart* (1920) 28 CLR 419, per Isaacs and Rich JJ at 429, [1920] HCA 68.

[993] See *R v Montgomery* [1995] 2 All ER 28 at 32.

[994] See *R v Sergiou* (1983) 5 Cr App R (S) 227 and *Kennedy v Lovell* [2002] WASCA 226.

[995] See *Re Colina* (1999) 166 ALR 545, [1999] HCA 57.

[996] See *Elias Padura v Stephanie Valakvi* (2012) N4894, [2012] PGNC 254; *Madang Development Corporation Ltd v Rabtrad Niugini Ltd* [2003] PGNC 113, (2003) N5259 and *Bank of South Pacific Ltd v Sekum* [2011] PGNC 176, (2011) N4588.

[997] See *Raikos Holdings Ltd v Porche Enterprise Ltd* [2011] PGNC 130, (2011) N4301.

See however: section 23 of the *Constitution of the Independent State of Papua New Guinea* ['Sanctions'].

## PUNISHMENT

When considering that the penalty for the offence of 'Contempt of Court' has no limit in the National and Supreme Courts, the punishment to be ordered is at the sole discretion of the Court, but subject to the general sentencing principles[998].[999]

Not every case of a wilful and deliberate interference in the administration of justice should attract a custodial sentence. Sometimes it is sufficient to impose a substantial fine, at least where there are circumstances which:

- explain the behavior; or
- tend to mitigate its seriousness.[1000]

Where the contemnor is bankrupt a fine is considered to be an inappropriate or inadequate sentence.[1001]

If the corporation is large the Court should consider the laws that govern the business and affairs of the corporation and determine what penalties are available for offences against those laws.[1002]

A fine should not be imposed on a corporation that will have an adverse impact.[1003]

---

[998] Refer also to the text titled 'Injia on Sentencing in Papua New Guinea and the Pacific'.

[999] See *The State v Enni Mathew and others (No. 2)* (2003) N2563.

See also: section 42(1)(b) of the *Constitution of the Independent State of Papua New Guinea* ['Liberty of the Person'].

[1000] See *New South Wales Egg Corporation v Peek* (1987) 10 NSWLR 72 at 84 and *Kennedy v Lovell* [2002] WASCA 226.

[1001] See *Australian Competition and Consumer Commission v Levi (No. 3)* [2008] FCA 1586; *Commissioner for Fair Trading v TLC Consulting Services Pty Ltd and others* [2011] QSC 374; *City Hall Albury Wodonga Pty Ltd and others v Chicago Investments Pty Ltd and others* [2006] QSC 31 and *Lade and Co Pty Ltd v Slack* [2006] 2 Qd R 531, [2006] QCA 294.

[1002] See *Newsat Limited v Telikom PNG Ltd and others* (2008) N3673, [2008] PGNC 227.

[1003] See *Newsat Limited v Telikom PNG Ltd and others* (2008) N3673, [2008] PGNC 227.

## PUNISHMENT

### [10.0] SEQUESTRATION

Sequestration is a process of the law of contempt.[1004]

Historically, a writ of sequestration was an old weapon of the Chancery Court to compel a party's obedience to mesne process or a decree and used for the purpose of enforcing compliance with such processes or decrees, rather than to punish disobedience.[1005]

Having regard to the important public interest that the armoury of remedies available to a superior court is designed to serve, there is no reason in principle why the undoubted power to order the sequestration of assets of a contemnor should not be employed to aid the effectiveness of other remedies to which resort may have been had.[1006]

Sequestration lies at the top end of the scale of severity in the means by which Courts can enforce their orders.[1007]

Sequestration should however be reserved for cases of extreme contempt or perhaps where a corporation does not have the financial capacity to pay a fine.[1008]

Sequestration entails the Court sanctioned seizure of the contemnor's assets.[1009]

Sequestration of the assets of a contemnor may be ordered by the Court as a means of coercing the contemnor to comply with the order.[1010]

---

[1004] See *Pratt v Inman* (1889) 43 Ch D 175, per Chitty LJ at 179.

[1005] See *Australian Consolidated Press Ltd v Morgan* (1965) 112 CLR 483, per Windeyer J at 501, [1965] HCA 21.

[1006] See *Australasian Meat Industry Employees' Union v Mudginberri Station Pty Ltd* (1986) 161 CLR 98 at 115, (1986) 66 ALR 577, [1986] HCA 46.

[1007] See *Howitt Transport v Transport and General Workers' Union* [1973] ICR 1, per Donaldson J at 11; *Showeering Ltd v Fern Vale Brewery* [1958] RPC 462 and *Quality Pizzas v Canterbury Hotel Employees' Industrial Union v Industrial Union* [1983] NZLR 612, per Richardson J at 617.

[1008] See *Newsat Limited v Telikom PNG Ltd and others* (2008) N3673, [2008] PGNC 227.

[1009] See *Raikos Holdings Ltd v Porche Enterprise Ltd* [2011] PGNC 130, (2011) N4301.

[1010] See *Australian Consolidated Press Ltd v Morgan* (1965) 112 CLR 483, per Windeyer J at 501, [1965] HCA 21.

See also: Australian Law Reform Commission, 1987, 'Contempt', Report No. 35, p. 299 and G Borrie and N Lowe, 1996, 'The Law of Contempt' 3rd ed., Butterworths, London, p. 606.

A writ of sequestration is directed to named sequestrators who are required to take possession of the contemnor's property and to retain it until the contempt has been purged and the Court has made appropriate orders.[1011]

The writ binds real and personal property from the time it is issued.[1012]

It places property belonging to the contemnor temporarily into the hands of sequestrators who, in the case of land, manage the property and receive the rents and profits.[1013]

When the property of the contemnor is actually sequestered and held under sequestration it is not confiscated.[1014]

The contemnor is deprived of the enjoyment of his or her rents and profits for the duration of the sequestration; but he or she does not forfeit the property in them.[1015]

When whatever is considered necessary to clear the contempt has been done, the sequestration is discharged by order of the Court and the sequestrators must then give up possession on having their costs and expenses.[1016]

By its nature, the writ of sequestration is available only for a civil contempt, ie., disobedience of, or non-compliance with, a judgment or order of the court, and not for a criminal contempt.[1017]

---

[1011] See *Australian Consolidated Press Ltd v Morgan* (1965) 112 CLR 483, per Windeyer J at 498, [1965] HCA 21; *Con-Mech (Engineers) Ltd v Amalgamated Union of Engineering Workers (Engineering Section)* [1973] ICR 620, per Donaldson J at 627 and *Trade Practices Commission v C G Smith Pty Ltd* (1978) 30 FLR 368, per Bowen CJ at 379, [1978] FCA 2.

[1012] See *Dixon v Rowe* (1876) 35 LT 548.

[1013] See *Australian Consolidated Press Ltd v Morgan* (1965) 112 CLR 483, per Windeyer J at 498, [1965] HCA 21.

See also: G Borrie and N Lowe, 1996, 'The Law of Contempt' 3rd ed., Butterworths, London, p. 606.

[1014] See *Australian Consolidated Press Ltd v Morgan* (1965) 112 CLR 483, per Windeyer J at 498, [1965] HCA 21.

[1015] See *Australian Consolidated Press Ltd v Morgan* (1965) 112 CLR 483, per Windeyer J at 498, [1965] HCA 21.

[1016] See *Australian Consolidated Press Ltd v Morgan* (1965) 112 CLR 483, per Windeyer J at 498, [1965] HCA 21.

[1017] See J Jacob, 'Sequestration for Contempt of Court', (1986), 39 Current Legal Problems 219, p. 220 and C O'Reagan, 'Contempt of Court and the Enforcement of Labour Injunctions', (1991), 54 Modern Law Review 385, p. 388.

It only lies against a person actually in contempt.[1018]

A writ of sequestration may be issued to enforce a fine imposed on a finding of contempt.[1019]

A writ of sequestration should not be issued in relation to the occurrence of a future uncertain event.[1020]

## [11.0] SUSPENDED SENTENCE

## [11.1] STATUTORY PROVISION

**Rule 49 Punishment**

'(1) Where the contemnor is not a corporation, the Court may punish contempt by committal to prison or fine or both.

(2) Where the contemnor is a corporation the Court may punish contempt by sequestration or fine or both.

(3) The Court may make an order for punishment on terms, including a suspension of punishment or a suspension of punishment where the contemnor gives security in such manner and in such sum as the Court may approve for good behaviour and performs the terms of the security'.

---

[1018] See *IRC v Hoogstraten* [1984] 3 All ER 25.

See however: *Webster v Southwark LBC* [1983] QB 698, although that case has been been questioned, see G Borrie and N Lowe, 1996, 'The Law of Contempt' 3rd ed., Butterworths, London, p. 606.

[1019] See *Australasian Meat Industry Employees' Union v Mudginberri Station Pty Ltd* (1986) 161 CLR 98, (1986) 66 ALR 577, [1986] HCA 46.

[1020] See *In re Lumley; ex parte Cathcart* (1894) 2 Ch 271 at 272; *Hulbert and Crowe v Cathcart* [1894] 1 QB 244 at 246 and *Lee v Walker* [1985] QB 1191 at 1200.

## PUNISHMENT

### [11.2] GENERAL PRINCIPLES

A Court may make an order for punishment on terms, including:

- a suspension of punishment[1021]; or
- a suspension of punishment where the contemnor gives security in such manner and in such sum as the Court may approve for good behavior and performs the terms of the security.[1022]

### [12.0] SENTENCING FACTORS

### [12.1] INTRODUCTION

When considering whether to punish a contemnor and, if so, the nature of that punishment, the factors that a Court should consider include:

- the objectives or purposes of sentencing a contemnor;
- the need to uphold and protect the effective administration of justice[1023];
- what punishment is required to express the Court's denunciation of the contempt[1024];

---

[1021] At common law, see:

- *Morris v The Crown Office* [1970] 1 All ER 1079, [1970] 2 QB 114, per Lord Denning MR at 125; *Harris v Muirhead* [1993] 2 Qd R 527; *Villiers v Villiers* [1994] 1 WLR 493 at 498; *Resolute Ltd and another v Warnes* [2001] WASCA 4; *Australasian Meat Industry Employees' Union v Mudginberri Station Pty Ltd* (1986) 161 CLR 98, (1986) 66 ALR 577, [1986] HCA 46; *Martin v Trustram (No. 3)* [2003] TASSC 80; *Doyle v London Guarantee Co* (1907) 204 US 599, [1907] USSC 38; *Con-Mech (Engineers) Ltd v Amalgamated Union of Engineering Workers (Engineering Section)* [1973] ICR 620; *Australian Competition and Consumer Commission v Goldstar Corp Pty Ltd* [1998] FCA 1441; *Lee v Walker* [1985] 1 All ER 781, [1985] QB 1191 and the observations of Munby J in *Harris v Harris* [2001] EWCA Civ 714, [2001] 3 WLR 765 at 774; and
- CJ Miller, 1976, 'Contempt of Court', p 12.

[1022] See Order 14, rule 49(3) ['Punishment'].

[1023] See *Australasian Meat Industry Employees' Union v Mudginberri Station Pty Ltd* (1986) 161 CLR 98 at 107, (1986) 66 ALR 577, [1986] HCA 46.

[1024] See *Buckby and another v Wharton and another* [2012] QSC 416; *Australian Securities and Investments Commission v Michalik* (2004) 52 ACSR 115, [2004] NSWSC 1259 and *Bydand Holdings Pty Ltd v Pineland Property Holdings Pty Ltd and others* [2009] NSWSC 584.

- the importance of bringing home to the contemnor the seriousness of the contempt[1025];
- vindication of the Court's authority[1026];
- the jurisdiction to commit for contempt exists so that the authority of the Courts can be maintained[1027];
- the circumstances of the offence[1028];
- the state of mind and subjective intention of the contemnor.[1029]

  The presence or absence of a specific intent to interfere in the administration of justice is certainly relevant to penalty.[1030]

---

1025 See *Australian Competition and Consumer Commission v World Netsafe Pty Ltd and another* [2003] FCA 1501; *Australian Competition and Consumer Commission v Hughes* (2001) ATPR 41-807, [2001] FCA 38; *Australian Competition and Consumer Commission v Info4PCCom Pty Ltd* (2002) 121 FCR 24, [2002] FCA 949 and *Commissioner for Fair Trading v TLC Consulting Services Pty Ltd and others* [2011] QSC 374.

1026 See *Registrar of Court of Appeal v Maniam (No. 2)* (1992) 26 NSWLR 309 at 314 and *Registrar of the Supreme Court v Nationwide News Ltd* (2004) 89 SASR 113 at 123, [2004] SASC 223.

1027 As observed by McHugh J in *Pelechowski v The Registrar, Court of Appeal* (1999) 198 CLR 435 at 463, [1999] HCA 19.

1028 See *R v General Television Corporation Pty Ltd* [2009] VSC 84; *R v The Herald and Weekly Times Pty Ltd and another* [2008] VSC 251 and *R v The Herald and Weekly Times Ltd* [2009] VSC 85.

1029 See *Public Prosecutor v Nahau Rooney (No. 2)* [1979] PNGLR 448, [1979] PGSC 23.

See also: *R v David Syme and Co Ltd* [1982] VicRp 16, [1982] VR 173 at 178; *Director of Public Prosecutions (NSW) v John Fairfax and Sons Ltd* (1987) 8 NSWLR 732 at 741; *R v Pacini* [1956] VicLawRp 84, [1956] VLR 544 at 546; *Attorney-General v Times Newspapers Ltd* [1991] 2 WLR 994, [1992] 1 AC 191 at 218, [1991] 2 All ER 398; *Australian Competition and Consumer Commission v Hughes* (2001) ATPR 41-807, [2001] FCA 38; *Australian Competition and Consumer Commission v Info4PCCom Pty Ltd* (2002) 121 FCR 24, [2002] FCA 949; *Australian Competition and Consumer Commission v World Netsafe Pty Ltd and another* [2003] FCA 1501; *Commissioner for Fair Trading v TLC Consulting Services Pty Ltd and others* [2011] QSC 374; *Legal Services Board v Forster (No. 3)* [2012] VSC 640; *Director of Public Prosecutions v Johnson* [2002] VSC 583; *R v The Herald and Weekly Times Pty Ltd and another* [2008] VSC 251; *R v The Herald and Weekly Times Ltd* [2009] VSC 85 and *R v Vasiliou (No. 2)* [2012] VSC 242.

1030 See *Attorney-General for New South Wales v Dean* (1990) 20 NSWLR 650 at 656.

The nature of the intent, if any, with which the person breached an order or undertaking will be relevant to penalty.[1031]

The intent of the contemnor may properly be inferred from the publication and the circumstances under which it was published.[1032]

- the reason or motive for the contempt[1033];
- the personal circumstances of the contemnor[1034];
- the existence or otherwise of any system in the relevant organisation for the prevention of the contempt[1035];

---

[1031] See *Australian Securities and Investments Commission v 1st State Home Loans P/L and another* [2002] QSC 55; *Australasian Meat Industry Employees' Union v Mudginberri Station Pty Ltd* (1986) 161 CLR 98 at 107, (1986) 66 ALR 577, [1986] HCA 46 and *Commissioner for Fair Trading v TLC Consulting Services Pty Ltd and others* [2011] QSC 374.

[1032] See *R v Tibbits* [1902] 1 KB 77 at 88.

[1033] See *Wood v Staunton (No. 5)* (1995) 86 A Crim R 183, per Dunford J at 185; *Principal Registrar of the Supreme Court v Jando* (2001) 53 NSWLR 527, (2001) 125 A Crim R 473, [2001] NSWSC 969; *Kennedy v Lovell* [2002] WASCA 226; *Chief Executive Officer, Department of Environment and Conversation v Szulc* [2010] WASC 195; *Corruption and Crime Commission v Allbeury, Silvestro, Chikonga, Smith (No. 2)* [2011] WASC 26; *Dental Board of Australia v Traianou* [2011] WASC 293; *Australian Securities and Investments Commission v Michalik* (2004) 52 ACSR 115, [2004] NSWSC 1259; *Commissioner for the Police Integrity Commission v Walker* [2006] NSWSC 964; *Trad v Pickles Auction Pty Ltd; In the Matter of Carl Trad* [2006] NSWSC 1177; *Principal Registrar of Supreme Court v Tran* [2006] NSWSC 1183; *Buckby and another v Wharton and another* [2012] QSC 416; *Registrar of the Court of Appeal v Gilby* [1991] NSWCA 235; *Legal Practice Board v Tee* [2009] WASC 5; *Legal Services Board v Forster (No. 3)* [2012] VSC 640; *Director of Public Prosecutions v Johnson* [2002] VSC 583 and *Bydand Holdings Pty Ltd v Pineland Property Holdings Pty Ltd and others* [2009] NSWSC 584.

[1034] See *Elias Padura v Stephanie Valakvi* (2012) N4894, [2012] PGNC 254.

See also: *Louis Vuitton Malletier SA v Design Elegance Pty Ltd* (2006) 149 FCR 494, [2006] FCA 83; *Commissioner for Fair Trading v TLC Consulting Services Pty Ltd and others* [2011] QSC 374 and *Metcash Trading Ltd v Bunn (No. 6)* [2009] FCA 266.

[1035] See *Peter Luga v Richard Sikani Commissioner, Correctional Services and The State* (2002) N2285.

See also: *R v David Syme and Co Ltd* [1982] VicRp 16, [1982] VR 173 at 180 and 182; *R v General Television Corporation Pty Ltd* [2009] VSC 84; *Director of Public Prosecutions (NSW) v John Fairfax and Sons Ltd* (1987) 8 NSWLR 732 at 741; *R v The Herald and Weekly Times Pty Ltd and another* [2008] VSC 251 and *R v The Herald and Weekly Times Ltd* [2009] VSC 85.

- whether the contemnor was aware of the consequences to himself or herself of what he or she did[1036];

- the size[1037] and nature[1038] of the contemnor's business.

  The size and nature of the contemnor's business is relevant not only to the objective seriousness of the offence, but also to the size of the financial penalty to be imposed in aid of deterrence.[1039]

  The Court is entitled to take into account the fact that the business of the contemnor is one of large size and substantial assets and that a fine that might be appropriate for an individual may be inadequate for an organisation of such size and assets.[1040]

  However, it has been said that it is not the function of the Court to impose a penalty that would put a company out of business or produce liquidation.[1041]

  Moreover, evidence of dire financial circumstances of a corporate wrongdoer could possibly justify leniency[1042];

---

[1036] See *Registrar of the Court of Appeal v Gilby* [1991] NSWCA 235; *Wood v Staunton (No. 5)* (1995) 86 A Crim R 183, per Dunford J at 185; *Principal Registrar of the Supreme Court v Jando* (2001) 53 NSWLR 527, (2001) 125 A Crim R 473, [2001] NSWSC 969; *R v Duncan* [2000] NSWSC 440; *Registrar of the Court of Appeal (New South Wales) v Craven (No. 2)* (1995) 80 A Crim R 272; *Australian Securities and Investments Commission v Michalik* (2004) 52 ACSR 115, [2004] NSWSC 1259; *Commissioner for the Police Integrity Commission v Walker* [2006] NSWSC 964; *Trad v Pickles Auction Pty Ltd; In the Matter of Carl Trad* [2006] NSWSC 1177; *Principal Registrar of Supreme Court v Tran* [2006] NSWSC 1183; *Buckby and another v Wharton and another* [2012] QSC 416; *Corruption and Crime Commission v Allbeury, Silvestro, Chikonga, Smith (No. 2)* [2011] WASC 26; *Legal Practice Board v Tee* [2009] WASC 5 and *Bydand Holdings Pty Ltd v Pineland Property Holdings Pty Ltd and others* [2009] NSWSC 584.

[1037] See *Attorney General (NSW) v TCN Channel Nine Pty Ltd* (1990) 5 BR 419.

[1038] See *Newsat Limited v Telikom PNG Ltd and others* (2008) N3673, [2008] PGNC 227.

[1039] See New South Wales Law Reform Commission, 2000, 'Contempt by Publication', Discussion Paper No. 43, Ch. 13 'Penalties and Remedies'.

[1040] See New South Wales Law Reform Commission, 2000, 'Contempt by Publication', Discussion Paper No. 43, Ch. 13 'Penalties and Remedies'.

[1041] See New South Wales Law Reform Commission, 2000, 'Contempt by Publication', Discussion Paper No. 43, Ch. 13 'Penalties and Remedies'.

[1042] See *Director of Public Prosecutions (Cth) v United Telecasters Sydney Ltd (in liquidation)* (1992) 7 BR 364, per Kirby J at 375.

- the general nature and purpose of the publication[1043] (including factors such as the extent to which the publication aspires towards 'seriousness' as opposed to sensationalism and the standard of its journalism)[1044]; and

- where a fine is sought, or else is being considered, the contemnor's financial means, together with their personal circumstances[1045].

## [12.2] AGGRAVATING FACTORS[1046]

A Court should also take into consideration any relevant aggravating factors.

Such factors may result in a more severe sentence than would otherwise be imposed.

Such factors include:

- any contempt of Court is a very serious matter.[1047]

  The seriousness transcends matters such as the personal dignity of the judiciary, or the rights of a particular litigant[1048];

---

[1043] See *R v General Television Corporation Pty Ltd* [2009] VSC 84.

[1044] See *R v David Syme and Co Ltd* [1982] VicRp 16, [1982] VR 173 at 180 and *R v The Herald and Weekly Times Ltd* [2009] VSC 85.

[1045] See *Smith v R* (1991) 25 NSWLR 1 and *R v The Herald and Weekly Times Ltd* [2009] VSC 85.

[1046] Refer also to the chapter titled 'Aggravating Factors' in the text titled 'Injia on Sentencing in Papua New Guinea and the Pacific'.

[1047] See *Public Prosecutor v Nahau Rooney (No. 2)* [1979] PNGLR 448, [1979] PGSC 23; *Sr Dianne Liriope v Dr Jethro Usurup, Chief Executive Officer, Modilon General Hospital and others* (2009) N3931, [2009] PGNC 244; *Pioneers Health Services Ltd v Gabriel Yer, Secretary of Department of Finance and The State* (2008) N3326 and *Pius Mark for and on behalf of the Council of the Mount Hagen Technical College v Korali Iki* [1995] PNGLR 116, [1995] PGNC 134.

See also: *Varnavides v Victorian Civil and Administrative Tribunal and another* [2005] VSCA 231; *Registrar of the Court of Appeal v Maniam (No. 2)* (1992) 26 NSWLR 309 at 314; *Attorney-General (NSW) v Whiley* (1993) 31 NSWLR 314 and *Bydand Holdings Pty Ltd v Pineland Property Holdings Pty Ltd and others* [2009] NSWSC 584.

[1048] As observed by Carr J in *Deputy Commissioner of Taxation v Hickey* [1999] FCA 259.

- the relative objective seriousness or gravity of the offence commited by the contemnor[1049] whilst taking in consideration the nature and circumstances of the contempt[1050], including the volume of money involved[1051].

  Insulting or offensive behavior directed towards the presiding Judge or magistrate is treated seriously because it often happens that a decision goes against one or other party in a trial. The unsuccessful party must accept the decision if the integrity of the trial process is to be maintained[1052];

---

[1049] See *Registrar of the Court of Appeal v Gilby* [1991] NSWCA 235; *Wood v Staunton (No. 5)* (1995) 86 A Crim R 183, per Dunford J at 185; *Principal Registrar of the Supreme Court v Jando* (2001) 53 NSWLR 527, (2001) 125 A Crim R 473, [2001] NSWSC 969; *R v Duncan* [2000] NSWSC 440; *Registrar of the Court of Appeal (New South Wales) v Craven (No. 2)* (1995) 80 A Crim R 272; *Kennedy v Lovell* [2002] WASCA 226; *Chief Executive Officer, Department of Environment and Conversation v Szulc* [2010] WASC 195; *Dental Board of Australia v Traianou* [2011] WASC 293; *Australian Securities and Investments Commission v Michalik* (2004) 52 ACSR 115, [2004] NSWSC 1259; *Commissioner for the Police Integrity Commission v Walker* [2006] NSWSC 964; *Trad v Pickles Auction Pty Ltd; In the Matter of Carl Trad* [2006] NSWSC 1177; *Principal Registrar of Supreme Court v Tran* [2006] NSWSC 1183; *Evenco Pty Ltd v Australian Building Construction Employees and Builders Labourers Federation (Qld Branch)* [2001] Qd R 118 at 128 and 137; *Buckby and another v Wharton and another* [2012] QSC 416; *Corruption and Crime Commission v Allbeury, Silvestro, Chikonga, Smith (No. 2)* [2011] WASC 26; *Legal Practice Board v Tee* [2009] WASC 5; *Legal Services Board v Forster (No. 3)* [2012] VSC 640; *Director of Public Prosecutions v Johnson* [2002] VSC 583; *R v General Television Corporation Pty Ltd* [2009] VSC 84; *R v The Herald and Weekly Times Pty Ltd and another* [2008] VSC 251; *R v The Herald and Weekly Times Ltd* [2009] VSC 85; *R v Vasiliou (No. 2)* [2012] VSC 242; *Bydand Holdings Pty Ltd v Pineland Property Holdings Pty Ltd and others* [2009] NSWSC 584; *Director of Public Prosecution v Australian Broadcasting Corporation* (1987) 7 NSWLR 588; *Director of Public Prosecutions v Wran* (1986) 7 NSWLR 616; *Director of Public Prosecutions v John Fairfax and Sons Ltd* (1987) 8 NSWLR 732; *Attorney General for New South Wales v Dean* (1990) 20 NSWLR 650 and *Registrar of the Court of Appeal v Maniam (No. 2)* (1992) 26 NSWLR 309.

[1050] See *Newsat Limited v Telikom PNG Ltd and others* (2008) N3673, [2008] PGNC 227.

See also: *Louis Vuitton Malletier SA v Design Elegance Pty Ltd* (2006) 149 FCR 494, [2006] FCA 83; *Commissioner for Fair Trading v TLC Consulting Services Pty Ltd and others* [2011] QSC 374; *Metcash Trading Ltd v Bunn (No. 6)* [2009] FCA 266 and *R v West Australian Newspapers Ltd; ex parte Director of Public Prosecutions* (WA) (1995) 16 WAR 508.

[1051] See *Kapil Salo and others v Peter Terry Gerari and others* (2005) N2923.

[1052] See *Rich v Attorney-General (Vic.)* (1999) 103 A Crim R 261, per Callaway JA at 283, [1999] VSCA 14.

- the level of culpability of the contemnor[1053];

- whether the contemnor was the holder of an official position and if so, the nature of the powers and legal obligations of such a position[1054];

- whether there has been 'a deliberate attempt' to interfere with 'the due and ordinary methods of carrying out the law'.[1055]

  If so, a grave offence has been committed and the punishment must be severe[1056];

- the implications of the contemptuous behaviour on the administration of justice[1057];

---

[1053] See *Public Prosecutor v Nahau Rooney (No. 2)* [1979] PNGLR 448, [1979] PGSC 23 and *Kapil Salo and others v Peter Terry Gerari and others* (2005) N2923.

See also: *R v Thomson Newspapers Ltd; ex parte Attorney-General* [1968] 1 All ER 268, per Parker LCJ at 269; *R v David Syme and Co Ltd* [1982] VicRp 16, [1982] VR 173 at 178; *Director of Public Prosecutions (NSW) v John Fairfax and Sons Ltd* (1987) 8 NSWLR 732 at 741; *JSC BTA Bank v Solodchenko* [2010] EWHC 2843 (Ch), [2011] 1 WLR 906; *Crystal Mews v Metterick* [2006] EWHC 3087 (Ch); *Kennedy v Lovell* [2002] WASCA 226; *Chief Executive Officer, Department of Environment and Conversation v Szulc* [2010] WASC 195; *Corruption and Crime Commission v Allbeury, Silvestro, Chikonga, Smith (No. 2)* [2011] WASC 26; *Dental Board of Australia v Traianou* [2011] WASC 293; *Louis Vuitton Malletier SA v Design Elegance Pty Ltd* (2006) FCR 494, [2006] FCA 83; *Commissioner for Fair Trading v TLC Consulting Services Pty Ltd and others* [2011] QSC 374; *Metcash Trading Ltd v Bunn (No. 6)* [2009] FCA 266; *Durack v Gallagher* (1983) 152 CLR 238, (1982) 44 ALR 272 at 286, [1983] HCA 2; *R v General Television Corporation Pty Ltd* [2009] VSC 84; *R v The Herald and Weekly Times Pty Ltd and another* [2008] VSC 251 and *R v The Herald and Weekly Times Ltd* [2009] VSC 85.

[1054] See *Peter Luga v Richard Sikani Commissioner, Correctional Services and The State* (2002) N2285; *Sr Dianne Liriope v Dr Jethro Usurup, Chief Executive Officer, Modilon General Hospital and others* (2009) N3931, [2009] PGNC 244 and *John Siune v Rendle Rimua and The State* (2013) N5282, [2013] PGNC 96.

[1055] See *Public Prosecutor v Nahau Rooney (No. 2)* [1979] PNGLR 448, [1979] PGSC 23, per Wilson J.

[1056] See *Public Prosecutor v Nahau Rooney (No. 2)* [1979] PNGLR 448, [1979] PGSC 23, per Wilson J.

[1057] See *Louis Vuitton Malletier SA v Design Elegance Pty Ltd* (2006) 149 FCR 494, [2006] FCA 83; *Commissioner for Fair Trading v TLC Consulting Services Pty Ltd and others* [2011] QSC 374; *Metcash Trading Ltd v Bunn (No. 6)* [2009] FCA 266; *Legal Services Board v Forster (No. 3)* [2012] VSC 640; *Director of Public Prosecutions v Johnson* [2002] VSC 583; *Durack v Gallagher* (1983) 152 CLR 238, (1982) 44 ALR 272 at 286, [1983] HCA 2; *R v The Herald and Weekly Times Ltd* [2009] VSC 85 and *R v Vasiliou (No. 2)* [2012] VSC 242.

- the extent to which the law has been brought into:
    - disrespect[1058]; or
    - disregard[1059];
- whether the contempt was seriously prejudicial to the public interest[1060];
- the real likelihood of interference with the due course of justice[1061];
- the practical consequence of the contemnor's failure to comply and its effect upon the effective administration of justice[1062];
- whether the contemnor appreciated the seriousness of the breach[1063];
- the costs incurred by the Court and other parties as a consequence of the contemptuous behavior[1004];

---

[1058] See *The State v Foxy Kia Tala; Re Corney Winjan* [1995] PNGLR 303, (1995) N1192.

[1059] See *Public Prosecutor v Nahau Rooney (No. 2)* [1979] PNGLR 448, [1979] PGSC 23 and *Sr Dianne Liriope v Dr Jethro Usurup, Chief Executive Officer, Modilon General Hospital and others* (2009) N3931, [2009] PGNC 244.

[1060] See *Von Doussa v Owens (No. 3)* (1982) 31 SASR 166; *Australian Securities and Investments Commission v Michalik* (2004) 52 ACSR 115, [2004] NSWSC 1259; *Buckby and another v Wharton and another* [2012] QSC 416 and *Bydand Holdings Pty Ltd v Pineland Property Holdings Pty Ltd and others* [2009] NSWSC 584.

[1061] See *Public Prosecutor v Nahau Rooney (No. 2)* [1979] PNGLR 448, [1979] PGSC 23.

[1062] See *Australian Competition and Consumer Commission v World Netsafe Pty Ltd and another* [2003] FCA 1501.

[1063] See *JSC BTA Bank v Solodchenko* [2010] EWHC 2843 (Ch), [2011] 1 WLR 906 and *Crystal Mews v Metterick* [2006] EWHC 3087 (Ch).

[1064] See *The State v Re Awaita; Contempt Proceedings* [1985] PNGLR 179, [1985] PGNC 29, (1985) N508 and *The State v Foxy Kia Tala; Re Corney Winjan* [1995] PNGLR 303, (1995) N1192.

- the extent to which the contemnor appreciated that a contempt was being committed[1065];
- the actual[1066] and potential consequences of the contempt[1067];
- the extent of the contemnor's awareness of the court order[1068];
- whether the prejudice is capable of remedy[1069];
- whether any remedial action has been taken[1070];

---

[1065] See *Australian Competition and Consumer Commission v Info4PCCom Pty Ltd* (2002) 121 FCR 24, [2002] FCA 949; *Australian Competition and Consumer Commission v World Netsafe Pty Ltd and another* [2003] FCA 1501 *and Commissioner for Fair Trading v TLC Consulting Services Pty Ltd and others* [2011] QSC 374.

[1066] See *Kapil Salo and others v Peter Terry Gerari and others* (2005) N2923; *John Siune v Rendle Rimua and The State* (2013) N5282, [2013] PGNC 96; *Sr Dianne Liriope v Dr Jethro Usurup, Chief Executive Officer, Modilon General Hospital and others* (2009) N3931, [2009] PGNC 244; *Elias Padura v Stephanie Valakvi* (2012) N4894, [2012] PGNC 254 and *Peter Luga v Richard Sikani Commissioner, Correctional Services and The State* (2002) N2285.

See also: *Legal Services Board v Forster (No. 3)* [2012] VSC 640; *Director of Public Prosecutions v Johnson* [2002] VSC 583; *R v General Television Corporation Pty Ltd* [2009] VSC 84; *R v David Syme and Co Ltd* [1982] VicRp 16, [1982] VR 173 at 178; *Director of Public Prosecutions (NSW) v John Fairfax and Sons Ltd* (1987) 8 NSWLR 732 at 741; *R v The Herald and Weekly Times Pty Ltd and another* [2008] VSC 251; *R v The Herald and Weekly Times Ltd* [2009] VSC 85 and *R v Vasiliou (No. 2)* [2012] VSC 242.

[1067] See *R v Thomson Newspapers Ltd; ex parte Attorney-General* [1968] 1 All ER 268, per Parker LCJ at 269.

See also: *Buckby and another v Wharton and another* [2012] QSC 416; *Wood v Staunton (No. 5)* (1995) 86 A Crim R 183, per Dunford J at 185; *Principal Registrar of the Supreme Court v Jando* (2001) 53 NSWLR 527, (2001) 125 A Crim R 473, [2001] NSWSC 969; *Australian Securities and Investments Commission v Michalik* (2004) 52 ACSR 115, [2004] NSWSC 1259; *Commissioner for the Police Integrity Commission v Walker* [2006] NSWSC 964; *Trad v Pickles Auction Pty Ltd; In the Matter of Carl Trad* [2006] NSWSC 1177; *Principal Registrar of Supreme Court v Tran* [2006] NSWSC 1183; *Registrar of the Court of Appeal v Gilby* [1991] NSWCA 235; *Legal Practice Board v Tee* [2009] WASC 5; *R v West Australian Newspapers Ltd; ex parte Director of Public Prosecutions* (WA) (1995) 16 WAR 508 and *Bydand Holdings Pty Ltd v Pineland Property Holdings Pty Ltd and others* [2009] NSWSC 584.

[1068] See *R v Pacini* [1956] VicLawRp 84, [1956] VLR 544 at 546.

[1069] See *JSC BTA Bank v Solodchenko* [2010] EWHC 2843 (Ch), [2011] 1 WLR 906 and *Crystal Mews v Metterick* [2006] EWHC 3087 (Ch).

[1070] See *R v General Television Corporation Pty Ltd* [2009] VSC 84.

- whether the contemnor intended to influence those who heard his or her public statements[1071];

- whether the contempt was committed in the course of a trial of a serious criminal offence[1072];

- whether the contemnor had the intention to directly interfere with the administration of justice[1073];

- whether the contemnor has any past disobedience[1074] whilst taking into consideration:

    - the public interest in the administration of justice[1075];

    - the period over which the convictions are spread[1076]; and

---

[1071] See *Director of Public Prosecutions (Cth) v Wran* (1987) 7 NSWLR 616 at 640.

[1072] See *Wood v Staunton (No. 5)* (1995) 86 A Crim R 183, per Dunford J at 185; *Principal Registrar of the Supreme Court of New South Wales v Jando* (2001) 53 NSWLR 527, (2001) 125 A Crim R 473, [2001] NSWSC 969; *Registrar of the Court of Appeal v Gilby* [1991] NSWCA 235; *R v Duncan* [2000] NSWSC 440; *Registrar of the Court of Appeal (New South Wales) v Craven (No. 2)* (1995) 80 A Crim R 272; *Australian Securities and Investments Commission v Michalik* (2004) 52 ACSR 115, [2004] NSWSC 1259; *Commissioner for the Police Integrity Commission v Walker* [2006] NSWSC 964; *Trad v Pickles Auction Pty Ltd; In the Matter of Carl Trad* [2006] NSWSC 1177; *Principal Registrar of Supreme Court v Tran* [2006] NSWSC 1183; *Buckby and another v Wharton and another* [2012] QSC 416; *Corruption And Crime Commission v Allbeury, Silvestro, Chikonga, Smith (No. 2)* [2011] WASC 26; *Legal Practice Board v Tee* [2009] WASC 5; *Legal Services Board v Forster (No. 3)* [2012] VSC 640; *Director of Public Prosecutions v Johnson* [2002] VSC 583; *R v Vasiliou (No. 2)* [2012] VSC 242 and *Bydand Holdings Pty Ltd v Pineland Property Holdings Pty Ltd and others* [2009] NSWSC 584.

[1073] See *Registrar Supreme Court v McPherson* (1980) 1 NSWLR 688, per Moffit P and Hope JA at 697 and Glass J at 711; *Director of Public Prosecutions (Cth) v Wran* (1987) 7 NSWLR 616; *Attorney General (NSW) v Dean* (1990) 20 NSWLR 650; *Director of Public Prosecutions v Johnson* [2002] VSC 583; *R v Slaveski (contempt)* [2011] VSC 643 and *Attorney General (NSW) v Mundey* [1972] 2 NSWLR 887 at 911.

[1074] See *Excel Noble Development Ltd v Wah Nam Group Ltd* [2001] 4 HKC 148 at 162; *Oriental Daily Publisher Ltd v Ma Chiu Sing* [2009] 2 HKLRD 558 and *Citybase Property Management Ltd v Kam Kyun Tak (No. 2)* [2003] 2 HKC 108.

See also: Australian Law Reform Commission, 1987, 'Contempt', Report No. 35, p. 299.

[1075] See *Citybase Property Management Ltd v Kam Kyun Tak (No. 2)* [2003] 2 HKC 108.

[1076] See *R v The Herald and Weekly Times Limited* [2009] VSC 85.

- the nature of the contemnor in the case of a corporation[1077];

- whether the contemnor sought to receive a benefit or gain from the contempt[1078];

- whether the contemnor has received a benefit or gain from the contempt[1079];

- whether a decision was made not to seek legal advice when the nature of the publication makes it obvious that it would constitute contempt[1080];

- whether the contemnor failed to show remorse[1081]; and

- whether the contemnor disregarded contrary legal advice[1082].

---

[1077] See *R v The Herald and Weekly Times Limited* [2009] VSC 85.

[1078] See *Australian Securities and Investments Commission v Michalik* (2004) 52 ACSR 115, [2004] NSWSC 1259; *Buckby and another v Wharton and another* [2012] QSC 416; *Bydand Holdings Pty Ltd v Pineland Property Holdings Pty Ltd and others* [2009] NSWSC 584; *Registrar of the Court of Appeal v Gilby* [1991] NSWCA 235; *Wood v Staunton (No. 5)* (1995) 86 A Crim R 183, per Dunford J at 185; *Principal Registrar of the Supreme Court of New South Wales v Jando* (2001) 53 NSWLR 527, (2001) 125 A Crim R 473, [2001] NSWSC 969; *R v Duncan* [2000] NSWSC 440; *Registrar of the Court of Appeal (New South Wales) v Craven (No. 2)* (1995) 80 A Crim R 272; *Commissioner for the Police Integrity Commission v Walker* [2006] NSWSC 964; *Trad v Pickles Auction Pty Ltd; In the Matter of Carl Trad* [2006] NSWSC 1177; *Principal Registrar of Supreme Court of NSW v Tran* [2006] NSWSC 1183; *Buckby and another v Wharton and another* [2012] QSC 416; *Corruption And Crime Commission v Allbeury, Silvestro, Chikonga, Smith (No. 2)* [2011] WASC 26 and *Legal Practice Board v Tee* [2009] WASC 5.

[1079] See *Kennedy v Lovell* [2002] WASCA 226; *Chief Executive Officer, Department of Environment and Conversation v Szulc* [2010] WASC 195; *Corruption and Crime Commission v Allbeury, Silvestro, Chikonga, Smith (No. 2)* [2011] WASC 26 and *Dental Board of Australia v Traianou* [2011] WASC 293.

[1080] See *Director of Public Prosecutions (Cth) v Wran* (1986) 7 NSWLR 616 at 642.

[1081] See *Newsat Limited v Telikom PNG Ltd and others* (2008) N3673, [2008] PGNC 227.

[1082] See *Sr Dianne Liriope v Dr Jethro Usurup, Chief Executive Officer, Modilon General Hospital and others* (2009) N3931, [2009] PGNC 244.

See also: *Attorney General (NSW) v Mirror Newspapers Ltd* [1980] 1 NSWLR 374 at 390.

## [12.3] MITIGATING FACTORS[1083]

A Court should also take into consideration any relevant mitigating factors.[1084]

Mitigating factors are usually unrelated to the circumstances of the offence.[1085]

The term 'mitigate' from which 'mitigation' is derived means:

> To lessen the seriousness of evil, harm, pain, etc.[1086]

Thus, circumstances or factors of mitigation are intended to make an offence less serious, and thereby lessen the severity or rigors of the prescribed sanction.[1087]

Such factors include:

- whether the contemnor pleaded guilty.[1088]

  A guilty plea should be treated as a mitigating factor, and a plea of guilty should attract a significant discount to the sentence that might have been imposed in its absence.[1089]

  The fact that the contemnor acknowledged the contempt and thereby spared the community the additional cost of a trial mitigates the seriousness of the contempt[1090];

---

[1083] Refer also to the chapter titled 'Mitigating Factors' in the text titled 'Injia on Sentencing in Papua New Guinea and the Pacific'.

[1084] See *JSC BTA Bank v Solodchenko* [2010] EWHC 2843 (Ch), [2011] 1 WLR 906; *Kennedy v Lovell* [2002] WASCA 226; *Chief Executive Officer, Department of Environment and Conversation v Szulc* [2010] WASC 195; *Corruption and Crime Commission v Allbeury, Silvestro, Chikonga, Smith (No. 2)* [2011] WASC 26 and *Dental Board of Australia v Traianou* [2011] WASC 293.

[1085] See *John Elipa Kalabus v The State* [1988-89] PNGLR 19.

[1086] See *The State v Iori Veraga* (2005) N2921, [2005] PGNC 43.

[1087] See *The State v Iori Veraga* (2005) N2921, [2005] PGNC 43.

[1088] See *Kapil Salo and others v Peter Terry Gerari and others* (2005) N2923.

See also: *JSC BTA Bank v Solodchenko* [2010] EWHC 2843 (Ch), [2011] 1 WLR 906; *R v General Television Corporation Pty Ltd* [2009] VSC 84; *R v The Herald and Weekly Times Pty Ltd and another* [2008] VSC 251 and *R v The Herald and Weekly Times Ltd* [2009] VSC 85.

[1089] See *Newman v R* [2002] FCAFC 136.

[1090] See *Attorney General (NSW) v TCN Channel Nine Pty Ltd* (1990) 5 BR 419.

- the timing of the plea.

  By analogy with sentencing in criminal cases, the earlier the admission is made the more credit the contemnor is entitled to be given[1091];

- whether the contemnor has co-operated[1092];

- whether the contemnor attempted to comply with the order and therefore, purge the contempt[1093];

- whether the contempt was motivated by fear of harm if evidence was given[1094];

- the extent to which the contemnor had acted under pressure[1095];

- whether the contemnor was placed in breach by reason of the conduct of others[1096];

- whether the contemnor has offered to pay costs[1097];

---

[1091] See *JSC BTA Bank v Solodchenko* [2010] EWHC 2843 (Ch), [2011] 1 WLR 906.

[1092] See *Sr Dianne Liriope v Dr Jethro Usurup, Chief Executive Officer, Modilon General Hospital and others* (2009) N3931, [2009] PGNC 244 and *Elias Padura v Stephanie Valakvi* (2012) N4894, [2012] PGNC 254.

See also: *JSC BTA Bank v Solodchenko* [2010] EWHC 2843 (Ch), [2011] 1 WLR 906 and *Crystal Mews v Metterick* [2006] EWHC 3087 (Ch).

[1093] See *Newsat Limited v Telikom PNG Ltd and others* (2008) N3673, [2008] PGNC 227 and *John Siune v Rendle Rimua and The State* (2013) N5282, [2013] PGNC 96.

See also: *Construction, Forestry, Mining and Energy Union v BHP Steel (AIS) Pty Ltd* (2003) 196 ALR 350, [2003] FCAFC 13.

[1094] See *Registrar of the Court of Appeal v Gilby* [1991] NSWCA 235; *R v Duncan* [2000] NSWSC 440; *Registrar of the Court of Appeal (New South Wales) v Craven (No. 2)* (1995) 80 A Crim R 272 and *Corruption And Crime Commission v Allbeury, Silvestro, Chikonga, Smith (No. 2)* [2011] WASC 26.

[1095] See *JSC BTA Bank v Solodchenko* [2010] EWHC 2843 (Ch), [2011] 1 WLR 906 and *Crystal Mews v Metterick* [2006] EWHC 3087 (Ch).

[1096] See *JSC BTA Bank v Solodchenko* [2010] EWHC 2843 (Ch), [2011] 1 WLR 906 and *Crystal Mews v Metterick* [2006] EWHC 3087 (Ch).

[1097] See *R v General Television Corporation Pty Ltd* [2009] VSC 84; *R v Herald and Weekly Times* [2008] VSC 251; *R v The Herald and Weekly Times Pty Ltd and another* [2008] VSC 251 and *R v The Herald and Weekly Times Ltd* [2009] VSC 85.

- the character and antecedents of the contemnor[1098], including whether the contemnor has a prior conviction for contempt[1099].

  A good record, such as no prior convictions for contempt, will invariably be taken into account in the contemnor's favour[1100];

- whether a genuine offer following judgment but before sentence was made to cooperate in the provision of information[1101];

---

1098 See *JSC BTA Bank v Solodchenko* [2010] EWHC 2843 (Ch), [2011] 1 WLR 906; *Wood v Staunton (No. 5)* (1995) 86 A Crim R 183, per Dunford J at 185; *Principal Registrar of the Supreme Court v Jando* (2001) 53 NSWLR 527, (2001) 125 A Crim R 473, [2001] NSWSC 969; *Kennedy v Lovell* [2002] WASCA 226; *Chief Executive Officer, Department of Environment and Conversation v Szulc* [2010] WASC 195; *Corruption and Crime Commission v Allbeury, Silvestro, Chikonga, Smith [No. 2]* [2011] WASC 26; *Australian Securities and Investments Commission v Michalik* (2004) 52 ACSR 115, [2004] NSWSC 1259; *Dental Board of Australia v Traianou* [2011] WASC 293; *Commissioner for the Police Integrity Commission v Walker* [2006] NSWSC 964; *Trad v Pickles Auction Pty Ltd; In the Matter of Carl Trad* [2006] NSWSC 1177; *Principal Registrar of Supreme Court v Tran* [2006] NSWSC 1183; *Buckby and another v Wharton and another* [2012] QSC 416; *Legal Practice Board v Tee* [2009] WASC 5; *Registrar of the Court of Appeal v Gilby* [1991] NSWCA 235; *Legal Services Board v Forster (No. 3)* [2012] VSC 640; *Director of Public Prosecutions v Johnson* [2002] VSC 583; *R v Vasiliou (No. 2)* [2012] VSC 242 and *Bydand Holdings Pty Ltd v Pineland Property Holdings Pty Ltd and others* [2009] NSWSC 584.

1099 See *The State v Foxy Kia Tala; Re Corney Winjan* [1995] PNGLR 303, (1995) N1192; *Kapil Salo and others v Peter Terry Gerari and others* (2005) N2923; *John Siune v Rendle Rimua and The State* (2013) N5282, [2013] PGNC 96; *Bewa Tou on his own behalf and on behalf of Isou Clan of Krissa Village, Vanimo, Sandaun Province v Papua New Guinea Forest Authority and others* (2003) N2490; *Newsat Limited v Telikom PNG Ltd and others* (2008) N3673, [2008] PGNC 227 and *The State v Lucas Sasoruo* [1997] PNGLR 676.

See also: *Attorney-General (NSW) v Macquarie Publications Pty Ltd* (1988) 40 A Crim R 405, per Kirby J at 410; *R v General Television Corporation Pty Ltd* [2009] VSC 84; *R v The Herald and Weekly Times Pty Ltd and another* [2008] VSC 251; *R v The Herald and Weekly Times Ltd* [2009] VSC 85; *Louis Vuitton Malletier SA v Design Elegance Pty Ltd* (2006) FCR 494, [2006] FCA 83; *Commissioner for Fair Trading v TLC Consulting Services Pty Ltd and others* [2011] QSC 374; *Metcash Trading Ltd v Bunn (No. 6)* [2009] FCA 266; *Director of Public Prosecutions (Cth) v Australian Broadcasting Corp* (1987) 7 NSWLR 588 at 615 and *Hinch v Attorney General* [1987] VicRp 62, [1987] VR 721, per Kaye J at 752.

1100 See *Sr Dianne Liriope v Dr Jethro Usurup, Chief Executive Officer, Modilon General Hospital and others* (2009) N3931, [2009] PGNC 244 and *Elias Padura v Stephanie Valakvi* (2012) N4894, [2012] PGNC 254.

1101 See *JSC BTA Bank v Solodchenko* [2010] EWHC 2843 (Ch), [2011] 1 WLR 906 and *Crystal Mews v Metterick* [2006] EWHC 3087 (Ch).

- the achievements of the contemnor in both his or her private and public life, including his or her contributions to the country[1102];

- whether the contemnor has demonstrated genuine contrition and proffered a full and ample apology[1103], including acceptance of the Court's authority[1104].

[1102] See *Bewa Tou on his own behalf and on behalf of Isou Clan of Krissa Village, Vanimo, Sandaun Province v Papua New Guinea Forest Authority and others* (2003) N2490; *Elias Padura v Stephanie Valakvi* (2012) N4894, [2012] PGNC 254 and *Sr Dianne Liriope v Dr Jethro Usurup, Chief Executive Officer, Modilon General Hospital and others* (2009) N3931, [2009] PGNC 244.

[1103] See *The State v Foxy Kia Tala; Re Corney Winjan* [1995] PNGLR 303, (1995) N1192; *Bewa Tou on his own behalf and on behalf of Isou Clan of Krissa Village, Vanimo, Sandaun Province v Papua New Guinea Forest Authority and others* (2003) N2490 and *The State v Raymond Tupundu* (1996) N1536, [1996] PGNC 10.

See also: *JSC BTA Bank v Solodchenko* [2010] EWHC 2843 (Ch), [2011] 1 WLR 906; *Wood v Staunton (No. 5)* (1995) 86 A Crim R 183, per Dunford J at 185; *Principal Registrar of the Supreme Court v Jando* (2001) 53 NSWLR 527, (2001) 125 A Crim R 473, [2001] NSWSC 969; *Kennedy v Lovell* [2002] WASCA 226; *Chief Executive Officer, Department of Environment and Conversation v Szulc* [2010] WASC 195; *Corruption and Crime Commission v Allbeury, Silvestro, Chikonga, Smith [No. 2]* [2011] WASC 26; *Dental Board of Australia v Traianou* [2011] WASC 293; *Australian Securities and Investments Commission v Michalik* [2004] NSWSC 1259 (2004) 52 ACSR 115, [2004] NSWSC 1259; *Commissioner for the Police Integrity Commission v Walker* [2006] NSWSC 964; *Trad v Pickles Auction Pty Ltd; In the Matter of Carl Trad* [2006] NSWSC 1177; *Principal Registrar of Supreme Court v Tran* [2006] NSWSC 1183; *Buckby and another v Wharton and another* [2012] QSC 416; *Gallagher v Durack* (1983) 152 CLR 238 at 245, (1982) 44 ALR 272, [1983] HCA 2; *Australian Competition and Consumer Commission v World Netsafe Pty Ltd and another* [2003] FCA 1501; *Commissioner for Fair Trading v TLC Consulting Services Pty Ltd and others* [2011] QSC 374; *Registrar of the Court of Appeal v Gilby* [1991] NSWCA 235; *Legal Practice Board v Tee* [2009] WASC 5; *R v General Television Corporation Pty Ltd* [2009] VSC 84; *R v The Herald and Weekly Times Pty Ltd and another* [2008] VSC 251; *R v The Herald and Weekly Times Ltd* [2009] VSC 85; *R v Vasiliou (No. 2)* [2012] VSC 242; *Bydand Holdings Pty Ltd v Pineland Property Holdings Pty Ltd and others* [2009] NSWSC 584 and *Superstar Australia Pty Ltd v Coonan and Denlay Pty Ltd (No. 2)* (1982) 65 FLR 432 at 436, [1982] FCA 190.

[1104] See *Legal Services Board v Forster (No. 3)* [2012] VSC 640; *DPP v Johnson* [2002] VSC 583 and *R v Vasiliou (No. 2)* [2012] VSC 242.

Where a contemnor has admitted the contempt, genuine contrition and a full and ample apology may reduce a penalty, although where the charges are contested, the absence of an apology does not carry any significant weight in the sentencing process.[1105]

The offer of an apology and an undertaking not to repeat the offence will mitigate the offence.[1106]

The apology must manifest contrition on the part of the contemnor; it must be sincere and not given grudgingly.[1107]

However, the offence of 'Contempt of Court' is a serious offence and should not be able to be met by an expression of regret and apology in the National and Supreme Courts[1108];

- whether the breach of the order was deliberate, intentional or unintentional.[1109]

  It is highly relevant to the question of penalty that the alleged contemnor disobeyed an order because he or she placed a construction on it that was not its true construction[1110];

- whether the contemnor has offered any explanation for his or her conduct.[1111]

---

[1105] See *Bovis Lend Lease Pty Ltd v Construction Forestry Mining and Energy Union (No. 2)* [2009] FCA 650 and *Commissioner for Fair Trading v TLC Consulting Services Pty Ltd and others* [2011] QSC 374.

[1106] See *Attorney General (NSW) v Macquarie Publications Pty Ltd* (1988) 40 A Crim R 405, per Kirby J at 410.

[1107] See *Attorney General (NSW) v Mirror Newspapers* (1980) 1 NSWLR 362 at 391.

[1108] See *Re Kennedy and McCann* [1976] IR 382 at 388.

For overseas comparative cases on sentence and mitigating and aggravating factors to consider in relation to scandalising a Court, see *Re Application by the Attorney General of Fiji* [2009] FJHC 8.

[1109] See *Re Perkins; Mesto v Galpin* (1998) 4 VR 505 at 512; *JSC BTA Bank v Solodchenko* [2010] EWHC 2843 (Ch), [2011] 1 WLR 906 and *Crystal Mews v Metterick* [2006] EWHC 3087 (Ch).

[1110] See *Universal Music Australia Pty Ltd v Sharman Networks Ltd* (2006) 150 FCR 110, [2006] FCAFC 41 and *Metcash Trading Ltd v Bunn (No. 5)* [2009] FCA 16.

[1111] See *Gallagher v Durack* (1983) 152 CLR 238 at 245, (1982) 44 ALR 272, [1983] HCA 2; *Australian Competition and Consumer Commission v World Netsafe Pty Ltd and another* [2003] FCA 1501 and *Commissioner for Fair Trading v TLC Consulting Services Pty Ltd and others* [2011] QSC 374.

An acknowledgment by the contemnor that a contempt was committed may be a mitigating factor[1112];

- whether there was no intention to prejudice[1113];
- whether the actions of the contemnor were spontaneous[1114];
- whether the contemnor was acting on legal advice[1115]; and
- the passage of time since the occurrence of the contempt[1116].

## [13.0] TECHNICAL CONTEMPT

Not every intentional disobedience involves a conscious defiance of the authority of the Court.[1117]

---

[1112] See *Australian Competition and Consumer Commission v World Netsafe Pty Ltd and another* [2003] FCA 1501; *Australian Securities and Investments Commission v Matthews* (1999) 32 ACSR 404, [1999] FCA 803 and *Commissioner for Fair Trading v TLC Consulting Services Pty Ltd and others* [2011] QSC 374.

[1113] See *R v David Syme and Co Ltd* [1982] VicRp 16, [1982] VR 173, per Marks J at 178.

[1114] See *Elias Padura v Stephanie Valakvi* (2012) N4894, [2012] PGNC 254.

[1115] See *Sr Dianne Liriope v Dr Jethro Usurup, Chief Executive Officer, Modilon General Hospital and others* (2009) N3931, [2009] PGNC 244.

See also: *R v Thomson Newspapers Ltd* [1968] 1 WLR 1 at 5; *Director of Public Prosecutions (Cth) v United Telecasters Sydney (Ltd) (in liq)* (1992) 7 BR 364 at 374; *R v Australian Broadcasting Corporation Ltd* [1983] Tas R 161 at 178; *Attorney-General (NSW) v Willesee* [1980] 2 NSWLR 143, per Moffitt P at 154 and Mahoney JA at 166; *Attorney-General (NSW) v Mirror Newspapers Ltd* [1980] 1 NSWLR 374 at 390; *R v General Television Corporation Pty Ltd* [2009] VSC 84; *R v David Syme and Co Ltd* [1982] VicRp 16, [1982] VR 173 at 180 and 182; *R v The Herald and Weekly Times Pty Ltd and another* [2008] VSC 251 and *R v The Herald and Weekly Times Ltd* [2009] VSC 85.

See however: *Newsat Limited v Telikom PNG Ltd and others* (2008) N3673, [2008] PGNC 227.

[1116] See *Legal Services Board v Forster (No. 3)* [2012] VSC 640; *DPP v Johnson* [2002] VSC 583 and *R v Vasiliou (No. 2)* [2012] VSC 242.

[1117] See *Australian Consolidated Press Ltd v Morgan* (1965) 112 CLR 483 at 500, [1965] HCA 21 and *Kennedy v Lovell* [2002] WASCA 226.

## PUNISHMENT

Judicial conservatism has, arguably, manifested itself in the development of the concept of 'technical contempt' which, in essence, is conduct that falls within the definition of 'Contempt of Court', but is nevertheless not regarded by the Court as conduct deserving of punishment in the particular circumstances of the case.[1118]

As stated by Cotton LJ in *Hunt v Clarke*[1119]:

> A penalty will not be imposed in its exercise unless the thing done is of such a nature as to require the arbitrary and summary interference of the court in order to enable justice to be duly and properly administered without any interruption or interference.

Whether the disobedience was 'casual or accidental and unintentional'; a Court may chose to exercise discretion to not impose a penalty.[1120]

---

[1118] See *Concord Pacific Ltd and Paiso Company Ltd v Thomas Nen – Managing Director, Papua New Guinea Forest Authority and the State* [2000] PNGLR 47 and *Peter Luga v Richard Sikani Commissioner, Correctional Services and The State* (2002) N2285.

See also:

- *Attorney-General v Times Newspapers Ltd* [1973] 3 All ER 54, [1974] AC 273 per Reid LJ at 301, Diplock LJ at 213 and Cross LJ at 325; *Attorney-General for New South Wales v Mundey* [1972] 2 NSWLR 887; *Victoria v Australian Building Construction Employees' and Builders Labourers' Federation* (1981-82) 152 CLR 25, [1982] HCA 31; *Director of Public Prosecutions (NSW) v John Fairfax and Sons Ltd* (1987) 8 NSWLR 732 at 742; *R v Sun Newspapers Pty Ltd; ex parte Attorney-General* [1993] 1 QdR 682 at 690; *R v Perkins; Mesto v Galpin* (1998) 100 A Crim R 324, per Brooking JA at 332; *John Fairfax and Sons Pty Ltd v McRae* (1955) 93 CLR 351 at 370, [1955] HCA 12; *Attorney-General v John Fairfax and Sons Ltd* [1980] 1 NSWLR 362 at 367; *Davis v Baillie* [1946] VicLawRp 76, [1946] VLR 486, per Fullagar, J at 493; *Re Perkins* (1998) 4 VR 505 at 512; *Advan Investments Pty Ltd v Dean Gleeson Motor Sales Pty Ltd* [2003] VSC 201; *Scott and others v Evia Pty Ltd and others* [2007] VSC 15; *Plating Company v Farquharson* (1881) 17 Ch 49, per James LJ at 57; *Stancomb v Trowbridge Urban District Council* [1910] 2 Ch Div 190 at 197; *Attorney-General; ex rel Leyton (Essex) Urban District Council v Walthamstow Urban District Council* (1895) 11 TLR 533 at 534; *Adlam v Noack* [1999] FCA 1606, per Mansfield J; *Rex v Ogilvie* (1928) 23 Tas LR 69, per Nicholls CJ at 76; *GCT (Management) Ltd v The Laurie Marsh Group Ltd* [1973] 14 RPC 432 at 438; *Michigan v Mathew* [1966] 3 RPC 47 at 53; *Marron v Salvemini; Re Scardigno* [1969] WAR 178 at 182 and *Evenco Pty Ltd v Amalgamated Society Of Carpenters, Joiners, Bricklayers and Plasterers of Australasia Union of Employees, Queensland and another* [1999] QSC 77; and
- AG Shott, 'Australian Supplement to Borrie and Lowe's Law of Contempt' 2nd ed., p. 120.

[1119] (1889) 58 LJ (QB) 490 at 493.

See also: *R v Payne* [1896] 1 QB 577, per Russell LCJ at 581.

[1120] See *Re Perkins; Mesto v Galpin* (1998) 4 VR 505 at 512.

However, it is not necessary to punish a contemnor. In some circumstances, an order for costs has been considered to be adequate to vindicate the public interest without the imposition of a penalty.[1121]

## [14.0] SUB-JUDICE CONTEMPT

As stated by Mason P said in *Harkianakis v Skalkos*[1122]:

> In punishing certain types of interference with litigants, the law is concerned to distinguish between proper and improper pressure.

Deterrence is the primary objective of the penalty to be imposed.[1123]

---

[1121] See *Concord Pacific Ltd and Paiso Company Ltd v Thomas Nen – Managing Director, Papua New Guinea Forest Authority and the State* [2000] PNGLR 47.

See also: *R v The Herald and Weekly Times Pty Ltd and another* [2008] VSC 251; *Director of Public Prosecutions (NSW) v John Fairfax and Sons Ltd* (1987) 8 NSWLR 732 at 742; *R v The Herald and Weekly Times Ltd* [2009] VSC 85; *Rex v Ogilvie* (1928) 23 Tas LR 69, per Nicholls CJ at 76; *GCT (Management) Ltd v The Laurie Marsh Group Ltd* [1973] 14 RPC 432 at 438, *Michigan v Mathew* [1966] 3 RPC 47 at 53; *Marron v Salvemini; Re Scardigno* [1969] WAR 178 at 182; *Sunibrite Products (Aust) Pty Ltd v Jabuna Pty Ltd* (1980) 47 FLR 73, [1980] FCA 4; *Brambles Holdings Ltd v Trade Practices Commission* (1980) 32 ALR 328 at 342; *Australian Competition and Consumer Commission v Australian Business Reports Pty Ltd* (1997) 19 ATPR 41-577 at 44,010; *Construction, Forestry, Mining and Energy Union v BHP Steel (AIS) Pty Ltd* [2003] FCAFC 13 and *Evenco Pty Ltd v Amalgamated Society of Carpenters, Joiners, Bricklayers and Plasterers of Australasia Union of Employees, Queensland and another* [1999] QSC 77.

However, in some cases costs have been awarded with no penalty for contemptuous behavior that was not considered to be of a technical nature, see *GCT (Management) Ltd v The Laurie Marsh Group Ltd* [1973] 14 RPC 432 at 438, *Michigan v Mathew* [1966] 3 RPC 47 at 53 and *Construction, Forestry, Mining and Energy Union v BHP Steel (AIS) Pty Ltd* [2003] FCAFC 13.

[1122] (1997) 42 NSWLR 22 at 30.

See also: G Borrie and N Lowe, 1996, 'The Law of Contempt' 3rd ed., Butterworths, London, p. 442 and D Eady and ATH Smith, 1999, 'Arlidge, Eady and Smith on Contempt' 2nd ed., Sweet and Maxwell, London, para. 11-261.

[1123] See *DPP (Commonwealth) v United Telecasters Sydney Ltd* (1992) 7 BR 364, per Kirby P at 376.

See also: New South Wales Law Reform Commission, 2000, 'Contempt by Publication', Discussion Paper No. 43.

## PUNISHMENT

A Court may take into account the fact that the fine imposed upon a corporation in reality punishes the shareholders, rather than those responsible for the contempt.[1124]

However, it is not necessary to punish a contemnor. In some circumstances, the prosecution itself, the burdens of the trial, the published findings of the Court and an order for costs will be adequate to vindicate the public interest.[1125]

In deciding whether a 'sub-judice contempt' involving wide publication of the contemptuous statement is serious enough to warrant imprisonment, it is relevant to consider inter alia:

- the real likelihood of interference with the due course of justice;
- the extent to which the law has been brought into disrespect or disregard;
- the culpability of the contemnor;
- the intention with which the act complained of is done; and
- whether the desire and need to protect society should override the interests of the contemnor.[1126]

## [15.0] DISOBEDIENCE CONTEMPT

### [15.1] GENERAL PRINCIPLES

It is in the public interest in the due administration of justice, as well as in the interests of the parties, that court orders are obeyed[1127] otherwise serious and lasting damage to the fabric of the law may result[1128].

---

1124 See *R v Wattle Gully Gold Mines NL* [1980] VicRp 57, [1980] VR 622 and *Hinch v Attorney General* [1987] VicRp 62, [1987] VR 721, per Young CJ at 732.

1125 See *DPP (NSW) v John Fairfax and Sons Ltd* (1987) 8 NSWLR 732 at 742.

1126 See *Public Prosecutor v Nahau Rooney (No. 2)* [1979] PNGLR 448, [1979] PGSC 23.

1127 See *Bakir v Doueihi and others* [2001] QSC 414.

1128 See *Australasian Meat Industry Employees' Union v Mudginberri Station Pty Ltd* (1986) 161 CLR 98 at 115, (1986) 66 ALR 577, [1986] HCA 46.

## PUNISHMENT

The public interest in the due administration of justice is a matter of vital importance.[1129]

There is an element of public policy in punishing civil contempt, since the administration of justice would be undermined if the order of any court of law could be disregarded with impunity.[1130]

If breaches of the orders of the courts were regarded as of little moment, respect for and observance of the law would inevitably deteriorate and, ultimately, pose a threat to social order.[1131]

The administration of justice must be protected by demonstrating that a Court's Orders must be obeyed, otherwise there will be consequences.[1132]

A breach of an order of a Court amounts to a serious misconduct as it operates against the entire system of justice.[1133]

If parties to litigation do not obey orders of the Court, that strikes at the system of administration of justice. It impedes the just resolution of issues between the parties. It must be punished in a significant way.[1134]

Contemnors need to realise that their perceptions do not constitute a licence to ignore court orders.[1135]

---

[1129] See *Peter Luga v Richard Sikani and The State* (2001) N2286 and *Kapil Salo and others v Peter Terry Gerari and others* (2005) N2923.

[1130] See *Kapil Salo and others v Peter Terry Gerari and others* (2005) N2923.

See also: the observations of Diplock LJ in *Attorney-General v Times Newspapers Ltd* [1974] AC 273 at 308.

[1131] See *Australian Meat Industry Employees Union v Mudginberri Station Pty Ltd* (1986) 161 CLR 98 at 115, (1986) 66 ALR 577, [1986] HCA 46 and *Pelechowski v Registrar, Court of Appeal of New South Wales* (1999) 198 CLR 435, (1999) 162 ALR 336, (1999) 73 ALJR 687, [1999] HCA 19, per McHugh J.

[1132] See *Pioneers Health Services Ltd v Gabriel Yer, Secretary of Department of Finance and The State* (2008) N3326.

[1133] See *The State v Charles Maniwa and Joseph Utura Maniwa* (2004) N2674.

[1134] As stated by Mansfield J in *Adlam v Noack* [1999] FCA 1606.

[1135] See *Australian Competition and Consumer Commission v INFO4PC.com Pty Ltd* [2002] FCA 949 and *Australian Competition and Consumer Commission v Purple Harmony Plates Pty Ltd (No. 3)* [2002] FCA 1487.

## PUNISHMENT

The primary concern in sentencing is to demonstrate to litigants that orders of the court are to be obeyed.[1136]

The party who has the benefit of a court order needs to be protected by ensuring that it is complied with and is not mere empty words.[1137]

It is for these reasons that a sentence by way of a fine is punitive, with the dual object of vindicating the authority of the Court and disciplining the contemnor.[1138]

The starting point for the process of reasoning in sentencing is the gravity of the offence. In the case of contempt of court involving contravention of, or failure to comply with, court orders, that means assessing the seriousness of the defiance of the Court's authority.[1139]

While it is possible for a contempt to be committed by a corporation without the corporation or its servants or agents being aware of a breach of the court order[1140], the question of intent is highly relevant in determining:

- how the contempt is classified; and
- the penalty to be imposed.[1141]

---

1136 See *Abu Dhabi National Tanker Co v Lam Ming Chi* [1998] 4 HKC 320 at 336.

1137 See *Pioneers Health Services Ltd v Gabriel Yer, Secretary of Department of Finance and The State* (2008) N3326.

1138 See *Pioneers Health Services Ltd v Gabriel Yer, Secretary of Department of Finance and The State* (2008) N3326.

1139 See *Vaysman v Deckers Outdoor Corporation Inc* [2011] FCAFC 17.

1140 See *Pioneers Health Services Ltd v Gabriel Yer, Secretary of Department of Finance and The State* (2008) N3326.

See also:

- *Stancomb v Trowbridge Urban District Council* [1910] 2 Ch Div 190 at 194 and *Re Garage Equipment Association's Agreement* (1964) LR 4 RP 491; and
- CJ Miller, 2000, 'Contempt of Court' 3rd ed., Clarendon Press, Oxford, p. 672.

1141 See *Pioneers Health Services Ltd v Gabriel Yer, Secretary of Department of Finance and The State* (2008) N3326.

See also: *Attorney-General v Times Newspapers Ltd and another* [1991] 2 WLR 994, [1992] 1 AC 191 at 217, [1991] 2 All ER 398.

## PUNISHMENT

The object of the penalty is:

- to punish conduct in defiance of the Court's order[1142];

- to serve as a coercive function by holding out the threat of future punishment as a means of securing the protection which the order is primarily there to do[1143]; and

- to vindicate the authority of the Court.[1144]

The consistent practice of the National Court has been to treat a conviction for a disobedience of contempt as warranting committal to custody.[1145]

However, Gray J made the following comments in *Vaysman v Deckers Outdoor Corporation Inc*[1146]:

> Restraint is appropriate in imposing sentences of imprisonment for contempt of court involving contravention of, or failure to comply with, orders of the Court. The authority of a Court can be brought into disrepute, rather than enhanced, by too great a tendency to punish severely in cases that do not warrant severity.

If the disobedience was 'casual or accidental and unintentional', this is relevant to penalty.[1147]

---

[1142] See *Lightfoot v Lightfoot* [1989] FCR 305 at 308; *Robinson v Robinson* [2001] EWCA Civ 2098; *Hale v Tanner* [2000] 1 WLR 2377 at 2381; *Australian Meat Industry Employees Union v Mudginberri Station Pty Ltd* (1986) 161 CLR 98 at 113, (1986) 66 ALR 577, [1986] HCA 46; *Capel v Caram Finance Australia Ltd* [1998] QSC 110 and *Commissioner for Fair Trading v TLC Consulting Services Pty Ltd and others* [2011] QSC 374.

[1143] See *Lightfoot v Lightfoot* [1989] FCR 305 at 308; *Robinson v Robinson* [2001] EWCA Civ 2098 and *Hale v Tanner* [2000] 1 WLR 2377 at 2381.

[1144] See *Australian Meat Industry Employees Union v Mudginberri Station Pty Ltd* (1986) 161 CLR 98 at 113, (1986) 66 ALR 577, [1986] HCA 46; *Capel v Caram Finance Australia Ltd* [1998] QSC 110 and *Commissioner for Fair Trading v TLC Consulting Services Pty Ltd and others* [2011] QSC 374.

[1145] See *Elias Padura v Stephanie Valakvi* (2012) N4894, [2012] PGNC 254.

[1146] [2011] FCAFC 17.

[1147] See *Re Perkins; Mesto v Galpin* (1998) 4 VR 505 at 512.

## PUNISHMENT

Notwithstanding that the proper construction of an order is not a matter of fact but a question of law[1148], it may be highly relevant to the question of penalty that the contemnor disobeyed an order because he or she placed a construction on it that was not its true construction.[1149]

However, a contempt involving disguised steps calculated to defeat the purpose of a Court order, could render it particularly serious.[1150]

## [15.2] CURRENT ORDER

Notwithstanding that the primary aim of contempt proceedings in cases where an order is still capable of being complied with is enforcement of the order, another purpose is to protect the effective administration of justice by demonstrating that the Court's orders will be enforced[1151].

Where a contemnor is found guilty of 'disobedience contempt' a sanction may be imposed not by way of punishment, but in order to compel compliance with the relevant Court order.[1152]

In the case of a failure to comply with a continuing order, compliance with which is still possible, the Court may sentence the contemnor to imprisonment indefinitely for the purpose of coercing compliance.[1153]

---

[1148] See *Universal Music Australia Pty Ltd v Sharman Networks Ltd* (2006) 150 FCR 110, [2006] FCAFC 41 and *Metcash Trading Ltd v Bunn (No. 5)* [2009] FCA 16.

[1149] See *Universal Music Australia Pty Ltd v Sharman Networks Ltd* (2006) 150 FCR 110, [2006] FCAFC 41 and *Metcash Trading Ltd v Bunn (No. 5)* [2009] FCA 16.

[1150] See *Australian Prudential Regulation Authority v Siminton (No. 2)* [2006] FCA 397.

[1151] See *Australian Meat Industry Employees Union v Mudginberri Station Pty Ltd* (1986) 161 CLR 98 at 107, (1986) 66 ALR 577, [1986] HCA 46 and *Witham v Holloway* (1995) 183 CLR 525 at 533, (1995) 131 ALR 401, (1995) 69 ALJR 847, [1995] HCA 3.

[1152] See *Stephen John Rose and John Charles Harrison v Neville Devete, Acting Solicitor-General and The State* (2007) N3327.

[1153] See *Stephen John Rose and John Charles Harrison v Neville Devete, Acting Solicitor-General and The State* (2007) N3327.

See however:

- section 23 ['Sanctions']; and
- section 36(1) ['Freedom From Inhuman Treatment']

of the *Constitution of the Independent State of Papua New Guinea.*

## PUNISHMENT

Once the contemnor complies, he or she is said to have 'purged' the contempt and may apply to be released *ex debito justitiae*, ie., forthwith.[1154]

As stated by Justice Breyer in *Turner v Rogers*[1155]:

> the contemnor 'carries the keys of his prison in his own pockets'.

The committal to prison is of a conditional nature, and remains in force until the contempt comes to an end, or a further order of the Court is made. When such an order is made, as soon as the contempt is purged, the contemnor is entitled to release.[1156]

When an order is made committing the contemnor until further order, the Court retains the power to determine whether the contemnor should be further punished, even if he or she purges the contempt. The purpose of making such orders is to endeavour to coerce the contemnor into purging their contempt by complying with his or her legal obligations.[1157]

---

[1154] See *Re Armstrong* [1892] 1 QB 327, per Williams J and *In re Freston* (1883) 11 QBD 545 at 554 and 557.

See also:

- *Hicks v Feiock* (1988) 485 US 624 at 638; *Gompers v Bucks Stove and Range Co* (1910) 221 US 418 at 442, [1911] USSC 79; *International Union, United Mine Workers of America v Bagwell* (1994) 512 US 821, [1994] USSC 43; *Australian Consolidated Press Ltd v Morgan* (1965) 112 CLR 483, per Windeyer J at 498; *Poje v Attorney-General for British Columbia* [1953] 1 SCR 516 at 519, [1953] SCC 34; *Hannaford (an examiner under the Australian Crime Commission Act 2002 v HH* [2010] FCA 1214 and *Corruption and Crime Commission v Allbeury, Silvestro, Chikonga, Smith (No. 2)* [2011] WASC 26; and
- Australian Law Reform Commission, 1987, 'Contempt', Report No. 35, p. 299.

In the United States contemnors who did not repent of their continuing contempts have been kept in prison for many years, see *Chadwick v Janecka* [2002] USCA3 273, 312 F 3d 597 (3rd Cir 2002) and *United States v Harris* 582 F 3d 512 (3d Cir 2009).

[1155] 564 US 10-10 2011 at 8.

[1156] See *Re Freston* (1883) 11 QBD 545.

See also: *Australasian Meat Industry Employees Union v Mudginberri Station Pty Ltd* (1986) 161 CLR 98, (1986) 66 ALR 577, [1986] HCA 46 and *Corruption and Crime Commission v Allbeury, Silvestro, Chikonga, Smith (No. 2)* [2011] WASC 26.

[1157] See *Corruption and Crime Commission v Allbeury, Silvestro, Chikonga, Smith (No. 2)* [2011] WASC 26.

A further possibility in these circumstances is a fixed term sentence coupled with a provision that the contemnor may apply to be released earlier on the ground that he or she has purged the contempt.[1158]

## [15.3] OUT-OF-DATE ORDER

Punishment can be imposed for a breach of an order even if the breach is incapable of remedy as a means of vindicating the Court's authority.[1159]

In cases in which non-compliance has ceased to be an issue the primary goal of contempt proceedings is to punish the contemnor for past disobedience.[1160]

Where compliance with the order is no longer possible a Court may impose a fixed term of imprisonment as a punitive sanction for past disobedience[1161], notwithstanding that the order may have been subsequently complied with[1162].

## [15.4] CONTUMACIOUS DISOBEDIENCE

A contempt which is not an accidental omission or performed through ignorance but is, rather, the result of a deliberate act of defiance resulting in a breach of a court order is properly viewed as contumacious.[1163]

---

1158 See Australian Law Reform Commission, 1987, 'Contempt', Report No. 35, p. 299.

1159 See *Australasian Meat Industry Employees' Union v Mudginberri Station Pty Ltd* (1986) 161 CLR 98, (1986) 66 ALR 577, [1986] HCA 46 and *Witham v Holloway* (1995) 183 CLR 525 at 530, (1995) 131 ALR 401, (1995) 69 ALJR 847, [1995] HCA 3.

1160 See Australian Law Reform Commission, 1987, 'Contempt', Report No. 35, p. 305.

1161 See Australian Law Reform Commission, 1987, 'Contempt', Report No. 35, p. 299.

1162 See *Phonographic Performances Ltd v Amusement Caterers (Peckham) Ltd* [1964] Ch 195, per Cross LJ at 199.

1163 See *Pioneers Health Services Ltd v Gabriel Yer, Secretary of Department of Finance and The State* (2008) N3326.

See also: *Witham v Holloway* (1995) 183 CLR 525 at 533, (1995) 131 ALR 401, (1995) 69 ALJR 847, [1995] HCA 3.

## PUNISHMENT

Contumacious disobedience is evidenced by deliberate defiance of judicial authority.[1164]

The standard of proof for such defiance is beyond reasonable doubt.[1165]

Historically, the sentencing options available to a Court at common law depended upon whether or not the disobedience was contumacious. 'Mere' disobedience attracted the sentence of open-ended imprisonment or sequestration of assets; whereas contumacious disobedience was punishable by fixed term imprisonment. A fine was not considered to be an appropriate sanction for any form of civil contempt.[1166]

Whilst it is not necessary to prove any subjective intent to deliberately disobey the order[1167], such intent is important in determining what is an appropriate penalty[1168].

The most serious class of contempt, from the point of view of sanction, is contumacious contempt.[1169]

---

[1164] See *Registrar, Court of Appeal v Maniam (No. 2)* (1992) 26 NSWLR 309 at 315.

[1165] See *Primelife Corp Ltd v Newpark Pty Ltd* [2003] VSC 106 and *Pico Holdings Inc v Voss* [2002] VSC 319.

[1166] See *Luga v Sikani, Commissioner of Correctional Services (No. 2)* [2002] PGNC 60, (2002) N2286.

See also: Australian Law Reform Commission, 1987, 'Contempt', Report No. 35, p. 314.

[1167] See *Stancomb v Trowbridge Urban District Council* [1910] 2 Ch Div 190 at 194.

See also: *Australian Competition and Consumer Commission v Hughes* (2001) AT PR 41-807, [2001] FCA 38.

[1168] See *Attorney-General v Times Newspapers Ltd and another* [1991] 2 WLR 994, [1992] 1 AC 191 at 217, [1991] 2 All ER 398.

See also: *Australian Competition and Consumer Commission v Hughes* (2001) AT PR 41-807, [2001] FCA 38.

[1169] See *Secretary for Justice v. The Oriental Press Group* [1998] 2 HKLRD 293; *Secretary for Justice v Choy Bing Wing* [2005] 4 HKC 416 at 445; *Registrar of the Court of Appeal v Maniam (No. 2)* (1992) 26 NSWLR 309, per Kirby P at 315 and *Kennedy v Lovell* [2002] WASCA 226.

## [16.0] REFUSAL TO GIVE EVIDENCE

A failure of a contemnor to give evidence is to be treated as serious contempt in the face of the Court.[1170]

It is serious because courts decide cases on the basis of evidence. If evidence is unjustifiably withheld, the administration of justice is impeded.[1171]

If witnesses will not give evidence, the process of law enforcement will be less effective and more people will suffer accordingly. There is a public interest in ensuring that, in this regard, disobedience of the law will be, and will be seen to be, punished.[1172]

Refusal to give evidence should not be deterred by admonition or by gesture: it is necessary that the punishment for it be direct, immediate and exemplary.[1173]

Personal deterrence may not be considered as a significant factor because it is not thought likely that the contemnor will find himself or herself again in the same circumstances.[1174]

---

[1170] See *Registrar of the Court of Appeal v Gilby* [1991] NSWCA 235; *Smith v R* (1991) 25 NSWLR 1; *Registrar of the Court of Appeal (New South Wales) v Craven (No. 2)* (1995) 80 A Crim R 272; *R v Duncan* [2000] NSWSC 440; *R v Taber and Styman; Re Shannon Styman* [2005] NSWSC 1329; *Trad v Pickles Auction Pty Ltd; In the Matter of Carl Trad* [2006] NSWSC 1177; *Principal Registrar of Supreme Court v Tran* [2006] NSWSC 1183 and *Corruption and Crime Commission v Allbeury, Silvestro, Chikonga, Smith (No. 2)* [2011] WASC 26.

[1171] As stated by Kirby P in *Smith v R* (1991) 25 NSWLR 1.

[1172] See *Registrar of the Court of Appeal v Gilby* [1991] NSWCA 235.

[1173] See *Smith v R* (1991) 25 NSWLR 1, per Mahoney JA at 23 and *Registrar, Criminal Division, Supreme Court of New South Wales v Glasby* [1999] NSWSC 846;

[1174] See *Trad v Pickles Auction Pty Ltd; In the Matter of Carl Trad* [2006] NSWSC 1177.

## [17.0] COMPARATIVE SENTENCES

### [17.1] CONTEMPT IN FACE

| Case | Penalty |
|---|---|
| *The State v Re Awaita; Contempt Proceedings* [1985] PNGLR 179, [1985] PGNC 29, (1985) N508 | K1000 fine |
| *The State v Foxy Kia Tala, Re Detective Constable Corney Winjan* [1995] PNGLR 303 | 6 months imprisonment suspended on conditions |
| *The State v Lucas Sasaruo* [1997] PNGLR 676 | K500 fine |
| *Re Passingan Taru and Contempt Proceedings* [1982] PNGLR 292 | K50 fine |
| *The State v Tana Kera* (unreported 24th July 1996) | K250 fine |
| *The State v Raymond Tupundu* (1996) N1536, [1996] PGNC 10 | K500 fine |
| *Re: Paul Luben and David Poka* (1987) N612[1175] | K50 fine |
| *Andrew Kwimberi of Paulus M Dowa Lawyers v The State* (1998) SC545, [1998] PGSC 9 | K100 fine |
| *Re: Contempt of Court; Re: Assistant Registrar, Philip Kaumba* (2004) N2763 | K1000 fine |

### [17.2] DISOBEDIENCE CONTEMPT

| Case | Penalty |
|---|---|
| *Public Prosecutor v Nahau Rooney (No. 2)* [1979] PNGLR 448, [1979] PGSC 23 | 8 months imprisonment |
| *Concord Pacific Ltd and Paiso Company Ltd v Thomas Nen – Managing Director, Papua New Guinea Forest Authority and the State* [2000] PNGLR 47 | Costs only |

[1175] See also: *David Gwaya Poka v The State* [1988-89] PNGLR 218, [1988] PGSC 27 in which the appeal was successful.

## PUNISHMENT

| Case | Penalty |
|---|---|
| *Bewa Tou on his own behalf and on behalf of Isou Clan of Krissa Village, Vanimo, Sandaun Province v Papua New Guinea Forest Authority and others* (2003) N2490 | K2500 fines suspended on conditions |
| *Pius Mark for and on behalf of the Council of the Mount Hagen Technical College v Korali Iki* [1995] PNGLR 116, [1995] PGNC 134 | 12 months imprisonment suspended on conditions |
| *Kapil Salo and others v Peter Terry Gerari and others* (2005) N2923 | 18 months imprisonment |
| *Newsat Limited v Telikom PNG Ltd and others* (2008) N3673, [2008] PGNC 227 | K5mil fine |
| *Philip Soon Kiat Yap v Tin Siew Tan, B and T Engineering Pty Ltd, Robert L Wong, William Baptiste and David F Tau* [1987] PNGLR 227, [1987] PGSC 21 | K5000 fine per charge |
| *John Siune v Rendle Rimua and The State* (2013) N5282, [2013] PGNC 96 | 12 months imprisonment suspended on conditions |
| *Sr Dianne Liriope v Dr Jethro Usurup, Chief Executive Officer, Modilon General Hospital and others* (2009) N3931, [2009] PGNC 244 | 6 months imprisonment |
| *Elias Padura v Stephanie Valakvi* (2012) N4894, [2012] PGNC 254 | 6 months imprisonment |

As regards the issuance of an order precluding a lawyer from appearing before any court until a fine is paid as a consequence of a conviction for contempt of court, see the observations of the Supreme Court in *Alan Robinson v The State* [1986] PNGLR 307.

## COSTS

A party has no entitlement to costs except under an order of the Court.[1176]

Whether an order is made for costs is always at the discretion of the Court[1177], not arbitrarily[1178], and in accordance with judicial principles.[1179]

As contempt proceedings are on the civil side of the Court, the ordinary rule that costs follow the event applies.[1180]

In other words, a successful plaintiff or defendant is entitled to recover his or her costs from the losing party.[1181]

---

[1176] See *Kumbu v Mann* [2012] PGNC 145, (2012) N4784.

See also: Order 22, rule 8 of the *National Court Rules 1983* ['Order for Payment'].

[1177] See *Sr Dianne Liriope v Dr Jethro Usurup, Chief Executive Officer, Modilon General Hospital and others* (2009) N3931, [2009] PGNC 244; *Elias Padura v Stephanie Valakvi* (2012) N4894, [2012] PGNC 254 and *PNG Ports Corporation Limited v Canopus No 71 Ltd* (2010) N4288.

See also:

- Order 22, rules 4 ['Powers of the Court Generally'], 5 ['Time for Dealing with Costs'] and 11 ['Following the Event'] of the *National Court Rules 1983*; and
- *Construction, Forestry, Mining and Energy Union v BHP Steel (AIS) Pty Ltd* [2003] FCAFC 13.

[1178] See *Kumbu v Mann* [2012] PGNC 145, (2012) N4784.

[1179] See *Karingu v Papua New Guinea Law Society* (2001) SC674, [2001] PGSC 10.

[1180] See *John Siune v Rendle Rimua, Secretary, Department of Petroleum and Energy and The State* (2013) N5110, [2013] PGNC 83; *Luchya Mussa Tikuye v Patrick Haines* (2009) N4434, [2009] PGNC 259; *Aisi Iuma Bore on behalf of Behori Clan of Furimuti Village v Clement Malaisa, Land Titles Commission* (2013) N5273, [2013] PGNC 92 and *Gaman Holdings Pty Ltd v Labu Holdings Pty Ltd* [2000] PGNC 47, (2000) N2016.

See also: *Hinch and Macquarie Broadcasting Holdings Limited v The Attorney-General for the State of Victoria* (1987) 164 CLR 15 at 89, [1987] HCA 56; *John Fairfax and Sons Pty Ltd v McRae* (1955) 93 CLR 351, [1955] HCA 12; *James v Robinson* (1963) 109 CLR 593, [1963] HCA 32; *Doyle v The Commonwealth* (1985) 156 CLR 510 at 516, [1985] HCA 46 and *R v Taylor; ex parte Roach* (1951) 82 CLR 587, [1951] HCA 22.

[1181] See *Karingu v Papua New Guinea Law Society* (2001) SC674, [2001] PGSC 10.

# COSTS

A Court may order either:

- costs on a solicitor client or an indemnity basis [also referred to as 'lawyer and client costs'] which comprise of the proper remuneration payable to a lawyer by his or her client for legal work performed and includes disbursements necessarily and reasonably incurred in the course of his or her employment[1182]; or

- party and party costs which comprise of the proper costs, charges and expenses reasonably and necessarily incurred by one party to a litigation to enable him or her to successfully, either complete or in part or in whole the prosecution of a claim or the defence of a claim.[1183]

  The amount of costs that can be recovered under this type of costs order is usually about two thirds (2/3) of the costs incurred on a solicitor client basis[1184] [1185].

The decision to award solicitor client costs in contempt cases is a discretionary one.[1186]

The law governing whether or not to order costs on a solicitor client basis is clear. Regard must always be had to the nature of the case.[1187]

---

1182 See *Karingu v Papua New Guinea Law Society* (2001) SC674, [2001] PGSC 10.

See also: Order 2, rules 34 and 35 of the *National Court Rules 1983* ['Solicitor and Client Basis'].

1183 See *Karingu v Papua New Guinea Law Society* (2001) SC674, [2001] PGSC 10.

See also: Order 2, rules 23 and 24 of the *National Court Rules 1983* ['Party and Party Basis'].

1184 See *Odata Limited v Ambusa Copra Oil Mill Limited and National Provident Fund Board of Trustees* (2001) N2106.

1185 See *Karingu v Papua New Guinea Law Society* (2001) SC674, [2001] PGSC 10.

1186 Contempt cases in which such costs were awarded, include *Concord Pacific Ltd and Paiso Company Ltd v Thomas Nen – Managing Director, Papua New Guinea Forest Authority and the State* [2000] PNGLR 47; *Degman Pty Ltd (in liq) v Wright (No. 2)* [1983] 2 NSWLR 354 at 358; *Marron v Salvemini; Re Scardigno* [1969] WAR 178; *Sunibrite Products (Australia) Pty Ltd v Jabuna Pty Ltd* (1980) 47 FLR 73, [1980] FCA 4; *In the Will of Mary Johnson* (1907) 24 WN(NSW) 124; *Flamingo Park Pty Ltd v Dolly Dolly Creation Pty Ltd* (1985) 5 FCR 169, [1985] FCA 123; *Australian Competition and Consumer Commission v Hughes* [2001] FCA 38; *Attorney General v Walthamstow Urban District Council* (1895) 11 TLR 533; *Lee v Aylesbury Urban District Council* (1902) 19 TLR 106 and *Stancomb v Trowbridge Urban District Council* [1910] 2 Ch Div 190 at 197.

1187 See *Beecraft No 20 Limited v Dr Fabian Pok as Minister for Lands and The State* (2001) N2125.

## COSTS

A plaintiff should not be out of pocket by reason of having taken proceedings to advance the public interest.[1188]

Another basis is to 'punish' the contemnor.[1189]

However, there is no rule of law as regards awarding solicitor client costs in contempt cases as a general rule.[1190]

In *Plating Co v Farquharson*[1191] the Court of Appeal said:

> Costs as between solicitor and client may sometimes be given.

However, such an order is appropriate:

- where the conduct of a party, either before or during the proceedings, can be said to warrant such an order[1192]; or

- in special or unusual circumstances where the justice of the case requires.[1193]

---

[1188] See *Australasian Meat Industry Employees' Union v Mudginberri Station Pty Ltd* (1986) 161 CLR 98 at 110, (1986) 66 ALR 577, [1986] HCA 46 and *McIntyre v Perkes* (1988) 15 NSWLR 417, per Rogers A-JA at 434.

[1189] See *Perkes v Landon* (1988) 15 NSWLR 408 at 414.

[1190] See *McIntyre v Perkes* (1988) 15 NSWLR 417, per Samuels JA at 424 and Rodgers A-JA at 436; *Adlam v Noack* [1999] FCA 1606; *LED Builders Pty Ltd v Eagle Homes Pty Ltd* [1999] FCA 1213; *Construction, Forestry, Mining and Energy Union v BHP Steel (AIS) Pty Ltd* [2003] FCAFC 13; *McNair Anderson Associates v Hinch* [1985] VicRp 30, [1985] VR 309; *Evenco Pty Ltd v Amalgamated Society of Carpenters, Joiners, Bricklayers and Plasterers of Australasia Union of Employees, Queensland and another* [1999] QSC 77 and *Colgate-Palmolive Company v Cussons Pty Ltd* [1993] FCA 536;(1993) 46 FCR 225.

[1191] (1881) 17 Ch Div 49 at 57.

[1192] See *PNG Aviation Services Pty Ltd v Geob Karri* (2009) SC1002 and *Kumbu v Mann* (2012) N4784, [2012] PGNC 145.

See also: *Construction, Forestry, Mining and Energy Union v BHP Steel (AIS) Pty Ltd* [2003] FCAFC 13 and *Re Wilcox; ex parte Venture Industries Pty Ltd (No. 2)* (1996) 72 FCR 151.

[1193] See *PNG Aviation Services Pty Ltd v Geob Karri* (2009) SC1002; *Kumbu v Mann* (2012) N4784, [2012] PGNC 145 and *PNG Ports Corporation Ltd v Canopus No. 71 Ltd* (2010) N4288, [2010] PGNC 203.

See also: *Construction, Forestry, Mining and Energy Union v BHP Steel (AIS) Pty Ltd* [2003] FCAFC 13 and *Colgate-Palmolive Company v Cussons Pty Ltd, Australian Transport Insurance Pty Ltd v Graeme Phillips Road Transport Insurance Pty Ltd* (1986) 10 FCR 177, [1986] FCA 85.

## COSTS

Although as a general proposition, solicitor client costs may be awarded where the Court finds the contempt proven, but does not impose a substantial penalty upon the contemner.[1194]

[1194] See *McIntyre v Perkes* (1988) 15 NSWLR 417, per Samuels JA at 426 and *Evenco Pty Ltd v Amalgamated Society of Carpenters, Joiners, Bricklayers and Plasterers of Australasia Union of Employees, Queensland and another* [1999] QSC 77.

# INDEX

## INDEX

# INDEX

## INDEX

# INDEX

Page

**W**

www.ingramcontent.com/pod-product-compliance
Lightning Source LLC
Jackson TN
JSHW062338160926
108328JS00012B/25
* 9 7 8 9 9 8 0 8 7 9 1 9 6 *